JAMES BALDWIN'S

TURKISH DECADE

JAMES BALDWIN'S

TURKISH DECADE

Erotics of Exile

MAGDALENA J. ZABOROWSKA

Duke University Press

Durham and London

2009

Designed by Amy Ruth Buchanan

Typeset in Quadraat by Tseng Information Systems, Inc.

Library of Congress Cataloging-in-Publication data

appear on the last printed page

of this book.

FOR MALINEK

CONTENTS

LIST OF ILLUSTRATIONS

PREFACE

Sightings

It is immensely important for the person who understands to be located outside the object of his or her creative understanding—in time, in space, in culture. For one cannot even really see one's own exterior and comprehend it as a whole, and no mirrors or photographs can help; our real exterior can be seen and understood only by other people, because they are located outside us in space and because they are others.

—**MIKHAIL BAKHTIN**, "Response," *The Dialogic Imagination*

The African American writer and activist James Baldwin (1924–87) was born in Harlem, thousands of miles and an ocean away from Orel, the birthplace of Mikhail Bakhtin (1895–1975), the Russian philosopher and literary critic who wrote the foregoing epigraph. Despite the linguistic, geographic, and cultural distances between them, Baldwin and Bakhtin explored, each in his own unique way, how the social environment shapes both the language and the consciousness of groups and individuals, and espoused cross-cultural dialogue based on the belief that the human desire for self-knowledge compels reliance on others as interpreters of our identities.[1] Surrounded by the historical and social upheaval of the Soviet Revolution and its aftermath, Bakhtin spent some time in political exile and later withdrew from public life into linguistic and literary study. He is best known as a literary theorist and as the author of numerous works of criticism, among them *The Dialogic Imagination* (1975), a volume that made Bakhtin's name, and that of his best-known concept, famous in the United States.

A descendant of southern black migrants to the promised land of the North, James Baldwin lived much of his adult life in France and Turkey but often returned to the United States to participate in the Civil Rights Movement, visit his family and friends, and confer with his editors and publishers.[2] Influenced by his international sojourns, and especially the little-known one in Istanbul, he wrote novels, plays, and essays that explored Americanness as inflected by race, class, gender, sexuality, and nationhood, within and outside U.S. borders. His world-famous two-essay volume *The Fire Next Time* (1963) called on Whites and Blacks "to dare everything" to "end the racial nightmare, and achieve our country, and change the history of the world" (141). It virtually prophesied the riots in American cities in the late 1960s. His works resound with a powerful mix of voices, and he commands complex sentences and emotions that make his style inimitable—from the intensely autobiographical tone of his first essay collection, *Notes of a Native Son* (1955), through the passionate intellectual and prophetic argument of *The Fire Next Time*, to the confessional narrative persona of his second novel, *Giovanni's Room* (1956), the polyphonic storytelling consciousness of his third, *Another Country* (1962), and a kaleidoscopic intra- and international layering of scenes of black experience in the essay volume *No Name in the Street* (1972), and his last novel, *Just above My Head* (1979). Baldwin's books and ideas influenced generations of black writers, from Alice Walker, Maya Angelou, Audre Lorde, and Toni Morrison, through Suzan Lori-Parks, Edward P. Jones, and Hilton Als, to Essex Hemphill, Melvin Dixon, and Randall Kenan.

Despite his extraordinary influence on American letters, however, Baldwin's death in France in 1987 followed years of relative obscurity in the 1970s and 1980s, years during which his later works were not well received or widely read and when his name began disappearing from course syllabuses at American high schools and universities. The dimming of James Baldwin's literary star coincided with Mikhail Bakhtin's rise to prominence as one of the most popular international theorists embraced by literary and cultural critics in the United States. In Dale E. Peterson's words, Bakhtin was "an exotic and somewhat rough-hewn Soviet import" ("Response and Call," 761). In the 1980s and 1990s, a wide spectrum of scholars embraced Bakhtin's dialogism, polyphony, and double voice, concepts that were especially suited to the study of minority, multicultural, and marginalized traditions and authors. Not surprisingly, Bakhtin's ideas soon found their way into the groundbreaking works of African American critics, who explored black expressive traditions, celebrated "a plurality of [gendered] voices,"[3] and challenged racialized literary canons by means of creating "a new narrative space for representing the . . . so-called black experience."[4]

Baldwin may not be a dialogic writer in the classic Bakhtinian sense, but his works lend themselves to rich dialogic interpretations. His little-known extended visits in Turkey throughout the 1960s, the subject of this book, compel a new narrative space, a new telling of his life and of his black experience, as well as new readings of his works. As a scholar trained in literary, American, and African American studies, I have embraced this project because of its interdisciplinary and dialogic appeal. As an immigrant and a feminist, I was also compelled by the intense conversations between the political and the personal that I encountered while conducting research in Turkey and while writing every page of this book.

Growing up in communist Poland, I had heard of Bakhtin long before I learned of Baldwin's existence. In an instance of cross-cultural exchange, years before attempting Bakhtinian readings of James Baldwin's works as an international scholar, I may have seen his face on Polish national television around 1982. That first, real or imagined, sighting of James Baldwin in an unlikely location coincided with an event at the Polish United Workers' Party headquarters in my hometown of Kielce, where many high school students like myself had been herded to welcome a delegation of visiting Yemeni students earlier that day. After I returned home, I glimpsed a television program that featured African Americans, their faces vivid and moving, but their voices muted with the dispassionate voice-over of the Polish narrator.[5] The program referred to events in the United States, whose documentary footage the Polish propaganda ministry deemed important enough to include in a series of mind-numbing shows that exposed and critiqued American imperialism domestically and internationally.[6] Perhaps because they resonated with my naive conceptions of race and racism at the time, the images of the African Americans on the TV screen connected in my mind with those of the students from the People's Democratic Republic of Yemen. We welcomed the Yemeni students and cheered for their country's striving toward "socialist progress"; all of us obediently applauded the same slogans at the Party headquarters. But in reality the smiling Yemeni students seemed nearly as remote and foreign to us as the serious American black men and women on television. Perhaps to us they all seemed merely

1. Architecture (yalı) along the Bosphorus, Boğaziçi,
Istanbul, 2005. Photo by author.

a part of the state's propaganda machine—just as we must have appeared
to them.

Several years later, as a student of American literature at Warsaw University, I learned that James Baldwin was an important writer when we
hosted the poet Nikki Giovanni, whose conversations with him had been
transcribed as *A Dialogue* and published in 1973. But we did not read any of
Baldwin's works in my M.A. seminar in American literature, where New
Criticism reigned and Ralph Ellison was revered as "innovative and modernist" and the only important African American writer.[7] I next encountered Baldwin, and finally read him, for my Ph.D. exam in twentieth-century
American literature, after I had managed, not exactly legally, to leave Poland
in 1987, the year of his death. The setting was Eugene, Oregon, and the book
Go Tell It on the Mountain (1953), Baldwin's stirring first novel, which I read

between stints as a maid and graduate teaching fellow (GTF) in American studies and composition.[8] As I was finishing my dissertation on East European immigrant women writers in 1992, with Eva Hoffman's "It is in my misfittings that I fit" (164) taped to the screen of my Mac Plus computer, I read Baldwin's second novel, *Giovanni's Room*, to "get away from my field." When I found myself coteaching that novel in my first academic job, at a private liberal arts college in the South, I realized that I had gotten far away from anything remotely familiar. I was as intrigued when some of my predominantly white, Baptist, and privileged undergraduate students complained to the dean that my colleague and I were "promoting homosexuality" by having them read *Giovanni's Room* as I was by those who claimed that "a black writer should not write white books" or that "Baldwin was making everybody fall in love with Giovanni, regardless of gender."[9]

This experience of "getting away from my field" and the attendant revelations, shocks, punishments, and lessons of my early career helped me to embrace more fully the interdisciplinary imperatives of scholarship in American and African American studies. A productive sense of dislocation—literary, geographic, political, and regional—became my modus operandi in the years that followed my immigration from Poland to the United States in 1996. As a newly minted "resident alien," I soon realized that I could not continue teaching "my immigrant writers" until I knew enough about black writers, and especially Baldwin and his contexts.[10] This meant not simply learning more about African American literature but rather coming to terms more fully with what my first book on Mary Antin and Anzia Yezierska had already taught me: how incredibly "worldly"—in Edward Said's elegant formulation—all literature is.

I offer these observations not to indulge my immigrant nostalgia but to explain how an international trajectory that has led me to Baldwin's works has also partially shaped this project on Baldwin in Turkey. I come from a country whose ties with Turkey have a long and complicated history; I was born and raised in a region that was, and might still be considered, part of the Orient.[11] Ever since teaching *Giovanni's Room* in the American South, I have been on the road with Baldwin, whom I saw more and more as putting a completely new spin on being an immigrant writer. I visited Paris and Saint-Paul de Vence in France; Istanbul, Ankara, and Bodrum in Turkey; as well as the American South, and Harlem and Greenwich Village in that country-within-a-country of New York City. As I read everything Baldwin wrote many times, and talked to people who knew him, I also taught his works in the United States and Denmark, always returning to Poland for visits with family, during which my mother would sometimes ask with a puzzled smile: "But why would you not write about *your own* people?" This book is a product of my international peregrinations in Baldwin's footsteps and an answer to my parents in the Old Country, to whom I owe my first understanding of what Baldwin said so well in *The Fire Next Time*: "If you know whence you came, there is really no limit to where you can go."

In a 1970 interview, Baldwin proclaimed, "I don't believe in nations any more. Those passports, those borders are as outworn and useless as war."[12] While he was privileged to travel and live all over the world, he was still defined by his nationality and race until the end of his days. Thirty years after his passing, nationalisms of all stripes flourish, and walls and borders are still with us, more than ever in this time of brutal military conflicts around the world. James Baldwin lived in no less troubling times than ours and was vocal about the writer's responsibility to speak truth to power; we should be reading him today. In an interview from 1970, he explained: "My talent does not belong to me. . . . It belongs to you; it belongs to everybody. It's important only insofar as it can work toward the liberation of other people. . . . I didn't invent it. I didn't make myself, and I wouldn't have chosen to be born as I was, when I was, where I was. But I was, and you do what you can with the hand life dealt you."[13] Baldwin's deceptively fatalistic approach to authorship was an expression of strength, not resignation. It enabled him to persevere in his vocation as a poet and prophet, as he liked to call himself, despite his experience of racism and homophobia and despite his inability to find peace in his home country.

Baldwin's acclaimed first novel, *Go Tell It on the Mountain* (1953) includes a scene that encapsulates the richness of his perspective on being black and male and American. The teenage protagonist, John Grimes, confronts his face in the mirror, "as though it were, as it indeed soon appeared to be, the face of a stranger, a stranger who held secrets that John could never know" (30). This compelling moment is signature Baldwin in its reliance on literal and metaphorical reflections and refractions of the gendered and racialized American self that his protagonist encounters. At the same time, it aptly illustrates Bakhtin's claim that self-knowledge depends on a confrontation with the other. When John Grimes "tried to look at [his face] as a stranger might, and tried to discover what other people saw," he saw only his physical features, or "details: two great eyes, and a broad, low forehead, and the triangle of his nose, and his enormous mouth, and the barely perceptible cleft in his chin" (31). Bakhtin's statements in the epigraph that "one cannot even really see one's own exterior" and that it "can be seen and understood only by other people" help us to understand that while John sees his physical reflection in the mirror, he can look at himself only through his father's eyes.

This moment of intense self-perception echoes Du Bois's well-known concept of double consciousness and Bakhtin's notion of double-voiced discourse, as John realizes that both he and his father see blackness and maleness through the eyes of white American culture.[14] In John's eyes the "barely perceptible cleft in his chin" suddenly becomes "the mark of the devil's little finger" because that is what his unforgiving, self-hating, and fanatically religious father saw in his stepson (31). Baldwin's third-person narrator stresses that John desires "to know: whether his face was ugly or not" (31), but also to know how to free himself from his father's projections, that is, how to know himself, his humanity and beauty as a black male, by means of love and acceptance of others. While Go Tell It on the Mountain ends with hope that such love and acceptance are within John Grimes's grasp, Baldwin's own life story as a transnational black gay writer suggests that the price they exacted from him necessitated estrangement and exile.

In "Intellectual Exile: Expatriates and Intellectuals" (1993), Edward Said evocatively links immigration and intellectual dissent in ways that help to represent Baldwin's predicament as a transnational black writer: "Exile is a model for the intellectual who is tempted, and even beset and overwhelmed, by the rewards of accommodation, yea-saying, settling in. Even if one is not an actual immigrant or expatriate, it is still possible to think as one, to imagine and investigate in spite of barriers, and always to move away from the centralizing authorities toward the margins, where you see things that are usually lost on minds that have never traveled beyond the conventional and comfortable."[15] As we know well from the examples of Henry James, Richard Wright, Nella Larsen, Gertrude Stein, George Lamming, and many others, writers abroad often tell us as much about where they are speaking from as their actual birthplaces. We need them and we need literature to make sense of who we are and where we stand. I hope that reading Baldwin now through his unexpected location in Turkey, and through the lens of the migratory literary misfittings that I deploy in these pages, will make the tale of transnational American literature even richer.

Baldwin's intensely personal rhetoric, imagery, and concern with the American self echo a large body of works in American literary history, including those of Emerson, Whitman, Douglass, and Du Bois, and challenge the genre of what Sacvan Bercovitch has termed "Auto-American-Biography."[16] Writing about the uniquely Baldwinian, black queer variation on this genre compels a critic to be sensitive to—and often suspicious of—the ways in which the complex interplays of experience, ideas, and interpretation inform writing and reading literature. I have been especially aware of this as a scholar positioned between the autobiographically inflected traditions of immigrant and African American writings, in which issues of identity politics, self-reflexivity, self-positioning, and self-representation are centrally located and hotly debated.

This project has grown from years of research, thinking, and writing and records as much the results of a scholarly process as those of a complex personal journey. Perhaps because I have been captivated by Baldwin's perspective on authorship as unapologetically autobiographical, at times I cannot help reading his writings and experience through the lens of my own story as an immigrant scholar, and hence an outsider-participant in American culture and academy. Such an approach also echoes my training in feminist theory and my commitment to acknowledging the self-reflexive side of scholarship and teaching in literary and cultural studies.[17] While retracing Baldwin's steps through Istanbul, interviewing numerous people who knew and loved him, and engaging archival material, theory, and literary criticism, I have been aware that my experience of getting to know this writer echoes to a certain extent John Grimes's experience with the mirror in *Go Tell It on the Mountain*. That is, I initially, and perhaps naively, approached my task as constructing a kind of mirror that would reflect a clear image of James Baldwin's face to my readers. I soon realized that I was no more able to project this image without including the visions that others had of him than I was able to write about Baldwin in Turkey without occasionally having to grapple with myself as an author of this book.[18] Hoping that my autobiographical intrusions will be helpful to some of my readers, I felt compelled to include them by the following passage from Baldwin's 1985 essay "The Price of the Ticket," which echoes his better-known statement from *The Fire Next Time*: "To do your first works over means to reexamine everything. Go back to where you started, or as far back as you can, examine all of it, travel your road again and tell the truth about it. Sing or shout or testify or keep it to yourself: *but know whence you came*" (xix). By having led me from Poland, through the United States, to Turkey, this project has helped me to relocate American literature as a transnational tradition and to reinvent myself as a critic reconciled with the idea that doing one's "first works over" is never done.

In the chapters that follow, I focus on how Baldwin's residences in Turkey throughout the 1960s helped him to reshape his views on sociability

and national identity as much as on race and sexuality and hence significantly influenced his articulations of Americanness across the Atlantic. The
accounts of his person and works by his Turkish hosts, friends, and collaborators shed light on a crucial decade in his life, and specifically on the
period following the publications of *Another Country* (1962) and *The Fire Next
Time* (1963), a period that has been unjustly neglected by scholars.[19] I hope
that this study of Baldwin's Turkish decade and his relationships with Turkish artists and intellectuals will add an important chapter to the emerging
field of transnational African American studies.[20] By putting in dialogue
Baldwin's articulations of the erotic and exile and by locating that dialogue
between Turkey and the United States, I show that his revolutionary works
exploded limiting notions of authorship, place, and national identity and
helped to build dialogic bridges across cultures.

In a statement that echoes Baldwin's own definitions and suggests his
influence on a younger generation of black writers, the lesbian poet and
essayist Audre Lorde terms the erotic the "creative energy . . . [and] knowledge [that] empowers us, [and] becomes a lens through which we scruti-
nize all aspects of our existence."[21] When writing about his exile, Baldwin,
as if anticipating some of Edward Said's more recent statements, refers to
it as a condition that "saved my life . . . [by making me] able and willing
to accept [my] own vision of the world, no matter how radically this vision
departs from that of others" (*Price of the Ticket*, 312). These two notions of the
erotic and exile crossbreed and fertilize each other in Baldwin's works and
stand at the center of his project of making the writer's art a tool of social
justice. I offer *James Baldwin's Turkish Decade: Erotics of Exile* as homage to this
effort by one of the greatest American writers, with hopes that it will contribute to increasing our energies, knowledge, and vision in this troubled
world.

Plan of the Book

This book's narrative design pays heed to chronology but focuses on the
effects and influences that Baldwin's attachment to Turkish places, culture,
and people had on his works rather than on the events of his life alone.
Hence while I take note of Baldwin's trips to the United States and elsewhere, and of the many Americans and African Americans who move in and
out of his life throughout the decade, I pay particular attention to the accounts and representations of Baldwin in Turkey as a black and queer writer
from the United States.[22] That is, I examine how his works, his person,

and his activism were received, interpreted, and often misconstrued and misread by the Turks, and show how this new archive of knowledge from an unexpected location enriches our understanding of what and how Baldwin wrote at the time and how he functioned as a transatlantic black intellectual. Consequently my readings of the works he wrote there, especially *Another Country* and *No Name in the Street*, deliberately privilege Turkey as an authorial location and cultural context that explicitly and implicitly shaped the form and content as well as the literary imagination of these works.[23]

Throughout the chapters that follow the introduction, I interweave sections that bring together scholarship and literary critical readings with those that relay the results of my primary research in Turkey and that have been inspired by, and organized around, the accounts of Baldwin's friends and collaborators whom I have interviewed for this project. Such a design allows the reader either to focus on the more scholarly or more narrative chapters or to read all of them as an ebb and flow of different kinds of material. I hope that it will appeal to audiences outside the academy.

Chapter 1, "Between Friends: Looking for Baldwin in Constantinople," employs an array of original sources—unpublished letters, interviews with Turkish subjects, and local archives—to explore Baldwin's entry into the artistic and intellectual circles of Istanbul, where he relocated both from his home country and his migrant home in France. Using Sedat Pakay's film *James Baldwin: From Another Place* and his evocative photographs of Baldwin in Turkey as a visual framework, I discuss Baldwin's reception by the Turks as an "Arap," or dark-skinned stranger, and queer American. At center stage of the chapter are interviews with Baldwin's friend Engin Cezzar and his wife Gülriz Sururi. This oral history material is cast in the context of the memoirs in which Cezzar and Sururi offer their impressions of their friendship and collaboration with Baldwin for the contemporary Turkish audience.

In chapter 2, "Queer Orientalisms in *Another Country*," I read closely Baldwin's second novel, which he rewrote and finished in Istanbul in record time, and which bears an important, and yet unexplored, Turkish imprint. I show how, while creating a complex image of the mid-twentieth-century American self and New York City in *Another Country*, Baldwin inserts implicit and explicit references to Turkish culture into its key interracial and sexual encounters. Such deployment of Orientalist imaginary and erotica opens up a new reading of Vivaldo's and Ida's affair as an example of how love and its very possibility have been debased by racism that extends beyond the United States. I read the novel's closing scene, inspired by Baldwin's friendship with the poet Cevat Çapan and featuring a young Frenchman's immigrant arrival in the United States, as an allegorical representation of the process of semi-acculturation and de-Americanization that Baldwin experienced in Turkey.[24]

Chapter 3, "Staging Masculinity in *Düşenin Dostu*," focuses on Baldwin's debut as a director of John Herbert's play *Fortune and Men's Eyes* (1967), which was performed at the Sururi-Cezzar Theater in Istanbul in 1969 and 1970 and revolutionized the Turkish stage. *Fortune and Men's Eyes* recounts power struggles and sexual violence among white inmates in a Canadian correctional facility for young males; in a provocative Turkish translation, the play under Baldwin's directorship became a great local and national success. I examine the circumstances of its production, staging, and reception in Turkey on the basis of local publications and my interviews with the play's translators, Oktay Balamir and Ali Poyrazoğlu. I include as well an interview with Baldwin's assistant and interpreter, the journalist and cultural critic Zeynep Oral, who became a key Turkish expert on Baldwin. Baldwin used the play as an opportunity to participate in Turkish culture and to explore the trope of the "prison house" that in his later works he would juxtapose with images of gendered domesticity (e.g., *If Beale Street Could Talk, No Name in the Street, Just above My Head*). Along with migration and passage, theater and incarceration became his central metaphors as he continued to live in Turkey and traveled back and forth to the United States, where he confronted the "Blacks' Old Country" on several trips to the southern states.

Chapter 4, "East to South: Homosexual Panic, the Old Country, and *No Name in the Street*," retraces Baldwin's journeys between 1957 and 1971 to what he called the American "Southland," which inspired his two-essay volume written in Turkey, *No Name in the Street*. I read this work, against its general negative reception by critics, as a seminal text that provides a powerful commentary on race and gender relations and what I call "regional homosexual panic" as they entered the American literary imagination in the turbulent 1950s and the 1960s. I show how Baldwin's engagement with Turkish culture and politics at the time of the book's writing and his advocacy on behalf of political prisoners at home and abroad provide rich contexts for his autobiographical encounters with urban segregation, racial and sexual violence, and homophobia in the United States. Bearing a distinct Turkish stamp in form and content, *No Name* also anticipates and elucidates Baldwin's later, little-discussed novels *If Beale Street Could Talk* and *Just above My Head* and helps to explain his feelings of entrapment in the American "house of bondage" on the one hand and his desire for a Turkish "home on the side of the mountain" on the other.

The conclusion, "Welcome Tables East and West," reads his last, unpublished play, cowritten with the African American theater director Walter Dallas, as a kind of literary testament in the context of Baldwin's late writings on gender and sexuality. Begun in Istanbul and completed in France, *The Welcome Table* shows how Baldwin's engagements with his and his friends' interpretations of Turkish notions of sociability helped him not only to establish his art as his home and hearth in the world but also to claim femininity and queer and transgender subjectivities as artistic inspirations. Anticipated in *No Name*, whose experimental form and radical message on race and sex caused some critics to accuse Baldwin of "madness," *The Welcome Table* echoed his preoccupation with feminine narrative perspectives and authorial personae in the essays "The Preservation of Innocence" and "Here Be Dragons," the novels *Go Tell It on the Mountain* and *If Beale Street Could Talk*, and the play *Blues for Mister Charlie*.

ACKNOWLEDGMENTS

Like the people who write them, books depend on and are sustained by complex and changing relationships with others. This one has led me to many who share my enthusiasm for James Baldwin's works—colleagues, students, artists, archivists, and interview subjects in Turkey, the United States, France, and Switzerland. Some of them have become close friends in the process, some disappeared from my life. So many others had fleeting contact with various parts of my work—commenting on my ideas at conferences, discussing my writing after guest lectures or workshops, or volunteering observations about Baldwin and information about resources—that I fear I cannot include them all here. Before I begin, then, let me apologize for that, as well as thanking all for their support and encouragement. This project has occasioned a veritable welcome table.

First, I would like to thank the anonymous readers for Duke University Press, and the editors who oversaw my book's transition from a manuscript to published volume: Reynolds Smith, who encouraged me to focus exclusively on Turkey and whose colorful tales of his own hippie-year travels in Istanbul added an unexpected bonus to our meetings; Bill Henry, who served as the copy editor; Pam Morrison and Sharon Torian, who helped to make the final product appear worthy of its subject; Amy Ruth Buchanan, who designed the beautiful cover and oversaw the placement of Sedat Pakay's wonderful photographs and other visuals throughout the volume.

Second, I began planning this book during my last year at Aarhus University in Denmark, and so I would like to thank my colleagues at Engelsk Institut, Gender Studies-"Cekvina," and American Studies Center Aarhus (ASCA), especially Prem Poddar, Kirsten Gomard, Tim Caudery, and Dale Carter, as well as all my students, especially Klaus Dik Nielsen and Carmen Maier, for their early encouragement and support. I am also grateful to Aarhus University's Forskning Aufdeling for sponsoring my trip to France and to the Center for Kulturforskning, where I held a fellowship in 1999 under the directorship of Niels Ole Finnemann, for intellectual and linguistic challenge and sustenance.

I also wish to thank Professors Genèvieve Fabre and late Michel Fabre for their hospitality and kind advice during my first trip to Paris following in Baldwin's footsteps. Jill Hutchinson, late David Baldwin's partner, welcomed me into Chez Baldwin in Saint-Paul de Vence in the summer of 2000; it was during an enchanted afternoon spent at the welcome table in Jimmy's garden that I decided to follow Baldwin from France to Turkey. In 2007, at another table, in Epesses, Switzerland, an interview with Lucien Happersberger brought the research on this project to a close. That momentous coda was enabled by the hospitality of Boris Vejdovsky and his wife Marianne Vejdovsky-Massy.

My first research trip to Istanbul in 2001 coincided with an international conference organized by the University of Michigan in collaboration with Boğaziçi Üniversitesi and Sabancı Üniversitesi, in which I was invited to participate by Fatma Müge Göçek and Michael Kennedy. As a scholar and friend, Müge has been indispensable in helping me to find links to my subjects in Turkey. I also thank Ayşe Öncü, Kim Fortuny, Aslı Tekinay, and Cevza Sevgen of Boğaziçi Üniversitesi for providing contexts, contacts, and explaining local customs.

The Turkish interviewees for this project—Engin Cezzar, Gülriz Sururi, Cevat Çapan, Zeynep Oral, Sedat Pakay, Oktay Balamir, Ali Poyrazoğlu, and Avni Salbaş—were hospitable and generous with their time and information; they showed me that Baldwin's legacy of humane love was alive and well, more so in Turkey than anywhere else. Others I talked to and corresponded with in the United States and Turkey, as well as in the United Kingdom and Switzerland—David Leeming, John Freely, Minnie Garwood, Walter Dallas, Irvin Schick, Brenda Rein, Kenton Keith, James Campbell, and Lucien Happersberger—were as welcoming and helpful; they shared with me personal memorabilia and stories that could fill another book, and they patiently corrected some of my factual errors. I am honored to have been in the presence of this distinguished crowd of Baldwin's friends and to have their words and memories to work with in this book. Çok teşekkür ederim/Dziękuję.

Numerous colleagues at the University of Michigan's Program in American Culture and Center for Afroamerican and African Studies deserve my deepest thanks: Michael Awkward, Kevin Gaines, Philip Deloria, Sara Beth Blair, Sandra Gunning, Jonathan Freedman, Jim McIntosh, Jay Cook, Penny Von Eschen, Arlene Keizer, Alan Wald, Carroll Smith-Rosenberg, Patricia Yeager, Tiya Miles, Paul Anderson, June Howard, Matt Briones, Lawrence Davis, Nadine Naber, and Hannah Rosen. They have read various parts or all of the manuscript as it metamorphosed through workshops and presentations over the years. Their critique, advice, and sincere belief in me have been indispensable (including painstakingly close readings of my prose—thanks, Jim!). Coleman Jordan (ebo) helped with key visual and video documentation during my first trip to Istanbul and in Paris in 2000. I also want to acknowledge the assistance of staff in both of my units, the Program in American Culture and the Center for Afroamerican and African Studies, especially Judy Gray, Don Sims, Mary Freiman, Marlene Moore, Tabitha Rohn, Chaquita Willis, and Amy Roust.

Colleagues from other institutions who contributed invaluable editorial advice include Kenneth Warren, who led the American Culture Program Manuscript Workshop (for the first draft of the book) and who has been a model scholar and critic. Other long-distance supporters, Marlon Ross and Thadious Davis, encouraged my nascent ideas to take shape as we met at conferences. Nicholas F. Radel, a dear friend and colleague of many years, has lent a helping hand many a time when I was stuck in the middle of a chapter or grappling with early modern queer theory; as my adopted American sibling, he is living proof that Jimmy's ideal of brotherly love includes transgender attachments.

Students I have taught or worked with as an advisor at the University of Michigan while writing this book—Menna Demesie, Shanesha Brooks Tatum, Deidra Wheaton, Jan Bernabe, Jennifer Beckham, Anya Cobler, Shaun Henderson, Craig Derbenwick, Sean Field, Aymar Jean, Tim Pruzinsky, Ebony Thomas, Dale Vieregge, Charles Gentry, Charles Sabatos, Dallavis Christian, Maria Paz Esguerra, Monica Huerta, Erik Morales, Veronica Pasfield, Monica Sosa, Donavan Williams—have been sources of inspiration and joy and have helped me grapple with many theoretical conundrums along the way. I am also grateful to Charles Sabatos, my past advisee in Comparative Literature, for first alerting me to the Turkish references in Another Country.

Special thanks are due to Aslı Gür, who has been my inveterate research assistant, bicultural guide extraordinaire, and translator in both Ann Arbor and Istanbul. Ian McBride assisted with compiling the bibliography, while Tayana Hardin accompanied me through the labyrinths of index making and proofreading.

This project has received generous financial support from the University of Michigan's Rackham Graduate School, Office of the Vice Provost for Research, as well as from my home units, the Program in American Culture and the Center for Afroamerican and African Studies. I also wish to thank the American Research Institute in Turkey, Tony Greenwood and Gulden Güneri in Istanbul and Bahadır Yıldırım and Pelin Gürol in Ankara, for hosting me during my research trip in 2005. Andre Elizee and Diana Lachetenere at the Schomburg Center for Research in Black Culture were helpful guides in the early stages of archival research; Label Bleu (France) gave me the gift of the jazz CDs (*A Lover's Question* and *Bandarkâh*) featuring Baldwin and his family members; Steffen Pierce of the Harvard Film Archive, Dick Fontaine, and Jerry O'Grady provided rare film material and resources. The Turkish publishers Doğan Kitap and Yapı Kredi Yayınları, as well as the authors İzzeddin Çalışlar and Gökhan Akçura, allowed me to cite from their works and reproduce invaluable images. Sedat Pakay, who has become a close friend as we have talked about his work and friendship with Baldwin over the years, provided the exceptional artwork for the cover and many of the photographs without which this book could not begin to communicate the richness of its visual context.

Throughout the process of writing this book, and accompanying transitions in my life, I have been sustained by the support and understanding of exceptional women. My sister by blood, Gosia Zaborowska, provided inexhaustible understanding and occasional tough love from Warsaw and Kielce; my adopted sisters, Justyna Magdalena Paś, a tireless collaborator who dispensed encouragement and editorial assistance over the last six years, and Tracey Rizzo, my "twin" and hero of feminist resilience for nearly two decades, have always been there for me in Ann Arbor, Asheville, and Ottawa. Nicole King has provided intellectual inspiration and sisterly support ever since we first discovered our shared passions for scholarship and parenting as professor-moms. June Howard, Sandra Gunning, Abby Stewart, Barbara Allen, Maria Diedrich, and Carroll Smith-Rosenberg have been my mentors, editors, and role models. Brenda Rein joined my East-West sisters following our interview in 2006.

My last and deepest thanks go to my extended families in Poland (the Zaborowscy and Cicirkos) and the United States (the Jordans), and especially to my son, Cazmir Thomas-Jordan Zaborowska (Malinek), to whom I dedicate this book. Malinek has shared with me the darkest and brightest moments of this project, and has supported me in ways that I can never repay: Thank you for letting me know that you "love me the most in the world"/ "kocham cię najbardziej w świecie," even on the days when I had little time for you. Cazmir/Malinek makes Baldwin's last lines from *Nothing Personal* hit home: "For nothing is fixed, forever and forever and forever, it is not fixed; the earth is always shifting, the light is always changing, the sea does not cease to grind down rock. Generations do not cease to be born, and we are responsible to them because we are the only witnesses they have."

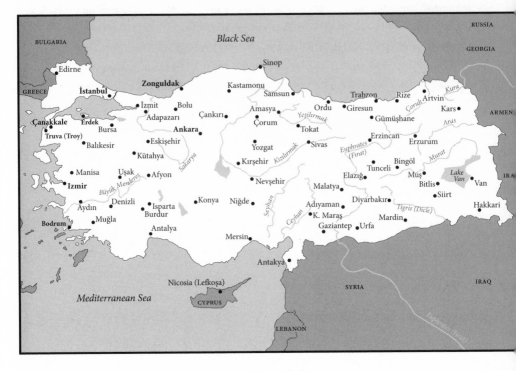

Turkey, 1961–81

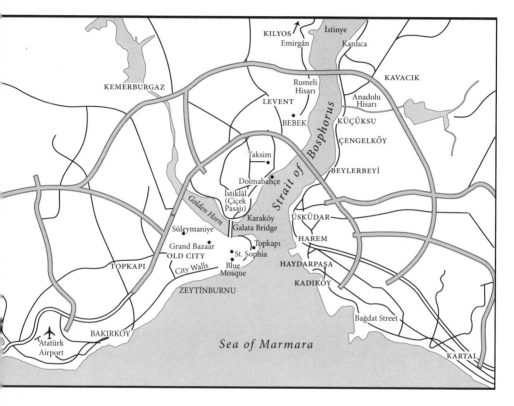

James Baldwin's Istanbul

2. Sedat Pakay, *From Another Place*. James Baldwin in street, Istanbul, May 1970.

INTRODUCTION

From Harlem to Istanbul

"Perhaps only someone who is outside of the States realizes that it's impossible to get out," James Baldwin's voice-over proclaims in a short film by the Turkish director and photographer Sedat Pakay, *James Baldwin: From Another Place* (1973). Pakay's little-known cinematic gem records the writer's movements through the city of Istanbul over a three-day period in May 1970 and frames Baldwin's assertion with seductive photography of private interiors, city streets, and a boat ride on the Bosporus. Like no other existing documentary, the black-and-white film captures the profound paradox of Baldwin's transatlantic vantage point by showing how he both belongs and remains an outsider in the teeming half-European, half-Asian Turkish metropolis. Baldwin's work has occupied an oddly similar position in American literary history and African American studies, as it has been woven in and out of the sometimes overlapping and sometimes discrete canons: American, black, and queer. Like Pakay's camera, this project attempts to bring the conflicting and often contradictory depictions of Baldwin's person and writings together.

In eerie ways and from an unlikely location, Pakay's compelling portrait of the black gay writer in Istanbul echoes the paradoxes of how African Americans were represented in the United States from the middle of the twentieth century onward. Caught between the hypervisibility of racist and oversexualized heterosexist images of African American bodies pervading popular culture and the political invisibility resulting from systemic discrimination by the state's institutions and the population at large, American Blacks were erased and displaced, often violently so. Having to fight for their most basic civil rights in the country that prided itself on the ideals of democracy yet allowed rapes and lynchings to go unpunished, they were trapped in, and simultaneously exiled from, their homeland as "undesirable subjects." While this predicament shaped James Baldwin's life and career to a large degree and forced him to leave the United States in search of writing havens, it also provided a powerful subject for his works that recast blackness, nationhood, and the erotic in a transnational context.

One of the most important American writers of the last century, James Baldwin was marked by his lower-class background, his blackness, and his homosexuality and for much of his adult life found life in semi-exile in France and Turkey easier than in the United States.[1] His illegitimate birth in poverty in Harlem in 1924, his struggle to attain education while helping to raise his eight siblings, and his conflict with a preacher stepfather who disapproved of his intellectual aspirations and berated him for being "ugly" compounded his perception of himself as an outsider and interloper.[2] His parents' slave ancestry and migration north from Louisiana and Maryland added to his sense of displacement and entrapment and, in addition to his illegitimacy, provided powerful and challenging subjects for his works.[3] Baldwin's early passages within New York City, down and up along the island of Manhattan, suggested the shape of his travels to come. As a teenager, he commuted every day from Harlem to the Bronx to attend high school, and then to New Jersey to work at menial jobs. Soon afterward he moved away from Harlem to Greenwich Village, where he began his career as a writer and struggled to come to terms with his sexual identity.[4]

Young Jimmy's journey from the uptown storefront churches of Harlem, where he served as a teenage preacher, to the predominantly Jewish and secular De Witt Clinton High School in the Bronx, where he apprenticed as a poet, writer of short stories, and editor of a literary journal, the *Magpie*, was dramatic. As his long-term assistant, friend, and biographer David Leeming stresses in his 1992 biography of Baldwin, the young man's Bronx journey involved tough lessons about surviving and deploying his excessive visibility as one of the few Blacks at the school, and the only one who represented the Fireside Pentecostal Assembly Church: "[His congregation] would have been scandalized had they been able to watch their favorite boy preacher prancing about with a tambourine in front of several laughing Jewish boys, imitating in song and dance the saints stricken by the power of the Lord at the foot of the cross."[5] While at De Witt Clinton, Baldwin formed friendships with Emile Capouya, Richard Avedon, and Sol Stein that later flourished into important connections and collaborations: Stein edited Baldwin's first essay collection, *Notes of the Native Son*, for Beacon Press in 1955 and became a lifelong friend; Avedon became a famous photographer and collaborated with Baldwin on a unique photo-text volume, *Nothing Personal* (1964); Capouya, who became a publisher, introduced Baldwin to the painter Beauford Delaney, whom Baldwin considered his artistic and spiritual father.

His second important transition, to Greenwich Village, where he worked as a waiter and occasional musician while trying to publish his early writings, took place after stints doing menial labor in New Jersey, or "New Georgia." This move also implied performances of a new identity and another betrayal, as he moved away from home after his stepfather's death, thus abandoning his mother and siblings for what his guilty conscience considered the narcissistic career of a writer.[6] The poet Harold Norse, whom Baldwin met when he was nineteen, evokes Greenwich Village after World War II as "an oasis of liberation to which, from all over America, young men and women flocked to express their socially unacceptable lifestyles."[7] Norse, older by a few years and white, immediately placed Baldwin in a hierarchy of racial stereotypes: "His half-starved, gaunt face . . . looked much older" (111), and his "wild eyes bugging out alarmingly" gave him the "crazed look of a junkie about to kill for a fix" (110). Despite Jimmy's small frame, he saw him as "ready to cut our throats for a quarter" (110). But Norse soon realized that Baldwin had approached him and his friend with similar apprehension: "I was worried. . . . Two white men skulking in the mist in the early hours can only mean trouble for a defenseless black boy" (110). Baldwin's comment evoked the brutal history of American race relations, which made Norse adjust his reading of him from pathological to pathetic, from a potential assailant to a victim, who was "discriminated against by both races," caught up "in a ghetto, outside the mainstream . . . an oddity in Harlem" and an "alien in the white world" (111).

Black, small, queer, and crazy-looking, Baldwin appeared to Norse the uttermost foreigner, out of place even in the bohemian Greenwich Village, and in a sense exiled long before he actually left his homeland. "Being queer was even worse than being black, Jewish, and poverty-stricken," Norse stresses, because "among bottom dogs gays were the bottom" (112). But while Baldwin's skin color made him a victim to Norse, his racialized queerness made him exotic: "His brown parchment skin reflected a silvery glow like an ancient African mask" (112). Still, Norse would often get tired of Jimmy's "desperation [over racism, which] was so intense that I felt guilty for being annoyed" (174). This comment would echo two decades later in his critiques of Baldwin's later works and in Norse's references to their brief affair in his *Memoirs of a Bastard Angel: A Fifty-Year Literary and Erotic Odyssey* (1989), which he somewhat incongruously dedicated, "For James Baldwin. In fond memory of our twenties."[8]

Unlike his ambivalent relationship with Norse,[9] Baldwin's friendship with Beauford Delaney (1901–79) and his soon-to-become-contentious relationship with Richard Wright (1908–60) helped him to embrace the process of becoming a writer.[10] These two black mentors and successful artists helped Baldwin to see himself as valuable and gifted enough to follow his vocation, despite his inability to attend college. Delaney, a son of a preacher and gay like Baldwin, opened up a whole new world to him by sharing his art and tastes in music, colors, and shapes and by introducing him to other famous black artists, Marian Anderson among them, who were "not meant to be looked on by me as celebrities, but as a part of Beauford's life and as part of my inheritance" (*Price of the Ticket*, x). Impressed with sixty-some pages of the novel that Baldwin was struggling with at the time, which would almost a decade later become *Go Tell It on the Mountain* (1953), Wright helped Baldwin to obtain a Eugene F. Saxton Foundation Fellowship and recommended him to Harper and Brothers. Baldwin idolized Wright, and when the older writer left for Paris in 1946, Baldwin "saw in his departure a future path for himself" (Leeming, *James Baldwin*, 50).

Baldwin's brief romance with the Left, perhaps in part encouraged by Wright's stint with the Communist Party, dates from around the time he entered the scene in the Village.[11] He befriended a young black man, Eugene Worth, whom he "loved with all my heart," and who was a member of the Young People's Socialist League (YPSL).[12] Worth persuaded Baldwin to embrace Trotskyism for a short time. Finding himself an "anti-Stalinist when America and Russia were allies," Baldwin soon realized that "it may be impossible to indoctrinate me" (*Price of the Ticket*, xiii). His alliance with the Left—"of absolutely no interest," as he stresses (xii)—ended with a painful loss that he would recall many times and that inspired the description of the suicide of Rufus Scott, the black jazz drummer in his third novel, *Another Country* (1962). Worth killed himself by jumping off the George Washington Bridge two years before Baldwin took off for Paris in 1948. For the rest of his life, Baldwin would regret that he had somehow failed to save him: "We were never lovers: for what it's worth, I think I wish we had been" (xii). After a long struggle, he was finally able to write the scene of Rufus's suicide—one of the hardest things he had ever written, he claimed—while on his first long visit in Turkey.

Before he found himself in Istanbul completing *Another Country*, Baldwin spent nearly a decade in France, where he realized that "Europe had formed us both [American Blacks and Whites], was part of our identity and part of our inheritance" (*Price of the Ticket*, 172).[13] His famed and well-documented flight to Paris took place on Armistice Day in 1948 and initiated his literary life in transit among cultures, languages, and continents. This departure, not to France but *away* from New York City, as he stressed repeatedly, compounded his feelings of estrangement from his country and guilt toward his family. When he attained international renown with the publication of *The Fire Next Time* in 1963, exactly two decades after Baldwin the elder's death on the day of the Harlem riot that his stepson described so vividly in "Notes of a Native Son" (1955), James Baldwin was still in search of a place where he would fit in as a black and queer writer. His intra- and international journeys are vital to understanding him as a migratory writer, a "witness dedicated to blurring the distinction between patriotism and expatriatism, citizenship and exile," as the literary critic Joshua Miller aptly defines him ("Discovery," 338).[14]

Baldwin's transitions from Harlem to Paris and then to Saint-Paul de Vence in the south of France, where he bought a house and remained for the rest of his life, have received much attention in the scholarship published during his lifetime and after his death from cancer in 1987.[15] But few scholars except for the biographers—David Leeming, James Campbell, Fern Marja Eckman, and William J. Weatherby—have followed Baldwin to Istanbul and Turkey. And yet that city and country had considerable impact on his career that must be taken into account today, when scholars of the African diaspora proclaim the importance of the "outer-national sites" for studying canonical African American literature (Edwards, *The Practice of Diaspora*, 4).[16]

Baldwin's little-known Turkish decade, a period roughly between 1961 and 1971, stands chronologically at the center of his multiple journeys—from the Harlem ghetto and Beauford Delaney's Greenwich Village studio, where he first learned "how to see," through the churches and lecture halls and freedom marches in the South, to the salons of jet-setting international literati and the vistas of southern France of his later years. It was an important period of artistic incubation and thematic and formal experimentation to Baldwin that was bracketed by the innovative form of his third novel *An-*

other Country (1962), and the complex essay structure of his little-read fourth collection, *No Name in the Street* (1972). For readers of American literature, Baldwin's Turkish sojourn helps us to embrace more fully the transnational dimension of mid-twentieth-century black literary culture; it helps us to see that "certain moves, certain arguments and epiphanies, can only be staged beyond the confines of the United States, and even sometimes in languages other than English," as Brent Hayes Edwards recently observed (4–5).[17]

Baldwin's Turkish period is also vital to reassessing his contribution nationally and internationally, as we witness the emergence of transnational African American studies. This new field expands and challenges Paul Gilroy's famous formulation in 1993 of the Black Atlantic cultures and has produced interdisciplinary projects by, among others, Bill Mullen, Penny Von Eschen, Nikhil Singh, Maria Diedrich, Kevin Gaines, Tyler Stovall, Michelle Wright, and Melanie McAlister. While *James Baldwin's Turkish Decade* hopes to contribute to the rich conversations in this field, it also engages in dialogue with another emergent field, one that plays on the margins and borders between African American and gender studies, and feminist and queer theory, a field that E. Patrick Johnson and Mae G. Henderson have recently defined as "black queer studies."[18] While relating Baldwin's prolonged stays in Istanbul and other parts of Turkey, this book engages the part of the world that has been persistently eroticized, exoticized, and Orientalized but little understood by the West. My subtitle, *Erotics of Exile*, plays on the stereotypical associations of the East and Islamic cultures with sensuality, on the one hand,[19] and Baldwin's insistence that his prolonged forays abroad must be defined as exile, on the other.[20] It also targets the intersections of race, sexuality, gender, and location that Baldwin explored in his works and rethought and recast amid his new milieu.[21]

As I show in the chapters that follow, Baldwin's attention to the intertwining of the erotic and race in a transatlantic context, and his embrace of what we would today call a "queer" identity, was sharpened and enabled by his Turkish exile precisely because he was free there from the American notions of race and sex. In my research for this book, I have tried to trace the influence of Turkey and its people on the texts that emerged from a prolific period in Baldwin's life, as well as acknowledging his occasional participation in exoticizing and stereotyping Turkish culture. I have done so by bringing together archival material—interviews with Baldwin's Turkish friends, unpublished letters, scholarly and journalistic accounts, photographs and film—with new critical interpretations of his works. Deploying a mix of theoretical tools and methods, from contextualized close readings and biographical accounts, through feminist and cultural studies approaches, to oral history and black queer studies, I offer this book as a contribution to the emergent dialogue on where and how we position the study of African American literature and culture in the twenty-first century.[22]

Looking for Baldwin in the East

Although it provided James Baldwin an excellent vantage point on his homeland and a lens through which to assess the aftermath of the Civil Rights Movement, Turkey may seem a somewhat unexpected location for studying this writer in the context of African American literature and culture.[23] It lies outside the geographic reaches of the African diaspora delineated by Paul Gilroy's landmark project *The Black Atlantic*, and while it fits more easily with the spectrum of international locales taken up by the more recent work in transnational African American studies, it challenges a scholar with the difference of language and cultural context. As Leeming cautions, Turkey was an important location to Baldwin, but not as important as France, where he was a part of a large, vibrant, and well-documented African American community and chose to spend his last years.[24] Unlike France, which is the fictional setting for several of Baldwin's works, Turkey does not appear prominently in any. Nevertheless it made the creation and completion of these works possible as an authorial setting and as such is worthy of careful and thorough consideration. Few American readers know that Baldwin's works and presence have had lasting resonance in Turkish culture, whereas his fans in that country are not only aware of his residency among them but now have two translations of *Another Country* to compare,[25] as well as brand-new ones of *The Fire Next Time* and *Giovanni's Room*.[26] They know that he formed important alliances with local artists and intellectuals and directed a play whose daring focus on prison homosexuality dramatically changed the Turkish theater scene. As Ali Poyrazoğlu, of the original Turkish cast of *Fortune and Men's Eyes* (*Düşenin Dostu*) and currently a prominent actor and director, contemplates restaging the play to celebrate Baldwin's legacy, we can only hope that his endeavor—when and if it comes to fruition—will be recognized in the United States as an integral part of the writer's larger transatlantic story.

Located on the margins of continents—between Europe and Asia, in the vicinity of North Africa and the Middle East—Turkey provided a haven where Baldwin worked on some of his most important, and arguably most American, works: *Another Country, The Fire Next Time, Blues for Mister Charlie,*

Going to Meet the Man, Tell Me How Long the Train's Been Gone, One Day When I Was Lost, and *No Name in the Street.*[27] Some of them would not have seen the light of day without the support of Baldwin's devoted Turkish friends, Engin Cezzar, Gülriz Sururi, Zeynep Oral, Cevat Çapan, Oktay Balamir, and Ali Poyrazoğlu, as well as the cultural newness and "breathing space" that their hospitable country afforded him. Turkey was an alternative location, a space of exile, but also a nurturing dwelling place after Baldwin had spent nearly a decade in France and Western Europe and failed to reestablish a permanent residency in his homeland upon his return in 1957. It became a hideaway during the depressed years following the assassinations of Malcolm X, Medgar Evers, and Martin Luther King Jr., all of whom Baldwin knew and considered friends. As a dramatically different location far removed from his home country, Turkey also provided a powerful lens through which he reimagined himself as a black and queer writer and readjusted his view of American race relations as the 1960s drew to a close. As Baldwin was fond of saying about people, countries, and works that punctuated profound moments in his career, Turkey "saved my life."[28]

Baldwin's first visit to Turkey took place in the fall of 1961. He went at the invitation of Engin Cezzar, a Turkish actor from the Yale Drama School whom Baldwin befriended in New York and cast as Giovanni in the Actors Studio production of *Giovanni's Room* in 1957. Jimmy, as his friends there called him, came to Istanbul with little money, depressed by a trip to Israel, and with a severe case of writer's block that made him desperate to finish *Another Country.* Local hospitality, the love and care of his hosts, and the peace of mind that surprisingly came to him in the middle of bustling Istanbul worked wonders. In a matter of months, fed, housed, and entertained by the extended Cezzar-Sururi-Çapan family, he rewrote and finished his long-overdue novel and returned to the United States to celebrate its publication and bestseller success.

After Baldwin had come back to Turkey a few months later, he established a pattern of remaining there for extended periods of time, returning home for visits with family and publishers, and traveling elsewhere that would last throughout the 1960s. While in Istanbul, he worked with abandon and socialized in a similar manner, as I was told by several of his friends, among them John Freely, a writer and physics teacher at Boğaziçi Üniversitesi (Bosphorus University), and Avni Bey, an Afro-Turk who worked as a bartender in Divan Hotel, one of Baldwin's and his friends' favorite hangouts.[29] Following the phenomenal success of *The Fire Next Time,* Baldwin became an international celebrity sought after by the Turkish press, cultural establish-

3. James Baldwin, Marlon Brando, David Baldwin, and David Leeming in Urcan Restaurant, Istanbul, 1966. Reproduced by permission of Doğan Kitap and İzzeddin Çalışlar.

ment, and high society. His increasing fame and need to stay in close contact with his American publishers and editors at a time when Turkish telecommunications and postal services did not work very well were among the reasons why he decided to move to France in 1971. Baldwin's last Turkish sojourn, "an interlude of almost idyllic calm," took place in the early fall of 1981, when he spent perhaps the happiest months of his life with his brother David, Cezzar, and Sururi at a farmhouse in Bodrum, a resort on the Aegean Sea (Leeming, *James Baldwin*, 358).

Baldwin's long-awaited financial success in the mid-1960s made it possible for him to afford his own accommodations in Istanbul, some of them quite spectacular, and to entertain lavishly. He soon became a magnet attracting other Americans and African Americans who came as either visitors or collaborators.[30] Lucien Happersberger, the Swiss man whom Baldwin met in his early years in Paris and described as the love of his life, came to visit in 1962, while he was going through his first divorce, from the mother of Baldwin's godson, Luc (J. Campbell, *Talking*, 209).[31] When the actor Marlon Brando dropped by in mid-1966, he was clandestinely transported around the city in Cezzar's little car while his limo served as a decoy to deflect the crowds of fans.[32] Jimmy's artistic mentor, the painter Beauford Delaney, came from Paris around the same time and quickly became a magnet for other artists; he painted Jimmy's portrait and a lovely vista of

4. James Baldwin, Bertice Redding and her children, Beauford Delaney, and dog,
Andromache, Istanbul, summer 1966. Photo by Sedat Pakay.

the Bosporus at night.[33] The U.S. State Department officer Kenton Keith
and his wife Brenda and their children, Pamela and Vincent, visited often,
and as often invited Jimmy to dinner at their house in Balmumcu, where
they also hosted the musicians Sonny and Linda Sharrock.[34] The singer Bertice Redding, revered by the Turks for her eccentric style and blonde wigs,
came to chat and cook with Jimmy. Redding's entourage included a teenage
daughter, an adopted orphaned Turkish boy, a Swiss husband, and a puppy,
as evidenced in evocative photographs of the gatherings at Baldwin's house
that were taken by Sedat Pakay in 1966 and 1967. Ann Bruno, a white journalist from New York, was a frequent visitor, and Alex Haley stopped by on
his way to Africa to research *Roots* (Leeming, *James Baldwin*, 275). Baldwin's
beloved brother David came to spend some time with him as well.

When in 1969 Cezzar and his wife, the actor Gülriz Sururi, invited Baldwin to direct a play for their theater, John Herbert's *Fortune and Men's Eyes*
(1967), he employed the jazz musician Don Cherry, who happened to be
passing through town, to write an original score for the performance.[35] The
choreographer Bernard Hassell, who had met Baldwin in Paris, came to
Istanbul on his invitation and collaborated with the Sururi-Cezzar Theater
Company on a production of *Hair*. Hassell later became Baldwin's secretary

and relocated with him to the south of France in 1971. The most famous African American resident in Istanbul besides Baldwin was the multitalented entertainer Eartha Kitt, who had a house in the neighborhood of Üsküdar and sang a catchy and erotically charged song in Turkish about the area.[36] The musicians Sonny and Linda Sharrock visited with the Herbie Mann's band in 1971; they later recorded the original music soundtrack to Pakay's film about Baldwin. As Kenton Keith, who served as the U.S. cultural attaché in Istanbul at the time, explained to me in a recent interview, there was never a large colony of exiled or expatriate African Americans in Istanbul. Still, American Blacks appeared there occasionally: for example, some civil rights activists came through town, a few draft dodgers preferred Istanbul to other European locations, and some Blacks worked at the U.S. consulate, while a handful of the air force military personnel lived in the city, too.[37]

The enticing cosmopolitan metropolis of Istanbul was the place where Baldwin spent the most time while in Turkey, and he came to love both the city and its people. Amid bazaars, mosques, and ancient sacral and Atatürk period secular architecture, with gigantic ships, including many American warships, passing through the picturesque strait of Bosporus, he not only worked on the books that were published but also planned many that were never finished or realized. Among them was a project for a triple biography of Malcolm X, Medgar Evers, and Martin Luther King Jr., tentatively named *Remember This House*, and a novel on Muslim themes, *No Papers for Mohammed*, "whose roots were sunk in Turkey" (J. Campbell, *Talking*, 271), which would echo years later in Baldwin's last completed, and unpublished, play, *The Welcome Table* (1987).[38] At the end of the decade, frustrated by his experience with Hollywood, where he was invited to write a screenplay for a film based on Malcolm X's life and on Alex Haley's biography, Baldwin finished and published his unrealized scenario with Dial Press as *One Day When I Was Lost: A Scenario Based on "The Autobiography of Malcolm X"* (1972).[39] Among the papers that Baldwin left with Oktay Balamir, his friend and the translator of *Tell Me How Long the Train's Been Gone*, there is a stage adaptation of *Giovanni's Room* dated 1964 and one of Albert Moravia's *A Cultural Experiment* that bears the names James Baldwin and Gene Lerner and the date of November 1969.[40]

Despite his negative experience with Columbia Pictures at the time of his involvement with the Malcolm X project, Baldwin dreamed of making movies and wrote two screenplays directly linked to Turkish and Greek cultures in collaboration with Cezzar. Encouraged by his energetic Turkish friend, he also wanted to realize film versions of *Blues for Mr. Charlie*, *Giovanni's Room*,[41] and *Another Country*, none of which saw the light of day.[42]

When Cezzar visited Baldwin in his new Provençal abode in Saint-Paul de Vence between 1979 and 1980, he proposed that they write together a screenplay based on a play by a Turkish playwright, Güngör Dilmen, entitled *Kurban* (The Sacrifice). They completed a version, but it was never realized as a film.[43] On his last visit in Turkey in 1981, Baldwin and Cezzar wrote another script, *The Swordfish*, which Cezzar quotes in his memoir as having been an adaptation of a novel, *L'Espadon* (The Swordfish), by the Turkish writer Osman Necmi Gürmen, who lived in France and wrote in French.[44]

A few years later, on his deathbed, Baldwin asked David Leeming, whom he first met in Turkey, to read to him from that screenplay.[45] As Leeming recalls, "Since I knew Turkey well and had been several times to Greece and to Cyprus, he wanted my opinion on whether or not he had captured the atmosphere of that part of the world" (*James Baldwin*, 383). Clearly Turkey, its landscape, his life and work there, and friends who welcomed him easily and warmly years ago were much on his mind until the day he died. As Engin Cezzar stressed in our interview in June 2001, he was convinced that his friend Jimmy would eventually have written about his Turkish experience but was too busy with the "usual American matters" and "simply ran out of time."

Baldwin's biographies, by Leeming, Campbell, Weatherby, and Eckman, are the only texts that deal with his Turkish decade as an integral part of his life and career. They include similar albeit somewhat conflicting explanations for Baldwin's extended visits to Turkey. While Leeming aligns ethnically and linguistically diverse Istanbul and its people with Harlem, stressing the familiar,[46] James Campbell capitalizes on the city's erotic and exotic mystique, stressing the alien; Campbell's recent article, "Room in the East," comments on the Turkish publication of Baldwin's letters to Cezzar and emphasizes that he "treated Istanbul as a place of refuge all through the 1960s" (3). Weatherby's *James Baldwin: Artist on Fire* agrees with both while emphasizing that Baldwin was drawn to the new and unfamiliar, even the stereotypically "Eastern" qualities of Turkey: the "ancient city on the Bosphorus seemed to combine the Europe he knew with the Orient and Arab world that were both strange to him" (177).[47] Similarly capitalizing on Istanbul's alien appeal, Eckman describes it as a faraway haven that Baldwin retreated to when he was particularly needy of a refuge or "whenever closer hideaways fail[ed] to immunize him against his own social susceptibility" (148).

Of the biographies, Leeming's offers the most informed, personal, and detailed account of Baldwin's contacts with the places and people of Turkey, including glimpses of several Anatolian locations. Leeming met Baldwin in Istanbul in 1961 while teaching at Robert College—now Boğaziçi Üniversitesi—and later became his secretary and a close friend of the family, whom Baldwin entrusted with the care of his papers.[48] Leeming lived with Baldwin for several years after they met in Turkey, and quotes the writer's stock response to Turkish reporters' questions about his Istanbul sojourn: "[Baldwin] was in Istanbul because he was 'left alone' there and could work better there. The fact that Turkey was a Moslem country had nothing to do with it, 'except, perhaps, that it's a relief to deal with people who, whatever they are pretending, are not pretending to be Christians'" (*James Baldwin*, 263). Leeming stresses the importance of Baldwin's friendship with Cezzar and the intellectual and artistic community of Istanbul's unequivocal welcome of him as an artist and activist, regardless of his race and sexual orientation.

Leeming's biography also describes a disturbing incident during Baldwin's visit to the Anatolian village of Erdek that confirms that it was not always possible to get away from racism and homophobia in Turkey. Although embraced and respected by the villagers, Baldwin was one day beaten up by a bizarre "magician" and his assistant who came to visit Erdek with a show that offended and angered many local people. Baldwin told Leeming about having been entrapped with no clothes on and called a "nigger queer" during the attack; he suffered injuries so severe that he had to be taken back to Istanbul for treatment (266–68). Before they left Erdek, however, the concerned villagers sent a representative who told Leeming that the evil magician "had gone and would not be back" (268); the exact meaning of this proof of Turkish hospitality is left to the reader's imagination.

The villagers who took the frail American black man under their wing and all of Baldwin's Turkish friends referred to him as "Arap Jimmy," or, as Leeming explains it, "'Arab Jimmy,' a term roughly equivalent to 'Black Jimmy'" or a darker-skinned person (266).[49] As much as the term connotes someone of foreign ethnic and geographic origins, it does not, as Cezzar, Leeming, and others assured me, connote references to blackness and essentialized racial difference in the same way that "Negro" or "African" and "black" or even "of color" do in American culture. It means that a difference in appearance has been noted, but that this fact does not have further consequences on the person's everyday life in the way it does in the American context. Again, however, the incident with the magician and the racial slur he used proved that this was not always true. When I spoke to Avni Bey (Avni Salbaş), Baldwin's Afro-Turkish bartender friend, he had a slightly different take on blackness, given his experience and family background. He iden-

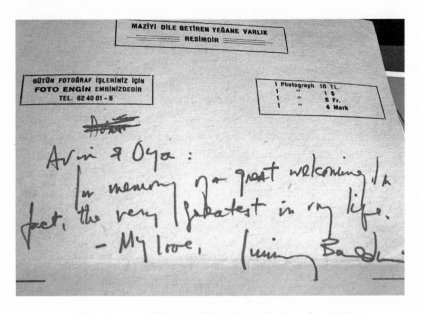

5. Baldwin's note to Salbaş, Istanbul, 1960s. Collection of Avni Salbaş.
Reproduced by permission.

tified his father as "South Arabian" from Mecca and "very dark," and his mother, who came from Anamur in southern Turkey, as "very light." Avni Bey was sent to Istanbul when he was eight, to be raised and educated by his Belgian godmother. A dignified old man who speaks beautiful English, he is aware and proud of his blackness and ethnic origins as an Afro-Turk, not a foreign "Arap."[50] When we talked, he showed me a photograph that he took of his wife, Oya, and of his aunt and Baldwin, as well as the note of thanks that Jimmy wrote him.

James Campbell's *Talking at the Gates: A Life of James Baldwin* (1991) does not dwell as much on the perceptions of Baldwin's race in Turkey as on the qualities of the place that welcomed him. Campbell stresses the sensual, "hermaphrodite Euro-Asian" aura of Istanbul, which "appealed to several different senses" and was a place "unique in Islam: ambitious to adopt Western appearances, it was oriental in its values, its manners, its atmosphere. . . . People were greatly hospitable" (208–9). He suggests that Turkish sociability nurtured Baldwin and its street culture helped him to feel positive about his sexuality: "Strangers were naturally sociable; young men had no shame in touching one another; homosexuality was quite common, and, in its underground form, accepted without fuss. . . . Baldwin himself, naturally gregarious, must have felt that he had landed in an ideal place—

6. Avni Salbaş in Avni's Pub, Istanbul, 2005. Photo by author.

another country, indeed" (209).[51] Baldwin's Istanbul period was an "exile of a different stamp from his first flight to Europe" (210), one that "afforded [him] another sort of freedom, from the treachery of language" (213). Baldwin's decision not to learn Turkish was a deliberate attempt to maintain his resident-outsider status as a "commuter exile." When considered from the United States and Western Europe, Campbell notes, Baldwin's "semi-residency" in Istanbul was considered a biographical "enigma" (208). For his readers and critics at home, James Baldwin was rooted very specifically as an African American writer, and so his location in exotic Istanbul and his identity simply "did not fit" (208).[52]

Straying away from the usual Western European and American trajectories into what Engin Cezzar called "our Babylonia," Baldwin sought a place not only where he could work undisturbed but also where he could shake off the stress of his busy life as a speaker and civil rights activist.[53] He saw it as a safe space compared to other destinations in the Middle East. As he recalled his first visit there in a 1970 interview, he went to Turkey after a tour of the Holy Land: "When I was in Israel it was as though I was in the middle of *The Fire Next Time*. I didn't dare to go from Israel to Africa, so I went to Turkey, just across the road" (Standley and Pratt, *Conversations*, 86).[54] Turkey was both "just across the road" as a central geographic location between Asia, Europe, and Africa and remote enough as a culture fairly alien to most Americans to become something like a safe house for Baldwin. In another interview from the same year, Weatherby reports, "Asked why he had come to Istanbul, he told reporters he had wanted 'a place where I can find out again where I am and what I must do. A place where I can stop and do nothing in order to start again'" (Weatherby, *Artist on Fire*, 302). In an interview with David Frost in 1970, Baldwin stressed the healing qualities of his Turkish hideaway as he painted Istanbul as a neither-here-nor-there liminal space, where it was "great to work." He liked it there precisely because it defied dichotomies of geography, religion, and culture by being "both in Europe and in Asia . . . neither Christian nor Muslim," and because there he could get away from identity labels and simply "try . . . to become a human being" (Standley and Pratt, *Conversations*, 93). Reporting for *Ebony* in the same year, Charles E. Adelsen saw Baldwin in Turkey as "the invited guest in the house" (46). In response to his question "Why Istanbul?" Baldwin pointed out again the unique quality of his Turkish haven as a space of personal renewal: "To begin again demands a certain *silence*, a certain privacy that is not, at least for me, to be found elsewhere" (44).

But when speaking of Turkey with his Turkish friends, Baldwin often stressed that to him the place of exile was not necessarily an unproblematic space of refuge. As he told Sedat Pakay in 1970, "There are no untroubled countries."[55] Like many other nations at the time, his temporary home had its own political tensions and had been scarred by a long history of conflicts, conquests, and defeats in the wake of its history as part of the Ottoman Empire. The military coup in 1960 and the subsequent liberal constitutional reform brought about unprecedented freedom of speech and an opening to the West that led to a vibrant period of experimentation and daring productions in the arts. By the time Baldwin got there, much was happening in Istanbul's cultural scene, and all his new friends were engaged in it. Given his lack of Turkish language and the highly educated and largely upper-crust intellectual circles in which he moved, he was not getting involved in local politics and relied on what his friends were telling him about Turkey's situation. Zeynep Oral, a journalist and translator who worked as Baldwin's assistant when he was directing a play for the Sururi-Cezzar Theater in 1969 and 1970, remembers that as the decade wore on, Baldwin became more interested in what was going on in his new home and regularly asked to be informed about daily press headlines.[56] When the government started cracking down on dissenting intellectuals and artists—for example, his close friend the Kurdish writer Yaşar Kemal was imprisoned for some time—he would organize petitions and use his standing as an internationally recognized writer and activist to support good causes.

A holder of a passport issued by the world's superpower, Baldwin considered himself privileged to be a "transatlantic commuter,"[57] yet he felt trapped by his Americanness. While his statement recorded by a *New York Post* reporter in Istanbul in 1968—that "he was in some ways that last unassassinated Negro of his generation"—may have exaggerated the extent of his actual physical danger, it conveyed his awareness of being a marked, or dangerously visible, man.[58] In letters to friends and family, Baldwin repeatedly expressed fears for his personal safety.[59] Recalling how the State Department had prevented Du Bois from attending the Congrès des Ecrivains et Artistes Noirs in Paris in 1955, Baldwin also worried that his passport might be revoked on one of his return visits to the United States. Leeming, who in 1958 had been "approached to work for American intelligence in Istanbul," remembered the sensation of being watched and the suspicions that he, Jimmy, and Baldwin's younger brother David harbored of some USIS employees who frequented their house on the Bosphorus. As Baldwin reported in a letter to Engin written on September 27, 1974, after scheduling a lecture tour in Germany, where *If Beale Street Could Talk* was a "smash" hit, USIS suddenly canceled his contract and "banned" him or announced that he was "unsuitable for use" (Leeming, *James Baldwin*, 308). This had to do with Baldwin's public denunciations of the Vietnam War and his advocacy on behalf of black prisoners. As he stressed in the letter, experiences like that made him realize that it was as impossible to get "into" America as to get "out" of it. He also commented on racism and discrimination across the world, upbraiding the Swiss for living in a "bank" rather than a nation and pointing out that in Germany, where he represented the "celebrated" witness to America's "Negro problem," this problem closely resembled that of the Turkish, Greek, and Spanish workers and their treatment in the former Nazi state.

Baldwin's awareness of the imperial presence of the United States in the world and of global racism increased and sharpened while he was living in Turkey. He was surrounded by friends who embraced radical leftist politics and were artists, writers, and intellectuals: in addition to Engin, Gülriz, and Yaşar Kemal, he befriended the poet and critic Cevat Çapan, drama teacher Hilary Sumner-Boyd, Irish American physics teacher John Freely, and literature scholar David Leeming—all from Robert College—as well as the eccentric artist Aliye Berger, actress Şirin Devrim, Armenian American expatriate Minnie Garwood, and feminist journalist Zeynep Oral. When Jimmy worked at Gülriz Sururi's and Engin Cezzar's theater in 1969 and 1970, he also met a young journalist and translator, Oktay Balamir, who worked for the British Council, and several actors, the flamboyant Ali Poyrazoğlu among them. Most if not all his Turkish friends strongly opposed the Vietnam War, American military presence in Turkey, and the civil and human rights violations by the United States at home and abroad. At the same time, they embraced American culture and Baldwin as its ambassador. In Pakay's film, while observing U.S. Navy warships on the Bosphorus through the window of his Istanbul apartment, Baldwin seems to echo some of the complex sentiments that motivated them all: "The American power follows one everywhere."[60]

Regardless of his fear that he was being followed, that his house was bugged, or that he might be "relieved" of his passport by the American government, as he wrote to Cezzar, Baldwin's sense of entrapment was also an artistic asset. Like other famous twentieth-century intellectuals and writers who had to negotiate multiple locations, cultures, and national allegiances—Frantz Fanon, Gertrude Stein, Edward Said, Salman Rushdie, and George Lamming, to name just a few—exile gave Baldwin a unique outsider-participant perspective on his country and the world. It made him one of the most powerful critics of twentieth-century American culture precisely because he embraced the mixed blessings of his condition with what Cornel West has recently described as "dramatic insights, and prophetic fire . . . [and] a rare intellectual integrity and personal anguish."[61] In Pakay's film, Baldwin explained his vantage point in simple terms of distance and scale: "One sees [one's country] better from a distance . . . from another place, from another country."

But while it allowed Baldwin a welcome distance from which to observe American culture, Turkey and the so-called East were baffling locations for his readers at home. Their bafflement had much to do with how Americans conceived of the world in the aftermath of its Cold War geopolitical divisions, which brought about myopic and racialized approaches to place and nationhood.[62] After World War II, the East included not only Asia but also Eastern Europe, or the scary, barbaric part of the globe staggering under Soviet domination.[63] Turkey, which seemed close enough geographically to be mistaken for a part of that little-known and demonized region, or at least to be seen as having been somewhat influenced by its Evil Empire qualities, was an ambivalent country in most Americans' eyes; it was among the "front lines of the Cold War, places that most tourists avoided."[64] It was a conglomerate of paradoxes: a NATO ally in the Korean War but also a state whose citizens protested the Vietnam War; a secular Muslim country and culture; both modern and ancient, immersed in the past and shockingly radical and modern.

Looking for Baldwin in Turkey then and now forces one to confront Orientalistic clichés about the East that have abounded in American popular culture. In twentieth-century Hollywood movies or dime novels, the Orient was either hyperexoticized or imbued with romanticized "authenticity" and mystique, at the same time as both approaches pictured the region as a reservoir of escapist, often erotic, fantasies for the West.[65] When considered relevant at all to African American culture in the mid-twentieth century, the Middle East was seen through the alliances that the Black Muslims sought with "both Arab culture and the forces of Arab nationalism," as well as the "moral geographies associated with religious communities," as Melanie McAlister claims (Epic Encounters, 86, 87).[66] As a black and queer writer,[67] Baldwin also stood out in sharp relief against a region that was stereotyped as exotic, erotic, and oversexed, as well as permissive toward homosexuality.[68]

And yet these defamiliarizations and dislocations of Baldwin and his works in the East can actually help us to overcome the splits along the lines of race and sex, genre and location, that have so far defined, if not entrapped, him and his legacy in the United States. Reconsidering how various aspects of identity functioned in the Turkish context and how their different configurations might have influenced Baldwin's thinking on Americanness opens up new perspectives on reading his writings today. Reminiscences of Baldwin by the Turks I interviewed for this project reveal him as both a familiar and somewhat anomalous figure—a perspective that sometimes echoes, and sometimes subverts, his representations in the United States, where, for example, the historian Carol Polsgrove construes him as an odd man in the Civil Rights Movement, while the literary critics Kendall Thomas, Dwight McBride, and Maurice Wallace approach him as one of the representative father figures.[69] In his Indians in Unexpected Places, the Native American historian Philip Deloria argues that "cultural expectations are both the products and the tools of domination . . . an inheritance that haunts each and every one of us" (4). Baldwin's legacy has been categorized according to the expectations that reflected the trappings of his identity as a black and queer man, that is, by privileging either race or sex. We have therefore inherited and been haunted by the black writer from Harlem of Go Tell It on the Mountain or by the gay writer from Paris of Giovanni's Room.[70] By destabilizing these notions, by offering an alternative location where they were played out and recast, Turkey helps us to understand and challenge their origins, rigidity, and arbitrariness.[71]

In the eyes of many of his American readers and critics, Baldwin's "Eastern hideaway" defined him according to a sexualized geography of the world, or what I call the "erotics of location." In 1970 *Ebony* magazine's Charles Adelsen described a "love affair" and "a kind of attraction for each other" between the writer and the "person-like," polysensual, and erotically charged city of Istanbul and placed them both on the "edge of the Orient" (44).[72] Such an approach could be seen as echoing a traditional way of regarding the exotic East as the locus of illicit erotic desire that must be tamed and rendered safe. As the cultural critic Irvin Schick theorizes it: "The West's sexual panopticism is indeed the construction of power over the Orient; it is appropriation through voyeurism, subjection by denuding" (*The Erotic Margin*, 15).[73] As he wrote to Cezzar in one of his letters, Baldwin was acutely aware that some of his readers, critics, and editors considered his Turkish visits a kind of "sex tourism" or "sex exile" — a perception that obviously revealed much more about their own voyeuristic approaches to race and sexuality than it "denuded" anything substantial about the writer.[74]

That the perceptions of Baldwin's race and sexuality sharpened in direct proportion to the distance separating him from the United States is clear from the critiques of his works and person that were published in the mid- and late 1960s. In a celebrity biography, *The Furious Passage of James Baldwin* (1966), Fern Marja Eckman sexualizes Baldwin's racial pain: "Baldwin tests everybody. . . . [His] anguish . . . spurts from him like semen" (243). He is the priapic black gay man who writes "hard," but also a gender-bending artist whose "labor pains are intense and prolonged" (120). The macho icon Norman Mailer famously called Baldwin's prose "perfumed," which Mailer's devotee Eldridge Cleaver dutifully repeated in his own attack on the author of *Another Country* in *Soul on Ice* (1968). Cleaver saw Baldwin as a sissy fearing the "stud" in himself, as self-hating and sick from the "intake of the white man's sperm," as "bending over and touching . . . [his] toes for the white man" (102). Even the unattributed article in *Time* magazine that featured Baldwin's face on the cover on May 17, 1963, and thus confirmed the peaking of his fame that year, denied that he was a civil rights leader and described him as "effeminate." While the United States postured as the home of true manhood, both white and black, not only could sissy men not be heroes or gay men not be manly there, but they were also considered foreign and outlandish. Not long ago, having heard my presentation on Baldwin's Turkish connections, a conference session participant took me aside to tell me that he was certain that Baldwin must have gone to Turkey for . . . the "Turkish baths!" Blinded by race (what would a black writer be doing in Turkey of all places?) and homophobia (a queer man would be there solely for the homoerotic allure of the hamams!), Baldwin's American audiences of all hues continue to see him as a displaced anomaly and a "sexual freak."[75] Baldwin anticipated this perception of himself by fellow Americans and used this very term to describe himself in No Name in the Street, a powerful autobiographical reconsideration of his relationship with manhood that was written in Istanbul and significantly influenced by his contacts with Turkish culture.

The critiques of Baldwin as either a race traitor or an angry panderer to Black Power, as some Whites saw the persona behind his later works, obscure his serious international involvement not only in antiracist but also in antihomophobic politics.[76] They leave out his increasingly prominent focus on the intersections of race, sexuality, and social space in his later works, such as Blues for Mr. Charlie, Tell Me How Long the Train's Been Gone, No Name in the Street, If Beale Street Could Talk, Just above My Head, and The Welcome Table, all of which have some ties to drafts, outlines, and planned projects in Turkey. Since his early essay "The Preservation of Innocence" (1949),[77] Baldwin insisted that race and sex must be approached as immutably interconnected and that homophobia was to be combated along with racism. His whole oeuvre can be bracketed between the publications of "The Preservation of Innocence," which surveys Truman Capote's and Gore Vidal's homoerotic novels of the late 1940s, and his late essay, "Here Be Dragons" (1985), originally published in Playboy as "Freaks and the American Ideal of Manhood," which ponders the vicissitudes of American manhood, as well as embracing androgyny and bisexuality.

Although many scholars in the 1970s and 1980s were resistant to Baldwin's theorizing of sex and gender, some critics commented on his innovative linking of race and sexuality long before it became all the rage in the twenty-first century. Besides Leeming's biography, which approaches Baldwin's works as complex parables of identity, Horace Porter's Stealing the Fire: The Art and Protest of James Baldwin (1989) claims that Baldwin "subliminally conflates race and homosexuality. . . . To . . . [him], sex and race, in America, are hopelessly intertwined" (153). Representing Baldwin as an icon of racial suffering, but by means of a gender-bending image of Hawthorne's Hester Prynne in blackface, F. E. Dupee's review of The Fire Next Time both castigates its author as an angry "Negro in extremis" who betrayed his European education and confirms that white critics saw blackness and nonnormative sexualities as interconnected. Baldwin's exhortations that liberation from racism must go hand in hand with liberation from sexual oppression were hard enough to swallow for his contemporaries when uttered explicitly in *Giovanni's Room* and *Another Country* and, more subtly, even in *The Fire Next Time*, where he discusses "sensuality" while contemplating religion, jazz, and national identity (60).

Baldwin's radical placement of bisexuality and interracial relationships at the center of *Tell Me How Long the Train's Been Gone*, which was written in his outlandish Orientalized location in Turkey, confused and embarrassed both his white and black audiences. In contrast, this novel was enthusiastically received when it appeared in Oktay Balamir's Turkish translation in 1973. As Lynn Orilla Scott argues, Baldwin's last novel, the hefty *Just above My Head*, was rejected due to its open celebration of black homosexuality (*James Baldwin's Later Fiction*, 122). Moreover, as Robert Reid-Pharr stresses, the "huge increase in the visibility of homosexual communities, particularly in the nation's cities," signaled, especially so for black communities, a sign of a "deep crisis . . . of identity and community that threw into confusion . . . the boundaries of (Black) normality" ("Tearing the Goat's Flesh," 378–79). No wonder, then, that even in 1984, just three years before his death, Baldwin felt he had to reinforce his point in an interview with Richard Goldstein: "The sexual question and the racial question have always been entwined."[78] Baldwin's insistence on sex and race as inseparable may seem unduly repetitive to today's readers, given our access to a wider spectrum of African American literature and criticism on the subject, but must be remembered as a revolutionary contribution that not only preceded the women's and gay rights movements of the late 1960s but also anticipated what is now cutting-edge scholarship in black queer studies.

Throughout the decade when America experienced its "greening," or sexual and civil rights revolutions, Baldwin's interviews and his correspondence with friends and family prove that he was well aware of the erotically charged allegations concerning his stays in Turkey and deliberately emphasized the working nature of his connection to that country.[79] His works written in Istanbul and his directing of John Herbert's play that explicitly focused on (homo)sexuality in a Turkish context can be interpreted, too, as evidencing Baldwin's awareness of, and reaction to, Western Orientalism, which he confronted perhaps most fully, and paradoxically, while living in a place that was their target, a place that he might once have stereotyped in similar ways himself. From *Another Country*, where Turkey and Istanbul provide shadow referents for New York City and the sexual encounters between its white and black inhabitants, through *Tell Me How Long the Train's Been Gone*, which was influenced by his friendship with the actor Engin Cezzar, to *No Name in the Street*, which echoes Baldwin's experience directing *Fortune and Men's Eyes* in Istanbul, he used Turkey as an authorial location and lens that allowed him to recast Americanness "from another place." Even his last completed work, the play *The Welcome Table*, harkens back to the notions of Turkish sociability that Baldwin experienced while working with Engin and Gülriz's theater company and on his last visit with his friends in Bodrum in 1981.

Turkey also provided Baldwin with a potent example of how much one's immediate environment—literally the very spaces where one lived, slept, and interacted with others—influenced one's ability to work. A few years before his arrival in Istanbul, Baldwin wrote a long letter to Sol Stein, his high school friend and editor of *Notes of a Native Son*, in which he described his writing using references to dwelling and confinement: "I don't, myself, think that I've seriously considered work as a penalty, though I do consider it my only means of understanding the world, and, in fact—at the risk of causing you to gnash your teeth—my only means of feeling at home in the world. I don't know what I think until I've written it. . . . Please, get over the notion, Sol, that there's some place I'll fit when I've made some 'real peace' with myself: the place in which I'll fit will not exist until I make it" (Baldwin and Stein, *Native Sons*, 96–97).[80] This letter, written in early 1957 while Baldwin was in Corsica struggling with early drafts of *Another Country*, describes his awareness that the only "place making" that he is capable of happens through writing.[81] He insists elsewhere in the letter that one's "inner" and "outer" "environments" are the same: "There is no such thing as an 'external environment.' . . . An environment is also an inward reality, it's one of the things which makes you, it takes from you and it gives to you, facts that are suggested by the word itself" (96–97). Baldwin explains here his tendency to flee from one place to another as having nothing to do with a desire to escape his national identity: "If I were trying to escape my environment, I wouldn't be covering the earth to do it. The best way to escape one's environment is to surrender to it." Exile, then, like his writing and mobility, became a form of dwelling to Baldwin. As he emphasized to Stein, "I don't think I'm romantic enough, any longer, to imagine that anything is ever escaped."

Baldwin explored this theme in Turkey while rewriting *Another Country*, and later while working on his fourth novel, *Tell Me How Long the Train's Been Gone*, and his fourth book of essays, *No Name in the Street*. The first and last of these three texts neatly bracket his Turkish decade, given that *Another Country* was finished and revised during his first visit there in 1961, and *No Name in the Street* was completed virtually on the eve of his departure for France in 1970. A best-selling novel describing the tumultuous romantic relationships and travels of a colorful group of New Yorkers in the late 1950s, *Another Country* has been the better known of these two works. *No Name in the Street*, on the other hand, was not received well and fell into obscurity soon after its publication. This unjustly neglected text offers a valuable introduction to the so-called late Baldwin, as it combines an autobiographical reevaluation of his life on the brink of the 1970s with a powerful examination of his visits to the American South, which he sees as a lens through which to approach American culture. It is also a follow-up testament to *The Fire Next Time*, in which Baldwin considers his waning reputation among younger African Americans in the context of gender and sexuality, and in which he relates his activism on behalf of political prisoners in the United States and in Europe. Finally, it offers an important reassessment of how Baldwin understood "intellectual activity" by the end of the 1960s.

Given the ravages of McCarthyism and the Cold War, but also what came after the civil rights reform legislation—the drive to embrace racial and sexual separatism and essentialism among many Blacks—Baldwin insisted in *No Name in the Street* that intellectual activity "must be, disinterested . . . [because] the truth is a two-edged sword—and if one is not willing to be pierced by that sword, even to the extreme of dying on it, then all of one's intellectual activity is a masturbatory delusion and a wicked and dangerous fraud" (31).[82] This passage implies a focus on both the intellectual and the erotic—"brilliance without passion is nothing more than sterility" (31)—that he embraced more fully in his nonfiction prose while living in Turkey. Framed by the rich vistas and aural textures of Pakay's *James Baldwin: From Another Place*, one of my key visual sources in the chapters that follow, Baldwin's pronouncements on the erotics of writing and intellectual activity signal as well his important contribution to locating sexualized and racialized Americanness in a transnational context.

Like France before, Turkey helped Baldwin to escape some of the racist and homophobic climate of his home country and saved him as a writer during a tough period in his life, but it did not make him into an expatriate. Unlike the white male hero figures of twentieth-century American literary history—Hemingway, Fitzgerald, and James—from whom Baldwin distances himself sharply in his 1962 literary manifesto "As Much Truth as One Can Bear," Baldwin saw himself as an exile rather than expatriate and was chastised rather than admired by others for his explorations of foreign places.[83] In 1968, when criticized by the *New York Post* for his prolonged stays in Istanbul, he replied that his presence in that ancient city signified "preparation, not flight," and that there was "no way except death to shut . . . [him] up," despite the fact that by that point, "what we called the civil rights struggle can be said to have been buried with Martin Luther King."[84] To the Turkish journal *Cep Dergisi* he stressed that his flight abroad was necessary to his productivity, and the critiques he kept receiving were in fact welcome: "I have been criticized for so many things, and for so long, that I am quite unable to look at the possibility of being criticized as a danger. The danger probably lies in the opposite direction" (Standley and Pratt, *Conversations*, 63).

Baldwin never avoided criticism, even when it hurt him to the core, as was the case when it came from other African Americans, such as Eldridge Cleaver or Amiri Baraka, who berated him for his sexuality and contacts with Whites. He also criticized his home country the more severely the longer it remained involved in Vietnam. He summarized his expanding view of the United States in the world in an interview with Sedat Pakay, recorded in Istanbul in 1970 during the production of Pakay's film: "And furthermore you look at other countries you cannot pretend that any country is free of the blood-guiltiness, which so dishonors my own." Baldwin's realization that no other state was free from the "blood-guiltiness"—exploitation, racism, and systematic murder—of which he accused his homeland was small consolation. As I was told by many of his Turkish friends, he claimed that American ignorance lay at the root of many of the world's problems. Recorded at the end of his Turkish decade, and never published, his interview with Pakay contains an indictment of "the most powerful country in the world, which is also the most ignorant, and in terms of action these days, is the most wicked." It is worth quoting at length:

> American ignorance is a new phenomenon, I think. It's not the ignorance of your peasant in Anatolia, or any peasant anywhere. . . . If you are dealing with people who do not know how to read and know they don't know how to read, it is at least conceivable that you can teach them how to read. If an African peasant doesn't know how to drive a tractor, or how to irrigate a barren field, he can be taught those things. But I don't know

what you do with the people who are ignorant in the way Americans are ignorant. Who believe they can read, and who read their *Reader's Digest*, *Time Magazine*, the *Daily News*, who think that's reading, who think they know something about the world because they are told that they do.

By placing American ignorance in a global context, and specifically in an unfavorable comparison with the problems of the so-called Third World, Baldwin stressed its magnitude and international impact. Speaking more directly and openly than he ever did when criticizing the United Sates at home, he also explicitly targeted the legacy of American exceptionalism and, implicitly, the American educational system for the inability of many to think independently. In a sweeping statement, and perhaps pandering too eagerly to his Turkish audience's anti-American sentiments, he castigated his compatriots, who "think that they know something about the world because they think that they are better than the rest of the people in the world, better than the other countries in the world . . . [and] have no respect for language, and they cannot read, and it means they cannot think." A grandson of a slave who never finished college because of his race and class, Baldwin must have felt that he had every right to be angry at Americans who did not use their privilege to learn more about the world.

In the same interview, Baldwin explained to Pakay another reason for his anguish and despair, that is, his belief that Americans lacked self-knowledge and self-reliance, those most American of characteristics extolled by founding fathers of the national letters such as Emerson and Thoreau: "They can never find out what's inside them, what they really mean, they can never divorce themselves from what they think they should think." As the "most fully Emersonian of democratic intellectuals in our history," as Cornel West defines him (*Democracy Matters*, 78–79),[85] James Baldwin devoted his life and career to exposing and battling his compatriots' ignorance about the world, about themselves, and about the various Others in their midst. As a black and queer writer, as we would call him today, Baldwin was marked as much by his racial as by his sexual otherness, and was thus doubly displaced and exiled in his home country, but was able to turn his marginalization into a catalyst for writing that redefined the meaning of American identity not only for the twentieth century but also for our own.[86]

James Baldwin Now

The publication of *Collected Essays* and *Early Novels and Stories* in the prestigious Library of America series in 1998 recognized James Baldwin as belonging to the national literary pantheon.[87] But while his books can now be tastefully displayed side by side with those of Henry James, Baldwin's favorite American writer, scholars are still disputing his oeuvre's worth along the lines of race, sex, and genre: whether Baldwin was "the defining voice" of black Americans during the Civil Rights Movement or sold out to the Whites,[88] whether in his attention to the erotic he set out to "illustrate [that] . . . Negroes . . . make love better . . . dance better . . . cook better,"[89] whether he was a better novelist or essayist. The majority of scholars, with several notable exceptions,[90] still split Baldwin's career into a period of artistic ascendancy and regrettable descent, from the publication of *Go Tell It on the Mountain* (1953) to the incendiary essay-epistle *The Fire Next Time* (1963), and from the play *Blues for Mister Charlie* (1964) to his last published work, the polemical essay *The Evidence of Things Not Seen* (1985). The tacit or in-your-face agreement that Baldwin's output after *The Fire Next Time* lacks merit, even among those who have not read his late works, is reflected in the very publication that has recognized him as a classic. We are yet to see the volume of his "late novels" from the Library of America.[91]

As we await new scholarship and new appreciation of this writer's later works, it is clear that Baldwin's Turkish decade stands at the crux of his biographical and authorial journeys. It helps us to trace his progress from the Harlem ghetto and Beauford Delaney's studio in Greenwich Village to the salons of international literati, and from the experimental novelistic form of *Another Country* to the complex essay structure of *No Name in the Street*. Positioning my project in conversation with past and present scholarship on Baldwin, I distance my readings from approaches that segregate the black writer from the gay writer and the novelist from the essayist.[92] Baldwin's Turkish sojourn helped him to articulate his key artistic and political concerns on the interdependence of race and the erotic in constructions of American identity, which should prompt more nuanced, transnational readings of his works across the fields of African American and American literary and cultural studies. And as much as placing Turkey at the center of his career helps us to read Baldwin's later works in a new light, it also provides us with critical tools for productively reassessing his earlier writings, especially those depicting migration, relocation, and transatlantic passage.

I read Baldwin's Turkish decade as a kind of voluntary exile, a temporal and spatial process of artistic incubation and discovery that resulted in new ways of seeing and conceptualizing (African) Americanness across the Atlantic. Edward Said's definition that stresses the in-between, neither-here-nor-there character of late-twentieth-century exile rings especially true given Baldwin's sense of entrapment in national identity: "For most exiles the difficulty consists not simply in being forced to live away from home, but rather, given today's world, in living with the many reminders that you are in exile, that your home is not in fact so far away" ("Intellectual Exile," 370). Said's notion stresses the inherent combination of geographic, linguistic, and intellectual factors that shape the exilic intellectual's "double perspective." Given Baldwin's conviction that the legacy of one's birthplace could not be escaped and his commitment to the fight for civil rights at home, while he was certainly immersed in, and appreciative of, Turkey as a kind of a houseguest, he lived there with a somewhat modified diasporic version of Du Bois's "double consciousness," what Said terms the "constant but tantalizing and unfulfilled touch with the old place."

Sedat Pakay's marvelous film captures the waning of James Baldwin's Turkish decade in 1970, but also the fact that the writer in exile found in the city of Istanbul a transitory home. Orhan Pamuk's recent memoir, *Istanbul*, describes the ancient metropolis as a place where someone like Baldwin could thrive and, perhaps temporarily, forget his own entrapments as a migrant: "Caught . . . between traditional and western culture . . . overrun . . . by wave after wave of immigrants, divided . . . along the lines of its many groups, Istanbul is a place where, for the past 150 years, no one has been able to feel completely at home" (115). As Baldwin's readers, we can try to imagine how he felt on that sea of strangers, but we will never know, of course, how he actually saw the city and his life there.

Speaking of his own exile and colonial and postcolonial experience as a West Indian, George Lamming stresses that "what a person thinks is very much determined by the way that person sees."[93] While interviewing Baldwin's Turkish friends, I experienced something similar, or how thinking is affected by point of view and ways of seeing, how there is often a contentious relationship between vision and rhetoric, memory and expression. As much as they tried to bring back how they saw Baldwin and what they thought when he was among them, they could offer only memories, often tinted with nostalgia, sometimes curiously autoethnographic, but always fascinating and enlightening. Many times Avni Bey's chuckle, "Memory is like the weather," went through my mind as I listened to their stories. I am profoundly grateful to him and all the other Turkish friends of Baldwin for welcoming and talking to me, as well as for showing me their beautiful city and other places in Turkey. In the end, when all the travels and research and endnotes are done, Baldwin's works are there to bring us closer to his thinking, and they, as always, offer us the best way of seeing him at home in the world.

ONE

BETWEEN FRIENDS

Looking for Baldwin in

Constantinople

In 1964 I saw a photograph of James Baldwin in a magazine. I was fascinated by his face, especially his bulging, vibrant eyes.

I was a high school senior in Istanbul, where Baldwin was then living. Through a friend I was able to secure an invitation to meet him. *Jimmy was very different from what I had envisioned:* reading his essays, I thought he might be an angry man, difficult and imposing. The person I met was warm, welcoming, and friendly. His eyes moved constantly, even when he sat quietly, thinking.

I photographed Jimmy many times. . . . I filmed him for three days in his apartment and around the city. That footage became the basis of a short film.

—SEDAT PAKAY

I first encountered Sedat Pakay's intense black-and-white short film *James Baldwin: From Another Place* (1973) excerpted in Karen Thorsen's documentary *James Baldwin: The Price of the Ticket* (1989).[1] It was the late 1990s, and I was teaching Baldwin at Aarhus University in Århus, Denmark, where my all-white students were intrigued and a little confused by the brief sequences from Pakay's small masterpiece.[2] We were as startled to learn that Baldwin went to Turkey as we were by the fact that someone there had become close enough to him to film him in his bedroom and ask about his sex life.[3] Amid the more comprehensive and traditional style of Thorsen's documentary, the fragments of Pakay's footage stood out as close and personal, erotic and seductive, unapologetic and direct. I soon managed to track down the filmmaker and obtain a copy of the film. I have been entranced by it ever since, and its rich imagery, soundtrack, and beauty of design and execution have been constant sources of inspiration and sustenance during the gestation of this book.

From Another Place was shot over three days in May 1970, when Baldwin was approaching the conclusion of his Turkish decade, and roughly six years after he and Pakay had first met. As a visual, dynamic, and metaphoric register of his progression through this decade by a local artist, the film makes an excellent introduction to Baldwin in Turkey. Its focus on both the familiar and unfamiliar, private and public, aspects of his life in Istanbul helps to locate both the famous African American writer and the person that he was at the time in his little-known writing milieu in the East. From the perspective of over thirty years since the film was made and released, and twenty years since Baldwin's death, Pakay's cinematic account offers both a gut-wrenching and comforting confrontation with the writer. It gives us the filmmaker's version of his friend Jimmy, to be sure, as From Another Place is both serious and tender as well as humorous and self-conscious in the touching way that personal memories often are.[4] It also offers a unique window on Baldwin's multivalent identity by questioning and subverting the popular perceptions of him as "angry . . . difficult and imposing." "Jimmy was very different from what I had envisioned," Pakay wrote of meeting Baldwin and photographing him throughout the 1960s in a brief note in a 1999 issue of Transition. This comment echoes the disconnect between the perceptions of Baldwin in Turkey and the United States after the publication of The Fire Next Time, but also the goal of Pakay's film to peer through the many layers of James Baldwin as a public and private person and a transnational black American.

While Pakay's film sheds new light on Baldwin's life outside the United States, it also drives home the fact that we have paid scant attention to how he was received and seen abroad and by non-Americans.[5] What did his Turkish friends think and remember about him? How did he fit in there as a black and gay American? And how did the Turks see him in their world as he worked through various entrapments and trappings of Americanness in the novels, essays, and plays he wrote there? As a cinematic register of Baldwin's private dwellings and passages through the public spaces of Istanbul, Pakay's film provides a good starting point as we try to answer these questions. While it lets us glimpse Baldwin through the lens of one gifted Turkish artist, it also helps us to understand the impact that Baldwin's Turkish period had on the central conflicts of his life and career: the desire to live in the world and the inability to escape America; the longing for stable domesticity; the articulation of a gospel of love and humanism in the face of his killing rage at American racism, homophobia, and imperial domination.

From Another Place begins by displacing and depersonifying Baldwin, as neither the location nor the time nor even the subject himself is made apparent in the opening shot, a close-up of a chin and hands on the off-white screen. The camera then glides down and focuses on slender fingers handling a strand of tespih, Turkish worry beads commonly used in Muslim prayers. We do not see the writer's face and hence do not know who he is, but we know that he is black from the glimpses of his body. We do not know where he is, but the tespih signals "somewhere in the East" for those in the know.[6] There are no signs of the times anywhere, so the historical moment captured with a 35 mm camera remains as blurry as its geographic and human referents. There is no music and no voice-over, only distant noises of the city in the background and the sound of the tespih sliding through Baldwin's expressive hands.

In the next scene, the camera slips inside an apartment, and we see a body in bed, a dark form under light covers. Pakay plays with the viewer's expectations of setting and character once again, as the person lying in bed could be anyone, just as the room could be any room, anywhere. Cengiz Tacer's photography and the impressionistic lighting of the scene magnify the effect of anonymity of place and person and invite comparisons with images of Baldwin's interiors that his readers carry around in their heads—we could be in Giovanni's room from the novel of the same title or in Arthur Montana's from Just above My Head.[7] Baldwin stirs, gets out of bed, walks to the window—a bright rectangle that echoes the bed's form and color—leans forward, and opens the curtains. Wearing only white briefs that gleam in the dimly lit room, he stretches his slight frame while looking out at a panoramic view of the water, mountains, and city. The moment we glimpse his face, we realize that Baldwin's body is almost nude. This is not how we are used to seeing famous writers.[8]

The Bosphorus, that picturesque passage between Europe and Asia at the heart of the ancient-modern-regional-cosmopolitan metropolis of Constantinople/Istanbul, fills the screen for only a split second. The cam-

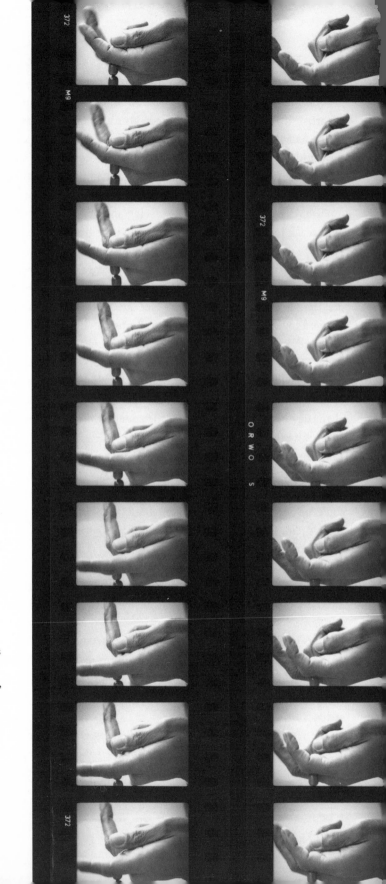

8. Sedat Pakay, *From Another Place*. Baldwin's hands with tespih (Muslim prayer beads), Istanbul, May 1970.

era seems to be looking at it through Baldwin's eyes, or over his shoulder, and this invites the viewer to approach the vista on the screen in a similar manner. There are large boats and barges on the water, one of them an American warship.[9] Baldwin turns and walks toward the camera, fetches a short, dark robe from a closet, turns his back to us, lights a cigarette, and sits down on the bed smoking, pulling the covers about him. The camera slowly closes in on his face. Unlike the first, anonymous shot of his body, this one is intimate, almost unbearable and embarrassing. James Baldwin looks at us closely, returning our voyeuristic gaze unflinchingly. His head appears large in the camera angle, slightly cocked to one side, his neck and eyes vulnerable.

Played against the soundtrack of Baldwin's captivating voice, which begins when we first see him in bed, this powerful opening links the viewer and the subject on-screen in a complex intimacy and an uneasy complicity brought about by Pakay's cinematic intrusion. All throughout, unlike the images of his body that sometimes obscure, sometimes amplify, his identity, Baldwin's voice is unmistakably his. He speaks informally, as if to a friend, in his direct, confessional mode, slightly breathless, often pausing to think or light a cigarette and inhale or exhale the smoke. As he moves about the room, gearing up for another day of work, he describes his sense of displacement and difficult role as a misunderstood artist in exile:

> I suppose that many people do blame me for being out of the States as often as I am. But one can't afford to worry about that. . . . One does, you know, you do what you have to do, the way you have to do it. And . . . *perhaps only someone who is outside of the States realizes that it's impossible to get out.* The American power follows one everywhere. But I am not any longer worried so much about that. I am worried about getting my work done, getting on paper, which is the best way for me, a certain record, which hopefully would be of some value to somebody, some day. . . . Being out . . . one is not really very far out of the United States. . . . *One sees it better from a distance . . . from another place, from another country.*[10]

Baldwin's take on his Turkish exile as a badly needed space for work and reflection is clear in this monologue on the complexities of his entrapment as an American. He feels guilty for being away from the United States, given his calling and responsibility as a black artist, and as the witness and poet that he liked to call himself. Despite criticism from both sides of the color line at home, he defends his way of doing work and employs his unlikely locale to cast Americanness in a transatlantic perspective, to produce a "record" from the vantage point of "another place . . . another country." He is always and foremost a writer: "My tool is my typewriter, my pen," he says.

From beginning to end, Pakay's film can be read as a visual, metaphoric register of Baldwin's progression through his decade in Turkey that highlights both the familiar and unfamiliar, private and public, aspects of place and person. We follow Baldwin through the city of Istanbul, which at once seems grittily real in his random encounters with passersby while evoking at the same time an exotic series of stage sets that have been carefully choreographed for the viewer's benefit. That is, Baldwin seems to be at times in, then completely outside, his element as we follow him to Eminönü, Yeni Cami (the New Mosque), and Mısır Çarşısı (the Egyptian or Spice Bazaar), where he feeds pigeons like a random tourist. When we see him near the busy Taksim Square, however, he looks over his shoulder with a questioning look and flashes us his magnificent, fond smile, as if it were just him and us, locked again in a fleeting moment of intense intimacy. Then we see him photographed by one of those tourist picture takers who sits him down, solemn and squinting in the sunlight, against a piece of textile background that is supposed to signify the authenticity of the location: "a souvenir from Istanbul."

Baldwin's voice-over fades to the music and vocals by Sonny and Linda Sharrock, and we see him walking and then colliding with a passing woman in a head scarf as he skirts a group of men surrounding a snake oil salesman. The salesman rushes toward the camera and for a split second blocks its eye with his hand, after which we see Baldwin walking in Beyazıt, the area of Sahaflar Çarşısı filled with *sahaflar*, or sellers of antique books. A man carrying a sizable bundle on his back negotiates the sidewalk nearby. The titles we glimpse on the bookstand where Baldwin stops hint at his contributions to Turkish culture: *Kara Yabancı* (Dark Stranger), the Turkish translation of *Another Country*; and *Düşenin Dostu*, the Turkish rendering of John Herbert's play *Fortune and Men's Eyes*, which Baldwin had just directed for the Sururi-Cezzar Theater. The book Baldwin chooses and holds up to the camera, *The FBI Story*, seems to carry us back inside his apartment, where we see *Life* magazine with photos of the Black Panthers spread on a cot. American power, politics, and pressures are never far away and in fact invade his private space and seem to haunt his dreams.

Baldwin is now sitting at his desk. The tespih resting beside his hands echoes the film's opening, and his typewriter and a glass of scotch hint at a break he's taking from writing. He is in profile, smoking and talking in-

9. Sedat Pakay, *From Another Place*. James Baldwin with back turned in a crowd, Istanbul, 1970.

tensely about his sexuality being "nobody's business," the camera zooming in on his hands and face, wisps of smoke trailing around his head. The political and the personal, race, sex, nationality, and location intertwine into fleeting formations as Baldwin emphasizes that love "saves" and "comes in strange packages" and that he has "loved some men and some women." That it is not he being interrogated but rather he who is interrogating American sexual conduct becomes clear only at the end of the scene, when he charges American culture, especially "American men," with sexual paranoia and homophobia. Exasperated by his fellow countrymen's ignorance of human history, he is cut off in midsentence when the camera makes us look through the window at two Roma men who wrestle with shackled dancing bears in the street below.

We also see Baldwin having his shoes shined around Taksim, the light-skinned shiner reaching over the elaborate decorations of his brass-and-velvet box, on which Baldwin's elegantly shod foot reposes for a moment—a hint at the reversal of epidermal hierarchies in the place far away from home. And then we are looking at Baldwin's serious profile and his dark, high-necked shirt, contrasting the lacy silhouette of the whitewashed Beylerbeyi Palace as he passes it and other yalı (buildings) on the water in a motorboat gliding over the gray waves of the Bosphorus. The last shot is of Bebek and the Özsüt teahouse, which has since been replaced by a McDonald's, alas.

The film closes on a witty note as Baldwin sits, flanked by two serious-looking Turkish waiters in tuxedos, or "penguins," as Sedat Pakay jokingly called them, and surrounded by a crowd of silent onlookers, all of them stern-faced Turkish men wearing dark hues. The last shot is another close-up of the writer's face. Jimmy is lost in thought, and there is a restlessness and intensity about him; he seems to be looking at us rather than just meeting our gaze. Setting a slim-wasted tea glass on a saucer, he says under his breath, as if continuing a soliloquy whose main part we have missed: "And . . . I've got to move and I've got to finish the book." And when, immediately afterward, the final credits begin to roll, we hear his last words: "And I've really got to get out of Istanbul." Both solemn and semislapstick, a nod toward cinéma vérité and the Keystone Cops, the scene makes us expect the three men onscreen either to begin philosophizing about life or to erupt into a riot of gags and piano music, if not both. Pakay's "brief but insightful work" leaves us wanting more and thus makes perfect sense as a coda to Baldwin's passage through Turkey, which has largely remained a mystery to his American readers (Leeming, James Baldwin, 309).

10. Sedat Pakay, *From Another Place*. James Baldwin in his studio, Istanbul, 1970.

11. Sedat Pakay, *From Another Place*. James Baldwin and waiters in a teahouse in Bebek, Istanbul, 1970.

While the film's release in New York in 1973 came shortly after the end of Baldwin's Turkish decade, Baldwin's third novel, *Another Country* (1962), could be seen as being marked by his arrival in Turkey and his first impressions of its people and culture. His inability to finish the book brought him to Istanbul in search of a new writing haven, whereas his subsequent recovery from writer's block there soon made the Turkish metropolis into his cherished home space. But before we look closely at the Turkish imprint on *Another Country*, which deserves a chapter of its own, let us consider the circumstances of Baldwin's entry into Istanbul. His Turkish friends shed light on his assimilation to the new space and his strivings to make it his transitory authorial home. Just as Pakay's film helps us to access Baldwin's connection to Turkey by providing intimate images of his private and public spaces in Istanbul, so the recollections of the men and women who first received him there, as well as glimpses of the actual spaces where he lived and worked, are indispensable to contextualizing his realities and representations as a black American writer in exile.

Heimat, or Home Spaces

The shock of Baldwin's arrival in Turkey in October 1961 was softened by his protective circle of friends, who made sure he could rest and write undisturbed or be entertained and shown around if needed. David Leeming, who met and befriended Baldwin at a party when *Another Country* had just been finished, emphasizes that the Turkish metropolis soon became the writer's "third home." It was so because "Istanbul was clearly a cast of characters for a man with Baldwin's instinctive interest in social and personal complexity" (*James Baldwin*, 194). At the same time, Baldwin was running away from home; as he told Ida Lewis in 1970, "It was very useful for me to go to a place like Istanbul at that point in my life, because it was so far out of the way from what I called home and the pressures" (Standley and Pratt, *Conversations*, 86).

The themes of home and homemaking weighed increasingly on Baldwin throughout his Turkish period. At one point he even seriously entertained the idea of buying a house in Istanbul to secure a more permanent writing base there. In the end, however, the city provided him only with a series of temporary dwellings. And yet Istanbul as a potential—and perhaps unrealized—space for domesticity was on Baldwin's mind for a long time after he left Turkey. In his last novel, *Just above My Head* (1979), the main character, the gospel singer Arthur Montana, thinks of buying a house in that idealized location when he grows tired of his fame.[11] Baldwin also wrote to David Leeming about the pleasures of domesticity in an unpublished letter of December 27, 1965, in which he mentions his reluctance to return to New York and how cozy and contained he felt in a "very nice" apartment in Istanbul, where he surrounded himself with food and "little gimcracks, like mirrors, and ash-trays," and life "looked very peaceful."[12]

Baldwin's increasing preoccupation with setting, place, and specific situations of dwelling and writing throughout the sixties inflected several letters to Engin Cezzar, with whom he also shared accommodations when they first met and worked on staging *Giovanni's Room* in New York in 1956. After Cezzar went back to Turkey, they wrote to each other for almost twenty years.[13] In one letter, Baldwin reports on his accommodations at the MacDowell Colony for writers in New Hampshire (letter 1, November 22, 1957), which was his "favorite writing sanctuary" (Leeming, *James Baldwin*, 148), and in another describes a "rather large" and "indisputably primitive" apartment in Paris (letter 4, September 23, 1957) that still allowed him to bear all kinds of things "more easily" (letter 6, August 12, 1958). A year later he mentions "a grim, inland room with a gas heater" and reports being the only guest in an "enormous, hideous hotel" in Cherry Grove, New York (letter 13, May 6, 1959). The first letter to Cezzar, now partially quoted in Campbell's article on the Turkish edition of Baldwin's missives to his friend, contains a significant statement which reflects the writer's longing for a haven and anticipates some of the actual locations where he would be living in Istanbul: "One of these days, I'm going to build myself a place to live and work at the side of the mountain or at the edge of the sea" (letter 1, November 22, 1957).

While living in Turkey, at one point practically next door to Cezzar in the Taksim Square neighborhood, he describes to him his apartment trouble in a note carried by his maid. Apparently Baldwin had to find shelter immediately, having been thrown out with his "sad tribe" of companions and family, because "the ancient Ottoman" who owned the building decided to no longer rent to anyone from Robert College. Apparently the landlord had been told not only about Baldwin's ties to the college but also that his books were "a scandal" and that he was a scandal, too. Baldwin ends the letter with an exclamation to the effect that the landlord should have known him in the days when he really *was* a scandal (note, letter 34, n.d.).

In 1968 Baldwin also reported to Cezzar on his efforts to secure a more permanent dwelling in New York, which Cezzar, a cosmopolitan graduate of Robert College, considered an adopted home. Jimmy's letter describes a lunch with his brother, David, "in Antibes," where they met with a house agent. Baldwin explains his interest in real estate by means of linking home and exile. He has been "looking at houses," but "with an eye to flight"; he would soon be talking about it all to Engin in Istanbul (letter 40, September 15, 1968). Throughout the years, Baldwin would send Engin requests for help in locating a new space after a visit in the United States. Often these would be rather short notices, speaking of his desire to move into new accommodations in a matter of weeks. In 1969 he wrote that he needed a summerhouse, where he would be "two" — arriving with a companion — and staying "until the fall" (letter 41, June 9, 1969). At the end of the decade, having also tried unsuccessfully to purchase a flat in Paris, he wrote about his desire to return to his unique writing haven of Istanbul, because the "entire world" had become "just about" uninhabitable and it was only in Turkey that he hoped to "get some work done" (letter 42, July 7, 1969).[14] This sentiment confirms as truth Baldwin's suspicion as a younger writer that making one's home might only be possible in one's work, a suspicion he voices in an undated letter to Sol Stein written in the mid-1950s when he was working on the short story "Sonny's Blues": "It will be nice to see the homestead [NYC] again. It would be even nicer if I could feel that I'd ever feel at home there. I'll tell you this, though, if you don't feel at home at home, you never really feel at home. Nowhere. I try to keep remembering something Peter Viereck told me, simply that you don't live where you're happy or, for that matter, unhappy: you do your best to to live where you can work" (Stein, *Native Sons*, 87).

In the 1960s, which Michael Thelwell describes as a period when "history and politics and literature . . . [were] inextricably intertwined," Baldwin's homemaking in Istanbul helps us to understand him as a writer and activist who was also deeply concerned about making the United States a better home for Blacks. Thelwell insists, "When it became clear that all of America's assumptions would have to be redefined—that the nature of discourse on the question of the Black presence and its meaning would have to change forever . . . Jimmy Baldwin . . . [was] the defining voice."[15] Baldwin's search for dwelling places and his desire for a permanent domestic space in Turkey paralleled his search for new literary expressions—a transformation that we can follow between the publications of *Another Country* and *No Name in the Street*, which bracket his Turkish decade.[16] Baldwin's home spaces in Istanbul provide an important physical framework for the works situated and emplaced in America that he wrote while living in Turkey.

Unlike the majority of his American locations, many of which have been demolished in the manner sadly typical of the U.S. culture of architectural erasure and ready-made replacement, all the buildings in which Baldwin lived in Istanbul still stand. But the fabric of the Turkish metropolis has preserved the physical settings of Baldwin's writing only by sheer accident; since his departure in 1971, Istanbul has been demolishing old buildings, expanding, and erecting new structures with increasing speed. The results of this building boom, as many of my interviewees pointed out, are not always pleasing to the eye. Aesthetic qualities of the new cityscapes aside, it was still exciting to me as a researcher and reader to see the surviving (for how much longer?) sites.

In her recent study of the houses of major Western writers and thinkers, Diana Fuss stresses the importance of "houses that sheltered and shaped the imagination of writers."[17] She argues that interiors shape how writers think, feel, and write because the "intensely private act of putting thoughts into words takes place in an environment enlivened by the sights and sounds, the textures and smells, and even occasionally the tastes of a fully embodied life" (215). This compelling description of a located and rooted writing process, however, seems to presume a settled lifestyle and signals privileged subjects.[18] How, then, can we talk about homemaking and writing in the case of writers who, like Baldwin, have been excluded, or choose to remove themselves, from the traditional racialized notions and trappings of bourgeois domesticity?[19]

In a study of "homemaking myths" of non-Anglo European immigrants, Orm Øverland stresses that they are "an essential feature of American ethnicity"; they are "expressions of an American identity created in the face of Anglo-American denials of such an identity" (Immigrant Minds, 21).[20] Øverland's trope of homemaking helps to explain the shifting hierarchies of immigrant whiteness and the competition to ascend to their top among various immigrant groups "in a nation where the indigenous people had always been seen as the absolute and defining Other" (13). In a daring comparison of the African middle passage and the "Irish middle passage" to the New World in "The Price of the Ticket" (1985), Baldwin anticipates some of Øverland's rhetoric by arguing that the notion of America as a safe house is a myth: "I know very well that my ancestors had no desire to come to this place; but neither did the ancestors of the people who became white and who require of my captivity a song" (xix–xx). Baldwin sees both groups as "shipwrecked forever, in the Great New World," and asks all Americans to "reexamine everything" in an attempt to "know whence you came"; they must all put their house in order, he prophesizes (xix). As a writer in exile who could not disconnect from his homeland, he also experienced what the exiled Polish poet Czesław Miłosz, who lived in the United States roughly at the time when Baldwin was in Turkey, explained as the inextricable link between writing and location: "Language is the only homeland."[21]

The postcolonial poet and critic Meena Alexander, a migrant writer in her own right, offers an evocative description of dwellings for authorial imagination: "And so the shelters the mind makes are crisscrossed by borders, weighted down as a tent might be by multiple anchorages, ethnic solidarities, unselvings" (The Shock of Arrival, 7). Alexander's notion of "unselving," which refers to temporary settling down and transitory emplacement, helps to expand Fuss's definition of "writers' lairs" in ways that are useful for reading Baldwin's dwellings in Turkey. The series of apartments and houses he occupied in Istanbul emerges as an enduring spatial narrative, a story that moves from one domicile to another and thus frames his life and work in that part of the world in literal ways. And this story is both literal and literary, as it brings together the material and metaphoric aspects of writing and dwelling in exile—a textured narrative of a life lived, friendships made, lovers lost and found, books written on pages and pages of typescript, long discussions over drinks and cigarettes, objects and bodies that were once dear and no longer exist. Unlike Baldwin, who migrated from the United States to write about it, Alexander claims her space in the United States as a migrant author by using her art to decolonize real and imagined places: "I write on paper to reclaim ground. . . . Marginality compels me to it, a territorial thing" (16).

My search for Baldwin's places in Istanbul has been a kind of reclamation, too, although I cannot begin to communicate it in poetic terms. The interviews, photos, videos, and newspaper clippings that I have brought back from my trips delineate a series of transitory domestic spaces that Baldwin moved through with his inseparable typewriter. I came to Istanbul in the spring of 2001 to meet and interview Engin Cezzar, determined to trek through the city to cover the same ground that Baldwin did, no matter that it was three decades since he had left Istanbul. I was certain that the city where he lived in the past retained an imprint of his presence and that I would be able to read it somehow. I anticipated that his friends, especially Cezzar, whose warmth and devotion were clear in Thorsen's documentary *James Baldwin: The Price of the Ticket*, would consider assisting a scholar they had never met. I was welcomed so warmly and generously that I felt as if I was a good friend, not an unknown Polish immigrant academic. Clearly, being serious about Baldwin opened doors and hearts in Istanbul. That is where my scholarship on this project entered one of its most exciting stages, by putting me in touch with extraordinary people who were part of Baldwin's life and agreed to help me to envisage it from my vantage point while learning and appreciating theirs. But before I could see the places where Baldwin lived, I had to listen to some stories. It soon became a pattern—a place would take shape through anecdotes, recollections, and confusions before I was able to see it, so that by the time I did, I was faced with both the literal and literary aspects of Baldwin's living quarters. They came with landscapes of memory, neighborhoods and hangouts, and diverse local flavors, sounds, and textures.

And yet throughout this experience I was able to see the writer as a person, friend, tenant, soul of the party, collaborator, or cranky guest behind what Baldwin's first host, Gülriz Sururi, remembers in her Turkish memoir *Kıldan İnce Kılıçtan Keskince* (Thinner than Hair, Sharper than Sword) as the "very famous [artist]" whose "books continuously made the top of the bestseller lists" and at whose house "it was very natural . . . to meet celebrities like Alex Haley, Marlon Brando" (429).[22] Sururi met Baldwin when he was still relatively unknown and poor; she remembers their meeting fondly and vividly, as a breakthrough in her own life: "Jimmy was the first ever foreigner [and black man] I had accepted into my house. I was shy and uncertain. But it was impossible for anyone not to feel relaxed with Jimmy in time."[23] He was in turn put at ease by his Turkish hosts and the friends of their relatives.

Baldwin met Engin Cezzar, Sururi's future spouse and business partner, through the New York Actors Studio production of *Giovanni's Room* in 1956. Cezzar was a gifted, handsome young actor still in his late teens and fresh from the Yale School of Drama. He graduated from Robert College, which kept sending a steady stream of talented actors to Yale, who were "automatically admitted," as Minnie Garwood, an Armenian American friend from Baldwin's early years in Istanbul, told me.[24] When we talked with Cezzar about the early days of his friendship with Baldwin in New York, he recalled being always on the move, looking for a "nest," at one point even rooming with Baldwin's family uptown like an adopted "tenth sibling" in their tenement apartment in Harlem (Sururi, *Kıldan İnce*, 324).[25] The day Cezzar and Baldwin first met, a mutual friend, the jazz pianist Lonnie Levister, brought Cezzar to Baldwin and introduced him with the exclamation "I've found the Giovanni!" Baldwin had long been searching for an actor to fit his image of the character and needed only one look at Cezzar to know that he had found his man. Their collaboration on the stage production of the novel started immediately, as they had to rewrite the original script that Baldwin had commissioned, which met with Cezzar's poignant evaluation: "Oh my god, this is shit!" Cezzar immediately urged his new friend, "You must do it yourself." He recalls the writing of the play in our interview:

> Jimmy was horrified at the idea. . . . Perhaps I made him feel that . . . he could do it. . . . So we sat together and made an outline, a synopsis, then a treatment of the *Giovanni's Room* production. And Jimmy started to laugh. On and on he would write. Whenever he had finished a scene we would work, discuss it, tear it to pieces, rewrite it. He was a very—how should I put it?—he was a very industrious writer. . . . Then it was finished, and it was a damn good play, I thought.[26]

Before long, they were staging the play with the Actors Studio cast: "a very brave play . . . for a subject nobody dared [to touch]." Soon they would refer

12. Engin Cezzar as Giovanni in the Actors Studio production of *Giovanni's Room*, New York, 1957–58. Reproduced by permission of Doğan Kitap and İzzeddin Çalışlar.

to each other as "blood brothers," a connection that endured many years, several major political upheavals in both countries, and severe personal ups and downs.[27]

The close connection between these transatlantic friends, who found each other because Baldwin needed someone to play with conviction the scene in which Giovanni spits on the cross, has several meanings. In our interview, Cezzar proudly refers to his distant North African ancestry[28]—his face a hybrid of continents and phenotypes and thus a visage very fit, indeed, to represent Turkey in Baldwin's transnational gallery of friends-and-family portraits.[29] Described in Cezzar's vivid manner, their multiple collaborations and fraternal roles in everyday life were often interchangeable, with one playing the elder sibling to the other as needed—Baldwin to Cezzar in New York, then Cezzar to Baldwin in Turkey. Cezzar said that he often felt like a "big brother" to Jimmy, no matter that Baldwin was some ten years his senior. With his performances, first as Giovanni in New York, then as Smitty in *Fortune and Men's Eyes*, the play that Baldwin directed in Istanbul in 1969, Cezzar would often embody the important male figures that Baldwin created and interpreted as he explored and theorized in his writing the issues of race, sexuality, gender, nationhood, location, and power.

There was also one of Jimmy's "really bad, dark days . . . [when] I had to bring him out of a black hole that he was crawling in emotionally, perhaps physically," remembers Engin. The crisis took place in Baldwin's apartment at 81 Horatio Street in the Village and involved Jimmy's broken heart and a glass smashed on the floor in a moment of despair and rage. Determined to help his "younger" brother overcome the loss of a lover and the ensuing despair, Engin, who referred to his ministrations in our interview rather cryptically, initiated a small ritual that, he emphasized, bound him and Jimmy together as "blood brothers." Although he asked me not to include this in my book at the time we spoke, Cezzar has in the meantime published a memoir, *Engin Cezzar'ı Takdimimdir* (Introducing Engin Cezzar) (2005), which describes the scene in detail, but without the context that I heard in the interview:

[Jimmy] never had a true friend before. He could not define what friendship is. One day I felt like it and said:

"Finding a new friend is a hard thing. You feel that you got it and then it does not work. I have a suggestion for you. You perhaps don't know friendship, but you do know brotherhood. You have many siblings. Let's be blood brothers. You are African. You can appreciate how serious I am. Let's be brothers, so that just like we act together now, we can support each other throughout our lives . . ."

"OK," he said. We cut our arms and rubbed the cuts against each other. So we became brothers. (53–54)

They subsequently celebrated their union with friends out on the town. Cezzar stressed, and made sure I wrote it down, "It was a gesture, but *nothing changed*. So I suppose we were blood brothers from the beginning, in spirit. That was 'the moment,' as Jimmy used that phrase quite a lot. That was 'the moment' for the ritual, for the scene. But as I say, nothing changed." I understood, but was a little surprised at the insistent tone of Cezzar's request. I would encounter similar, often vehement disavowals of any possibility of some more intimate, perhaps erotic, perhaps even sexual component of Baldwin's friendships in other interviews.

Apart from my speculations, which must remain just that, the blood brothers incident proved to both men involved—in Engin's evocative retelling and my interpretation of it through Baldwin's letters to Cezzar—that their friendship indeed embodied unconditional brotherly love.[30] Baldwin craved such connections in his private life, explored them in his works, and, in its general principle, saw brotherly love as the ultimate solution to individual and national problems of discrimination and inequality. In that respect, their relationship did and did not have anything to do with "blood" — just as Engin's retelling of "the moment" of their blood brotherhood ritual stressed its theatricality, his virtually having staged it for the benefit of rescuing his black brother from a depressive mood.[31] They simply loved each other like Vivaldo and Rufus in *Another Country*, platonically but passionately; they were artists who shared much, grew together, and learned from each other regardless of the cultural and geographic distance between them. When Baldwin published *Tell Me How Long the Train's Been Gone* (1968), his novel about theater written in Istanbul and dedicated, among others, to Cezzar, his friend telegrammed his congratulations and first-read impressions in a way that summed up the kind of intimate communication they shared: "Thanks baby for Black Christopher stop the Train is great . . . love engin" (letter 39, January 1968).

In Cezzar's memoir, *Engin Cezzar'ı Takdimimdir* (Introducing Engin Cezzar), an "as told to book" written with İzzeddin Çalışlar, Baldwin's blood brother mentions Jimmy's "incessant" homosexuality and stresses his own importance in saving him from despair by making him realize the meaning of true male friendship during their times together in New York. This retelling in print, and for the Turkish audience, of the story I heard in person makes me think about how much Baldwin may sometimes have been misread, unwittingly and with no ill intent to be sure, by his friends, who would try to make his stories fit the shape of their own. In the memoir, for example, the story of the ritual of blood brotherhood follows a passage of Engin's musing about his and Jimmy's idealistic youth:

> Our creativity increased when we cooperated. We were looking at the world with the same crazy, audacious, new eyes. We were two young fellows from opposite ends of the world meeting here, who were very different yet could understand each other very well. We were young indeed. With all the cells in our bodies. . . . We thought we could eliminate racism. We were supposed to be able to do that. (53)

Cezzar was thrilled that they worked well together, stressing, contrary to what Baldwin wrote and believed about interracial collaboration: "Jimmy had been . . . left with no belief in the possibility of working with a white man and had had no faith in the others" (53). While in the American context, Cezzar thus saw himself as white, but also as part of the multiracial and multicultural scene of bohemian New York, which he loved and relished. In Istanbul, on the other hand, he became an older brother, who occasionally aggrandized his role in saving Jimmy from the evils of Harlem streets:

> We stayed friends all our lives. He came to Turkey and stayed here. He became world famous, yet we never broke up. Perhaps for the first time he made a real friend. He did not know what that meant. He grew up in the streets. Shoved around. He was discovering a new thing. (54)

While some of this confirms what I have been able to learn from other witnesses and interpreters of Baldwin's life, both American and Turkish, Cezzar's account oversimplifies Baldwin's life story by representing him as a passive victim of race and class who did not make any friends until he met Cezzar. That Cezzar might be ambivalent about his memories is clear when he states that he and Jimmy never broke up, though some forty pages later he discusses their breakup that followed an unsuccessful attempt to sell a movie script to Costa-Gavras: "My blood brother and I parted badly" (97).

These inconsistencies, however, can be interesting and revealing, as they suggest that Baldwin's friends perceived him in different, often conflicting, ways. In that vein, Cezzar's book credits Jimmy with streetwise authority when it describes their New York friendship. Despite having been "shoved around," Jimmy is also a jack-of-all-trades survivor, who teaches his younger Turkish friend bartending tricks when he is struggling to make it in New York:

> We think tipping is an Oriental custom, but it is an accepted source of income in New York, too. One day Jimmy said the magic words: "If you are a good barman, they tip you well." He introduced me to a bar owner. He was a huge man, one of Harlem's Mafiosi. The guy told me, "I won't pay you, but I don't mess with the tips you receive," so I started working. I learned the ways of the profession from him. "In the first drink, you will be generous and give 1.5 measures. He will get tipsy and will drink more. You should get the cash first, and then give him his drink. He will be drunk by the second shot anyhow. Then you may go easy on the measures." (55)

While Cezzar is quick to follow their advice on bartending, he establishes himself firmly as a straight male vis-à-vis his friend's more flamboyant and sexually ambivalent persona when he mentions his "skirt chasing" in the

East Village. Since Baldwin presumably cannot give him tips on that, Cezzar takes up another role model:

> There were times I worked as a gigolo, when I was short of money. Both the giver and the taker were happy . . . Jerry Orbach was my role model and partner in crime. I learned the ways from him. You stand by the bar; the chic girls approach and one starts chatting; and then we go to her place uptown. The more satisfaction she gets, the bigger the payment. (55)

Cezzar mentions his relationship with a supermodel who "had a nice big house on Hudson Street" and to whom Baldwin sent greetings in several of his letters to Cezzar. Jimmy ends some of them with "Kiss Pud for me" (letter 10, December 1958).[32] He also relishes the bars and famous jazz musicians that he and Baldwin listened to: "Miles Davis, Chet Baker, and Thelonius Monk used to play in the bars we frequented. These places were shedlike, smoky, drug filled, but uniquely spirited places" (56). Most of all, he cherishes his friendship with Baldwin in the Village: "We thought Washington Square was the center of the world" (56).

The friendship with Engin Cezzar was among the most enduring and sustaining relationships in Baldwin's life and is well documented in his letters. When Cezzar mentions their correspondence of over two decades in his memoir, he expresses a desire to have Baldwin's letters translated and published in Turkey:

> There are approximately seventy letters he wrote to me over the twenty-five years [of our friendship]. When Yapı Kredi [publishing house] asked me to translate his books, I recommended Seçkin Selvi as the best translator and mentioned the letters. They were immediately interested and started to translate, but then they gave up. The letters are still waiting. (54)

The memoir does not explain why the project was abandoned, and reproduces the complete text of one of the 1962 letters in Turkish translation. The original letter is long, beautifully written, and rich in detail. "Hideously overdue," it mentions Baldwin's trip to Paris, a bronchial illness that caused him to lose five pounds, his hopes for the "Oscar" (otherwise known as the National Book Award) for *Another Country*, and plans to collaborate with Elia Kazan on a Greco-Turkish film that might also involve Cezzar. Baldwin also requests help with sending his stuff, "including my suit—*which* suit?" to his close friend Mary Painter in Paris. He writes about his strong desire to work "in the cinema" and about the shooting of the television film based on his essay "Stranger in the Village," which featured his narration in English and French. The letter ends with pleas for news about Cezzar's and several other friends' situation ("Tunç and Şirin"), given the "recent convulsions" in Turkish politics that Baldwin had gleaned from the French media.[33]

The correspondence between Baldwin and Cezzar spans the years 1956 and 1974—from the moment they met until Cezzar left New York to return to Turkey, up to the time of Baldwin's departure from Istanbul and his acquisition of the house in Saint-Paul de Vence. There are only fifty-four documents in the file I have read, all by Baldwin, with the exception of a copy of a telegram Cezzar sent Jimmy after the publication of *Tell Me How Long the Train's Been Gone*. The letters provide an invaluable account of the friendship between the two men and a treasure trove of impressions, stories, and reports on the political situations in the United States, Germany, France, Senegal, and other places Baldwin visited. One letter refers to Turkey as a "much beloved" country, and another dwells at length on Baldwin's feelings of being "imprisoned" by his American passport. In many, Baldwin writes about the meaning of his work and craft as a writer living in between cultures and continents; he constantly reviews his relationship to the United States as a writer through the lens of race and politics. Sometimes he intercedes on behalf of friends in trouble or asks Engin to look out for one of his partners; he proposes plays that he would like to direct for the Sururi-Cezzar Theater; he sends itineraries; he cautions his Turkish friends against believing what is being written about him in the American papers. Observations about dwelling and search for home and haven are another consistent thread, as are repeated associations of Turkey with a haven and space of creative renewal. Baldwin mentions many people he knew in Turkey, enclosing "kisses" for Gülriz and messages for Cevat and Yaşar and others; the letters also contain advice on acting and always end with expressions of unchanging friendship and love for his Turkish brother or "M'boy"; there are terms of endearment in French, "Cao" or "Je t'embrasse"; there is an occasional plea that they not "lose each other" and that Cezzar "love [him] still."

As this book went into production, the Baldwin-Cezzar letters were issued by Yapı Kredi Yayınları, the Istanbul house that had originally been interested in the project and that by now seems to have secured a virtual monopoly on publishing Baldwin's works in Turkey. Entitled *Dost Mektupları* (Letters from a Friend) and translated by Seçkin Selvi, whom Cezzar had in mind when he first proposed the project, the volume includes an introduction by James Campbell, who describes it in a review in the *Times Literary*

Supplement: "Cezzar's book . . . is made out of roughly a hundred pages of Baldwin's letters, complemented by Engin's replies and by Baldwin's notes for their work together in the theater" ("Room in the East," 3). Campbell's reading of the correspondence emphasizes its development along "a route of lost innocence":

> The early exchanges between writer and actor are full of high spirits. "Must do something about my finances before March, when the current shoestring breaks," he wrote in January 1958. A month before, he had dashed off a note with no other purpose than to quote a poem by Marianne Moore, which he kept pinned above his desk. It was too good, too inspiring, not to be passed on:
>
> > What is there like fortitude!
> > What sap went through this little thread
> > To make the cherry red!
> > . . .
>
> In a letter written in 1959 from Paris . . . he makes a typical, preacher-like reference to a "healing" place in which the "muck of the Nile, the plane trees of Athens, and the Roman cross will come together and be transfigured and give us a new morality." (4)

While the letters to Cezzar expose all sides of Baldwin's character—"magnetic, compulsively sociable, elaborately extrovert, darkly introverted, depressive, magnificently generous, self-absorbed, self-dramatizing, funny, furious, bubbling with good intentions, seldom hesitating over a breach of promise"—they also reflect his increasingly more pessimistic reactions to the changing racial politics in the United States and to his own situation as a writer. By the mid-1960s, he contends with his position as one of the most sought-after black intellectuals, "'I'll just go on working. I'll probably become more and more famous and I'll manage that way.'" He was convinced that "'whatever move I make is, in the eyes of the American government a political move.'" While living in Istanbul, he felt "'hounded'" by the American press "'with their miserable, cowardly' surveys, and their insistent, wrong-headed question: 'What does the Negro want?'" In a gut-wrenching letter of April 12, 1968, having "'got[ten] into trouble in France, had to fight my way into England,'" he writes about another suit, the one that resurfaces in three year's time in print in a key moment early in *No Name in the Street*: "'Between 2 &3 weeks ago, I had to fly from Hollywood to NY to do a benefit with Martin [Luther King] at Carnegie Hall. I didn't have a suit, and had one fitted for me that afternoon. I wore the same suit at his funeral.'" Cezzar reads from the same letter in Thorsen's documentary, *James Baldwin: The Price of the Ticket*; he puts a strong emphasis on the part about the suit and the part where his friend tries to hold onto last vestiges of hope: "'I repudiate despair: but the daily necessity for this repudiation contains its own despairing comment'" (Campbell, "Room in the East," 5). Coming only two years after Baldwin's passing, Cezzar's impassioned delivery is both an artistic performance for the benefit of the camera and a vehicle for expressing grief of a bereaved brother. Indeed, what is there like the fortitude of friendship?

Friendships and connections to Turkey were crucial to me, too, as I was trying to make my way to Istanbul. I was put in contact with Cezzar through a grapevine of extraordinary Turkish women that stretched efficiently all the way from Ann Arbor, Michigan, to Boğaziçi Üniversitesi in Istanbul.[34] Engin graciously replied to my inquiries as one of "Jimmy's Babylonian friends" and consented to an interview. A few weeks later, as soon as I arrived in his city, he called me to arrange a meeting time. Soon, loaded down with photographic and video equipment, my erstwhile partner Coleman Jordan and I were being driven by Cezzar's amazingly fast, resourceful chauffeur to Cezzar's and Gülriz Sururi's apartment near bustling Taksim Square. We were welcomed by a beaming host in an elegant space filled with art, antiques, and books and framed with a breathtaking view of the Bosphorus.

After that first meeting—"when we just sit and chat to get to know each other," as Engin remarked, "please, do not take any notes yet"—we met several more times and got a lot done. Cezzar was even more personable and charming than he seemed to be in Thorsen's film, and sounded like a bohemian artist from Greenwich Village in the late 1950s. When we parted that first evening, he shook our hands warmly and said, "Okay, baby, tomorrow we work. Be ready!" And so we did, and stayed busy for several intense days. We talked, walked, and drove all over town, with Engin weaving yarns a mile a minute in his hip American English and showing us the houses where Baldwin lived, filling us in on local color, translating street names, and instructing Coleman, who videotaped some of our escapades, as a director would a cameraman: "Reverse shot now! We actors love being on camera, you know." He was delighted by the fact of my being Polish—"Yeah, Jimmy would have loved that!" His attitude was contagious: "Right on, baby, you go for it and get it done!"

We heard several versions of his first meeting with Baldwin in New

York and their subsequent collaboration on many theater- and film-related projects. Sometimes Engin would laugh at my questions, shake his head, and say, "Oh, really, I forgot all about that; that's very funny. What year was that? Can't remember, better look it up. David [Leeming] was very good with the dates. It's all there." But then, perhaps prodded by the auto-ethnographic impulses that propel the complex mechanisms of memory, he would remember details and tidbits and illustrate the story in question in ways no scholarly biography could capture.[35] When we proposed that he show us where Baldwin used to live, Cezzar immediately loved the idea and metamorphosed into a genial guide around his city. This indefatigable man, who studied at an elite drama school in the United States and embraced the complex role of Giovanni while still in his late teens, returned to his home city at the age of twenty to play Hamlet for 180 performances, which catapulted him into national stardom overnight. Despite his sporadic efforts for some years to return to the United States, he never came back to this side of the Atlantic, focusing instead on building an impressive career in Istanbul, throughout Turkey, and elsewhere in Europe.[36] Unlike Baldwin, Cezzar embraced the state of being rooted and made the best of it; he is clearly at home where he is, in love with his city; his pleasure at showing us around was palpable.

As he told us, after Baldwin first showed up on their doorstep unexpectedly, he stayed with Cezzar and his new bride, Gülriz Sururi, in their small apartment in a yellow modernist block of flats near Taksim Square. The house still stands at the crossing of the streets Saray Arkası and Çifte Vav.

When we walked on the street Çifte Vav, Engin started explaining to us the meaning of its name. What we understood at the time was that it had something to do with the doubling of the letter *w*. Having consulted with Irvin Schick, I received the following interpretation that provides an interesting context for Baldwin's dwelling there: "Here is the basic idea: the letter *vav* (or *waw* in Arabic) can be either a vowel (in which case it is pronounced o or u) or a consonant (in which case it is pronounced v or w). The doubling of *vav* has a particular symbolic meaning in Islamic mysticism. The letter *vav* has a numerical value of 6, so two of them written side by side become 66, which is the numerical value of "Allah." In other words, *çifte vav* is a numerological cypher for God. It was common to draw a double *vav* in religious art." So we have it on good authority that Baldwin, the former pentecostal preacher from Harlem, lived on a street of God in Istanbul, as behooves a true prophet, albeit one from quite a different religious and geographic universe than that of Islam.

We walked to his house from Engin's impressive abode hand in hand; sunshine filled the streets, and a bright green truck with "Tang" painted on it in huge white letters was parked nearby. On the way, we also passed another of Baldwin's apartments in the area, one that stands practically behind what Engin calls "the Palace," the large gated building of the German Embassy. Engin told me that Baldwin had moved there after having stayed with Cevat Çapan and his family near Bebek while Engin did his army service. (I later learned from another interviewee that Baldwin had lived there only in late 1969.) At one point, Engin pointed at the sidewalk on the corner by the embassy gate and told us that one day Jimmy had seen a black man sitting there on the ground, playing jazz. It was Don Cherry, who happened to be in town with his Swedish wife, Maki, and two kids, Nenah and Eagle Eye. Cherry would later write the music for Baldwin's production of *Fortune and Men's Eyes*.

Before Baldwin moved to more affluent abodes following the financial success that came with the publication of *The Fire Next Time* in 1963, Engin found him yet another small flat in the neighborhood around Taksim, on Ebe Hanım Sokak (Saros Apt. 4). I am counting three Baldwin-occupied buildings in the area of a couple of city blocks. The area has changed somewhat since Baldwin's time, Engin told me, but its topography and major landmarks have remained the same. Some of the oldest, charming wooden houses and structures are now gone, replaced by rather drab socialist-realist looking concrete atrocities, one of them an unfinished, huge parking-garage-like ruin that made our skin crawl.[37] The whole neighborhood seems to be a metaphor for Baldwin's complex transnational allegiances at the time: the African American located in Istanbul, overlooking the Bosphorus, which divided and linked continents and through which international ships passed day and night; he had as his neighbor the embassy of Germany, whose history filled him with dread, and prompted him to make comparisons between its Nazi past and other racist projects in his home country and elsewhere. While holed up in his study and writing, he was away from it all, in a room of his own, yet he remained entrapped in his focus on America in the world.

All of this was going through my mind as we attempted to see the interior of Cezzar's apartment, in which Baldwin had made his entry into Istanbul on that memorable night in October 1961 and promptly begun rewriting *Another Country*. Since the place was occupied, we managed to persuade a caretaker to let us through the house and into the courtyard in the back. We looked up at the windows behind which, decades earlier, Baldwin had wrestled with his third novel while his hosts were building their careers and life together as the stars of the Turkish theater.[38] From Taksim we drove to Bebek, a neighborhood near the campus of the former American missionary school, Robert College, now the prestigious Boğaziçi Üniversitesi. Baldwin stayed on the first floor in another modernist apartment building there, one that is now partially screened by foliage but still overlooks the water and the rich residencies and hills on the Anatolian coast.

I was relieved to see this building at last, as this was where Baldwin had finished *Another Country* while living with Engin's brother-in-law, Cevat Çapan, and his family. Although Baldwin had offered to find a hotel instead of imposing on Cezzar's kin, his friends thought such an idea preposterous. Campbell quotes Baldwin writing to his agent, Bob Mills: "'They all considered this to be an insult. . . . I've gained a little weight here and this is taken, apparently, as an enormous justification for Turkey's existence.' Life . . . has been 'very restful'" (*Talking*, 209). According to the local hospitality codes, it all made sense, of course—he was family and had to be hosted by his (new) kin. Lodging with Çapan thus extended Jimmy's Turkish familial circle, as well as offering him ample opportunity to meet local people and some Americans associated with the academic community that his host was part of as a faculty member at Robert College.

It was also in that house, at the famous party during which he finished *Another Country* on Çapan's kitchen counter, that Baldwin met David Leeming, with whom he ended up discussing for hours their favorite writer, Henry James. Leeming, a Princeton graduate who had written a dissertation on James (and who decades later generously shared with me his memories of Baldwin in several interviews), would soon become a close friend and subsequently join the family, or Baldwin's "tribe," as an assistant and secretary. Leeming spent several years with Baldwin in Istanbul and received his blessing to write his definitive biography. His impressions of several of the Istanbul lodgings appear in *James Baldwin: A Biography* (1994) and *Amazing Grace: A Life of Beauford Delaney* (1998). When in 1966 Baldwin asked Leeming to escort Beauford Delaney and another friend from Paris to Istanbul, his assistant embarked on one of those life-changing journeys that Baldwin seemed so talented at arranging for others. From the beginning, Leeming "had the distinct sense that this was all a kind of test" (*James Baldwin*, 271). Having driven all across Europe with Delaney, who suffered from severe schizophrenia and often heard voices that threatened to kill him—in Baldwin's words, Delaney was a "cross between Brer Rabbit and St. Francis"— Leeming completed what seemed a tough rite of passage into Baldwin's tribe (270–74). He sums up his experience thus: "I understood that through Beauford I had learned something terrifying about the hidden inner pain that is the most terrible result of racism—a pain that no mere law can relieve. I had also learned a great deal about the anguish that motivated James Baldwin" (272).

Beauford Delaney quickly became "a legend in a city built on legends" (273). Soon after his arrival, Baldwin found a new place to live near Bebek, in Rumeli Hisarı, close to Robert College, where they all spent many months until the summer of 1967. This large, impressive house had once belonged to a nineteenth-century intellectual, Ahmet Vefik Pasha, and soon was called by everyone "the Pasha's Library" (274). Baldwin's entourage at the time included occasional visitors such as Marlon Brando, the singer Bertice Redding and her family, and the writers Alex Haley and Geoffrey Wolff, as well as Turkish friends such as the writer Yaşar Kemal and his wife Tilda, and the talented Robert College student Sedat Pakay, who would take many photographs during his visits and persuade Baldwin to make a documentary film about him in Istanbul in 1970.

On a beautiful day in June 2001, Engin's chauffer drove us to see the Pasha's Library. We sped along beside the sparkling waters of the Bosphorus, past white rows of yachts moored in the marina, past mosques old and new and residential buildings that climbed the hills or sloped down to the water on the European and Asian sides. The streets and neighborhood around the house were quiet, shaded with old trees, and had an air of privacy and affluence. We walked around the property on tiptoe and looked at the large red-brick house and into the garden through an iron gate with an attached guardhouse, where no one answered our polite knocks. Emboldened, we peered through the wrought-iron gate and climbed it high enough to see more of the building and the grounds, all situated beautifully and overlooking the Bosphorus toward the Asian shore. This was the house that for some time fulfilled Baldwin's dream of the ideal writer's abode that he had described to Engin in a letter written from the MacDowell writers colony in New Hampshire a decade before, "a place to live and work" and located "at the side of a mountain or at the edge of the sea" (letter 1, n.d.). This opulent domicile signified as well that he had arrived at last; he was living like a true pasha, with an entourage of friends and family, and commanding the best views of the most beautiful city in the world.[39]

As if to confirm Baldwin's ascendancy to the ranks of local semiresident aristocracy by 1966, the Pasha's Library sits near a fifteenth-century fortress of Mehmed II, better known as Fatih Sultan Mehmet, cited in

English-language sources as "the Conqueror," given his victory over Constantinople. We walked to see the towering, roughly hewn stone structure and took photographs while Engin told us stories about his performance of *Hamlet* on the ramparts. There again they were, the blood brothers at work, chiseling their respective "master stones," as Baldwin sometimes referred to work. Jimmy the "Pasha" was writing *Tell Me How Long the Train's Been Gone*, the novel about "'surviving success' in America" (Leeming, *James Baldwin*, 278), ensconced in his pasha's *köşk*, or villa, while in the fort next door Engin was performing the play that had brought him home to Istanbul. To me, seeing the unexpected Turkish settings that witnessed Shakespeare's drama in Cezzar's rendering and Baldwin's scenes of solitary writing about American blackness was in some ways more dramatic, more poignant, than visiting the actual Helsingør in Denmark.

While in his luxurious abode, complete with a day cook, his usual entourage of friends and family, and two adopted stray dogs (white and black, Andromache and Flea) (*James Baldwin*, 274–75), Baldwin worked regularly and contemplated ideas for some new projects, such as *The 121st Day of Sodom*, "a takeoff on Sade . . . 'a drawing room nightmare of six adventurers' in the south of France" (275) that would later metamorphose into his last completed and unpublished play, *The Welcome Table*. Leeming also remembers that Baldwin was keen to develop a "modern *Othello* musical" about "two Negro men and a Greek girl in Greece" (274). In an interesting parallel, Cezzar had starred as Othello, in blackface, in 1954–55 at Robert College, in a production directed by an American teacher, Hilary Sumner-Boyd, and then at his and his wife's theater company in 1963–64; I have no information on whether Baldwin saw the latter performance, but it is likely that he did. Fascinated with actors and their craft and influenced by his daily contacts with Engin and Gülriz, Jimmy created in *Train* an alter ego who is a famous black theater star, Leo Proudhammer. Bisexual and famous, but alienated and embattled, Proudhammer clearly echoes Baldwin's own and Cezzar's experience, as well as their theatrical collaboration over the years.[40]

The last stop on our journey following Baldwin's living spaces throughout the city was not far from the Pasha's Library, along the busy coastal road in Bebek, where Baldwin rented his last long-term abode—a wooden house surrounded by a white fence on the European shore of the Bosphorus. An enormous traffic bridge now dwarfed the building, and when we stood under this roaring, floating thoroughfare, the noise of passing cars and trucks was so overwhelming that I could hardly understand what Engin

13. Engin Cezzar as Othello, Istanbul, 1960s. Reproduced by permission of Doğan Kitap and İzzeddin Çalışlar.

was saying. It seemed that he was not sure which house was Baldwin's, after all, as the bridge had changed the area considerably, although the houses themselves, he assured us, were untouched. After walking around and peek-ing over picket and wire fences, we settled on a white structure from whose balcony you must have been able to see the ancient city center—the angle seemed right to Engin. But we could not be sure. The light made me think about Pakay's silhouette portrait of Baldwin taken from another location, the Galata Bridge, looking toward the Golden Horn, with Süleymaniye Mosque darkly outlined in the distance. But there was no time for reveries. We quickly left the area and its deafening roar; we would see the house from the water in just a few days, quite unexpectedly, when we took a boat ride through the strait.

When we returned to his place, Engin told us that Baldwin's search for a home in Istanbul had had to be suspended indefinitely by the end of the decade. He had to travel a lot and felt restless again after his years in Turkey. Leeming also emphasizes Baldwin's disappointment with Hollywood and his unrealized and, as he felt, undermined and underappreciated scenario for the Malcolm X film as important factors behind this restlessness (*James Baldwin*, 303). Ironically, despite his extensive efforts to do justice to Malcolm X as the African American hero in the late 1960s, Baldwin was also facing "increasing criticism" from "the young radicals he had tried so hard to cultivate," many of whom saw him as a "Tom" (304). After his trip to France following the staging of his controversial *Fortune and Men's Eyes*, and very likely driven by a desire for a new haven in which to enact yet another "unselving," Baldwin decided to leave Istanbul.

Kankardeşi (Blood Brothers) and Can Yoldaşı (Bosom Friends)

Having seen the places where Baldwin lived in Istanbul, I was able to interview Engin Cezzar's wife, Gülriz Sururi. Our conversation took place on the last of the few days we spent together, and I was eager to hear what Gülriz had to say about her friendship with Jimmy and their living and working together after his arrival in Turkey. We had met her only briefly on our first day at their apartment, but then this impeccably elegant and self-consciously attractive older woman seemed to remove herself from the scene, as if wanting to place Engin at center stage. He in turn explained to us that she was shy because she did not feel that her English was adequate to conduct an interview without a translator. "Shy" is not an adjective one would use to describe Gülriz Sururi, as we soon found out, but perhaps Engin was referring only to her reluctance to struggle with her English. (I had a feeling, though, that she understood what we were saying quite well.) She finally graciously agreed to talk to us and be videotaped in the process. We worked as a team, with me asking the questions, Engin serving as an interpreter, and Coleman videotaping us all with great patience and dexterity, as he did throughout that whole trip.

When they shared their apartment in 1961, Engin and Gülriz remember that Baldwin worked intensely, usually at night, and sometimes they would not see much of him when their schedules did not coincide. Occasionally they would share late-night feasts after their return from the theater, and these soon became pleasant social transitions into Baldwin's nocturnal work periods. On many a morning, however, no matter how late he had worked, he would gather with them for a "round a table"—to read aloud the results of his efforts, explaining, describing, and asking for advice: "He would read the pages in English, then I would translate it into Turkish for Gülriz," Engin told me. He stressed repeatedly their mutual penchant for collaboration and sharing, another proof of their brotherly affinity, as well as Baldwin's desire to include Gülriz in his work.

Along with their regular "morning critical sessions," Gülriz remembers vividly her first, life-changing impression of Baldwin. Her story reflects some of the spellbinding effect that Baldwin often had on women:

> Engin had told me everything about Jimmy, and I was to meet a black man for the first time in my life. We were having a big party at home for the wedding. When I answered the door, there he was: an uncomely, tired, bedraggled "Arap." We faced each other for a moment, then with sparkling eyes he smiled, kissed, and hugged me. I did the same. He walked in and he was introduced to the whole Istanbul intelligentsia just like that. In a few minutes I discovered what beauties this ugly Arab possessed.

The "Arap" soon became Jimmy. His metamorphosis from ugly to beautiful in Sururi's eyes went hand in hand with a transformation from man to child as they got to know each other:

> Jimmy was like a child, an innocent child to be protected. I felt that we could, maybe, form a family. I felt that I should care for him and that he needed my affection. In the house, he used to follow me around, in the kitchen. He was always asking [me about] and learning new things.

Immediately, and unbeknownst to Engin, Gülriz and Jimmy formed a strong alliance as "bosom friends," or one side of that alternative family triangle that she imagined. As she recalls in the first volume of her memoir, her seemingly infantile guest helped her overcome her shyness and skillfully drew her out as an interlocutor. Tables turned often between them, especially when Engin found out about their closeness:

> I am speaking English with James Baldwin when we are alone in the house. I stop talking right away when Engin is back home. One day, when Jimmy tells him about what we were talking about, Engin is surprised. He says: "Why did you hide from me that you speak English?" "This does not count as 'speaking,'" I say. And I still don't speak when Engin is around. I am ashamed like a child. (Kıldan İnce, 324)

Decades after that scene, it was clear to me during our interview that in their relationship Engin was protective of Gülriz, perhaps in a similar way

14. Cezzar, Sururi, and Baldwin, Galata Bridge, Istanbul, 1969.
Reproduced by permission of Doğan Kitap.

he used to be of Jimmy as his "big brother." They must have made a striking family triangle at the time. (I later heard this confirmed by several of my other Turkish interlocutors.) At one point, when I mentioned Gülriz's distinctive beauty, Engin exclaimed, "Of course, of course! But forty years ago! Can you imagine what she looked like then?" Yes, I could easily imagine her as a young actress[41] pioneering breakthrough performances and productions in Turkish theater. Sururi came from a prominent Istanbul family that had been involved with the stage for generations. She mentions in her memoir that when she and Engin were to be married, his family rejected her at first, not for lack of class credentials but because of their reluctance to have an "actress" and a divorcée married to their son. Although deceptively shy at first—she was a great actor, after all—Gülriz was no wilting violet, as shown by her many accomplishments, and her candid and clearheaded writing.[42] I was sure I could sense an iron will and discipline behind the feminine charm she cultivated on the surface, although at first she seemed to be aloof, delicate, and fragile, and so in need of her husband's protection. Perhaps he was in some need of her vulnerability?

Later on, I found out more about the power she wielded over her partner and career and about the rocky history she and Cezzar had had as a couple, as they divorced and remarried, only to separate again after our meeting. Like Jimmy, Gülriz was older than Engin when they met. I learned later that she had also helped him considerably with his career. Engin, on the other hand, seemed to be a brilliant prodigy who never stopped on his way to the top. He had energy and cheer enough to be everybody's "big bro." During our visits, he took us under his wing, me especially, much in the same manner. When he learned that I was pregnant, he made sure I rested, ate well, and drank gallons of tasty ayran—a salted yogurt and water drink that Engin served margarita style in glasses rimmed with salt ("For strong bones for the baby!"). He and Gülriz did not have children—"There was no time! There was so much work to do in the theater."

When Gülriz described her relationship with Baldwin, she would stress, somewhat competitively, that she and Jimmy quickly developed a bond to rival that of the "blood brothers" and that they created their own spaces of intimacy. She talked about their cavorting in her kitchen, for example, where Jimmy sometimes cooked for them and their frequent guest the African American singer Bertice Redding. Leeming includes a photograph by Sedat Pakay of one such kitchen gathering in his book, with Baldwin in a flipped-up hat at the stove preparing what looks like fish, and Redding sitting to one side and wearing a bright scarf on her head.[43] That neither Gülriz nor Engin is in the picture implies them as observers, with Pakay framing and photographing the scene and capturing a moment in Baldwin's daily life in Istanbul. Redding appears in many other photographs by Pakay, an impressive woman in an array of blond wigs, who the overawed Engin called "A real big mama." I would learn later on from Sedat Pakay that Redding adopted an orphaned Turkish boy, who appears in some of Pakay's photographs, which also feature Bertice's white Swiss husband and her beautiful teenage daughter.

Gülriz assured me that she loved their kitchen chats and visits with friends; they would be discussing "love" and confiding in each other, sometimes with giggles, sometimes with tears. Perhaps not surprisingly given the scant attention that has been paid to women in Baldwin's life, the fact that he formed strong friendships with many of them, in all the places he lived, has not generally been noted.[44] Gülriz stressed several times Baldwin's attractiveness as a friend for Turkish women who met him—his warmth, sensibility, and delicacy. Although I did not ask her to comment on Baldwin's comportment as a gay man, Gülriz seemed to read my thoughts and emphasized that she never viewed Jimmy as simply "gay." He was "foremost a person to her"—a perfect combination of gendered qualities that made for a warm, compassionate, and irresistible friend "for anybody." She laughed as I tried to describe for her what my students often imagined his magnetism and charisma could have been like, how, between his texts and images, we tried to imagine his real-life erotic-neurotic personal appeal.

Although we could not talk directly, as the conversation progressed, we exchanged more and more nonverbal signals that helped to steer us toward more intimate topics. Gülriz remembered her relationship with Jimmy only in snippets of impressions but seemed determined to give me her version and make sure that I got it. As we became more comfortable with each other, her answers took me in new directions. I wanted to know more about how Baldwin was received in Turkey and how he may have felt there as a black and gay man, and as an American, so far away from home. But Gülriz was not as concerned with painting a picture of Baldwin in exile as with showing him in the new family setting that he soon entered and helped to form in that part of the world. Like Cezzar, she wanted to make me see that he really fit in and was a part of their lives, rather than just passing through as a transatlantic commuter.

I quote hereafter a series of fragments from the transcript of Gülriz's replies to my questions, which I interweave with quotations from the first volume of her memoirs.[45] As a scholar and critic, I cannot resist including a commentary on what Sururi has to say, but I hope that this arrangement will nevertheless give her story some space and freedom inside my project.

When she told me about her early days in Baldwin's company, when the two of them would often be left alone at home, she emphasized their closeness and shared sensibility: "I used to look into his big, melancholy eyes and understand what he was thinking. I cannot explain what this understanding is. A positive current, definitely. I think it was an artistic understanding, a common treading ground." Comparing the interview with the memoirs, it is clear that in the story meant for the Turkish public, much in the way that Engin also does, Gülriz is more concerned with representing how Baldwin fit into their professional life and how he offered expertise as someone who knew much about theater. At the same time, both accounts complement each other, as we encounter in them Baldwin the serious writer and international celebrity, but also a close friend who relished communal domesticity and witnessed and contributed to the couple's success during the 1960s:

> While Jimmy was living with us, we used to talk about theater every night. That was a subject I never got tired of. I used to forget the time on those nights. Engin and I loved going shopping in the fish market. Fish was our favorite food. Despite the fact that we had hired help, we used to cook together. Engin was preparing Antep style raw meatballs. We used to prepare various mezes and bulgur pilaf à la Antep for ourselves. (325)[46]

When Baldwin accompanied them to the theater, he would become a critic and friendly mentor to her:

> Jimmy watched me perform. He criticized and evaluated me [as an actor]. He suggested plays for me to take on. And these discussions brought us closer together. . . . We used to discuss theater in general, and specific plays. We were planning to do "Blues for Charlie" in our theater. We used to talk about Engin and Yaşar Kemal and his [Baldwin's] friends in Istanbul.

But when she recalls a similar scene in the memoir, when they talked about what roles she should play, she emphasizes how intimate and comfortable they were with each other. Here she is the great star of the national stage, and she aligns herself with the divas of Western theater and film:

> He used to reach for my hair, for my bangs, and uncover my forehead and say, "You should play Jeanne d'Arc." Then he would let the locks of hair fall back into place on my forehead and say, "No, no, you should play Cleopatra!" (325)

Baldwin validates this alignment by the laying on of hands and by being the one who links her beauty to iconic and mythic heroines. Here he plays an unlikely role for an African American at the time, as a de facto westerner who legitimizes Sururi's claim to be recognized not just as a great Turkish actress but as a great world actress, period. Given Baldwin's own ambition to be a great writer, not just a "Negro writer," it is easy to imagine that he would have been sympathetic toward his friend's aspirations.

That Gülriz cherished the friendship that she and Jimmy shared and that she wanted to convey its depth and paint its best picture is clear from her accounts.[47] That she would dwell on the best parts of the story in the memoir was, of course, obvious, just as it was obvious that she would focus on what was of interest to her Turkish audience. When I pushed her at one point to say more about what race and Baldwin's blackness meant to her, and how she felt about his sexuality, she let her guard down slightly. I truly appreciated her honesty but was rather shocked, too, when she admitted to using what in my ears were racial slurs as terms of endearment to refer to her friend: "We were both born under the sign of Leo. So we sometimes called each other 'Lion.' Like Jimmy the Lion or Gülriz the Lioness. Sometimes I called him 'Yamyam.'"

Yamyam is Turkish for cannibal. Is that how Gülriz the Lioness saw Jimmy the Lion? Was it yet another instance of that chuckling "genteel racism" that one encounters all over the world?[48] My American experience, references, and contexts said yes, although Gülriz's and Engin's smiling faces and friendly manner conveyed something quite the opposite. The matter was obviously much more complicated.

"He *loved* being called Yamyam," Oktay Balamir, a translator and Baldwin's close friend in 1969–70, told me in 2005 as he recalled their escapades to Club 12, a famous gay and transgender hangout where Jimmy was a guest of honor. The nickname was mere loving banter and insider talk, Balamir said, "because, after a while, he became one of *us*, an İstanbullu." Like race, Balamir also wanted me to understand, Baldwin's erotic choices and lifestyle were not made a big deal of either: "Jimmy's homosexuality was never apparent in Turkey. . . . People looked up to him as an idol . . . as an intellectual." "But sometimes," Balamir chuckled, thinking of how little people in the street actually knew about African American culture and politics, "they thought that he was . . . a Black Panther!"[49] The chuckle referred also to Baldwin's fashion sense, which was a far cry from the required hypermasculine Panther garb of military vests, berets, and combat boots. Sedat Pakay told me about another instance of misrecognition that seemed both funny and slightly more plausible than the others. Some people took Jimmy for the world-famous Brazilian soccer star Pelé, with whom he shared such features as skin color, lithe frame, and expressive eyes. It seemed to his friends that such moments were amusing to Baldwin, much in the same way that being called Arap and Yamyam was. They all confirmed that he loved the attention and awe he inspired, even among those who would hope to run into black soccer stars rather than black American writers in Turkey.[50]

I realize how complex the issue of cross-cultural translation of racialized language is, and also how much my perceptions of the representations of race, and race-related humor, have been conditioned by my American education and experience. At the same time, the ease with which we often justify and presume the innocence of race-related objects and jokes that can be found outside the United States troubles me. When I first heard "that word" from Gülriz, I immediately cast a worried glance toward Coleman, remembering a Little Rascals movie we had seen together just months before our trip to Turkey. Coleman, who is black and loved the Rascals' television series, wanted me to see a feature film inspired by the series. He obviously had not seen the film before, because he was as shocked as I was to see a white man in grotesque blackface, sporting a grass skirt and the inevitable bone through the nose, run around the screen chasing little kids and screaming, "Yam-yam, eat them up! Yam-yam, eat them up!" I also recalled our discussions of the "Jolly Nigger" money banks (which looked like they came from the pages of Ralph Ellison's *Invisible Man*) that we saw on sale at several tourist resorts when we lived in Denmark in the late 1990s. Around the same time, a Danish colleague from Aarhus University showed us a book for kindergarten children from the 1950s titled *Lille Sorte Sambo* (Little Black Sambo) that made me remember a poem, "Murzynek Bambo," that was included in our Polish primer as an example of socialist notions of multiculturalism.[51]

When Baldwin first walked through the snow-covered village in the Swiss Alps that he describes in his essay "Stranger in the Village" (1953), he encountered unanimous awe among its inhabitants, to whom his blackness meant that he was "simply a living wonder" (*Price of the Ticket*, 81). They all wanted to touch him, to feel his hair, and the kids, who referred to him as "*Neger!*" (81), adored him, as can be seen in the footage from a television program inspired by "Stranger in the Village" that was included in Thorsen's documentary. In the essay, Baldwin also describes the annual village custom of "buying" African natives "for the purpose of converting them to Christianity," a process that included collecting money to be forwarded to the missionaries in Africa, and children blackening their faces and dressing up as such happily saved "natives" (82). He sums it all up in a way that makes my own perceptions clearer: "The syllable hurled behind me today [*Neger!* in Switzerland] expresses, above all, wonder: I am a stranger here. But I am not a stranger in America and the same syllable riding on the American air expresses the war my presence has occasioned in the American soul" (85). Still, he cautions, "The ideas on which American beliefs are based . . . came out of Europe . . . [including] the very warp and woof of the heritage of the West, the idea of white supremacy" (87). When Zeynep Oral explained to me that having read *The Fire Next Time* made her realize her own whiteness for the first time, I understood that Jimmy's presence in Istanbul must have occasioned some changes in the Turkish soul, too.

But not all of Jimmy's Turkish friends regarded themselves as being implicated in transnational racialized hierarchies as openly as Oral did. When words like "Arap" or "Yamyam" or even the n-word rolled off tongues easily, I was told, they were used warmly and jokingly, as "terms of endearment." Gülriz, Engin, and later Oktay assured me that it was so while recounting parties and nights on the town with the Arap. Still, I could not shake my unease and agree that when spoken with love in another country, words that kill at home could suddenly become harmless banter. Baldwin's experience in Switzerland must have prepared him for what he encountered in Istanbul, no matter how İstanbullu he might eventually have become with time. In an interview with Henry Lyman, in which he discussed his poems, he emphasized that to him the n-word designated not only American black people but also all "the dispossessed . . . those without power . . . those excluded" everywhere.[52] His works teach us that love is complicated, especially love in foreign climes; they also teach us that words retain their power, that they are always immediate and raw, no matter how far away from home we are. That is why in "Stranger in the Village," he, a lone American black gay man, smiles at the snowy scenery and the white villagers' attention but admits that the "smile-and-the-world-smiles-with-you routine . . . did not work at all" because while he sensed "no element of intentional unkindness, there was yet no suggestion that I was human" (*Price of the Ticket*, 81).[53]

Loèche-les-Bains in 1951 was of course not the same as Istanbul in 1961 or in 1971. Still, no matter how much Baldwin was loved in Turkey—and he was loved much, as was clear in my every interview and meeting—he was ultimately racially marked in the eyes of his friends, even if his friends were not aware of that. He was marked, of course, not in the extreme, malignant, and even deathly ways he would be marked in the white supremacist culture of the United States. But he was marked as a foreigner, as a charming guest who had to be recognized for, and named because of, looking different. Why else would those who loved him, who wanted him to feel at home, to be a citizen of their city, need to call him by names other than Jimmy? And if they wanted to call him by nicknames, which would be understandable, why would they use those that targeted the color of his skin?[54] In 1984, in a preface to a new edition of *Notes of a Native Son*, Baldwin quoted Doris Lessing's preface to her *African Stories*: "Colour prejudice is not our original fault, but only one aspect of the atrophy of the imagination that prevents us from seeing ourselves in every creature that breathes under the sun" (xvi).

As if in response to my thoughts and ambivalent reaction to the Yam-yam story, Sururi soon steered the conversation toward how well Baldwin dressed and how cultured, dashing, and dignified a presence he was. The image she conveyed then was far from the domesticated, petlike Jimmy the "Arap" that might have been read in her earlier comments:

> I always remember him as very well dressed. He arrived in my life looking like a bedraggled street boy. But as time went on and he became famous and rich, he dressed to kill [Engin translates the phrase as "like a killer"]. I remember his seal-skin coat and hat. And he was always wearing very original rings. He never took off the good luck charm ring that I had given him. When we met in Paris, he was a real Parisian-host to us. Also at Saint-Paul de Vence.

When I asked her about what she had read of his works, she made it clear that she "prefer[red] Jimmy's novels and essays to his plays. . . . Especially *The Fire Next Time*." I am certain that she would have reached for Turkish translations, so she must have read *Giovanni's Room*, *Another Country*, *If Beale Street Could Talk*, and *Tell Me How Long the Train's Been Gone*, some of which, to a lesser or greater degree, Baldwin wrote in Turkey. Now, I am not sure about *The Fire Next Time*, as the only translation I know of came out in January 2006. Perhaps Engin would have read it to her while translating it from the

English? I would later learn from my other interlocutors that this book, like everywhere else, was Baldwin's "most widely read text in Turkey." Apparently it must have been so only among the English-speaking elite.

The mention of *The Fire Next Time* brought up Baldwin's politics, and Gülriz recalled their similar outlooks:

> Another common ground was politics. We in Turkey were involved in a very strong leftist movement. So our political outlooks [with Jimmy] were similar. The black problem in America and the Kurdish problem in the Near East were very similar. Jimmy was quoted as saying "The Kurds are the Niggers of Turkey." I knew a lot about the black problem in America before I knew Jimmy. I had read a lot. I did not learn anything new from Jimmy. . . .
>
> But to hear from Jimmy's mouth his woes [about racism] was another experience. . . .
>
> I also remember (I can't remember the names) that Jimmy was very mad at some American artists of the day. He found most of them unsincere in terms of the black problem. . . .
>
> We were so close in those days that I was corresponding with Paula Maria [Baldwin's youngest sister].

I am far from trying to discredit the sincerity of Sururi's leftist convictions, not to mention the important intellectual movement that she was a part of when she and Baldwin met. At the same time, her comments on how much they shared in terms of politics sometimes struck me as rehearsed and shallow. Baldwin's supposed statement concerning the Kurds being "the Niggers of Turkey" seems a mere restatement of what he had said about the Arabs in France. Oktay Balamir denied that the Jimmy he knew some years later would have said anything like that, and laughed at this instance of Sururi's autoethnographic self-fashioning. Although Sururi never visited the United States, her knowledge of racism there came from the Turkish media and from reading, which, in addition to Baldwin's testimonies, were reliable sources. But did she really know enough about the Kurdish situation? I would learn later from Zeynep Oral that the problem of how the Kurds were then seen vis-à-vis race and class could not be represented so simplistically or be seen as equivalent to the so-called black problem in the United States.

When we discussed Baldwin's sexuality, Gülriz stressed her distate for labels and stereotypes while also expressing her views concerning gay men: "Jimmy was not a typical 'gay.' He was a real human being." Many things are lost in translation, it is true, but this statement jolted me, because she seemed to mean it as a compliment. So Jimmy was better than "typical gay men," whatever that meant, because he was human? Seeing my puzzled look, Gülriz explained her statement using references to her occupation as an actor that also reflected her views on gender:

> Because of my profession, I have known and lived and worked with a lot of gays. I could always decipher their admiration or hatred, or friendship, or love toward me. I have seen Jimmy with Simone Signoret, and some [other female] friends here in Turkey. He treated them as if they were as good as male friends (but not boyfriends). We were friends. It did not matter whether I was a man or a woman. He liked me, chose me as a human being. He also admired me as the young and beautiful, talented star of the Turkish stage.

Her memoir addresses the gay issue in much the same manner, so I am positive that what I heard in my interview was a recitation that came from Gülriz's book *Kıldan İnce*:

> Homosexuals had always attracted my attention. Lately the visibility of gays increased, and like in the rest of the world, maybe a little belatedly, this issue surfaced in Turkey, too. I had the acquaintance of many homosexuals in various circles and among the artists. I had friends and enemies among the ones who were out of the closet, in the closet, platonic, professionals, and the ones who had not yet realized who they were despite their mature age. My observant self would be piqued as soon as I saw them. Closed boxes pique interest and curiosity, just like that. [But] I could not establish friendships with gays who openly talked about their sex life, just like I never liked my women friends who talked openly about their sex life either. But I would never exchange my intelligent friends for anything in the world, those who have a balanced life and who have the ability to be accepted in any circle easily, those who neither hide anything, nor talk about it needlessly. (428)

Gülriz then took this last thought further and explained that she preferred sexual freedom but without affirmation and contestation, if not politicization, of sexual identity: "I have always avoided vulgarity. I am for people feeling free about their sexual life. However, that life should be honest and open. The person should be able to choose his own sexual life" (429). When we turned to how Baldwin conducted his love life, she stressed that she was a willing confidante to him, but made sure I realized that she preferred to discuss feelings rather than acts:

> Yes, he would talk about his love affairs. I knew some of them. A few became our houseguests, too.
>
> For Jimmy what mattered was LOVE. He did have short sexual adventures. One-night stands. But Jimmy was always in love. Jimmy always loved what ran away from him. Most of his loves were platonic.
>
> Also, I knew many women in Turkey who fell in love with Jimmy. Because of his personality, his genius. His reactions to them were warm, friendly, brotherly.

Definitely not on a hunt for X-rated material, I was nevertheless interested in the erotic and explained to Gülriz how, as a black male, Baldwin was stereotyped sexually in the United States. I wanted to know how free he would have been from such stereotypes in Turkey and where the gay life of Istanbul was located at the time. Still, she focused on his feelings and loving nature instead of telling me where he might have hung out and how he seemed to others as an openly gay, homosexual, bisexual, or queer—to string together all the adjectives used to describe his sexuality—man. I respected that as a sign of her loyalty to her friend and as a refusal to discuss what she saw as his private life. At the same time, I was dissatisfied as a critic who agreed with Barbara Smith's claim that Baldwin's sexuality was integral to his identity. Like Essex Hemphill, I wanted to know "Who did he love?" Knowing what he wrote in Turkey and how sexuality and the erotic were central to *Another Country* and *Tell Me How Long the Train's Been Gone*, for example, I regretted not hearing about his everyday observations and experience of these aspects of life in Istanbul.

We ended the interview on a rather sad and sentimental note. I must admit to having succumbed to Sururi's evocative closing statements, which were delivered with beautiful poise:

> I see Jimmy in my dreams. His eyes very prominent. And every time I dream of him something very nice happens. When I am down and under I think of Jimmy. I miss him. If he were here he would understand, he would find a solution, I think. This is how I remember Jimmy.

As Sururi writes in her memoir, Baldwin was "one of those people whose inner beauty reflects on the outside" (324). I am stunned that she thought him unattractive—"Once I got accustomed to him, I even found Jimmy beautiful, even though I thought him to be very ugly when we first met," her book explains (324). I would hear the same opinion about Baldwin's ugliness from several other Turks and would be at a loss, again, whether I should read it as a racialized expression or not, given that race operated rather differently in Turkey than in the United States in the 1960s, and given the important fact that Baldwin thought of himself as ugly, too, and must have talked about it with his friends. For Sururi, it took getting to know the person, the "human being" behind the African mask, behind the Arap image that—no matter how much they deny its having anything to do with racial hierarchies—all Turks, like everybody else, carry in their heads as a marker and maker of difference. It may be fitting that it was only Sedat Pakay who peered into the space between the inside and outside, who looked deeply at and into the man. His beautiful photographs clearly show it.

Baldwin was popular and the soul of the party, I learned from our conversations with Engin and Gülriz, but he could be a demanding and daunting houseguest at times. He drank a lot, for example, and Gülriz told me that she managed to provide alcohol for him when times were lean by preparing homemade "yellow vodka" according to the recipe of a famous artist, Aliye Berger, who kept her liquor in a bathtub and whom Jimmy met on his first night in Istanbul and deeply admired. In Gülriz's book, this anecdote appears as an occasion to provide a detailed recipe of that Turkish equivalent of moonshine to her readers (do try this at home) (Sururi, Kıldan İnce, 324).[55] Since it was published during his lifetime, I wonder if Baldwin ever saw Sururi's book and learned about the parts devoted to him, as I know that he went to Turkey for a long visit in 1981. I regret now as I write this, some three years after our interview, that I did not think to ask her about that.

Between the accounts of Gülriz and Engin, I learned some other interesting trivia. For example, jewelry was important to all of them, as a symbol of presence and absence in human relationships. When they got engaged, Engin and Gülriz decided not to wear traditional engagement rings, so as not to lose them somewhere in the dressing room, as actors typically do. They opted instead for "Mevlevi medals on our necks," as Sururi's memoir explains (323).[56] Jimmy loved to wear jewelry on his hands, especially a ring he got from Gülriz, as she told me. In one of the letters, he refers to Engin's "Magic Ring," too. No matter how many there were, we can see one of these heavy silver rings—symbolic perhaps of his quasi-wedded state to his Turkish family—on his finger in Sedat Pakay's film and in many photographs throughout the period. During one of his later visits, when he was "rich and famous," Baldwin gave Gülriz a heavy turquoise necklace that he had brought from Mexico. She handed it to me as we were saying goodbye in the hall after the interview; she wanted me to look at it and touch it; it was heavy and warm and had been lying in a large bowl on the sideboard, across from the entrance to their apartment. She told me that it was her good luck charm, her talisman, and that she held it in her hands every day. I left her apartment thinking that it was guarding her and Engin's space; indeed, it must still be there, welcoming visitors, its blue warding off the evil eye, glowing with reminders of Jimmy's blues, laughs, and many gifts.

Although I saw Gülriz mostly in her domestic space during our interview, from the collection of photographs I saw, I was able to glimpse her and others at work and play outside that space. The photographs come from private archives and local papers, and many of them show Baldwin being entertained, working on *Fortune and Men's Eyes*, walking through town, playing on the beach. One photograph reproduced earlier in the chapter, my favorite, shows Jimmy, Gülriz, and Engin walking across the scenic Galata Bridge. They are a young, vibrant, happy family, indeed. I also wandered through the top level of the apartment when we took a break to see the portrait of Gülriz by Beauford Delaney, which she was not very fond of. I liked it quite a bit, and thought, romanticizing shamelessly but also feeling somewhat troubled about all that I had just learned, that it showed the young woman whom Jimmy enabled to speak English behind her husband's back, whom he called "Lioness" while mussing her hair, and to whom he confessed his love affairs while she called him "Yamyam."

There were two more paintings by Delaney, Jimmy's spiritual and artistic father. One was an image of the night lights on the Bosphorus, all navy blues, indigos, swirling whites, and scintillating yellows. The other was a portrait of Baldwin as a serious young artist in Turkey. He is wearing a bright, textured shirt against a background of bright yellows, purples, pinks, and tans that could be Hagia Sophia, or just a hill looming on the horizon over the Bosphorus, or his very own and omnipresent "mountain." There was no portrait of Engin in the house, or at least we did not hear about one having been painted by Delaney. A portrait of sorts, however, does emerge from the interviews we held at his place and the letters that Baldwin wrote to his friend between 1956 and 1974.

Unlike Jimmy and Gülriz, Jimmy and Engin shared a past in the United States and planned to make it possible for Engin to continue having a career there even as he achieved success in Turkey. This never came to be, causing much frustration on both sides, especially, I imagine, to the ambitious Cezzar, who might easily have tried his luck in Hollywood. Nevertheless, de-

15. *Left to right*: Engin, Beauford Delaney, Gülriz's portrait by Delaney, Gülriz,
and Jimmy. Reproduced by permission of Doğan Kitap.

spite the mixed blessings that the failure of these plans must have brought,
as I have learned from the letters and from our conversations and trips with
Engin throughout his city, their brotherly relationship survived Baldwin's
Turkish sojourn and whatever ups and down they had to deal with over the
years.[57] As Baldwin writes in one of his late missives, he carried Cezzar's
symbolic protective talisman wherever he went: hoping that "planes don't
crash," he confirmed that he was still wearing his ring and announced his
return to Paris the first week of September (letter 43, n.d.).

Baldwin's letters to Cezzar and the stories that emerge from my interviews seem to be carrying on a fascinating dialogue across the Atlantic.
Engin makes it clear that he never saved copies of his letters to Jimmy; "I
never collect what I write. . . . Once I've sent it off, once it's out there, it's out
[of] my hands, gone." When in our interview I suggested that he write his
memoirs or a book on Jimmy, Engin laughed: "I couldn't. A film [maybe],
or I could write a play. I hate writing. . . . I can't do that. I just keep taking
notes, and sticking them away, hiding them somewhere . . . I hate it. But
I love writing screenplays." They complement each other in strange ways,
these African American–Turkish brothers, one a consummate writer who
would love to act, the other a consummate actor who hates writing. And it

seems fitting that Cezzar would take over as the self-appointed elder of the two, given that he invited, welcomed, and hosted Baldwin in Turkey. When we talked in his apartment, four decades after Baldwin's arrival on his doorstep, Cezzar was proud of having nurtured his friend when he needed it, and stressed that their connection escaped simple verbalization:

> Let's face it—I *saved* Jimmy in a very, very bad period in his life. He was losing his health, losing his objectives, his motivations . . . broke as hell. The man had to be taken care of. It so happened that I was insisting, that I knew the situation—I said, "you come here"—to save himself. I don't want to sound like he came to Istanbul and that was a renaissance or whatever. I was a friend who was offering him my friendship, my house, my family, my food, my bed. In a situation where he could rest, he could write, not worry about food, drink, or where he was going to sleep that night. He had a room in my house. I had just married, working really hard, and just left him alone. Until the time when he recovered, and he became notorious—the notorious nigger of Istanbul![58] So this is the evolution—you take it from there. It was that year when he finished *Another Country*, in that house, under those very horrible conditions.[59] We were not hungry, not dirty, but it was not luxurious.

Cezzar was proud of the magic that Istanbul worked on his friend and of the role he played as Baldwin's Turkish host and anchor:

> Something got into him, from down and out in Paris, and in London and in New York, to Istanbul, the finishing of the novel, the discovery of Istanbul and the people who were so loving around him; everybody loved Jimmy. It must have influenced him, impressed him, must have made its imprint somewhere in his subconscious. And we didn't talk about it, but anytime he came back, it was probably for the same reasons, not in exactly the same terms or conditions. One must always have friends, and places one can trust, and wholly . . . trust. Everybody craves that. So I suppose it's that kind of first impression, a first rebirth that, sort of, brought him back.

Cezzar also emphasized the unspoken connection between them and their several collaborations as artists:

> There was such solidarity. We were also working together. We had three projects going—three came through, actually. "Hair" came through—he was co-producer. . . . And Jimmy started his career . . . as a director

[here]. He had his writing brother in Istanbul. . . . So working together, creating together, was another [factor], I'm sure. I mean, you don't talk about these things . . . you feel these things.

As I read the transcripts of my interviews with Engin in the context of Baldwin's fifty-four letters to him that I have been able to examine, more parallel stories emerge that seem to bring them even closer together at certain points in their lives as transatlantic kin.

Cezzar left the United States some ten years after Baldwin had left for Paris, and although he went back to Istanbul, the city of his birth, he was not set on staying there forever and thus also searched for a haven to recover and regroup as an artist. He remembers his departure from the New York harbor, following a bad bar fight that later found its way into *Another Country*—a subtle Turkish inflection in the scene in the novel when Rufus and Vivaldo are attacked by a white mob. Engin was nineteen going on twenty at the time, and Baldwin was about thirty-two:

> [Jimmy always said,] "Let's cross the oceans." How did I leave—maybe that's important? That's the last vision I have of Jimmy, on the Brooklyn docks. He was waving goodbye, for now. We had had this horrible accident—a fight in the Village—and I was hospitalized, had eight stitches in my head, and my jaw was broken. I really had a tough time. My girlfriend took care of me. I had this paranoia. I lost all my jobs. I was teaching; I was [doing things] at the UN; I had auditions. I couldn't walk out into the street.

Cezzar's departure from America took place after this "accident" that almost cost him his life; the fight also brought him closer to Baldwin as he was to leave the United States for Turkey, where their blood brotherhood would flourish in a few years. Quite fittingly, Cezzar's vision of his black friend on the day of his departure has Baldwin framed against the chains hanging along the Brooklyn docks—an obvious metaphor for Baldwin's inability to escape his homeland, his birthplace, and the mixed blessings of his birthright as the bastard child of the American "house of bondage." Cezzar's memory of this parting scene might also be read as a possible inspiration for the pivotal moments of migrant departure and arrival in the short story "This Morning, This Evening, So Soon," which Baldwin wrote around that time. Cezzar's desire in the late fifties and early sixties to return to the United States could also be framed as an immigrant's longing for the Promised Land. Baldwin was aware of his friend's aspirations and tried to help him. But he also told Ida Lewis in an interview conducted in 1970 for *Essence* that "the people of Istanbul . . . know nothing about what the black man has gone through in America. They still think of America as a promised land. . . . They don't know that that dream which was America is over" (Standley and Pratt, *Conversations*, 87).

For his part, Cezzar's narrative of Baldwin's longing for "another country" and arrival in Istanbul departs from how Gülriz Sururi sees it, with her focus on herself *receiving* Baldwin as a somewhat intimidated host. Her husband's account echoes the familiar narrative of (im)migrant passage, but from a vantage point of someone standing between the worlds, someone who facilitated Baldwin's transition onto a new stage. Engin's description of Jimmy's arrival is both dramatic and autoethnographic, as it has both the unexpected guest and his host performing a stunning entrance in front of an audience of natives:[60]

> And two rings [at the door], in comes this little, bedraggled . . . hungry, reeking [Jimmy] . . . a battered suitcase in his hand—into the middle of this party with the whole of the Istanbul intelligentsia—artists, activists, writers, anybody who is nobody . . . nobody who is anybody . . . is there such a term? I'm just making it up, I think, but you know what I mean. In walks Jimmy. I say, "Welcome home, Jimmy." I say, "Oh, hose him off immediately." I say, "Friends, Romans, countrymen, this is Jimmy Baldwin, of literary fame, the famous black American novelist." He was in the middle of the party and he met everybody that ever came into his life in Istanbul that night. He finally fell asleep in the lap of an actress—a very big actress, huge—[*inaudible*], she lives in America now, a very interesting person, actually. And he fell asleep in her lap, the party was over, and he went into his little room to his little bed. And that was the beginning of that space.[61]

While the new space Baldwin inhabited in Istanbul was becoming a specific place for him, Engin witnessed and facilitated Jimmy's education about everyday life in Turkey. Baldwin, who must have been familiar with some of the Orientalist Western notions about Turkey as an exoticized and eroticized location, was stunned at what he saw as the overall homoerotic atmosphere of the city. For example, Cezzar recalled his friend's shock at seeing Turkish men walk the streets hand in hand:

> When Jimmy was here—one of the first days—he said, "Wow, Engin, here people walk hand in hand and nobody turns their head." I said,

"Jimmy, they're not gay. They're mostly soldiers who are on leave. They've come to Istanbul and they're afraid of losing each other so they go like this, not 'hand in hand'" [*laughs*]. "They walk so they don't lose each other." Jimmy was so torn. "No, people don't [just] walk hand in hand."

When we discussed sexual conduct and homosexuality in Turkey between the past and the new century, Cezzar chuckled about the suppression of discourse concerning what had been a widely known lifestyle—"It's the Mediterranean, for crying out loud!"—and mentioned the new movements and identity politics that emerged in Turkey in the 1990s:

> It's an unspoken, unadvertised way of life here. It's all over. My god, it's the imperial Ottoman Empire. All the sultans had wives, and boys. A harem for wives, a harem for boys. Nobody questioned anything. So it's that kind of tradition, plus the rural tradition, plus the military. It exists.[62]

But when I asked him about the visibility and outspokenness of gay, lesbian, and other queer movements, he hesitated and said that while the practice was widely accepted, it was not spoken about:

MZ: So it was all walks of life.

EC: All walks of life. Starting high up—that's very interesting—starting from the very highest, to the . . . [lowest], political prisoners. You could write volumes about it. It's unspoken, but it's there. It should not be a shock to anybody, really. . . . In general, you don't see it in the streets very much. Unless they're a transvestite. Jesus Christ, they are so brave. . . . There is hostility insofar as they form their ghettos. But that becomes very dangerous. And whatever is around the ghetto . . . there have been many rough, violent things against them.

This discussion emerged when we turned to the allegations already mentioned in the introduction, ones that really offend me and all of Baldwin's Turkish friends in their stereotypical assumption both about the visitor and about the land that took him in—namely, that Jimmy came to their country for the sake of the famed "Turkish baths."[63] I was trying to come up with a polite way of framing a rather crude question about this that Engin answered very directly, globalizing for me his friend's emplacement as a kind of a transatlantic queer:

I'll tell you something very funny. . . . Baldwin's lovers were French, American—the ones that came to Istanbul. Baldwin didn't have a very deep affair with a Turk in Istanbul. Can you believe that? Nothing like the affair he had with Alain, the French boy. Nothing like the affair he had with Lucien. Nothing like the big love story with Arnold back in Harlem. He did not have a serious love affair in Istanbul. . . . He must have had one-night stands. He had relationships with lots of people. But he did *not* come to Istanbul for that. That was the *least* attraction for Jimmy in Istanbul!

I was a little taken aback by this statement. Cezzar seemed to be giving with one hand and taking away with another as he both affirmed and diminished the importance of Baldwin's sexuality. Perhaps, like other Turkish artists and intellectuals of that generation, he was trying to be progressive while at the same time maintaining certain secure, mainstream, heteronormative identifications, a kind of decorum that I also noticed in Gülriz. I also double-checked the facts about Baldwin's affairs in Turkey against Leeming's biography, where I found a statement about Jimmy's "Greco-Turkish lover" who was around when Baldwin lived at the Pasha's Library (*James Baldwin*, 275).[64] I also learned later that Baldwin was romantically involved with another Turkish man at the end of his last prolonged stay in Istanbul.

Not surprisingly, from a discussion of cruising and lovers we got into one on the meaning of eroticism and "love" to Baldwin and how they were reflected in his works. Cezzar spoke of his friend's virtually Kierkegaardian— that's what it sounded like to me—pursuit of an ideal lover, an impossible scenario à la *Don Juan* that Cezzar agreed with me had always been coupled with Baldwin's search for an idealized domestic and artistic setting.[65] Baldwin's conviction that the function of the artist is akin to that of the lover is clear, as his erotics of domesticity and work space intertwine with rich images of places dreamed up, perceived, and experienced. When we talked, I mentioned to Engin many scholars' interest in Baldwin's theorizing of love on several literal and metaphoric levels: brotherly love, love between blacks and whites within the nation, compassionate love for all humans, and spiritual love that transcends institutionalized religion. I wanted to know what other kinds of love Cezzar and Baldwin talked about besides the kind one cries over on a friend's shoulder. Cezzar told me:

Besides the crying on my shoulders, [*inaudible*] I think there is nothing unsaid about Jimmy's concept [of love]. . . . There are no secrets . . . Jimmy had no secrets. . . . The one thing, and the last thing Jimmy told [*inaudible*]

[was]: "Don't ever lie to yourself, and don't lie to your audience. Don't ever lie" . . . That is the secret. . . . It was a pleasure for him . . . to share his secrets. Thereby, to enlighten them [his friends and listeners], to help them to understand themselves, from their own secrets. . . .

Let's face it, Jimmy is an expert humanist. He's an expert on human relationships. . . . [He concludes a long narrative with:] "My shoulders are wet!"

We moved back and forth in our discussion without paying much attention to chronology. So I was not surprised when Cezzar returned once more to the beginning of the trust and mutual support that he shared with Baldwin in the fifties in New York, practically since they had first met. The story of their scraping by together as artists working hard for a break echoes to a degree the way that the fictitious David and Giovanni managed together in Paris in the novel that actually brought Engin and Jimmy together:

We were always broke in New York. But it was nice. I had a little money coming in. From my UN job. And we used to get together over drinks, so it was a matter of who was going to pay for drinks tonight. Whoever has the money pays for the drinks. Rough days, but later on, the money was coming in. Checks were coming in, royalties were coming in, bestsellers, and all that jazz.

That Engin quickly became an adopted member of the Baldwin family was clear, too. He knew everyone and admired Baldwin's connection to his mother, Berdis, and to his sisters, brothers, and all the nephews and nieces that soon started coming into his international life. He called his sister, Gloria Smart, his "great friend." He laughed about Jimmy's dislike of his trips to New York when he lived in Turkey but added quickly that his family was a magnet that always made those trips right, despite Baldwin's paranoia concerning his safety in the United States and the way that his government perceived him, along with his art, activism, and politics:

His mother—he's very fond of his mother. He's very fond of Paula Maria, the baby sister. I loved her. All his nephews and cousins . . . and Gloria [Baldwin's sister]—Jimmy always goes back to them. How should I put it? He was a world citizen. Not of his own choice, but he became one. In spite of the fact that he always bitched about it: "I have to go back. I have to go to Israel. I have to go to Paris. I hate going to New York." He did hate going to New York, and he was scared shitless of going back to New York because he had this paranoia that they were going to take his passport away from him. For years. . . . But he had to go to the States. He had the Civil Rights Movement. He had to be there for the march on Washington. He had to be at Martin Luther [King]'s funeral. So all these connections are very real. And therefore, from the get-go, it was impossible for a person who's so colorful, full of life, dynamic, and beautiful like Jimmy to stay in one place. It would have stagnated him and he knew this, instinctively. As I say, we never discussed it—this is the first time I've said anything out loud. . . . We shared everything.

Elia Kazan, the Istanbul-born, Greco-Turkish theater and film director, was Baldwin's close friend; Jimmy wrote in a blurb on the cover of Kazan's *America, America* (1962): "This is a marvelous story. Not many Americans have dared to face the truth of why they came to this continent, or what happened once they did. Gadg baby, you're a nigger, too."[66] Kazan remembers in his autobiography how much trouble Baldwin sometimes had to go through to be able to travel: "[In 1964] he went to Washington to see Hubert Humphrey and demand to know why he'd been refused a visa to go to Europe. 'Because every time you go to Europe, you besmirch America,' Humphrey had explained. Jimmy answered, 'When I read that a black meeting place in Alabama has been bombed, tell me what to say, M. Humphrey.' Jimmy got his visa."[67] It is poignant that the experience of Baldwin and other Blacks abroad—W. E. B. Du Bois and Paul Robeson, for example—proved that American citizens were suffering from the post–World War II nightmare common among immigrants from the oppressed third world countries and the second world of the Soviet bloc. In that nightmare, shared by millions of all colors, one's passport would be taken away, and one would be locked forever behind the barbed-wire borders of one's prison-homeland.[68]

Along with the issues of travel, governmental surveillance, and personal safety, Engin's and Jimmy's sharing of spaces and ideas included their thinking about religion. To a degree, it was something both used as artists, each in his own way. Cezzar acted in many plays that took on the clashes between secular and religious Islamic law, one of which, *Kurban* (The Sacrifice), by the Turkish playwright Güngör Dilmen, brings together the Greek myth of Medea with the marital drama in a Muslim household in a Turkish village.[69] In the production from the same year, with Gülriz playing the female lead, Engin played the husband who insists on taking a second, younger wife, which leads to a tragic ending for his whole family. The play later served as an inspiration for one of the movie scripts that Cezzar and Baldwin wrote together during his last stay in Turkey.

EC: "The Sacrifice." The title . . . was "The Sacrifice," but we changed that hundreds of times. Jimmy always changed names. Every day he changed names. If I say, "Wow, this is it!" three days later he says, "Fuck it—it's this." So the last one was "The Sacrifice." And it didn't go through.

MZ: But was the script ever finished?

EC: The script was finished. [I have it] in Turkey, of course. But Costa [Gavras] didn't like it. He had liked the idea, the synopsis, the treatment. But he didn't like it [the script] this time. And I was in such a fucking position because this was Jimmy's friend. So I said, "All right, go tell Jimmy." He said, "I can't. You do that." I said, "Are you kidding? We coauthored, we wrote it together. I want you [to] say to Jimmy that you don't like his script." He said, "No way." Costa copped out. I like to think, I'm not sure, but I like to think that it was for a political reason because the government in Greece changed at that time. . . . Costa was called to Greece for many projects [around 1974]. And the Greek minister of culture was an avid Turk hater. And I want to think that it was this influence that made Costa cop out. Maybe it wasn't, maybe it was just a personal evaluation. Anyway, it was tragic.[70]

While in Bodrum in 1981, Baldwin and Cezzar worked on another script, this one based on the novel L'Espadon and titled The Swordfish; they also attempted to produce it with the director Costa-Gavras, but it never came to be.[71]

The discussion of Kurban brought us back to religion as a topic. Engin explained to me at length his dislike of religious fanaticism and fundamentalism in any shape and form in the "three book religions" he was familiar with—Judaism, Christianity, and Islam. His outrage at the ravages and terror wreaked by organized religion was echoed less than three months after our visit, when the terrorist attacks of 9/11 brought East and West together yet again tragically and not entirely unexpectedly. In his comments, Cezzar clearly echoed Baldwin's thinking about embodied faith and individual responsibility, as well as the violent fallouts of worldwide Christianization; perhaps it also resounded with their many discussions on the subject:

One is worse than the other! Muslims, Christians, Jewish. They are the worst, the most fanatical believers. And they kill for it. What kind of teaching is that? If you can't teach somebody, you kill them, get them out of the way. So for me these three religions are the same. I've seen the best and the worst of all these religions. Embodied in certain people of course, how else can you see it?

The first time he and Jimmy had a chance to confront the issue of religious conflict, interestingly enough, came in New York, in 1957, when they were working on the staging of *Giovanni's Room* for the Actors Studio. Cezzar contextualized displays of religious feelings and theatrical spectacles within what seemed to be a notion of performance of faith involved in both cases. He was also very clued into Baldwin's own ambivalences about his upbringing in the black church and legacy as a preacher:

> I'll tell you a funny thing, and Jimmy is very funny. In *Giovanni's Room*, when we did the play, there is a scene when Giovanni spits on the cross. Jimmy said, "I get such pleasure in watching a Muslim spitting on the cross." There you are, decipher this! [*laughs*]. As if I were a devout Muslim. Well I wasn't, *I was an actor, of course*. But that was his interpretation. It's a quote, a great quote from Jimmy. I'm sure there must have been other such quotes in our lives I can't remember right now, maybe from the letters I find. We must have discussed this subject in more detail. He was a preacher . . . I never met such a religious person as Jimmy. *Not a believer but religious*. The way he uses the Bible. All these quotes, all from the Bible, so well chosen, so appropriate. He was always great with the Bible inside out. And he did not hate the Bible, but he hated Christians, the Christian culture. It's quite a concept to delve into.

When he had a chance to live in a Muslim country, Baldwin could not help comparing favorably the unknown culture he had just entered to the one he had fled. It seems that in Turkey, among many different "Islams" and far from the ghetto he had grown up in, he was exorcising his experience of racism at home and even his having been "saved" as a teenager in his Pentecostal storefront church in Harlem. And yet when asked about his approach to Islam by the journal *Cep Dergisi*, he said: "The Moslem question does not enter into my reasons for being here at all, except, perhaps, that it is a relief to deal with people who, whatever they are pretending, are not pretending to be Christians. I am not now, and will never become—at least not by my own desire—an expatriate. For better or for worse, my ties with my country are too deep, and my concern is too great" (Standley and Pratt, *Conversations*, 59–60). As he put it in one of his letters to Engin, there is no escape from the country of one's birth, especially the "freest of them all"—America.

Cezzar helped me to see how, for Baldwin, comparisons of his extensive experience with Christian cultures and his relatively superficial ones with Islam in Turkey often seemed to evolve into a kind of competition in which he would pitch the religions against each other like teams in a contest. He also made it clear that despite having lived in Turkey for a long time, and in Istanbul specifically, which is itself "another country" within Turkey, Baldwin hardly experienced the raw realities of local Islamic orthodoxy. They agreed on one thing, though—the best way to experience the effects of a religion on society was to observe what it did to that society and the individuals within it. Cezzar told me:

> He always harped on the fact that this is a Muslim country instead of Christian. Therefore, in his terms, it was much more—what's the word? Lenient? . . . not the castrating horrors of Christianity. He found the Muslims more to his taste. Of course, no way because of the Black Muslims, naturally that must have been the starting point in his mind about the Muslim religion. . . . But then he lived in a Muslim country, he studied the religion, per se. He was dealing with Muslim people, none of them were very religious. On the contrary, very nonreligious. . . . Still, it was a Muslim country, a Muslim culture. His shoeshine boy was a Muslim boy, his grocer was a Muslim. Those kinds of everyday relationships with another country, another culture. But in this culture it was always the religion he brought forth. He always put Turkey as a Muslim country against the Christian countries.

Engin's comments, not for the first time, sounded to me as if he were engaging in a kind of self-Orientalizing scrutiny. It was as if he were looking at his own culture from the outside, perhaps trying to imitate a Western gaze or employing the New Yorker outlook he had acquired while living in the Village in the 1950s. (And he was all those identities as a cosmopolitan Turkish artist.)

Despite being a rare sight as a black man in the streets of Istanbul, Engin claimed, Jimmy could feel more invisible and private there than at home. It was hard to believe, again, because, as I said before, even among the ethnically mixed Turkish people Baldwin was called "Arap" (Arab), so the color of his skin was clearly emphasized with that name. Still, it is true that he did not have to worry about not being served at a restaurant or being attacked by cops while in a "good" neighborhood; and in his later years, his hypervisibility would make him a star. I regretted that I was not able to interview his good friend the Kurdish novelist Yaşar Kemal, hoping that he, as an ethnic minority in Turkey, might have a different opinion. Campbell quotes Kemal saying something that confirms the complexity of Turkish approaches to blackness: "As far as I was concerned, Baldwin was not black . . . for there are no 'blacks' in Turkey in that sense. We didn't experience the slave trade; we don't have the category; there are only people with darker skins" (*Talking at the Gates*, 210). Given the history of the Ottoman Empire's trade contacts with North Africa and the presence of black slaves, male and female, in the sultan's palace, the statement is not accurate.[72]

In cases when Baldwin brought up the issue of race himself, his nationality seemed to override his color in the eyes of his hosts. For example, when he mentioned feeling at home in Turkey to Kemal, Campbell reports: "Kemal, who has been imprisoned several times on account of his political allegiances, is not a man to be lighthearted about Turkish liberties, but he understood why Baldwin experienced relief from racial pain in Istanbul. . . . [Baldwin] used to tell Kemal: 'Yaşar, I feel free in Turkey,' to which Kemal replied: 'Jimmy, that's because you're an American'" (211). Baldwin's national allegiances were a complex matter to him, but to his friends abroad, his U.S. citizenship guaranteed his international mobility and access to hard currency. He was noticed because he was black, but he was left alone because he was American.

We ended the discussion about Baldwin almost where we started, at Cezzar's "welcome table," circling back to Baldwin's initial experience of hospitality and sociability in Istanbul, which led to his writing the early parts of his last finished play, *The Welcome Table*, while in Turkey. Engin stressed the symbolic importance of the image of a table around which friends meet to recover from their journeys and share stories: "He always had a 'welcome table,' at Saint-Paul de Vence or in Istanbul." Cezzar regretted that Baldwin decided to settle for good in another country but understood his desire to be in a place where he could speak the language well as he got older: "He would never have learned Turkish. Can you imagine? A resident here in a sea of strangers?"[73] Czesław Miłosz's invocation of "language as the only homeland" resounds again in my mind and is revised by Baldwin.[74] By 1971 he traded the Muslim city, where he could be somewhat private and seen partaking of the pleasures of a metropolis without speaking its language, for an unlikely location, a French Catholic village, where he would be excessively visible as the only black person, no matter that he spoke the language well. Despite the obvious differences between Turkey and France, the dwelling and working paradigm that Baldwin had tested in Turkey would work in the south of France, too. He would be left alone there; he would be able to "breathe freely" while the phones and faxes worked to keep him in touch with the homeland from which he saw no escape. He would return to Turkey in 1981 for what he told Engin was the happiest vacation in his life, which they spent together with Gülriz and David Baldwin in the coastal village of Bodrum.

At the end of my interview with Cezzar, I repeated the question with which we had begun our conversation a week before. Looking at photographs, remembering the sunny months with Jimmy on the beach in Bodrum and their collaboration on the screenplays, speaking of their plans for more projects to come, Cezzar was more willing to speculate on the reasons for the relative absence of Turkish settings in his friend's works:

MZ: So why do you think he didn't write about Istanbul in his fiction?

EC: Why should he? Jimmy writes about black places, black people. He might have later on.

MZ: You were saying he didn't have time.

EC: I don't think he had time. Who knows? Maybe one of his later novels would've taken place in Istanbul. It would have been about what he learned from Istanbul, from the people. I'm sure he would have. I took it for granted that he would one day, but I don't think he had time.

The lack of time Cezzar emphasized refers as much to Baldwin's packed schedule as to his death at sixty-three. Assuring me that they "*always* talked about [new] projects," Cezzar smiled and stressed what seemed to make him even more content than a whole novel by Baldwin about Turkey might have. Quite simply, he was glad that he had "saved" his friend and that Baldwin had come to love his Bosphorus outpost and felt at home and at peace with his Turkish surrogate family: "He loved the water; he loved the sea. He watched the ocean; he watched the beach." This connection between the location and its people, and the lens on his work and life they afforded him is clear in Baldwin's letters to his friend and blood brother. Cezzar and his city helped him navigate between the temptations and perils of home and exile; they enabled him to understand further the peculiar imprisonment of his Americanness.

Perhaps that is one of the reasons why Baldwin finally had to leave Turkey. He could not go back to the United States; a few years later he would tell Sedat Pakay something that sounds disturbingly resonant for our own day: America "has dragged [itself], and may well have dragged the world, onto the very edge of a kind of unimaginable conflict, which could be the end of all of us, and has done it out of a really weird determination to protect something called the American way of life, which used to be called manifest destiny" (Pakay, *From Another Place* interview, 1970). He was to remain in search of a home, in exile, and in transit, but would carry his Turkish experience with him. His first impressions of Turkey made their way into *Another Country*, and his residence in Istanbul and interaction with its people affected the shape and content of his subsequent works. Like the tespih in Pakay's film, which is there in Baldwin's hands in the opening scene and can mean much or little depending on how we read it, his stays in Turkey imprinted to a degree everything he wrote during the decade. And while these impressions and imprints exist in his works more implicitly than explicitly, they come into sharper focus once we try to see Baldwin in Istanbul the way that Pakay did, that is, as his own person in his own world and both inside and outside the always new and shifting worlds of the others around him in his transient locale in the East.

16. Sedat Pakay, James Baldwin in bed, Istanbul, 1970.

TWO

QUEER ORIENTALISMS IN

ANOTHER COUNTRY

While Sedat Pakay's *James Baldwin: From Another Place* captures the ending of Baldwin's Turkish decade on film, it is Baldwin's third novel, *Another Country* (1962), that marks the beginning of the decade in fiction. The novel's perpetually unfinished manuscript brought Baldwin to Engin Cezzar's door in the fall of 1961. As Jimmy wrote to Cezzar in 1958, *Another Country* was only half finished at the time; it was "infinitely more unpublishable," it was "intransigent," but also black, "erotic," and powerful; it made his life miserable.[1] At work on it for nearly ten years, Baldwin mentioned in another letter that *Another Country* made him feel as if he were giving birth following a long-term pregnancy. He described the novel as "terribly active," as if it were a baby "pushing itself out" (letter 13, May 6, 1959).[2] Once on the Bosphorus, however, Baldwin was able to complete and rewrite *Another Country*, or deliver this tough baby, in about two months of intense labor.[3] The stories by those who witnessed his arrival in Turkey and lent editorial and moral support as he was finishing the manuscript confirm the importance of Istanbul as a location and lens through which we should reassess this work today. As the novel was being molded into its final form in exile in the East, *Another Country* also became a record of sorts of Baldwin's contacts with the new places, peoples, and cultures of Turkey.

Baldwin told the Turkish journal *Cep Dergisi*: "The principal reason that I find myself in Istanbul is that I am a writer, and I find it easier to work here than I do anywhere else. I am left alone here."[4] While he loved the solitude, he also embraced the cultural newness around him. He was in a foreign place, surrounded by a language he did not speak or read and by people whose ways of life and thinking were dramatically different from his own. Some of his friends, perhaps to emphasize that their Jimmy and their country did fit together, would dwell on affinities rather than analyzing productive differences. Engin Cezzar pointed to "something ancient . . . in this land . . . as ancient as [Baldwin's] African blood" and stated what David Leeming would later confirm in his biography, that Istanbul's Old City reminded Baldwin of Harlem.[5] But Baldwin enjoyed and embraced the unfamiliar and anomalous aspects of his life in Turkey: "It was . . . a place to work and a place to live . . . another way of life. . . . A set of assumptions that was not mine . . . [that could] teach you a great deal."[6] This statement is also revealing in regard to Another Country, the hardest of all his novels to complete because of its daring subject, and because its writing made Baldwin confront his increasing need for safe spaces to work away from the United States, and for havens where he could give time to personal recovery. That a country poised liminally between East and West, historically Orientalized and eroticized by Western writers, travelers, and artists, would fulfill such a role surprised some of Baldwin's readers and critics. Viewed from New York or Paris, Istanbul was a part of the mythologized Eastern world that since the eighteenth century, as Edward Said's magisterial Orientalism describes it, had served as a reservoir for Western exotic fantasies and imperialist designs.[7]

Part of the Orient, Turkey was seen as a site of foreign excess and danger, where one could lose one's intellectual and artistic grip. When illustrating the critics' rejection of Baldwin's later works, specifically his fourth novel written in Istanbul, Tell Me How Long the Train's Been Gone (1968), Thorsen's documentary flashes a line from the New York Times: "Too much . . . Turkey."[8] The line appeared on September 21, 1979, in John Leonard's review of Baldwin's last novel, Just above My Head (1979), which was not written in Turkey, but whose "aggravating sprawl" is explicitly linked to Baldwin's forays abroad. Turkey was associated with what Leonard calls Baldwin's "lapse" or his "[having] wandered for years in either a parenthesis or a doldrum" following The Fire Next Time, large parts of which were written in Istanbul.[9] Leonard wishes he could "wring" the neck of Baldwin's stray new novel, as it is so "swollen and bloated," and he criticizes Baldwin's "epileptic compulsion to connect with the realities of developing black America" while living in other countries. While Leonard thus infantilizes the ever-developing "black America" and pathologizes Baldwin as its writer, he also significantly locates the source of Baldwin's "lapse" in his third novel, or "about 100 pages into 'Another Country,'" the book that in fact brought Baldwin to Istanbul.[10]

That Istanbul provided Baldwin with a unique and compelling space to finish *Another Country* and write his later works can be seen in a powerful sequence from Pakay's film. About two-thirds into *From Another Place*, Pakay takes us into the private space of Baldwin's study. The camera pans across a small and sparsely furnished room dominated by a table and a typewriter; we can see a newspaper spread on a narrow bed that reveals photographs of several Black Panthers.[11] Although we are in the writer's inner sanctum, the question that Baldwin is answering on the soundtrack has nothing to do with writing but rather addresses the profane matters of sexuality, specifically his own. "What can I say . . . it is not to be spoken about to the world," Baldwin responds at first, defending his right to privacy. But then he goes on, compelled to be a witness, and links his personal story of having loved "some men and some women" to a global landscape of the history of sexuality and the specific problem of homophobic paranoia plaguing "American men." Pakay shows Baldwin sitting near his typewriter, smoking and fingering a cigarette and a cigarette holder, with a Muslim tespih lying on the table and a drink standing nearby.[12]

This moment in which the main tool of Baldwin's trade (the typewriter), a cultural artifact that marks his Turkish location (the tespih), and an image that recalls his distant home in the United States (the newspaper) all come together as he is discussing his sexuality can be read as a key to Pakay's film. The scene also represents a convergence of factors central to my reading of *Another Country* as a pivotal text that ushered in Baldwin's later works and helps to explain their shift in focus and form. I contend that in his third novel, Baldwin uses Turkey as a location and lens—a place to write *from* and one *through which* to see and reassess American culture. Although set in New York and centering on American characters, *Another Country* was revised in Istanbul, on the "erotic margin" of Asia and Europe, and articulated a turning point in Baldwin's views on race and sexuality in a transnational context.[13] It is in this third novel that the "black writer" from Harlem who wrote *Go Tell It on the Mountain* and the "gay writer" from Paris who wrote *Giovanni's Room* became a "black gay"—and as I will show throughout this chapter—a "black queer" writer.

Another Country articulates most fully Baldwin's insistence on the indivisibility of race and sex and their dependence on location and migration,

17. Sedat Pakay, *From Another Place*. James Baldwin at typewriter, 1970.

themes that would remain central for the rest of his career. By juxtaposing a close look at the context in which *Another Country* was written in Turkey with close readings of several key moments in the novel, I show how Baldwin engages a way of seeing and representing cultural difference of the part of the world known as the East. I argue that he does so to internationalize and interrogate dominant American and Western notions of racialized sexuality and heteronormative dominance. My reading of Baldwin in Istanbul performs a similar task to Bill Mullen's reading of Richard Wright as an "Occidental tourist" in marking his "hybrid and peculiar Orientalism" (*Afro-Orientalism*, 46, 47). Unlike Mullen, who claims that Wright's sense of dichotomies underlying his Western identity sharpened the more he wrote about the so-called Orient, I claim that Baldwin's residence in Turkey facilitated his departure from such dichotomies toward a kind of third space of queerness that helped him to revise his notions of Americanness at a critical historical juncture.

This chapter unfolds in two parts that are in dialogue with each other. They can be read independently or together, given their focus first on the biographical and theoretical contexts of Baldwin's writing *Another Country* in Istanbul and second on close readings of moments in the novel where Baldwin brings together discourses on the East with those on queer sexuality. The first part includes interview material with Turkish subjects, as well as definitions of the terms "Orientalism" and "queer" that may be familiar to some readers and helpful to others. The second part reads closely the instances in the novel where Baldwin shows us how Western notions of Eastern exoticism are present even in the erotic and racial experience of his American characters and thus provide a broader context for regarding whiteness, blackness, and sexuality in the mid-twentieth-century United States. My reading of *Another Country* focuses on the spectacular and fantastic associations of the imaginary East with decadent erotic desire and nonnormative and interracial sexuality and demonstrates how Baldwin sets out to "refunction and rearticulate" Orientalism "against itself" on its pages (Lowe, *Critical Terrains*, 5).[14]

Another Country was Baldwin's novelistic response to the Civil Rights Movement in its insistence that racial and sexual oppression are inextricably interlinked, that they are private and political, domestic and transnational. It is in this novel that Baldwin broke ground for *The Fire Next Time* and its final invocation to white and black Americans to come together "like lovers" in the struggle against American and global imperialism, and where he embraced interracial dialogue and both sensual love and agape, or spiritual love. In *Another Country*, he also anticipated some of the themes of his second play, *Blues for Mister Charlie* (1964), in which racist sexual violence results from the clash of white and black machismos, as much as from failed interpersonal relationships and state policy. As Marlon Ross poignantly puts it, *Another Country* "is exactly a prolegomenon for a revolution that is (homo)sexual and racial simultaneously, that the fire next time cannot merely be a fire that sears the racial existence of Americans but must also be one that disrupts their sexual psychology" (JB *Now*, 19).

The Context: The "Killer" Novel and the City

No matter his striking African appearance and nickname as "Arap," as a U.S. citizen Baldwin was a westerner to the Turks, marked by his passport, language, currency, clothes, access to travel, and foreign mannerisms.[15] On his first visit to Istanbul, he was also to some degree an American tourist, but one endowed with the mixed blessings of a double vision, or a particular form of Du Bois's double consciousness that Baldwin developed because of his racial and sexual marginalization at home. He could thus discover and observe with a keener eye the local rules of sociability and how race, gender, and sexuality were negotiated in another country. For example, Istanbul's curious mix of Muslim dogma and state-enforced secularism resulted in dramatically different gender relations and homosocial negotiations of public spaces. This was especially true concerning the open and often deceptive homoeroticism among men, which took Baldwin some time to understand, as he told Cezzar. This has not changed much since then and helps us to imagine Baldwin's scenes of writing in Turkey.

"It's such a men's culture. Just look at them—out and about, drinking tea, so close and so happy," Oktay Balamir, who became Baldwin's close friend during the production of *Fortune and Men's Eyes* in 1969 and 1970, told me during an interview in 2005.[16] Balamir and I strolled through downtown Ankara and saw numerous groups of men in the streets. There were similar scenes in Istanbul and Bodrum. One could certainly see more women in the public spaces of Istanbul in 2005 than in Pakay's film from 1970, but one still noticed many closely knit male groups and couples holding on to each other. Men occupied tables in dense groups, drinking tea and smoking, playing board games, reading, getting ready for prayer, or simply people watching. In Maureen Freely's novel *The Life of the Party* (1984), which fictionalizes the rowdy international crowd at Robert College in the sixties, it is clear that men dominate public spaces. Given local presumptions about

18. Sedat Pakay, *From Another Place*. James Baldwin at a cafe outdoor table, 1970.

foreign women's lasciviousness, the female characters in Freely's novel are always wary of walking alone and of being bareheaded in public without male escorts.[17] In Pakay's film, we follow Baldwin strolling through mostly male crowds or surrounded by silent male onlookers; once he bumps into a women in a scarf; another sells him pigeon feed around the Spice Bazaar. Browsing through books in the Beyazıt Sahaflar market, drinking tea in a cafe in Bebek, Baldwin is either being looked at by silent male Turks or trying to see inside a circle of men captivated by a street snake oil salesman in Eminönü. Many of Pakay's photographs catch Baldwin with ordinary people throughout the city: having his shoes shined in Eminönü, admiring a young child, being given a pin by schoolchildren at the monument of Atatürk in Taksim Square.

Pakay's visions of Baldwin freeze-frame him as being comfortable, though transient, in Turkey, a place that was exotic and foreign to most Americans. In her study of American popular culture after World War II, Melani McAlister claims that it was steeped in "Orientalism" and that it used "a certain type of lens" to imagine and regard what was considered the mythic realm of the East. Orientalism continues to be the "stuff of children's books and popular movies: a world of harems and magic lamps, mystery and decadence, irrationality and backwardness" (Epic Encounters, 8). As a source of coveted artifacts and narratives, McAlister observes, the East has been a locus of desire for the exotic, a source of what Edward Said has termed the "iconography of sexual desire" (Orientalism, 63). As a location and lens, the East provides a wide range of erotic fantasies for the Western traveler, consumer, and artist: "the possibility of . . . reverie, release, sensual pleasure . . . an exhibition, a spectacle, even a dream" (Epic Encounters, 22).[18] Orientalist paintings reflect and enable these dreams and pleasures by focusing on "the magnificent nudity of Oriental males. . . . lust . . . [and] slave markets," imaginings that catered "to the buyer's prurient interest in erotic themes." The East was an "ideal milieu for an artist who could never have depicted such subjects in a Christian or Western setting" (Germaner and İnankur, Orientalism and Turkey, 42). The cultural historian Irvin C. Schick links fantasies of "oriental sexuality" to specific urban spaces and architectural structures that supplied the European literary imagination, and by extension the North American imagination since the eighteenth century, with "an entire arsenal of fictionalized devices such as the harem, the public bath, the slave market, concubines, eunuchs, polygamy, and homosexuality" (The Erotic Margin, 1).[19]

Like structures and landscapes taken out of context, Western visions of the East have been "fragmentary" and synecdochic; they represent the Orient as the "stage on which the whole East is confined" (Said, Orientalism, 128–29). The "European imagination" that created this stage was for centuries nourished by a "fabulously rich world" of characters and literary fantasies, "settings, in some cases names only, half-imagined, half-known; monsters, devils, heroes; terrors, pleasures, desires," that included "the Sphinx, Cleopatra, Eden, Troy, Sodom and Gomorrah, Astarte, Isis and Osiris, Sheba, Babylon, the Genii, the Magi, Nineveh . . . Mahomet, and dozens more" (63).[20] While Baldwin's enormous erudition made him familiar with this rich world of exotic imagery, with what Obeidat calls "an alien, if somewhat confrontational, alternative World" of the Muslim Orient (132–33), it also taught him that Western visions of that world were never schematic and predictable but "heterogenous and contradictory," as they reflected changing goals of Western colonialism, historical developments, and geopolitical shifts (Lowe, Critical Terrains, 5).

By the time Baldwin went to Turkey, there emerged, for example, what Christina Klein terms "Cold War Orientalism," or a concerted effort of the "middlebrow intellectuals" to explain the U.S. expansion into Asia by means of "an ideology of global interdependence rather than one of racial difference" (16). By relying on "a network of sentimental pathways between the United States and Asia," Klein points out, cultural productions such as the musical The King and I "paralleled and reinforced the more material pathways along which America's economic, political, and military power flowed" (17). A similar situation existed with Euro-Asian Turkey, which became a NATO ally in the 1950s and hosted U.S. Navy ships and military bases. Istanbul and Ankara also hosted American cultural attachés, State Department officers who organized events that promoted American musicians, writers, and visual artists.[21] As Baldwin told Ida Lewis, while in Turkey he "learned a lot about dealing with people who are neither Western nor Eastern." A liminal country that was hard to categorize according to the Cold War divisions of the world, Turkey was a "satellite on the Russian border," where one learned about the "brutality and the power of the Western world" by "living with people whom nobody cares about, who are bounced like a tennis ball between the great powers" (Conversations, 86). To Pakay, Baldwin spoke about Turkey as a geopolitical spectacle, where he saw "the cynicism of power politics and foreign aid . . . functioning everyday in . . . [a] sort of a theatre."[22]

Positioned on the "West–East axis," Turkey partook in the long history of what Howard Winant calls the encounter of "absolutist Europe with the

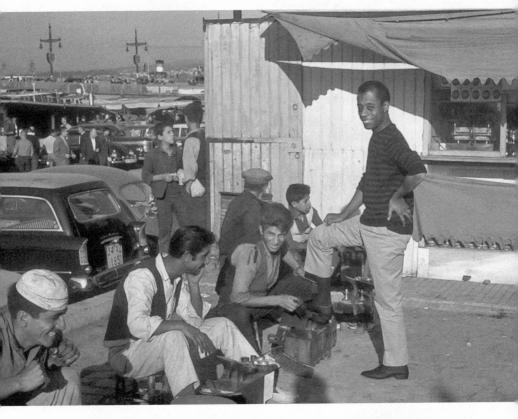

19. James Baldwin and shoeshine in Eminönü, summer 1965. Photo by Sedat Pakay.

20. James Baldwin and children in Taksim Square, summer 1965.
Photo by Sedat Pakay.

Islamic world [which] was a crucible of race consciousness" (*The New Politics of Race*, 132).[23] Baldwin's contacts with Turkish intellectuals and artists—many of whom looked white but were not considered so by American and Western European standards—helped him to realize that he was observing people who creatively reacted to and reshaped Western discourses about the East. The feminist scholar Reina Lewis stresses that the West "was never a sole arbiter and owner of meanings about the Orient . . . [because] Orientalism was a discourse framed by the responses, adaptations and contestations of those whom it constructed as its objects" (*Rethinking Orientalism*, 2). Sheltered from the less congenial parts of Turkish reality—illiteracy and poverty—by his privileged friends, Baldwin confronted his geopolitical assumptions about the East–West divide with the daily experience of living among the Westernized and secular upper crusts of Istanbul. He read books about the history of the city and talked with his friends John Freely and Hilary Sumner-Boyd from Robert College, who were at that time working together on an extensive guide, *Strolling through Istanbul* (1972).[24] Apart from long conversations about politics with his Turkish friends, Baldwin enjoyed people watching in the streets, walks and sightseeing, and visits to teahouses, cafes, and restaurants.

Baldwin's daily observations would sometimes trigger comparisons between Turkish and American approaches to power, race, and sex, and what, years later in his interview with Sedat Pakay, he called the Blacks' and the Turks' shared "peculiar relationship to the West."[25] His growing awareness of local history and politics provided a rich context for his writings on American racial strife amid the complexities of the Cold War in *The Fire Next Time*. Few realize that parts of that work, which catapulted Baldwin to international fame, were in fact composed in Turkey, and it was his decade there that helped him to see the East as one of the key subjects and theoretical paradigms in the lexicon of Western imperial domination.

Baldwin's sense of the positive "energy" of Turkey, as he called it in the interview with Pakay, also had something to do with the personal freedom he experienced there as a man who loved other men. In a culture that drew the lines of gender and sexuality strikingly differently, he did not stand out; he was not vilified; he was not questioned about his boyfriends; he was left alone. This leads me to another central term of this chapter besides "Orientalism." *Another Country* marked a turning point in Baldwin's career, as it provided him with a space to question American binary constructions of race and sexuality and to arrive at an articulation of what we would today call a *queer* identity.[26] Let us recall the basic meaning of the term "queer" when Baldwin came of age in Greenwich Village in the 1940s. At that time, "queer" designated male same-sex desire, but more recently the gender studies scholar Eve Sedgwick has interpreted the term as meaning "across"—as in "across genders, across sexualities, across genres, across 'perversions'" (*Tendencies*, xii). Important for my purposes, this term suggests movement, experimentation, and resistance to received notions of knowing and being. "Queer" suggests thinking, subjects, and states that are nonbinary, "transitive—multiply transitive . . . antiseparatist . . . [and] antiassimilationist"; it is "relational, and strange" (xii). In short, in Sedgwick's terms, queerness seems to reside at the center of Baldwin's novel. To echo Robert Reid-Pharr's definition of queerness and his reading of *Another Country*, it also refers to the ways in which we relate to our bodies and to each other through the body when engaged in acts of transgressive desire and interracial sex; it relates to the fact that Baldwin the black queer writer puts "his own body on the line" in a novel that self-consciously crosses the boundaries of race and sex (Reid-Pharr, "Dinge," 75–76, 84).[27]

Baldwin's articulation of queerness in *Another Country* took form as he was negotiating the complex web of relationships with his Turkish friends and lovers and revisioning Americanness from another place of Istanbul. In this sense, then, his Turkish location and lens influenced his vision of queerness and, as I will show in the next part of this chapter, encouraged him to engage and interrogate the Orientalist imaginary in his novel. Edward Said calls attention to more innocent gestures of Orientalization, that is, to writers using the East's "unimaginable antiquity, inhuman beauty, boundless distance" as sources of inspiration. Like Byron and Victor Hugo before him, Baldwin could be seen as engaging both in the experience and the imaginative rendering of that location "as a form of release, a place of original opportunity" (*Orientalism*, 167).[28]

On the last page of *Another Country* Baldwin wrote, "Istanbul, Dec. 10, 1961," thus affirming the centrality of the city and date to the final shape of the novel. David Leeming, who met Baldwin as this last line was literally being written down, confirms the novel's unequivocal tribute to the Turkish metropolis. He came across Baldwin calmly finishing the book with a lively party going on around him:

> The setting into which I then strolled consisted of a kitchen counter covered with seemingly disorganized papers mingled with glasses and Turkish hors d'oeuvres at which, on a high stool, sat a small black man with huge eyes who paid no attention to me as he scribbled furiously on

one of the pieces of paper until he abruptly stopped and stared for some time at what he had written. "God," he said, "it's finished." As it turned out, he had just written the last words of Another Country. For the first time he looked at me. "Hey, Baby," he said, "I'm Jimmy." "I'm David," I said. He looked at me quite seriously for what seemed a long time before breaking into a large smile. "I like that name," he said, "it's special to me. Let's have a drink." (James Baldwin, 195–96)

The scene took place in the house of Cevat Çapan—a poet, critic, and teacher—who at the time was married to Engin Cezzar's sister, Mina, and hosted Baldwin during Engin's service in the army.[29] Leeming, who had the same first name as Baldwin's favorite brother, David, and would later manage Baldwin's papers and write up his life, confirmed during our recent interview in New York that the meeting in Çapan's kitchen "changed his life."[30] Baldwin would often lecture on Henry James, the writer they both loved, to Leeming's classes at Robert College; Leeming lived with him as his secretary in Turkey for several years; they remained lifelong friends. They saw each other for the last time just days before Baldwin died in his house in the south of France. In an unpublished letter from 1966, Baldwin wrote his friend that he had brought him "great good luck."

As Leeming wrote three decades later in his biography, "Istanbul was clearly a cast of characters for a man with Baldwin's instinctive interest in social and personal complexity" (194). On my first visit in Istanbul, I met one of those characters, Cevat Çapan, in a stuffy, densely packed cafe near Taksim Square, where he participated in a panel on poetry and literary criticism. There were many outspoken students, and Çapan answered their questions in a husky voice, chain-smoking all the while. When we talked afterward he was happy to answer my questions about Baldwin and assured me, "We treated him as a brother." Jimmy moved into their house in Bebek, near Robert College, and loved being across the street from the water. Not only was it in Çapan's kitchen that Baldwin actually finished Another Country and met David Leeming, but Çapan also read the whole typescript that Baldwin had reworked while staying at Engin and Gülriz's place, and gave him final editing suggestions.[31]

Another Country does not include acknowledgments, so we will never know exactly how much Çapan's advice, or the editing sessions with Gülriz and Engin, actually shaped Baldwin's novel. As Çapan told me with much pride and joy, he felt privileged that his "brother Jimmy" took his editorial advice to heart while finishing Another Country. He was especially captivated by Yves's immigrant entry to New York and asked Baldwin simply "to stop [the novel] there," with the scene that made a great coda to the story about boundary crossings. Unlike Baldwin's American critics, Çapan loved the book and considered Baldwin "a very good novelist." Çapan's observations of white Americans in Turkey echoed his and Baldwin's comments about the novel's focus on the pitfalls of interracial communication: "You could just touch it, it was very obvious that . . . whites were not psychologically or spiritually equipped to understand blacks."[32] In contrast, he and Baldwin "could talk about *any* writer, no matter the race"; they could talk about anything without shame.

When he hosted Baldwin, Çapan taught English at Robert College, today's Boğaziçi Üniversitesi, and found in his American brother a kindred spirit with whom to discuss literature, theater, and politics. He remembered that Jimmy "was working all the time." Baldwin also began his interactions with university students in Turkey.[33] He sometimes lectured in Çapan's classes and was a great hit with the young people, who loved his charisma and passionate convictions and read *Giovanni's Room*, *Go Tell It on the Mountain*, and *The Fire Next Time*.[34] As a teacher of American poetry, Çapan credited Baldwin with making him go beyond the white European modernist canon that was then prescribed fare at Robert College. Jimmy introduced him to the blues singer Bessie Smith and explained that her lyrics should be regarded as poetry. Çapan would subsequently teach Smith's blues side by side with T. S. Eliot's verse and argue for regarding black vernacular as closer to the national poetic form: "Of these two poets who came from the same American town, only Smith was genuine and powerful." He emphasized: "This was my privilege, to be able to talk like this [with and] thanks to James Baldwin."[35]

When Jimmy and Cevat talked shop, they did so intensely. They shared a love of Henry James's novels and discussed African American writers, as well as race and sexuality. Çapan recalled his friend's dislike of Hemingway, whom Baldwin accused of fabricating "false representatives of manliness," and his general disdain for any kind of "false identities." The subject of machismo and whiteness came up often during parties with the Robert College crowd. "It was very educational to watch" Baldwin's arguments with other Americans, which would inevitably spiral toward issues of interracial sexuality. Jimmy was especially merciless toward the so-called white liberals, a prominent group in *Another Country*, and would inevitably ask a WASP interlocutor point blank: "*Would* you let your sister marry a black man?"

In a 1964 interview with Tektaş Ağaoğlu, who translated *Giovanni's Room* into Turkish the same year, Baldwin emphasized his disgust with the white racist preoccupation with miscegenation and the American obsession with black sexuality. His comment also related to *Another Country*: "When everybody gets into bed with such myths in their minds, sexual relations between blacks and whites, even between whites and whites and blacks and blacks run into a gridlock."[36]

Baldwin's openness to transgressive desire, his charismatic manner, and his interest in testing the racial and sexual tolerance of his interlocutors influenced how they approached him. "You know, some Robert College people . . . quite a few promiscuous ones . . . took interest in Jimmy's homosexuality," Çapan revealed. While objectifying him, such people would often "be astounded when he [Baldwin] took them to task" for doing so. Çapan saw Baldwin as open and truthful in his dealings with others, even if that meant being uncomfortable and making others so: "Jimmy was not afraid of being alive, of what he was"; he did not fear "coming into contact with *any* people; . . . he was genuine, honest, friendly, while the others were not, and felt guilty [about it], but would not admit it." As if signing on to Baldwin's anger at some of his compatriots, Çapan's cool intellectual poise shifted as he indicated how "limited and arrogant" many Americans seemed to him when they patronized the Turks and Turkey as backward while boasting about being in Istanbul on a civilizing mission to "teach democracy." He did not make it clear whether or not he actually told the offending Americans what he told me: "We have more to teach *you* than you could ever give us."[37]

As a writer, Baldwin amazed his Turkish friends by conversing in whole paragraphs that would later find their way into his essays or fiction. In that he was similar to Yaşar Kemal, a Kurd and one of the best-known Turkish writers in translation, whom Baldwin met at the time. "A huge gruff peasant from the southern mountains, who had escaped from and documented in several novels . . . the oppression of his people by an unfair economic and class system" (Leeming, *James Baldwin*, 194), Kemal could, Çapan recalled, "recite his manuscripts from memory. . . . Having come from an oral tradition, he could repeat whole sections by heart." Kemal loved Baldwin's novels and when interviewed in Thorsen's documentary claimed that *Another Country* was his favorite. Baldwin was happy when the novel was translated into Turkish in 1970, so that Kemal, who did not speak English, could finally read it.[38] Çapan chuckled at the memory of the small-framed Jimmy and the giant Kemal as bosom friends; the two men had no language in common but hit it off and communicated nonverbally or through him as a translator. "It was a very touching and human experience," Çapan said; it taught him much about the human need for contact and closeness, "something that I was able to learn from Jimmy." As if reciprocating for his help with negotiating linguistic boundaries in Turkey, Baldwin acted as a mentor, elder brother, and cultural translator when Çapan went to the United States on a Fulbright fellowship. Jimmy wrote him introductory letters to writers "like Toni Morrison and others," but Cevat admitted that he felt "too shy to use them."

The interviews with Çapan and Leeming, as well as conversations with Minnie Garwood, a close Armenian American friend whom Baldwin called "sister," and the American Irish expatriate John Freely, both of the Robert College scene, confirmed the thick cross-cultural contexts in which Baldwin reworked *Another Country*. All his Turkish friends agreed, too, that he came to love Istanbul. By the time Baldwin got there, his urban imaginary included Harlem and Greenwich Village, Paris, London, and other places at home and abroad. Italo Calvino's *Invisible Cities* (1972), published at the end of Baldwin's Turkish decade, provides an image of a Western traveler that sheds some light on what Baldwin's first view of Istanbul may have been like:

> The man who is traveling and does not yet know the city awaiting him along his route wonders what the place will be like. . . . In every city of the empire every building is different and set in a different order: but as soon as the stranger arrives at the unknown city and his eye penetrates the pine cone of pagodas and garrets and haymows, following the scrawls of canals, gardens, rubbish heaps, he immediately distinguishes which are the princes' palaces, the high priests' temples, the tavern, the prison, the slum. . . . Each man bears in his mind a city made only of differences, a city without figures and without form, and the individual cities fill it up. (34)

Calvino's interplay between interior and exterior cities helps to elicit the interplay between Baldwin's international (Western) urban imaginary and his expectations and perceptions of the (Eastern) city of Istanbul. The imperial traveler in Calvino's allegorical text is unmistakably an Orientalist. Baldwin might not have been impervious to the Orientalist mystique, but as a descendant of peoples shaped by the legacies of slavery and colonialism, he was endowed with a complex transnational vision that helped him to see beyond that mystique.

Historically contingent and hybrid, Baldwin's urban imaginary was also partially shaped by African American art and culture, especially the myriad visions of the city he absorbed from poetry and the blues, paintings and photography. He credited his mentor Beauford Delaney with teaching him how to see and specifically how to depict the urban landscape: "I remember standing on a street corner with the black painter Beauford Delaney down in the Village, waiting for the light to change, and he pointed down and said, 'Look.' I looked and all I saw was water. And he said, 'Look again,' which I did, and I saw oil on the water and the city reflected in the puddle. It was a great revelation to me. I can't explain it. He taught me how to see, and how to trust what I saw" (*Conversations*, 235).[39] In this moment of epiphany, the homophonic "I" and "eye" merge as Baldwin repeats the action of looking to understand and see what Delaney is pointing at. He notices the "oil on the water" and the city it reflects "in the puddle," but only after having ventured across the boundaries of his imagination, that is, having embraced his mentor's way of seeing. The trick is for the writer to see the way the painter does, so that he can render any location, body, and reflection of the world in his own colors. This moment between Baldwin and Delaney reveals a way of seeing momentarily untainted by racist culture, a dialogic moment between black artists who are creating their common "inheritance" (*Price of the Ticket*, x).

Baldwin's emphasis on the interplay of vision and writing, or writing as a way of seeing, is directly linked to *Another Country*, in which book 3 begins with a rhetorical question from Shakespeare's Sonnet 65: "How with his rage shall beauty hold a plea, / Whose action is no stronger than a flower?" This question, and possibly the last line from the sonnet, can be read as a tribute to Delaney and to the power of writing and seeing in the face of a racialized world: "That in black ink my love may still shine bright."[40] Baldwin dedicated two important works to Delaney, the collection of short stories *Going to Meet the Man* (1965) and his long essay *No Name in the Street* (1972).[41] In a letter to Engin written in 1961 shortly before his arrival in Istanbul, he begged him to help care for Delaney, "my great, my oldest friend," who had helped him "grow up" and was now ill and in need of being moved from Greece to Turkey.[42] Years later, Baldwin would recall the East as one of the locations and visions that his mentor had helped him to imagine for the first time from his "small studio" in the Village, which "Beauford, simply by his presence, had transformed, transmuted into the most exclusive terrace in Manhattan or Bombay" (*Price of the Ticket*, x).[43]

Having moved from the eastern American location of Manhattan to the Eastern city of Istanbul, Baldwin confronted personal issues that had to do with *Another Country*'s fictional and autobiographical setting in New York City.[44] To an interviewer, he described his birthplace as "one of the loneliest places in the world" (*Conversations*, 49), while in his novel he presented New York as "the city that never slept," whose weight "was murderous" (*Another Country*, 4). He also blamed it for his inability to work at home and hence for his exile: "It's always been difficult for me to write in New York. . . . Now it's impossible. I've always hated this city, and yet it's where I was born and where my family is. So, in another way, . . . I love it. I can't entirely escape it, but I can't work in it. . . . I'm going to continue spending half my time abroad doing what I should be doing and the other half here—doing what I have to do" (*Conversations*, 33).[45] Writing his third novel about New York City was painful to Baldwin. In 1959 he wrote to Cezzar in graphic terms that he was trying to "kill" *Another Country*, which was "expiring," but whose blood it was impossible to get "off the walls" (letter 15, August 13, 1959). In 1966 he told Fern Marja Eckman that it was the "easiest" to read of all the novels he had written, but was emphatic: "That book almost *killed* me," and "I never could finish that book properly—until I was in *Turkey*."[46] Remembering Baldwin's work on the early drafts at his summerhouse in Connecticut, William Styron described his "terrific almost schizoid wrenching" and physical suffering over *Another Country* and recalled Jimmy saying, "I'm not really in control of what I'm trying to do." His younger brother David confirmed this in Thorsen's film, claiming that Jimmy felt that his characters were getting away from him; he would often tell David, "This person is not speaking to me,"[47] discussing his characters as if they were real people with whom he had to wrestle for his daily writing quota.

Given the trial of writing *Another Country* before Istanbul, it seemed that Baldwin's new exilic location worked miracles on his craft and mood. But how could Istanbul, the third city in Baldwin's life after New York and Paris,[48] be a space of healing? The architect Lebbeus Woods contends that built forms can facilitate post-traumatic healing and self-renewal in places scarred by violence and military conflict through what he calls "freespaces."[49] Comparing freespaces, or areas where life begins to flourish among the ruins, to scabs and scars on a wounded human body, Woods sees them as zones of material suturing and survival on the organism of a city. In these freespaces, the human will to survive and rebuild asserts itself in opposition to the forces that have brought about material destruction: "Traditional links with centralized authority, with deterministic and coercive systems are disrupted," and "existence continuously begins again, by the re-invention of itself" (*War and Architecture*, 21). Delaney's studio was Baldwin's freespace in the East Village, and the city of Istanbul he encountered in 1961 was another with its architectural scabs and scars, its mixed peoples, religions, and fashions as idiosyncratic and hybrid as its history. A two-faced metropolis, straddling the past and present and spanning two continents over a waterway through which the whole world passed, Constantinople-Istanbul allowed him to recover from stress and escape the racist violence of America. As Leeming observed, it also helped him to attempt new and difficult things as a writer.[50]

The new and difficult things that Baldwin embarked on in Turkey had to do with the personal and political issues that had always preoccupied him—race, sex, migration, and national belonging for Whites and Blacks—which he now saw in an increasingly transnational perspective.[51] Baldwin also came to Turkey to heal after a series of profound personal traumas. As all his biographers agree, in addition to frequent traveling, which could take a toll on anyone, Baldwin lived his private and public life dangerously, working long hours when others slept, drinking and smoking more than was good for him. His work habits were not always so by choice, given his political commitments, frequent need for cash, and tight schedule as an activist. In stark contrast to his vitality, cheerfulness, and seemingly inexhaustible stamina during periods of productivity, he occasionally suffered bouts of severe depression and several times attempted suicide before 1961. While he claimed to have fled racist New York in 1948 to "avoid certain death,"[52] he attempted to take his life for the first time a year later, following the "stolen sheet" incident during his early, lean, and desperate days in France, which he described in the essay "Equal in Paris" (1955). Another attempt took place in 1956 in the midst of writer's block related to early drafts of *Another Country* and an unraveling love affair. Forming a "strange leitmotif in Baldwin's life," there would be several other, "half-hearted" attempts at suicide that were linked to periods of depression and troubled love life, all of which remained invisible to the media (Leeming, *James Baldwin*, 119–20). When Engin Cezzar told me in 2001 that when he had first welcomed Baldwin to his home, "the man really needed to be taken care of," he expressed a sentiment that his grateful friend would echo repeatedly, saying that Turkey had "saved" his life.

The Text: Through the Orient Queerly

Baldwin's personal and professional salvation in Turkey hinged on the completion of *Another Country*, whose complex plot and characters caused him much anguish, but whose publication marked his coming-of-age as an American novelist. In the essay "As Much Truth as One Can Bear,"[53] which Baldwin wrote in Istanbul and published in the *New York Times* soon after *Another Country*, he outlines his literary manifesto:

> In my mind, the effort to become a great novelist simply involves telling as much of the truth as one can bear, and then a little more. It is an effort which, by its very nature—remembering that men write the books, that time passes and energy flags, and safety beckons—is obviously doomed to failure. . . . [But] one must be willing . . . to locate, precisely, that American morality of which we boast. And one must be willing to ask one's self what the Indian thinks of this morality, what the Cuban or the Chinese thinks of it, what the Negro thinks of it. Our own record must be read. And, finally, the air of this time and place so heavy with rhetoric, so thick with soothing lies, that one must really do great violence to language, one must somehow disrupt the comforting beat, in order to be heard.[54]

Baldwin's invitation to ask "what the Indian . . . Cuban or the Chinese" thinks of American and Western morality echoes his interrogations of American sexual and racial conduct in *Another Country* and places the domestic themes of this "great novel," as well as the ubiquitous "what the Negro thinks," in an international context. The essay rejects the American white literary canon—the "chill embrace of T. S. Eliot," Faulkner's "soupy rhetoric," and Hemingway's "sexless and manufactured" heroines ("As Much Truth," 11)—and encourages young writers to abandon its worn-out themes, to "turn our backs forever on the big two-hearted river." Writers must examine their societies and lead them to change by means of Jamesian "passion" and the romantic "madness" of art and while doing "great violence to language" to forge new expressive forms. These were the principles that Baldwin embraced in *Another Country*, where he focused on "the particular" in the manner of Dostoyevsky. In "As Much Truth," Baldwin claims that Dostoyevsky used the particular to show "something much larger and heavier" about his people and the world because morality "must be perpetually examined, cracked, changed, made new."[55]

In a 1963 interview for the *New York Herald Tribune Books*, he confirmed the special place of *Another Country* in his literary development: "I think . . . [it] is my best novel so far. Not because I achieved everything I wanted to in it—in that respect, I'm only at the beginning of my life as a writer. But *Another Country* was harder and more challenging than anything I'd ever attempted, and I didn't cheat in it. I didn't tell any lies; at least I wasn't aware of telling any. I know some critics said the characters were cardboard and that I had become more of a polemicist than a novelist. I deny it. I'm much too good a pro to have let that happen. That book saved my life as a writer—in my own eyes" (*Conversations*, 33–34). *Another Country* proved to be not only one of Baldwin's many saving devices but also one of the most important works of mid-twentieth-century American literature. Although not a favorite with reviewers, many of whom rejected its structural innovations and resisted its frank treatment of sexuality and interracial relationships, and despite having been publicly denounced for obscenity in Montana, Louisiana, and Illinois, it became a bestseller and the best known, besides *The Fire Next Time*, of all of Baldwin's books.[56]

Another Country's popularity proved that it had answered a profound need for frank representations of sexuality and race at the time of the Cold War and during a decade when discussions of black civil rights largely excluded matters of gender and homoeroticism. Baldwin flew from Istanbul to New York for its publication and presided over a memorable party that Dell Press threw for him at Small's Paradise in Harlem. In August 1962 he wrote Cezzar from the "middle of the air," while flying to Dakar with his sister Gloria, that *Another Country* was selling a thousand copies a day and had received some "incredible reviews." One of them in *Jet* magazine, he reported, stated "bitterly" that Baldwin knew nothing "about Negroes." That was "probably true," Baldwin wrote, speaking against essentialist views of race, because he didn't "believe" that they ("Negroes") existed.[57] In another letter to Cezzar written from Barcelona (letter 31, May 12, 1962), he reported on his plan to be in New York on June 10 "for *Another Country*" and included an excited note that Gadge (the nickname of Elia Kazan) was considering making a film based on this novel "after his Turkish film."[58]

Another Country opposed stereotypes of whiteness and blackness and purposefully lacked fixed identities. It was "shapeless" in terms of plot, characters, and setting, he told Leeming (*James Baldwin*, 200). It thus reflected what in "Notes for a Hypothetical Novel" (1960) Baldwin called the "enormous incoherence" and the "bottomless confusion which is both public and private, of [the] American republic" (*Price of the Ticket*, 241, 243). Nonetheless *Another Country* is a carefully designed triptych of books whose titles and epigraphs signal Baldwin's intention about its place in Anglo-American literary history as a work by a black writer, the peculiar product of the West that in *The Fire Next Time* he calls "the American Negro." The first book, "Easy Rider," takes its title and epigraph from W. C. Handy's blues lyric and gestures at the blues-and-jazz character of the composition that follows: "I told him. Easy riders / Got to stay away, / So he had to vamp it, / But the hike ain't far."[59] Book 2, "Any Day Now," evokes Joseph Conrad's novel of colonial desire in the South Seas, *Victory* (1915): "Why don't you take me in your arms and carry me out of this lonely place?" The title of book 3, "Toward Bethlehem," echoes W. B. Yeats's poem "The Second Coming," but its epigraph comes from Shakespeare's Sonnet 65 — "How with this rage shall beauty hold a plea" — which also echoes in Baldwin's rhetorical question about the fate of black people ("What will happen to all that beauty?") in *The Fire Next Time* (140).

Book 1 begins with Rufus Scott, a young black jazz musician, whose lonely trek through New York City one night ends with a suicidal leap from the George Washington Bridge into the Hudson River. Rufus's tragic end follows an affair with a poor white southern woman whom he abused, Leona, and ushers in the other main characters: his close friend, a struggling Irish-Italian American writer named Vivaldo Moore,[60] who fails to see Rufus's pain and impending doom; Vivaldo's former teacher, a Polish American writer named Richard Silensky, and his WASP wife, Cass; Eric Jones, a gay white southerner from a rich family, who is an actor and lives part time in France; and Rufus's younger sister, Ida, who is studying to become a singer and becomes involved with Vivaldo.

In book 2, where Eric is the central character, we glimpse idyllic visions of his life in the south of France with his young French lover, Yves. Back in New York to act on Broadway, Eric awaits Yves's arrival and becomes involved with Cass, who is suffering in her marriage with Richard, now a commercially successful author. Eric, Baldwin's alter ego of sorts, derives his affirmative humanistic stance from his rejection of racism and his queerness; in flashbacks, we see his sexual initiation in the arms of a black friend, LeRoy, in the South, as well as his courtship of Yves in Paris. This part ends with Cass's and Richard's fight after he has discovered her affair with Eric.

Book 3 focuses on Vivaldo's and Ida's unraveling love affair as she, stricken with grief and rage, attempts revenge on Rufus's friends for their failure to see his suffering and their inability to look beyond their own dramas to save him. Hurt by Vivaldo's possessiveness and jealousy, Ida has slept with a married TV producer, Steve Ellis, who helps to advance her singing career. But in a final confrontation with Vivaldo, Ida comes clean about her betrayal, while he, who has in the meantime slept with Eric, Rufus's onetime lover, is still unable to face his ambivalence about his black lovers, embattled whiteness, and unacknowledged queerness.

As Baldwin told Eckman, the most challenging and personal part of *Another Country* was Rufus Scott's suicide. Tormented and ultimately destroyed by racism and self-hatred, Rufus is the only major black male character in the novel. Yet he dies on page 88 of a text of 436 pages. Although he exits the plot so early, all the action and other characters remain connected to him by a web of complex relationships in a kind of extended American-nation-as-family drama.[61] Rufus is "the black corpse floating in the national psyche" (Leeming et al., "The White Problem"), the "ghost who haunts . . . Vivaldo's most intimate interactions" (Reid-Pharr, "Tearing the Goat's Flesh," 382). Rufus's story hinges on the possibility of queer desire as a liberating force in the novel, the force that could surmount racial oppression, even though, or precisely because, Rufus as a black male has been destroyed by racism and homophobia. Although some critics see Eric and the "optically white" Vivaldo (81) as the characters who embody "queerness,"[62] I argue that it is Rufus and his blackness that stand for the central and transgressive object of queer desire.[63]

In an interview with John Hall in 1970, Baldwin explained his preoccupation with this character:

> Writing is a polite term for [experimenting]. . . . Let's take *Another Country*. . . . A lot of people in that book had never appeared in fiction before. . . . There's an awful lot of *my* experience which has never been seen in the English language before. Rufus, for example. There are no antecedents for him. He was in the novel because I didn't think anyone had ever watched the disintegration of a black boy from that particular point of view. Rufus was partly responsible for his doom, and in presenting him as partly responsible, I was attempting to break out of the whole sentimental image of the afflicted nigger driven that way (to suicide) by white people. (*Conversations*, 104)

Echoing his critiques of Harriet Beecher Stowe and Richard Wright in "Everybody's Protest Novel" (1949), Baldwin intended Rufus to become an alternative to the socially determined characters of the slave Tom in *Uncle Tom's Cabin* and Bigger Thomas in *Native Son*.[64] Sexless and docile Tom and oversexed and violent Bigger represent the two types of black masculinity entrenched in the nineteenth- and twentieth-century American literary imagination and provide the background against which Baldwin cast Rufus as a black male with "no antecedents." Rufus dies destroyed by the very city where he was born, but also as a complex subject "partly responsible for his doom."[65] His suicide has been caused as much by racism as by his abuse of his white lovers: Eric, whom he rejected and ridiculed, and Leona, whom he drove to insanity by beatings and rapes. He thinks about Eric and asks Leona for forgiveness as he jumps to his death from the "bridge built to honor the father of his country." Rufus is a bastard son of America but also refuses the affection of his own family; he is the victim but also a victimizer; he makes a decision to kill himself because he knows that he has gone too far, that the "pain would never stop [and] he could never go down into the city again" (*Another Country*, 87).

Baldwin's retrospective statement of authorial intent concerning this character is important for another reason. As Leeming emphasizes, Rufus Scott was the "embodiment not only of the collective tragedy of racism but of the personal crisis that James Baldwin left America to escape" at the time he went to Istanbul (*James Baldwin*, 201–2). Katy Ryan observes about Rufus Scott's death that "suicides lead to places" and stresses the importance of "a peculiarly American kind of fall in its most famous city" ("Falling in Public," 114). For that reason, Baldwin's American city of New York must be read through the Turkish city of Istanbul, where he arrived at the final form, the characters, and settings of *Another Country*.[66] In Istanbul-Constantinople, where Thanatos and Eros are inextricably woven into the fabric of the city, Baldwin's wrestling with Scott's suicide scene recalled a personal trauma caused by the tragic death of Eugene Worth, his youthful "bosom companion" (Eckman, *Furious Passage*, 162). Worth was a light-skinned black man who, like Rufus, jumped off George Washington Bridge in 1946 after a disastrous interracial love affair. Baldwin wrote about Worth in 1985: "I would have done anything whatever to have been able to hold him in this world."[67] Baldwin told Eckman that his autobiographical and authorial anguish influenced the final structure of the novel: "Once I got the suicide scene licked—that was the beginning of the book, y'know—I was able to write the *last* scene with Ida and Vivaldo, which is at the *end* of the book" (162).[68] While this bracketing confirms the importance of Rufus as a representative black man in a novel about the state of the American self and society in the late 1950s, it also links his fate with the focal interracial love story of the Irish-Italian immigrant Vivaldo and Ida.[69]

Several critics agree about the structural and thematic links between the beginning and ending sections of the novel,[70] but the central scene of

Rufus's suicide has rarely been seen as a generative moment in Baldwin's authorship.[71] In early 1961, a few months before his arrival at the home of Sururi and Cezzar, Baldwin, who often employed childbirth metaphors, reported to Eckman that he was "astonished that he hadn't 'fatally miscarried' during his long pregnancy," having "revamped his concept of the book three times" (Furious Passage, 158). The gestation process consisted of erecting and then ripping down the "scaffolding" for the novel (158), which seemed to be never ending, until Baldwin's "perspective snapped into focus and he seized control of his book" after he had settled to work in Istanbul (162). Reading Another Country through the lens and location of that city reveals that some of its scaffolding, or main structural elements, use references to the East as an exotic realm. A close scrutiny of its key erotic and interracial encounters helps us to see, too, how Baldwin's queer and Orientalist imaginaries come into dialogue and conflict in its narrative.

Another Country is dedicated to Mary S. Painter, a white American economist, whom Jimmy loved and with whom he kept in close touch throughout his life (Leeming, James Baldwin, 77, 377).[72] The book opens with an epigraph from Henry James's preface to Lady Barbarina (1888), a short novel on the Jamesian themes of class, marriage, and national and cultural differences between Europeans and Americans, signaling interesting literary historical connections: "They strike one, above all, as giving no account of themselves in any terms already consecrated by human use; to this inarticulate state they probably form, collectively, the most unprecedented of monuments; abysmal the mystery of what they think, what they feel, what they want, what they suppose themselves to be saying" (Art of the Novel, 209).[73] James compares here the Americans and the English while referring to the ancient Assyrians and the city of Nineveh, the location that Said lists as being among the key sites that historically fed Western literary imagination of the East (Orientalism, 63, 167). Like the exotic and remote symbols, shapes, and scripts on Nineveh's walls and monuments, the Americans and the English appear impervious and closed off to the world and thus come to represent the opacity of what James ironically calls "the dear old Anglo-Saxon race" (Art of the Novel, 208). While the metaphor of Nineveh is Eastern, the identities of the characters in James's novel are decidedly white, Western, and urban and are much concerned with eugenics and racial purity.[74]

Along with the epigraph from James, the title of Another Country[75] signals Baldwin's engagement with the East by echoing a famous line from the fourth act of Christopher Marlowe's The Jew of Malta (ca. 1589):

Friar Barnardine: Thou hast committed—
Barabas: Fornication? But that
Was in another country; and besides
The wench is dead.[76]

Barabas is the Orientalized title character, in Nicholas Radel's description, a stereotype of an avaricious Jew, who "delights in various evil deeds" and as "the foreigner would have been linked to villainy, heresy, sodomy, devilry . . . [and thus] to non-Christians, the Turks," and other foreign and heathen figures.[77] Marlowe's play embraces a sweeping vision of the East as a locus of evil, sexual perversion, and paganism that reigned in the European imagination since the eleventh century. The Orient emerged from the early modern period as a stage set, a playground for imagination, "a living tableau of queerness" (Said, Orientalism, 103).[78] Stressing the importance of religious and erotic stereotypes to that imagination, Marwan M. Obeidat explains that "Western attitudes toward Islam followed certain themes which relate to religion, power, and sexual laxity." Like other non-Christian systems of belief, including Judaism, the Muslim faith was seen as a "corrupt religion based on false beliefs" and thus corruptible to those who observed it (34); it was a small step from heresy to sexual perversion.[79]

While gesturing at the history of literary representations of Orientalism, Another Country also plays with distinctly African American expressive forms. It is a blues song and a parable (Leeming, James Baldwin, 204). As Cornel West stresses, border crossing, formal innovation, and heterogeneity lie at the heart of black expressive cultures but also hybridize and transform Western forms: "There is no jazz without European instruments" (Prophetic Thought, 4). In his novel, Baldwin was aiming at what Henry James called "perception at the pitch of passion," but while modeling "himself after [black] jazz musicians rather than other writers . . . especially Miles Davis and Ray Charles," he wanted to write a book that had no antecedents (Leeming, James Baldwin, 206). The publisher's blurbs advertising the most recent Turkish translation of Another Country, Bir Başka Ülke (2005), translated by Çiğdem Öztekin, pick up on its transnational artistic appeal: "You could have met the jazz musician Rufus, his sister Ida, writer Vivaldo, homosexual Eric and his French lover Yves, married couple Cass and Richard from Greenwich Village, and the other unforgettable characters of that novel today while walking in Beyoğlu. Another Country is that real and that contemporary."[80]

Beyoğlu is the happening area at the heart of Istanbul, where crowds of artists and bohemian youths congregate every night much like Baldwin's characters did in Greenwich Village in the 1950s. But in New York City, the central black characters in *Another Country*, Rufus and Ida, the jazz artist siblings from a churchgoing family in segregated Harlem, are constant reminders of the painful American history of racism, slavery, and sexual violence. That history underlies all the romantic and erotic entanglements in Baldwin's narrative. Why, how, and where people survive this American condition and learn to negotiate the complex web of erotic desire as black and white Americans depends in *Another Country* on whether or not they become successful and fulfilled artists.[81] Baldwin explained his own relationship with his art in somewhat fatalistic terms: "You don't decide to be an artist, you discover that you are one; it is a very great difference. What you do, you do because you must. The way fish breathe water writers write; if they don't they'll die" (*Conversations*, 31). He also emphasized the importance of self-knowledge as a liberating force: "One needs an image in order to see oneself and be released from oneself. One has an image of oneself that is always at variance with the facts; the great effort is somehow to see that I in my mind and I in life are not the same. Something connects them, but the effort is to bring these two things together, to fuse the reality and the image" (31).

Vivaldo is a writer and seeker of self-knowledge in the sense that Baldwin describes here, and so is Rufus a jazz musician, Ida a singer, and Eric an actor. They all struggle with the process of fusing the "reality and the image" as artists, but also in how they see themselves and relate to those around them. Their identities and relational struggles are reflected in several intense moments throughout *Another Country*, especially in its interracial queer encounters. These moments feature lovemaking, migrations, arrivals, and departures and fuse the erotic with the American and European locations where the novel's action takes place. They also refract the invisible city of Istanbul where Baldwin came to terms with them and committed them to paper.[82]

Baldwin's most immediate autobiographical link to Istanbul in the novel is the racially motivated beating that Rufus and Vivaldo experience in an Irish bar early on, following an angry outburst by Vivaldo's prejudiced white girlfriend Jane (*Another Country*, 31–36). The triangle of friends and lovers in that scene—an ambivalently sexed WASP woman (Rufus says to Vivaldo, "She dresses like a goddamn bull dagger," or butch lesbian [31]), a "whitened" Irish-Italian immigrant, and a black man—makes the encounter symbolic and historically representative of American race and gender relations. The fight ends with the men's narrow escape from a northern version of a lynch mob riding to the rescue of white womanhood in distress. The scene re-creates an actual brawl that Baldwin and Cezzar were involved in while in New York in 1956. As Yi-Fu Tuan explains, the experience of place "can be direct and intimate, or it can be indirect and conceptual, mediated by symbols" (6). Baldwin's and Cezzar's experience in New York was direct but was treated symbolically in the novel; it was also directly and symbolically linked to both New York and Istanbul, given that Jimmy and Engin lived, and that Baldwin worked on the novel, in both places. Rufus's thoughts in the aftermath of the fight seem to echo Baldwin's feelings about his lifelong friendship with Cezzar. Like Baldwin and Cezzar in New York when they first met and became close friends, and later in Istanbul as Baldwin struggled to finish Another Country, Rufus "depended on and trusted" Vivaldo (Another Country, 36). Leeming describes the relationship between Cezzar and Baldwin as "platonic but profound": "Whatever the basis of Baldwin's original interest, he respected Cezzar's intelligence and his abilities and was more than willing to maintain the friendship without a sexual component. They referred to each other as 'my brother' and meant it" (James Baldwin, 148).

Although Rufus and Vivaldo were never sexually involved, there is homoerotic tension between them that is apparent in the bar scene. Rufus's intense dislike of Jane, the "phony white chick" (Another Country, 35), may have something to do with both racial and erotic jealousy, as well as homophobia. After the fight, for which Vivaldo blames and curses Jane, Rufus realizes his love for Vivaldo and his dependence on him. But he also realizes his friend's power to cause him pain. By fighting other whites side by side with Rufus, Vivaldo declares the superiority of their homosocial bond over his heterosexual and racial bond with Jane. He becomes to Rufus "unlike everyone else that he knew in that they, all the others, could only astonish him by kindness or fidelity; it was only Vivaldo who had the power to astonish him by treachery" (36). This is the moment when Rufus opens himself up to being hurt by saying yes to love, love across color lines and love that challenges the lines drawn by heteronormative sexual behavior. We know that Rufus is capable of queer desire from his affair with Eric, whom Rufus has abused and treated as a "hideous sexual deformity" (46). Eric in turn has held on to the memories of the moments when Rufus "had looked [on him] with love" (238).

In another bar scene, on the night of Rufus's suicide, when he and Vivaldo go out and run into Jane, Vivaldo does indeed betray his friend. Rufus has just resurfaced after weeks of having been lost to the streets of New York in the aftermath of Leona's breakdown, but instead of going home to his family in Harlem, he knocks at Vivaldo's door. But Vivaldo chooses to spend the night with Jane over attending to his friend. Vivaldo's indifference to Rufus's and to other people's suffering provokes some questions: Has Vivaldo's rejection of Rufus on the night when they talked about, and thus obliquely confessed to, "wishing" to be queer (51), when Rufus needed to be held and loved, and when his white friend was too afraid to reach across "that quarter of an inch" to touch him (343), contributed to his destruction? Has Rufus died so that Vivaldo could test, fulfill, or render safe his queer potential as a white ethnic? And will Ida, with whom Vivaldo promptly falls in love as if to erase his guilt over Rufus's destruction, be sacrificed in a similar way? Rufus's connection to Ida and Vivaldo and the semi-incestuous triangle of desire they form at the core of *Another Country* suggest that this may be so. When Vivaldo first meets Ida, she is a teenager, and he imagines her as boyish and androgynous (103), an attractive body that is a clear reflection of Rufus's.[83]

In Vivaldo's eyes, Ida's connection to her brother parallels as well her dislocation into the realm of the foreign and exotic as a woman of color. This connection and dislocation are stressed by means of a series of explicit and implicit images and situations scattered throughout the novel. First, we encounter Ida's exotic shawl, a gift that Rufus bought for her in England while he was in the army. The shawl comes from India via London and signifies the presence of the colonized globalized world and Western imperialism in the background of Baldwin's novel (7). Ida is resplendent in the shawl, and when Rufus looks at her, he sees for the first time "the beauty of black people." The beauty of the object, its origin, and of Ida blend together, as Ida is now draped in the allure of India and becomes an image to be admired in Rufus's eyes: "She became associated with the colors of the shawl, the colors of the sun, and with a splendor incalculably older than the gray stone of the island on which they had been born" (7). Rufus is unable to reconcile his vision of Ida, his Afrocentric vision of her as a beautiful descendant of African royalty, with the reality she faces as a black woman in the United States: "Ages and ages ago, Ida had not been merely the descendant of slaves. Watching her dark face in the sunlight, softened and shadowed by the glorious shawl, it could be seen that she had once been a monarch. Then he looked out of the window, at the air shaft, and thought of the whores on Seventh Avenue. He thought of the white policemen and the money they made on black flesh, the money the whole world made" (7).

Like Rufus's thoughts about his sister, Vivaldo's thoughts about his relationship with Rufus cannot escape the legacies of American history and the clash between image and reality. Vivaldo fails Rufus because he cannot escape the rivalry and violence inherent in American male homosocial bonding, especially bonding between men of different races. In fact, neither man can escape what Baldwin calls the "obscenity of color": "Somewhere in his heart the black boy hated the white boy because he was white. Somewhere in his heart Vivaldo had feared and hated Rufus because he was black" (134). This unspoken racial hatred between the two friends is the reason why Vivaldo is not able to see his friend's pain and need on the last night of Rufus's life; it is the reason why, betrayed and rejected, Rufus walks away into death. Subsequently Ida becomes an opportunity for Vivaldo to make amends to her dead brother. As he explains to Cass at Rufus's funeral: "I think she has something to forget. . . . I think I can help her forget it" (125). But Vivaldo is looking for forgetfulness himself, and so he uses Ida as his fantasy hideaway; he enters her "splendor" and rich colors to escape Rufus as much as the "gray stone island," their home, whose only hues are white and black.[84]

When Vivaldo recalls first having met Ida when she was about fifteen, it is clear that even then he saw her as a potential target, prize, and prey. The memory of her causes him to masturbate (142), which as a form of auto-erotic expression does not have to be seen as objectifying but foreshadows Vivaldo's exotic fantasies of Ida in their future lovemaking. Like Ida's reappearing colorful shawl, the memories of Rufus and the closeness and erotic tension between them reappear throughout the novel, thus inextricably linking the black siblings and Vivaldo in a fantasy ménage à trois. The shawl is "old-fashioned and rather theatrical" (144) and "brilliant" (146), a symbolic reminder of their erotic triangle, as well as its transnational implications. As Vivaldo walks with Ida in the Village before they first make love, he fantasizes about her exotic looks and ancestry that, like her shawl, "she [was] wearing . . . especially for him" as "his girl" (143–44). He also enjoys the "small clouds of male and female hostility . . . [that] Ida accepted . . . with a spiteful pride" like some foreign aristocrat (145). This scene echoes Ida's royal image in Rufus's mind at the beginning of the novel and suggests a larger context for white and black men viewing black women as exotic and foreign.[85]

The scenes where Ida is represented as a colorful female fetish gesture to the East as a fantasy location where sexual and racial longings can safely be played out. Other moments in *Another Country* where the East provides a direct or symbolic reference for the action confirm the centrality of Rufus to the plot. For example, when Eric and Yves are seen in their idyllic hideaway on the French Riviera, male nakedness and bathing are linked with the hammams, the famed Turkish baths that have stirred the Western homoerotic imagination for centuries.[86] Eric, who prefers prudent showers, contemplates the "Oriental opulence which overtook Yves each time he bathed," an image "abruptly overwhelming, of Yves leaning back in the bathtub, whistling, the washrag in his hand, a peaceful abstract look on his face and his sex gleaming and bobbing in the soapy water like a limp cylindrical fish" (201). Immediately following this reference to erotic images of male bathers in the hamam, Baldwin introduces an oblique reference to Rufus via Eric's recollection of his first male lover, who was black: "[Yves's] image was somehow the gateway, of that moment, nearly fifteen years ago, when the blow had inexorably fallen and his shame and his battle and his exile had begun" (201).[87]

Through the gateway of memory, Eric recalls his first love, LeRoy, and their fateful lovemaking in the vicinity of the train tracks dividing their small Alabama town. This recollection brings together the memory of his homosexual initiation and racial transgression with a descendant of his family's slaves "down south" with his happy contemplation of his white European lover's body in the south of France. Eric focuses on Yves's penis specifically, and in his mind this vision is linked to Yves's penchant for "Oriental opulence" (201). This transnational and interracial connection also evokes violence and Eric's exile as a young queer in Alabama, where "his increasing isolation and strangeness was held, even by himself, to be due to the extreme unpopularity of his racial attitudes" (200). Even as a child, he felt that he had to hide his love for his surrogate black parents, Grace and Henry (197), and when he and LeRoy are about to have sex for the first time, LeRoy makes it clear that as a gay man, Eric might be under a threat of violence, that is, lynching, as much as the black LeRoy: "You better get out of this town. Declare, they going to lynch you before they get around to me" (206). The interracial and Euro-American queer connection is made even stronger when Eric realizes that "there was something in Yves which reminded him of Rufus" (192). The similarity in Eric's eyes of his African American and European lovers reflects Eric's interregional, international, and interracial mobility. His southern origins and his traversing of the boundaries of race, sex, region, and nation in search of love are juxtaposed with the "Oriental opulence" and boundlessness of homoerotic desire that he embraces with Yves; homosexuality is clearly another country, foreign and remote, but attainable. The stereotyped homoerotic Orient in this instance serves as a space of fantasy escape for queer desire, the space away from the closet of the home country, and one through which it is possible to see one's home and origins anew.

Eric is the most sexually liberated and mobile character in *Another Country*, and his search for love and artistic fulfillment takes him across all kinds of geographic boundaries—from the American South to the North, then all over France, and finally back east to New York. As if anticipating Baldwin's confrontation with his home city when he returned from Istanbul to celebrate the release of *Another Country*, when Eric arrives from France after a three-year absence, he sees New York's density and its mixed population as exotic and alien. In his returned immigrant's eyes, New York seems to be a city like Italo Calvino's, "very strange indeed." On approaching it, Eric employs the stock Orientalist stereotype to explain his perceptions: "It might, almost, for strange barbarity of manner and custom, for the sense of danger and horror barely sleeping beneath the rough, gregarious surface, have been some impenetrably exotic city of the East" (230). Like James in the preface to *Lady Barbarina*, Baldwin employs imaginary ancient cities and civilizations as a lens to regard the West and westerners. Like "Carthage and Pompeii" (230), Eric thinks while looking at New York through the kind of lens that Beauford Delaney helped Baldwin to create, the city seems to have been "dismissed" by time and "to have no sense whatever of the exigencies of human life." It gives one a feeling that "a kind of plague was raging, though it was officially and publicly and privately denied" (230–31). In Baldwin's boundary-crossing novel, the plague has everything to do with race and sex.[88] The New York that Eric sees is framed transnationally; it is in North America but also displaced from it to the barbaric East, and it is filled with characters who are often seen and see themselves through various Orientalist lenses.

We encounter one such character in the rich and famous producer and villainous seducer of Ida, Steve Ellis, to whom Istanbul is a glamorous travel destination. This white man, short in stature but powerful in social status, is not, however, yet another incarnation of the Man. Given how the other characters see him and his "older" and "talkative" wife (*Another Country*, 161), Ellis might be a descendant of Jewish immigrants.[89] Vivaldo's implied anti-Semitism in the passage describing Ellis seems to warrant reading stereotypes of the second-generation Jewish immigrant into the representations of Ellis's character. Moreover, his last name echoes the name of the famous immigrant processing station on Ellis Island. Steve Ellis is the successfully Americanized immigrant who has made it big, who "worked hard" (164) and grabbed the American Dream by the collar; he resembles the likes of Samuel Goldwyn and other Jewish immigrants from Eastern Europe who were active in the American entertainment industry in the first half of the twentieth century. When Vivaldo looks at Ellis, he instantly hates him, while another young writer at the party where they meet cautions that, as a presumably native-born Jew, Ellis "too, can become President." That comment is followed by "At least he can read and write" (168), which echoes the assumptions about the illiteracy and barbarism of immigrants.[90] Rich, clever, powerful, hardworking, and driven, Steve Ellis has Istanbul as one of the world's pleasure- or business-related destinations at his fingertips (164). Jewish by implication, he also fits in the lore and imaginary geography, as well as carrying the "false faith," of the realm known as the East.

Like Marlowe's Jew of Malta, Ellis is a sexual predator, and in the course of the novel he becomes involved with Ida after having been smitten with her beauty and vitality. They meet for the first time at Cass and Richard's party, where Ida and Vivaldo appear on their first romantic date. Ellis promises to help Ida to advance her career as a singer, gives her his business card, and invites her to visit his office. Vivaldo, who is hoping to begin a sexual relationship with Ida, is instantly jealous because of what he reads immediately and obsessively as an inevitable economic and sexual transaction between a powerful white man and a powerless black woman. Ellis takes a passing interest in Vivaldo's book project as potential television material but quickly decides that Vivaldo does not possess anything that might attract him. He also accuses Vivaldo of feeling superior toward others: "You think that most people are shit and that you'd rather die than get yourself dirtied in any of the *popular* arts. . . . Man, you're too touchy" (163). Vivaldo is touched, indeed, and immediately and rudely lets Steve know that he dislikes him. Then he hurts Ida's feelings with his racist and sexist suspicions and assumptions about her intentions concerning Ellis's invitation. As if echoing Vivaldo's history of sexual transactions with black prostitutes, Ida tells him, "You think I'm nothing but a whore. That's the only reason you want to see me" (169).

Although Steve Ellis is perhaps the least developed character in *Another Country*, he is also an important one, a white male–whitened ethnic–Orientalized Jew who leads us back to Rufus as the central presence—that "floating corpse"—in Baldwin's text. On the one hand, Ellis is linked to Rufus indirectly through his attraction to Ida. On the other hand, somewhat like the scene with Yves in the bathtub, the scene when we first encounter Ellis is a gateway that leads us to how race and the erotic cut across national borders. That is, the scenes with Eric and Yves (with Rufus and LeRoy present in Eric's mind) and Ellis and Vivaldo (with Ida present in both their minds) bring together blackness, the erotic, and the imaginary East in these characters' imaginations. They thus allow Baldwin to revision, in a very different landscape and historical moment, what Henry James suggests in the preface to *Lady Barbarina*, where Nineveh is the lens through which the reader is expected to apprehend the "dear old Anglo-Saxon race."

Said's *Orientalism* provides a compelling explanation of how, in the eyes of the West, the various human types "all hang . . . together" because of the definitions "made from the outside by virtue of vocabulary and epistemological instruments designed both to get to the heart of things and to avoid the distractions of accident, circumstance, or experience." Vivaldo seems to think in such terms, the terms that "obliterated the distinctions between the type—*the* Oriental, *the* Semite, *the* Arab, and *the* Orient—and ordinary human reality" (*Orientalism* 231, 230), and his perspective on others positions him as the White Man and an Orientalist (226–27). As a writer and student of the human soul, Vivaldo should know better, but he is unable to learn from experience, preferring instead to live in his head.

Vivaldo's hostility toward Steve Ellis is tinged with anti-Semitism, just as his remarks to Ida about Ellis are tinged with racism and sexism, in the moments when he measures himself against his rival in the homosocial arena. Vivaldo sees them all caught up in the marketplace of sex and money:

> Then, as Ellis poured himself another apple jack and he poured himself another Scotch, he realized that the things which Ellis had, and the things which Richard was now going to have, were things that he wanted very much. Ellis could get anything he wanted by simply lifting up a phone; headwaiters were delighted to see him; his signature on a bill or check was simply not to be questioned. If he needed a suit, he bought it; he was certainly never behind in his rent; if he decided to fly to Istanbul tomorrow, he had only to call his travel agent. He was famous, he was powerful, and he was not really much older than Vivaldo, and he worked very hard. (*Another Country*, 164)

Vivaldo competes with Ellis in the erotic arena, not so much for Ida's attention as for the possession of her, as he thinks: "[Ellis] could get the highest-grade stuff going; he had only to give the girl his card. And then Vivaldo realized why he hated him. He wondered what he would have to go through to achieve a comparable eminence. He wondered how much he was willing to give—to be powerful, to be adored, to be able to make it with any girl he wanted, to be sure of holding any girl he had. And he looked around for Ida" (164).

Vivaldo sees Steve Ellis, "a short, square man with curly hair and a boyish face" (160),[91] in terms of his mobility, access to goods and sex with females, or as cosmopolitan, wealthy, and oversexed. That the first destination to which he imagines Ellis flying is Istanbul may not be accidental, as it places Ellis in a relationship to the East as both an imaginary and actual geographic context. Such a displacement implies that Vivaldo gets even with Ellis the Jew by putting him in his place, that is, by relegating him to the ubiquitous imaginary "East" of the evil heathens, while positioning himself, a whitened ethnic, as an American. This allows Vivaldo to express his anti-Semitic thoughts about the other man, thoughts that are revealed even more fully when Vivaldo watches Ellis getting closer to Ida in the course of the evening. Once again, Vivaldo focuses on the other man's face, which he sees as "becoming greedier and more vulnerable" (166). This vision may reflect Ellis's growing desire for Ida, but coming from Vivaldo, it also seems to link stereotypical Jewish avarice to sexual predation, as well as implying Ida's complicity and sexual laxity, or at least her desire for the purchasing power that Ellis represents.[92]

In the marketplace of American masculinities, in comparison with the wealthy and powerful Ellis, Vivaldo possesses only the dubious "capital — of understanding and gallantry" toward Ida that he has "patiently amassed and hoarded" and sees vanishing as his jealousy and dirty insinuations about her conversation with Ellis provoke their first fight (167). When he asks her forgiveness after she tells him that he made her feel like a whore, she says, "All you white bastards are the same" (169). This is a comment as much about Vivaldo's behavior as about Ellis's but fails to make Vivaldo realize the extent of Ida's awareness concerning the traffic in women and racialized sex that has just taken place in their charged and historically tortured triangle of a whitened Jew, whitened Italian-Irish immigrant,[93] and forever black African American woman. Vivaldo's expressions of love in their reconciliation scene are followed by his waking up to "a failure more subtle than any he had known before," after he and Ida have made love at his place (172). Vivaldo's inability to give Ida an orgasm, or rather her unwillingness to share a genuine one with him, leads Vivaldo to a series of thoughts that place her in the role of a racialized sexual object. In Vivaldo's erotic fantasy, she becomes a fetish, an object, a houri in a dream harem.

Having realized that Ida is not a virgin — "He wondered who had been with her before him; how many, how often, how long . . . [and if they] had been white or black" (172)—Vivaldo likens her to land and architecture. These are common references denoting colonial possession of foreign territories, whose conquest has been traditionally represented with metaphors of rape and penetration, with the male-identified conqueror taking possession of the female-identified land.[94] For Vivaldo to see himself as white, Ida's black body must become part of a hybrid colonial fantasy shot through with the elements of a Western fairy tale: "that incredible country in which, like the princess of fairy tales, sealed in a high tower and guarded by beasts, bewitched and exiled, she paced her secret round of secret days" (173). These images evoke cheap romances and exotic erotica.[95] Vivaldo, the failed novelist, seems to fancy himself a knight on a mission to rescue a virgin princess who has been saving herself for him, locked safely away from the attentions of other men; her "fairness" serves as a kind of racial and sexual marking, an imaginary chastity belt. Much as Vivaldo's earlier imagery of Ellis displaced the Jewish man to the East, now his fairy tale scenario displaces Ida, the black American woman, into the unbound fairy tale land. Given the proliferation of erotic imagery inspired by Eastern fantasies à la One Thousand and One Nights in American popular culture at the time, Vivaldo is thus able to deracialize Ida as a "fair princess" and, as their lovemaking progresses, to reracialize her as an exotic foreign female fetish.[96] This evasive maneuver helps to deflect his thoughts from his dismay at Ida's not being a virgin and, more important, from the associations of black female sexuality with violence and promiscuity, specifically with the black prostitutes in Harlem that he has been visiting in search of sexual gratification. Hence he is straining to escape to an imaginary location untainted by the American history of violence against black women's bodies and by his own sexual transactions with them.[97]

But when morning comes, Ida's "wild and tangled" hair, "unpainted lips," and "darker" skin make her look like "a little girl" who also reminds him of "all the sleeping children of the poor" (173). As soon as she is awake, Ida is black, lower-class, and American again. Vivaldo asks her to love him and sets out to prove his love to her, having extracted her confession that she has "never loved a white man" before (175). He attempts to initiate intercourse while "trying to empty his mind of the doubts and fears that filled it." This moment marks another transition into an imaginary East and another racial and sexual transaction. While Vivaldo is hoping to make love in an "attentive" way this time (177), he tries to metaphorically restore Ida's virginity.[98] In this fantasy, she is like "a virgin, promised at her birth to him, the bridegroom; whose face she now saw for the first time, in the darkened bridal chamber, after all the wedding guests had gone" (175).[99] This lurid scenario harkens back to what Irvin Schick terms Oriental "ethnopornography" or "xenological erotica" (77–79). Again, given the availability of that imaginary, Vivaldo's desire to view Ida as a bride or harem slave, a body completely at his mercy, echoes a long literary tradition of gendered and eroticized approaches to the Orient.[100]

Like the bodies of exotic women that Western travelers encountered and fantasized about, Ida appears to be an extension of the collective body of all the women of color that Vivaldo is lusting after, including the actual whores of Harlem, and perhaps the houris from fantasy harems.[101] He imagines her as a trembling bride-slave in his power: "There was no sound of revelry anywhere, only silence, no help anywhere if not in this bed, violation by the bridegroom's body her only hope" (175). As they continue foreplay, he comments aloud on the "many different, crazy colors" of her body at the same time as in his thoughts he likens her blackness to "the entrance to a tunnel" (175). When he gets closer to climax, he lets loose his fantasies of possessing a dark continent, which seem to echo Conrad's epigraph in book 2 of *Another Country*. Vivaldo feels that Ida "opened up before him, yet fell back before him, too, he felt that he was traveling up a savage, jungle river, looking for the source which remained hidden just beyond the black, dangerous, dripping foliage" (177). Having thus made his black female lover into a metonymic vagina-aperture-cave-tunnel–jungle river, Vivaldo then embarks on a rape and deflowering fantasy that implies his desire for empowerment and Ida's subordination, submission, and violation. When he thinks he is feeling her pleasure, he perceives it as torture and murder: "He felt a tremor in her belly . . . as though something had broken there, and it rolled tremendously upward, seeming to divide her breasts, as though he had split her all her length" (178).

These images in Vivaldo's mind serve to blot out the American national taboo, or the white-black sexual tableau that he enacts with Ida. But he fails to escape racism and sexism through an alternative vision of "another country" of love because, by yielding to Orientalist fantasies, he reaffirms the racism and sexism at their core. Baldwin makes this clear in the description of Vivaldo's thoughts after Ida gets out of bed: "He watched the tall, dusty body, which now belonged to him, disappear . . . in the bathroom" (179). After her metaphorical rape and murder, Ida has become a body, an object and image that, once possessed and violated, loses its exotic allure and becomes interchangeable.[102] But as such, she could also be a stand-in for Rufus, his safely exorcised extension, blood relation, and legacy, whom

Vivaldo can now use to ease his guilty conscience. Like other Orientalists, Vivaldo presumes the superiority of his perspective, knowledge, and right to conquer and possess the black woman or any exotic body he chooses. Just as there was no room for Rufus in his life, there is no room in his mind for Ida as a subject independent of him or someone who can and does "imagine him back." Ida voices some of her thoughts on the subject much later in the novel, in a conversation with Cass, when she reveals her painful awareness of her situation as a black woman in the midcentury United States: "You don't know, and there is no way in the world for you to find out, what it's like to be a black girl in this world, and the way white men, and black men, too . . . treat you" (347).

Contrary to what Eckman reads in the novel's sexual scenes as Baldwin's "glorified . . . apotheosis of love" (Furious Passage, 165), the lovemaking between Ida and Vivaldo shows how love and its every possibility have been debased by racism and sexism that transcend the borders of the United States. By focusing on Vivaldo's observing consciousness in the scene, Baldwin is able to explore—at the risk of having Ida's consciousness made invisible—how a white American man might experience sex with a black woman and what he might be thinking in the process. What I am suggesting here is that Baldwin uses Vivaldo's erotic fantasy of the East to highlight the ways in which white and Western preconceptions shape erotic and racial experience in the whole world. However much Vivaldo romanticizes what is going on by framing himself and Ida within an imaginary of a fairy tale or a wedding night in the seraglio, Baldwin's description taps the reader's imagination with the repressed images of rape and violence against the slave and free black women who were Ida's foremothers.[103] Baldwin makes Vivaldo's Orientalization of Ida, his displacing of his guilty fantasy to some vaguely Eastern neverland, serve the purpose of deflecting his attention from domestic racist and sexist history and from his guilty conscience as a white man (or whitened, second-generation immigrant).[104]

As if to strengthen the link between Vivaldo and Rufus, who seems to be nearby wherever Ida is, including in Vivaldo's bed, Baldwin draws a striking parallel between Vivaldo's and Rufus's fantasies during their first sexual encounters with Ida and Leona. At the beginning of book 1, Rufus takes Leona brutally on a balcony at a jazz party in Harlem. They drink and smoke a joint, and he promises to give her pleasure and not to hurt her (23), but all the while is enacting a brutal rape fantasy of a white woman in his mind (22). Before they begin intercourse, however, he imagines Leona momentarily as a princess enveloped in the magical lights of the city surrounding them, much as Vivaldo would later imagine a fairy tale setting with Ida. His vision of poor, white-trash Leona as a fairy tale heroine might be as much the result of marijuana as of Rufus's excited imagination and suppressed longing for romantic love (19). At the same time, as Vivaldo will do with Ida, Rufus reduces Leona to her genitals when he first looks at her and assesses her as potential prey: "Pussy's just pussy as far as I'm concerned" (13). Later Rufus imagines both her death and his own and "a hundred black-white babies" as he shoots his "venom" into Leona and imagines a "lynch mob arriving on wings" to kill him for violating a white woman (22). By juxtaposing these sex scenes between a black man and a white woman, and a white man and a black woman, Baldwin thus shows us that both men cannot help debasing the females they are having sex with, and that they both resort to fantasies that displace them from their American contexts. He commented on the importance of racial and sexual national stereotypes in an interview with Tektaş Ağaoğlu for *Yeni Dergi* (New Journal) in which he discussed *Another Country*: "When a white boy sleeps with a black girl, he is sure that she will be satisfied. . . . What goes on through the black girl's mind, that is another matter" (19).

These complicated moments exclude Leona's and Ida's thoughts and might be framed in the context of Marlowe's *The Jew of Malta*, as well as being traced to the early modern notions of sexual and racial difference vis-à-vis an imaginary East. When accused of having committed "fornication," Marlowe's Barabas repudiates the accusation by saying that it was in "another country; and besides / The wench is dead." Like a fantasy, it may never have happened; what is permitted in faraway lands may not be permitted in the civilized West. Baldwin knew Elizabethan plays well, all of Shakespeare and especially *Othello*, and would have been aware of the role that various figurations of the Orient played in them. As Daniel J. Vitkus writes, "from the perspective of English Protestantism," which migrated to, and was transformed in, the New World colonies where white American manhood was born, "the Flesh, the Church of Rome, and the Turk were all believed to be material means for the Devil to achieve his ends. Conversion to Islam (or to Roman Catholicism) was considered a kind of sexual transgression or spiritual whoredom" ("Turning Turk," 145–46). A white ethnic with a Catholic background, Vivaldo attempts to overcome his sexual and racial hang-ups by means of relegating his sexual and racial transgression with Ida to "another country" of the exotic and heathen East.

But then, we might ask, could this desperate imaginative effort on Vivaldo's part be an attempt to actually save himself and Ida from the trappings of American racialized identity? That is, while Vivaldo is hoping to veil himself—in an ironically self-revealing way to the reader—from his sexual obsession with black bodies and from his desire for their racist possession and violation, might he not also be trying to veil Ida from being their object? While this may be true, by resorting to a seraglio ravishment fantasy where a white supremacist scenario à la Baldwin's short story "Going to Meet the Man" might be expected to appear, Vivaldo affirms the racist context of his actions. By yielding to his notions of the exotic, he reveals a wider, transnational context for the American nightmares of race, sex, and violence that he has been trying to escape.

This is an admittedly harsh reading of Vivaldo, whom Baldwin tries to make a sympathetic character later in the novel. At the same time, it adds depth to the process of growth he undergoes in the course of *Another Country*, and helps us to contextualize his admittedly narcissistic suffering as a white queer ethnic who is afraid to embrace his liminal identity. Caught in the American nightmare, Vivaldo wants to possess Ida's blackness because he despises his whiteness and misses Rufus, at the same time as he wants to claim blackness and benefit from it in sexual terms as Ellis does. Vivaldo is uncomfortable with, and confused about, his sexuality and race because, as I have argued elsewhere, for whitened ethnics like him the process of cultural assimilation or Americanization compels racialized heterosexualization.[105] As an Italian-Irish American, Vivaldo cannot assimilate fully into manhood in the New World until he can assert his machismo and join the white heteronormative consensus of men in power.[106]

When he first confesses his whoring in Harlem to Cass, the white wife of his former mentor, Richard, whom he also sees as a rival as a successful writer, Cass tells him, "What a good American you are" (*Another Country*, 97). Her biting irony confirms that she recognizes, too, that sexual domination and violation of black female bodies or female bodies of color are the price of whiteness and heteronormative masculinity. Vivaldo's defensive response to her statement confirms that he knows it, too, but that he also sees her, the WASP wife of another whitened ethnic, Richard, as a prize in the marketplace of American masculinities: "I haven't said they were any better than white chicks."[107] The interracial and interethnic sexual competition that Vivaldo wages with Ellis, Rufus, and even Richard helps to explain his anxiety about race and sex vis-à-vis his fantasies of identification with blackness when he is interacting with other black characters and locations in the novel.[108]

To push this interpretation further, Vivaldo's erotic fantasies of fairy tale scenarios and the exotic East may have something to do with his repression of queerness, which is manifested through his desire to see himself as belonging in the world of the escapist fantasy of romance and sex, on the one hand, and in the black world of real America and Harlem, on the other. Before Vivaldo and Ida become lovers, we witness his wandering in Harlem and "his fancy that he belonged in those dark streets uptown precisely because the history written in the color of his skin contested his right to be there." Being in the black part of the city gives him a sense of power: "He enjoyed this, his right to *be* being everywhere contested; uptown, his alienation had been made visible and, therefore, almost bearable. . . . He had felt more alive in Harlem, for he had moved in a blaze of rage and self-congratulation, and sexual excitement" (132). The blaze of sexual excitement Vivaldo feels in Harlem brands the moment when he and Ida have sex for the first time. While his longing for blackness can be read as racist, it also hints at a desire for love and freedom outside the strictures of the American national story that has been cloven into black and white, hetero and homo, normal and perverse. Vivaldo's desire for blackness embodied by Ida—but also by Rufus, whose love Vivaldo refused to see and reciprocate—may also be read as desire for queer liberation.[109]

As much as Ida is Vivaldo's guilty fantasy, she could also be a potential means to his salvation,[110] and thus an extension of the victimized queer figure at the heart of *Another Country*, her brother Rufus.[111] Vivaldo does eventually acknowledge his guilt for his indifference toward his black friend. And, as he confesses to Cass on the day they attend Rufus's funeral in Harlem, this may not be the only death he feels his indifference may have caused. The story he tells Cass concerns a sport popular among young Italian males from Brooklyn, where Vivaldo comes from, which was picking up, raping, and beating up queers from the Village: "There were seven of us, and we made him go down on all of us and then we beat the piss out of him and took all his money and took all his clothes and left him lying on that cement floor, and, you know, it was winter. . . . Sometimes I still wonder if they had found him in time, or if he died, or what" (112). Vivaldo finishes his story not with true remorse but with whining self-pity: "Sometimes I wonder if I'm still the same person who did those things—so long ago." To which Cass, who becomes increasingly important as a listener and commentator in the novel, responds to him in her thoughts: "No. It was not expressed. . . . Perhaps . . . because Vivaldo's recollections in no sense freed him from the things recalled. He had not gone back into it—that time, that boy; he regarded it with a fascinated, even romantic horror, and he was looking for a way to deny it" (112). Like Vivaldo's fantasy of the East and visions of Ida, this memory of a real event fails to liberate him.

This is because Vivaldo cannot see that "the queer" he raped, beat up, and left for dead was a person like himself, that it could have been himself or Rufus or Eric who was violated that night, given their location in the Village, that quintessentially queer neighborhood of New York. As a writer, Vivaldo observes life and writes things down; he creates paper characters, passions, and pain but refuses to enter and be touched by the real-life experiences that surround him. Even his sorrow and guilt about Rufus are like a memory of an experience not quite lived when he insists to Cass that his pain and whatever happened to him were the "same things" as what happened to Rufus and other Blacks. Cass tries to set him straight: "They didn't . . . happen to you *because* you were white. They just happened. But what *happens* up here [in Harlem] . . . happens because they are colored. And that makes a difference" (113–14). It also makes a difference that the violence that Vivaldo participated in during his youth happened because of the identifiable queerness of the person they targeted. Similar to race, but not always, queerness marks a body, and when it does mark like race, it makes that body visible and vulnerable. Vivaldo's resistance to queerness means resistance to being marked and singled out, to being made visible or ceasing to be shielded by his hard-earned whiteness.

And yet things begin to change when Vivaldo realizes that Ida has been unfaithful to him with Ellis, when he confronts his tormented thoughts one night as he is waiting to hear from her. In this moment he likens her to a fallen Eastern city, and himself to a conquering army raping and pillaging: "When he entered that magnificent wound in her, *rending and tearing! rending and tearing!* was she surrendering, in joy, to the Bridegroom, Lord, and Savior? or was he entering a fallen and humiliated city, entering an ambush, watched from secret places by hostile eyes?" (308). He admits to being afraid of Ida and imagines a castrating woman: "They were always threatening to cut the damn thing off." He recalls his Catholic upbringing, "And what were all those fucking confessions about? *I have sinned in thought and deed.* . . . What a pain in the ass old Jesus Christ had turned out to be, and it probably wasn't even the poor, doomed, loving, hopheaded old Jew's fault" (308). This is a significant moment because, threatened with the loss of Ida, Vivaldo for the first time begins wondering what she might be thinking and how she might feel about him as a white man. He confronts himself as a reality and an image he might be to her: "What did she see when she looked at him? He dilated his nostrils trying to smell himself: what was that odor like for her? When she tangled her fingers in his hair, his 'fine Italian hair'?" He realizes that race as a social reality cannot be escaped, although he longs to change that: "Oh, Ida, he thought, I'd give up my color for you, I would, only take me, love me as I am! . . . And if she despised her flesh, then she must despise his. Who can blame her . . . if she does? and then he thought, and the thought surprised him, who can blame *me*?" (308). At the same time, his vision of sex with Ida as a conquest of an exotic city reveals his continued ambivalence about race and sex. Although he promises to give up his color for Ida—and thus recognizes that he has a color—he still wants to remain "as I am." This is a sequence in which Baldwin demonstrates Vivaldo's growth as a character, but also how trapped he is by his Americanness and Western notions of the racialized erotic. Even in his final confrontation with Ida, after she has confessed her affair with Ellis, he is unable to come clean about his romance with Eric and needs for her to comfort him, to stroke "his innocence out of him" (431).

Shortly before this moment, Vivaldo has been drinking alone in a bar, afraid to admit to himself that he knows that Ida is somewhere out with Ellis. In a sequence echoing the musing on "sad mortality" from Shakespeare's Sonnet 65 that Baldwin chose for the epigraph of book 2, he thinks of Rufus as he contemplates his own face in a mirror and the "odor, juices, sounds" of a sexy blonde sitting nearby, who might be a shadow of Leona (301). Finding himself thus in yet another queer erotic triangle, he then feels that "something in him was breaking" and imagines himself "briefly and horribly, in a region where there were no definitions of any kind, neither of color, nor of male and female. There was only the leap and the rending and the terror and the surrender. And the terror: which all seemed to begin and end and begin again—forever—in a cavern behind the eye" (302). This is a horrific vision as Vivaldo contemplates jumping off into the dark waters of death as Rufus did, and finally it brings about his realization that he has never really seen his friend, his pain and need. Vivaldo's failure was a failure of love as much as a failure of vision and perception; the "cavern behind the eye," or his mind, could not process what the eye could not see.

This moment helps us to regard the enormity of Vivaldo's failure to save Rufus, his retrospective agreement with Rufus's thoughts about Leona, "It's not possible to forget anybody you've destroyed" (51). When, early on, Rufus comes to Vivaldo on the night of his suicide, Vivaldo does not want to deal with his friend's pain: "He was tired—tired of Rufus' story, tired of the strain of attending, tired of friendship. He wanted to go home and lock his door and sleep. He was tired of the troubles of real people. He wanted to get back to the people he was inventing, whose troubles he could bear" (71). He chooses instead to spend the night with Jane, a kind of betrayal that Rufus once feared Vivaldo might be capable of inflicting on him. Vivaldo's choice to be left alone and get laid, but also his choice to be a writer attending to fictitious characters rather than saving his living friend, spells out Rufus's demise. At that moment, Vivaldo desires to leave blackness and Rufus behind, and as a white man, he sees this as a choice, just as after Rufus's death he wants to be able to leave America and travel to the East the way Ellis does. But Vivaldo's fantasy trip with Ida during sex is as far as he goes. He can be seen, then, as geographically stuck between downtown and uptown Manhattan, much as Rufus once was. Still, the color of his skin makes it possible for him to survive and fantasize that he could escape love and hate for Rufus, that he could leave behind blackness and his own racial and sexual ambivalence, that he is the creator of characters whom he can manage as a demigod writer. In other words, the murderous city around him, his mind and art, and how other people see him do not have the power to kill him. When he possesses Ida and indirectly Rufus, then, he enacts only a momentary escape, perhaps the way Kipling's White Man does when he possesses the world according to Said's troping of race in the colonized East, and thus finds himself alive but imprisoned in his own fantasy.

Vivaldo is not the only one who yields to the lure of the Orient to escape the realities and imaginary of American racism. When the unhappily married Cass Silensky considers her affair with Eric, she translates her state of fear, confusion, and lust through a simultaneous dread of, and attraction to, a symbolic, Orientalized image of masculinity, "some unspeaking, unspeakably phallic, Turk or Spaniard or Jew or Greek or Arabian" (*Another Country*, 287). Somewhat like Vivaldo, she imagines a tawdry scenario, as if her sexual transgression meant that "her body could become a trap for boys, and the tomb of her self-esteem." This fantasy is also conveyed in terms of travel and removal to a decidedly exotic location: "She had embarked on a voyage which might end years from now in some horrible villa, near a blue sea," where she would be living a Harlequin sexploitation scenario with her exotic and unspeakably foreign lover (287). That Cass imagines that oversexed male to be unspeaking signifies her association of racialized bodies, lust, and sexuality with the realms outside language and civilization. The WASPish Cass's articulation of desire for the "unspeaking Turk" may be an attempt to veil her erotic attraction to men of color in the novel, perhaps even to Rufus, but also toward Eric, whose queerness, Baldwin implies by repeatedly linking him with black men, might be seen as somewhat racialized.

To Cass, with her refined background and sheltered upper-middle-class and upwardly mobile life, interracial unions, violence, and injustice belong in "a vision of the world" from which she "felt herself holding back" (290).[112] But the material world of the other from which Cass is holding back—the police beatings of street boys in Paris that Eric tells her about, Rufus's death, which she can only imagine and repress, Ida's rage and pain that she witnesses—is not a vision but reality to her friends, and it touches her whether or not she wishes to be touched. Her choice of Eric for a lover, the man who has been marked by loving black men, signals her desire for blackness and exoticism; it is an attempt to escape her sheltered marriage as much as her narrow vision of reality. Like Vivaldo, she is a "good American" thus fleeing whiteness for a metaphorical blackness or racialized queerness that Eric embodies as Rufus's former lover. Cass's choice of a "dark," phallic, and foreign fantasy realm as a mythic location to exorcise and hide her sexual fears and longings confirms her desire to escape the reality of American race and sex relations. Unlike Vivaldo, however, she seems to be better equipped to face her predicament.

Cass's preoccupation with blackness and sex can be seen in the scenes at Small's, the Harlem bar where she goes with Ida to meet Ellis. While drinking with Ellis and his guests, she watches a black couple, a "large, ginger-colored boy dancing with a tall, much darker girl" (354–55). She is attracted to them both, and to the black man especially, and is jealous of the young couple's skill and their freedom on the dance floor. She studies the dance and reads an erotic language into it, an expression "so effortless, so simple" (355). What these young people on the dance floor are able to express is something "difficult and delicate, dangerous and deep," and as she watches them, she asks herself, "Why would it be forever impossible for her to dance as they did?" Even in her thoughts she uses "boy" and "girl" to refer to the couple and thus marks her distance from them as a white woman. She also watches Mr. Barry, a black guest at the table, and confronts her thoughts about the "jungle" howling inside him, behind the "carefully hooded and noncommittal eyes" (355). She thinks Barry must hate her and feels that "his hatred was connected with her barely conscious wish to have the ginger-colored boy on the floor make love to her" (355–56). As she flees home to her husband and children, she is besieged by a desire for a dark-skinned and Spanish-singing Puerto Rican cabbie, which she explains as a result of her "fall from—grace?" with Eric, a fall that had "left her prey to ambiguities whose power she had never glimpsed before" (364, 362). These feelings make her decide to reconcile with Richard, her immigrant husband from Eastern Europe. He is her protection against the "wilderness of herself" (362), but he is also someone whom she once saw as savage and sexual, someone whom she married because he was foreign and exotic in comparison with her patrician WASP family.

Like Vivaldo, Cass can travel only so far into the dark jungles and erotic terrors of her fantasies. Unlike him, she is more conscious of being stranded in her American fantasies of otherness and uses her new knowledge to reshape her situation and learn from her actions. This gives her courage to confront her queerly cuckolded husband—she slept with a man who is defined as a homosexual, rather than with Vivaldo, as Richard has thought. The husband stands up to the occasion like the archetypal brute "Polack" Stanley Kowalski, the violent immigrant from Tennessee Williams's *A Streetcar Named Desire*. Richard Silensky bloodies Cass's face as she confesses her affair, and having experienced what Leona experienced, Cass feels ready to stop "acting as the bulwark which protected [Richard's] simplicity" (*Another Country*, 373–77). This brutal and paradoxical realization of Baldwin's modern-day Clarissa, whom her husband calls "the icebound heiress of all the ages" (290), makes her confront the fact that her real and fantasy love for the immigrant man she once married has always had something to do with racial and ethnic difference, with the lure of the erotic forbidden. She acknowledges to herself that she left her family in an act of rebellion and embraced Richard's ethnic otherness and exoticism.[113] Significantly, she realizes this while recalling her first idyllic lovemaking with Richard, her deflowering in a "field of flowers." This pastoral fantasy, however, is accompanied by flashbacks of the "ginger-colored boy and the Puerto Rican" cabbie who recently stirred her lust (371). At least now Cass can tell the image and the reality apart as she arrives at a place in her country of love where she can be honest with herself and others.

The conclusion features another arrival, Eric's young French lover, Yves, who comes to New York and confronts the city inhabited by "angels" as a fresh-faced immigrant queer from the Old World.[114] "'Yves,' wrote Baldwin, is representative of "'all the innocent Europeans' who 'came seeking another country,' and 'I spent a whole book trying to convey what this innocent European was going to get himself into'" (Leeming, *James Baldwin*, 205). Like other white immigrants from Europe, Yves will have to deal with the conundrum of color as soon as he gets off the boat. His second issue will no doubt be a realization that, no matter the color of his skin, he will be marked by his queerness and foreignness, and that this might be an asset or a liability. His only hope is that he can turn his condition to his advantage. Ironically, after Rufus's fatal flight off the George Washington Bridge, Yves's landing promises a new life, as his entrance into the United States means a reunion with his older and more experienced lover, Eric, who has "saved" him from the streets of Paris and will serve as his bulwark once again. Perhaps, like Engin to Jimmy in Turkey, Eric demonstrates his love and devotion to Yves not only by having invited him to enter his home but also by not being afraid of losing him to the temptations of the New World. In his recently published memoir, written with İzzeddin Çalışlar, Engin Cezzar includes a chapter entitled "Jimmy," in which he proclaims: "*Another Country*, the novel Jimmy wrote [here], I believe is the novel of the century" (55).

The last scene of *Another Country* reflects and frames but also refracts Baldwin's authorial location in Istanbul. Its rich imagery of travel, arrival, and hope for a new beginning in a new land recalls countless immigrant narratives. It also echoes Baldwin's feelings about his third home in Turkey, where he underwent a de-Americanization and de-Westernization of sorts that allowed him to see his home country anew. In that sense, *Another Country* is a tribute—the best that a writer could give—to the city and people of Istanbul, where he reinvented himself as a kind of temporary immigrant and traveler from the West. Perhaps that is why the immigrant arrival in its conclusion appealed to Cevat Çapan, who admired Baldwin's worldliness and his ability to remain honest to his vision. By inserting the explicit and implicit Turkish references and Orientalist imagery into *Another Country*, Baldwin seemed both to embrace the stereotypes of the East as the erotic margin and to reject them as another form of racism. And while this strategy may not be entirely conscious, consistent, or clear throughout the text, it is there, pointing out the ways in which American notions of sexuality, race, and location have larger transatlantic contexts. Baldwin's doubly conscious, hybrid outlook informs the East–West urban imaginary and "imaginative geography" of *Another Country* and reveals in fictional form what Ronald Hyam formulated decades later in *Empire and Sexuality*, namely, that "sex is at the very heart of racism" (Bernstein and Studlar, *Visions of the East*, 2; Hyam, *Empire and Sexuality*, 203).

When we watch Baldwin strolling through Istanbul's Beyazıt book market in Pakay's film, only viewers familiar with the cover of the first Turkish translation of *Another Country* would recognize it as the volume that he picks up when he stops at a stand for a moment. The camera zooms in on the book's cover, and we glimpse the title, *Kara Yabancı* (Dark Stranger) (1970). This moment excludes non-Turkish viewers of Pakay's film while placing Baldwin in closer proximity with the citizens of his third home. When Baldwin replaces the book on the stand, his hand lingers on another volume lying next to *Kara Yabancı*. That book is *Düşenin Dostu*, the Turkish translation of John Herbert's play *Fortune and Men's Eyes*. As was the case with the first translation of Baldwin's third novel, the title of Herbert's play was changed in Turkish. Rather than alluding to the first line of Shakespeare's Sonnet 29 as Herbert did, Ali Poyrazoğlu and Oktay Balamir called the play *Düşenin Dostu*, "Friend of the Fallen."[115] Baldwin's involvement in the theater, both in Turkey and in the United States, gave him ample opportunity to be such a friend. His revolutionary staging of *Düşenin Dostu* is the subject of the next chapter.

21. James Baldwin's silhouette at Cezzar-Sururi window, 1965. Photo by Sedat Pakay.

THREE

STAGING MASCULINITY IN

DÜŞENIN DOSTU

It is a curious comment on the human race that it is only the truth that can shock us. It is perhaps a hopeful comment, too, for it implies that we are able to recognize the truth. A day is coming, hopefully, when the shock of recognition will be a joy and not a trauma, a release, and not a constriction: for it is absolutely and eternally true that all men are brothers, and that what happens to one of us happens to all of us.

—**JAMES BALDWIN**, Notes on *Fortune and Men's Eyes*

When Baldwin learned that Ingmar Bergman was staging his second play *Blues for Mister Charlie* (1964) in his Swedish theater,[1] he told a reporter in Italy that he was very pleased with that interpretation of the play: "They played it straight with all Swedes. No black face. They understood the play is about tribes, not races, about how we treat one another" (Weatherby, *Artist on Fire*, 265). Engin Cezzar, who regretted that his theater company's plan to stage *Blues for Mister Charlie* in Istanbul did not materialize, told me during one of our interviews that Bergman simply used black and white ties to signify the inhabitants of the segregated Black Town and White Town in Baldwin's play. Jimmy must have liked that deliberate signifying on the symbologies of race in Stockholm. He recalled having met the "Northern Protestant" on a visit to Sweden in 1960, which he described in the essay "The Precarious Vogue of Ingmar Bergman."[2] At the time, Baldwin was "struck by what seemed to be our similarities," by "something in the weird, mad, Northern Protestantism which reminded me of the visions of the black preachers of my childhood" (*Price of the Ticket*, 203). Baldwin's interest in international theater paralleled his focus on the domestic representations of identity as spectacle and performance as a playwright—from the church of Sister Margaret in his first play, *The Amen Corner* (1954),[3] to the battle of racialized machismos between Lyle and Richard in *Blues for Mister Charlie*. As in *Another Country*, he saw in his plays an opportunity to dwell on the "particular" but also to show "something much larger and heavier" about people, the world, and morality. He therefore embraced an invitation to direct a play for Sururi-Cezzar's company in Turkey, no matter that the play was by a white Canadian playwright, John Herbert.[4]

Baldwin agreed to direct Herbert's play on prison homosexuality, *Fortune and Men's Eyes* (1964), in Istanbul in 1969, at the very end of his Turkish decade. Its bravura production took the Turkish theater world by storm. The play's translator, Oktay Balamir, stressed that sympathy for the plight of American Blacks at the time embellished Baldwin's stardom with iconic status: "He was very, very popular. Here he was a famous American writer and an anarchist . . . a black American, a man that suffered . . . symbolizing a race that suffered in the States. . . . And so everywhere he went, ordinary Turks, women, men, children showed him sympathy."[5] But while Baldwin's success as the director marked his most publicly acclaimed contribution to his adopted culture, it seemed to be his least known triumph in the United States.

Unlike in Istanbul, where Baldwin was a coveted guest in the houses of wealthy socialites who clamored for his attention, in New York he was losing popularity as the sixties drew to a close. He was frustrated by the experience of staging *Blues for Mister Charlie* with the Actors Studio's Lee Strasberg and Cheryl Crawford on Broadway in 1964. Although the production was well received and attracted many Blacks, after the play's publication, Philip Roth dismissed it in the *New York Review of Books* as "banal," and Howard Taubman complained in the *New York Times* that it was filled with "stereotypes" and "caricatures" of white people.[6] Engin Cezzar liked the play, but in response to his desire to stage it in Istanbul, Baldwin wrote in a letter dated March 13, 1964, that he hesitated to let him do it because he worried that it might not be a hit, and that he was not sure what Engin's theater could "do" with it in Turkey; he was sending his friend the script nevertheless.[7]

Baldwin's fourth novel, *Tell Me How Long the Train's Been Gone* (1968), whose main character, Leo Proudhammer, is a middle-aged bisexual black actor recovering from a heart attack, and which focuses on how American theater refracts and re-creates social divisions of class and race, sexuality and gender, was not a hit with the reviewers at home, either.[8] Eliot Fremont-Smith wrote in the New York Times that the novel was "a disaster in virtually every particular," and Mario Puzo echoed other negative critiques in the New York Times Book Review by calling it "one-dimensional."[9] Train, as Baldwin liked to call it in his letters, arose from his longtime fascination with the world of the stage and reflected his experience as a playwright, director's apprentice, and also as a theatergoer in Turkey, where he saw several of Engin's and Gülriz's performances. In 1958 and 1959, just a few years after finishing The Amen Corner (1954), Baldwin assisted Elia Kazan while he was directing Archibald McLeish's J.B. (1958) and Tennessee Williams's Sweet Bird of Youth (1959) on Broadway.[10] Baldwin eagerly attended rehearsals and took notes for his mentor, but while he loved Williams's play, he "disliked J.B. with a passion" because he felt that MacLeish was patronizing. In his autobiography, Kazan refers to this as the clash of the "'different cultures, Harvard and Harlem'" (Kazan, A Life, 583).[11]

Tell Me How Long the Train's Been Gone, written in Istanbul a decade afterward, reflects some of that experience, as well as Baldwin's memories of his collaboration with the Actors Studio on the production of Giovanni's Room in 1956 and their fraught Broadway staging of Blues for Mister Charlie eight years later. Baldwin did not hold a high opinion of the American theater, and he made this clear as well in the pages of Train. He disliked the Method approach worshiped at the Actors Studio; he also had doubts about the racial politics on the main stages of the United States.[12] In a letter he wrote to Cezzar in December 1958, in which he conveys his excitement about having seen Lorraine Hansberry's play Raisin in the Sun, Baldwin makes clear what kinds of "truthful" and engaged theatrical productions he would prefer that Americans embraced: "I've rarely sat in a theater and felt an audience so intensely. They were really with it from beginning to end, groaning, laughing, weeping, hissing instructions to the actors ('Don't forget your flowers!' they wailed to Miss Claudia . . .)." After the show, Baldwin enjoyed witnessing Hansberry's celebrity: "I came out of the stage door with Lorraine . . . to face a great mob of people; 'that's the author!' somebody shouted; and I held Lorraine's bag while she signed autographs ('It comes once in a lifetime,' she said . . . and whipped out her fountain pen)." Baldwin particularly enjoyed the urban scene around them — "a wintry afternoon in this dingy city, with white folks and black folks with burning faces gathered around a frail little colored girl, and a heavy, black woman (Claudia). They stopped traffic, baby" — and the fact that "some of the glory even rubbed off on me," as he was asked for an autograph, too, by "a working man" who recognized him and told him that "he'd been giving *Notes* [of a Native Son] away for Xmas for years" (quoted in J. Campbell, "Room in the East," 5).[13]

In terms of its reception by readers and critics, *Train* did much better in Turkey than in the United States when it came out in 1973 as *Ne Zaman Gitti Tren*, riding the wave of Baldwin's popularity after the staging of *Fortune and Men's Eyes*.[14] The novel's translator, Oktay Balamir, who received much help and encouragement from Baldwin as he struggled with the novel's rich idiomatic expressions, spoke about it as a masterpiece and praised Baldwin's phrasing and captivating imagery, even though they were sometimes difficult to render in Turkish. "I had no idea how to translate 'The House Nigger'" (the title of book 1 in the novel), Balamir told me. "There are no Turkish equivalents, and that was an important expression." Eventually they settled on "Karaderililer," which means "the black-skinned ones," and seems to echo the title of the first translation of *Another Country, Kara Yabancı*, or "The Dark Stranger," as well as Baldwin's moniker "Arap."[15] Engin Cezzar, to whom the book was dedicated along with David Baldwin and David Leeming, agreed that it was a great work, but in a cable to Jimmy, recognized that it targeted a select audience. It was "not for people who have no love for children or actors."[16]

Baldwin's frustration with American audiences also had something to do with how deeply he was angered by Hollywood, which had invited him to write a script for a film based on Alex Haley's *The Autobiography of Malcolm X* but then made it impossible for him to do justice to its subject. He found himself fighting Columbia Pictures for virtually every line of his text and ended up walking away from the project after the studio imposed a cowriter on him.[17] His frustration and pain are clear in his letters to Cezzar from 1968, where he mentions the demonic "powers" of Hollywood and the sublime incompetence and unreality of the people he had to work with; he also justifies his own "tantrums" about the process and considers the possibility of Engin's acting in the film's Mecca sequence.[18] Campbell quotes a fragment from one of the letters: "'The California sun has scrambled their brains, the swimming pools have clogged their ears. . . . They are not wicked: they are simply sublimely incompetent'" (Campbell, "Room in the East," 5).[19] Legend has it that at one point Columbia considered casting Charlton Heston as Malcolm, "darkened up a bit" (Leeming, *James Baldwin*, 300); Sedat Pakay remembers hearing this verbatim from Baldwin during a visit in

Los Angeles when Baldwin was still working on the script.[20] On September 15, 1968, Jimmy wrote that, following several "monumental fights" with Hollywood, he "walked off" the Malcolm X project, which was a "very unprofessional" way to act, but necessary to convince the studio about doing things his way. He soon abandoned the project altogether and, along with his friends Jean and Beauford Delaney, made it "back to Istanbul, as far away from Hollywood as it seemed possible to get" (Leeming, *James Baldwin*, 302). Baldwin's qualifications as a screenplay writer aside, it is significant that a Malcolm X film did not materialize until 1992, when Spike Lee reworked parts of Baldwin's published screenplay, *One Day When I Was Lost: A Scenario Based on "The Autobiography of Malcolm X"* (1972).[21]

Everyone that I have interviewed in Turkey confirmed that Baldwin enjoyed directing *Fortune and Men's Eyes* immensely, despite its somber focus on violence and incarceration. It was a welcome diversion after what he perceived were the failures of the American culture industry to understand his later works; as he told the journalist Zeynep Oral, he felt that his "last book [*Train*] was banned" in his home country.[22] In Istanbul, Baldwin worked closely with his actors, implementing in his new role as theater director the creed about the artist as "lover" and "disturber of peace," as he would tell Ida Lewis of *Essence* during the play's run. The actors perceived the process of working with Baldwin as being "unlike anything anyone in the cast had ever experienced in the theater" (Leeming, *James Baldwin*, 306); in our interview, Ali Poyrazoğlu called it "life altering." In the newspaper *Her Gün*, Hilmi Kurtuluş credited Baldwin, "a director who knows his job one hundred percent," with the play's success.[23]

Düşenin Dostu, or "The Friend of the Fallen"

David Leeming called Baldwin's decision to accept Engin and Gülriz's invitation to direct Herbert's *Fortune and Men's Eyes* (1964) — translated into Turkish as *Düşenin Dostu*, or "Friend of the Fallen"[24] — "an act of love" (306). After *Another Country*, reworked by Baldwin with a little help from his friends and the city of Istanbul, the play would be something new to him and would entail creating a whole new set of relationships with his adopted home and family. Embracing this newness was all about love, too. Not only was Baldwin willing to take on a role he had not yet tried, but he was also overjoyed at being able to reciprocate, with a tangible contribution to Turkish culture, his friends' devotion and their city's hospitality. He was happy to have a chance to work on a large-scale project with Engin, to whom he wrote in one of the early letters about his tremendous excitement concerning the "intricacies" of the acting profession (letter 10, December 1958). In another letter, however, Baldwin referred to the same profession as "punishing" (letter 11, February 24, 1959). In the aftermath of *Fortune's* successful run, Baldwin would say that the play "saved" his life—just like Beauford, Paris, and Lucien, like Istanbul and Engin and Gülriz, and ultimately like Saint-Paul de Vence. This sequence of people and places, now enriched by a theatrical spectacle, registers what he considered moments of salvation, creative breakthroughs, and milestones in the complex story of his authorship and autobiography. Like his protagonist Leo Proudhammer in *Train*, Baldwin was lost and saved repeatedly; he kept on keeping on.

That Baldwin did not speak Turkish was the first major obstacle in his early work on *Düşenin Dostu*, and he needed to use a translator at all times because some of the cast did not speak English. The talented young journalist and critic Zeynep Oral, who had interviewed Baldwin a few years earlier for *Yeni Gazete*, agreed to be his assistant and translator. When one of the cast, Ali Poyrazoğlu, asked Baldwin in an interview for the company's newsletter *Tiyatro Dergisi* why he had decided to direct a play "in a language you don't speak and in a country whose theater you don't know well," Baldwin replied that "he was a playwright" who "directed the directors who directed his plays" and that his prior experience in the theater, his deep understanding of Herbert's play, and his artistic "instincts" made him confident enough to try.[25] Like several of his other enterprises in Turkey, this would be a highly collaborative and multilingual venture that would widen Baldwin's circle of close friends.

Paradoxically, even with the difficulty of working in another language, Baldwin ended up having more control over the final shape of Herbert's play in Istanbul than over his own *Blues for Mister Charlie* when it was staged on Broadway. At home in exile in Turkey, he was working with friends who were in the avant-garde of the local experimental art world, who were ready to try new things on their audience and trusted his vision and instinct. *Fortune's* explicit focus on the realities of a male prison—profanity, homosexuality, homophobia, homosocial struggle for hegemony, violence, trauma—gave Baldwin a unique opportunity to explore some of the issues central to his own work in the remote context of Turkey, with no worries about either finances or domestic politics. While he was sensitive to the ways in which the play might be received, he was also in the position of being a famous American writer who had been invited to bestow his authority on a cultural production in a city and country that respected and admired him, rather

New York'u Istanbul'dan seyreden yazar:

James Baldwin Hisarda son romanını bitirdi

Ahmet Vefik Paşa kitaplığında sanatçı zenci davasını savunuyor

Roportaj: Zeynep Blisel

Ünlü Amerikalı zenci yazar James Baldwin'i, Rumeli Hisarı'nın arka yamacında, 1800'lerden kalma ahşap bir köşkte, yazı makinesinin üzerine eğilmiş bulduk. Kendini, yazdığı satırlara vermiş, geldiğimizi hissetmedi bile.

Yemyeşil büyük bir bahçenin ortasındaki bu köşk, Ahmet Vefik Paşa Kütüphanesi. Yazar, kalmak için, bütün Boğaz'a hâkim olan bu köşkü kiralamış.

James Baldwin'in İstanbula gelip yerleşme hikâyesi epey eskiye dayanıyor. New York da Engin Cezzar'la tanışıp ahbap olmalarından bir müddet

dâvası yüzünden her şeyden önce Amerika'ya dönüp, bana düşen vazifeleri yerine getirmek istiyorum. Burada devamlı kalıp yerleşmem bir çeşit kaçmak olur ki, bunu ben yapmam. Yazar, memleketindeki zenci-beyaz meselesine, vereceği konferans ve konuşmalar, yazacağı eserlerle yararlı olacağına inanıyor, taşıdığı sorumluluğun karşılığını vermek istiyor. Nitekim Türkiye'ye gelmeden önce de James Baldwin bu alanda çok faal bir kimseydi. Hayatın güçlüğüne inanıyor. Ünlü sanatçı «Hayatım meslekle sosyal hayat arasında çok kompleks, karmaşık» demektedir.

James Baldwin'in Türkiye-

22. Zeynep Oral's interview with James Baldwin for *Yeni Gazete*.

than having to prove himself, as he always felt he had to in the United States. He insisted on being involved with all the aspects of the play's production, and Engin and Gülriz gave him a free hand in everything, including stage set, music, and lighting.

The Canadian playwright John Herbert wrote and revised *Fortune and Men's Eyes* between 1963 and 1966, basing much of its action on his personal experiences at a Canadian correctional facility for young men, where he served a term while in his late teens.[26] Much like the androgynous, sensitive, bookish character Mona (Jan) in his play, Herbert was imprisoned unjustly, having been attacked by hoodlums who, when discovered by police while robbing and beating a visibly queer youth, testified that they were acting in self-defense because the "pervert" had made a "pass" at them. Violence, homophobia, (homo)sexual panic, and male rape occupy the center of the play, whose main goal is to show how state institutions shape individuals in society and destroy its young in the process. These themes attracted Baldwin, who paid much attention to masculinity, sexual mortification, and violence between men throughout his works from his first published essay on homosexuality in American literature, "The Preservation of Innocence" (1949), through his piece dealing with André Gide's being a "husband and homosexual," "The Male Prison" (1954), to *Blues for Mis-*

23. James Baldwin and Engin Cezzar backstage in Sururi-Cezzar Theater, April 1970. Photo by Sedat Pakay.

ter *Charlie* and its focus on white-on-black violence and sexual competition among men, as well as practically all his novels until then.[27]

In the interview for the company's newsletter, *Tiyatro Dergisi*, Baldwin told Ali Poyrazoğlu:

> While I was sitting through the rehearsals [in the past], I always thought that I would make a good director. We will see. There is another thing . . . I know the play I am going to direct very well. I have been working on it for a long time. I can summarize it for you this way, so that you will understand how I will approach it and put it onstage. [The play] symbolizes masculine loneliness in this century. This is a universal problem for everyone everywhere in our age. Since Turkey is also living in the twentieth century . . . I believe I will be able to handle this by my instincts. . . . Perhaps the play might be banned. Then we can understand whether the twentieth century has arrived in Turkey or not. (*Tiyatro*, 10–12)

Baldwin's comments place issues of gender, homosociality, and male yearning for camaraderie at center stage of his interpretation of *Fortune and Men's Eyes*. They also hint at the gendered dynamics among the main power brokers behind the play, which was produced by Gülriz Sururi but translated and acted by an all-male "tribe" and "family," as Poyrazoğlu referred to them. Later Poyrazoğlu helped Balamir care for Baldwin when he fell ill with jaundice and was practically "abandoned" by Engin and Gülriz, who were too busy with their theater to "even knock at his door."[28] When Poyrazoğlu and I talked about his friendship with Baldwin, he described him in dramatic terms and admitted that he thought that Baldwin often deployed his pain and trauma as a "technique to produce writing. . . . His strategy was to step outside of himself." On the other hand, Poyrazoğlu saw Baldwin as a sensual man, who loved Turkish food and even learned how to cook it: "He wanted to try everything, learn everything—he was a writer!" To Poyrazoğlu, a flamboyant and whimsical actor whose diverse roles and several famous drag acts have earned him a huge following, Baldwin was a passionate and powerful writer, "among the biggest in the English language"; he was "like a beacon . . . in contrast to the color of his skin, he shed light around him." He saw him also as writing his characters as a theater director would and trying "to inhabit their skin like an actor," impressions that were no doubt influenced by Poyrazoğlu's close collaboration with Baldwin on Herbert's play.[29]

Fortune and Men's Eyes was first staged in New York City in 1967 and was subsequently published in a paperback edition by Grove Press.[30] Its London production in the same year coincided with Ali Poyrazoğlu's visit there, and he was so impressed and intrigued by the play that he immediately called Engin Cezzar in Istanbul to tell him about it and to propose that they try it at their theater.[31] Poyrazoğlu, Cezzar, and Sururi were at that time partners in a new dynamic theater company, Ümit Tiyatro, or Hope Theater. Having read Fortune, Engin immediately decided, "Let's offer the play to Arap!" They had the text translated by a vibrant young journalist and critic, Oktay Balamir, who was then in his early twenties and worked at the British consulate in Istanbul. Balamir was an eager and able translator, but in the case of Herbert's play, he needed help with its abundant prison slang and sexual profanity; he felt that the language was central to the action and wanted to create a whole new idiom to do it justice. Poyrazoğlu, the only gay member of the cast who was out at the time, came to the rescue and edited the play, and so he and Balamir appear together on the playbill as cotranslators. As Balamir told me, when he and Poyrazoğlu collaborated on the text, they felt that they were, in effect, discovering the "secret language of Turkish gay people."[32]

Balamir and Poyrazoğlu handled some of the idiomatic difficulties by

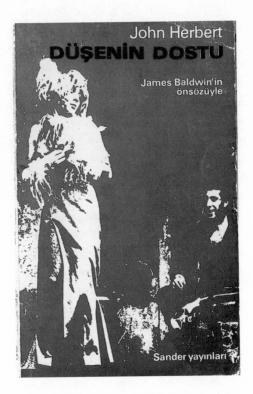

24. *Düşenin Dostu*, book cover of the Turkish edition,
published by Sander Yayınlari in 1970.

asking Baldwin for help, and he eagerly explained the meaning of the original expressions. They also turned to Turkish gay street slang and included
some Roma terms that they agreed would be accurate equivalents. In our
interview in his spacious summerhouse in Bodrum on the Aegean Sea,
Poyrazoğlu explained to me that the "Gypsy [Roma] slang" they used in the
Turkish translation was rooted in the history of the Ottoman Empire's theater, which evolved a form of "slang used by actors, puppeteers, and belly
dancers." These expressions survived in various forms and inflected Turkish
gay slang in the 1960s, which the translators also used and reworked in their
version of the play. In the aftermath of *Fortune*'s notoriety, the street then
adapted some of the expressions that were spoken onstage. Poyrazoğlu
chuckled at the circulation of some of these slang terms from prisons and
the prison they portrayed onstage to the street to the cafes and clubs. Balamir confirmed, "Turkish gays have a language of their own," and the play
"shocked the Turkish audience . . . because for the first time, onstage, they
heard how the Turkish gay people spoke, how they addressed one another.

. . . And since then, even today, many of these words are being commonly used in Turkish high society."[33]

Fortune and Men's Eyes consists of two acts and takes place in a prison cell of a juvenile male detention center; there are bunk beds and doorways to a shower room and prison corridor. There are three other characters besides the delicate and androgynous-looking Mona, or Jan, who occupy the cell: Smitty, a handsome and "manly" new arrival in his late teens, who is considered "green" and fair game for the more experienced inmates; Rocky, a hardened macho youth who is in for rape and soon declares his readiness to become Smitty's "old man" or protector; and Queenie, a large, flamboyant, bleach-blond gay burglar with a penchant for female impersonation, who wants Smitty for himself and in time helps him to dominate Rocky. The cast also includes Holy Face, a dyspeptic middle-aged guard, who is counting the days to his retirement and often seems as much oppressed by his job as his charges are. All the young men are products and victims of dysfunctional families, especially distant, absent, or criminal fathers, and have been shaped by the state-run social welfare and penal systems. This conjunction between "home" and "prison" as problematic spaces spells their destruction as society's unwanted children and must have appealed to Baldwin, who wrestled in his own life with issues similar to those plaguing Herbert's characters.[34] It is not clear whether Baldwin knew that when the play was staged in New York in 1967, David Rothenberg and Mitchell Nestor, who produced and directed it, cast a black actor, Robert Christian, as Mona.[35] In light of *Fortune*'s several references to race and sexual otherness as being interlinked, this androgynous character seems to embody the racialized queerness that was central to Baldwin's vision of the play.

The action of Herbert's *Fortune and Men's Eyes* spans several weeks, during which Smitty—in for the minor misdemeanor of possession of marijuana—declares his staunch heterosexuality and flaunts his possession of a girlfriend outside but quickly learns the rules of the game in the new homosocial world of inmates, guards, gang rapes, solitary confinement, sexual favors, and regular beatings. In act 1, we follow him from his beginnings as Rocky's rape victim and reluctant sex slave to his victorious fight to overpower his first "protector," which initiates his brief indenture to Queenie. In act 2, we witness preparations for a Christmas concert in which Queenie gets ready to perform in provocative drag, and Mona, also in drag, rehearses to recite Portia's speech from *The Merchant of Venice*. We also follow Smitty's triumphant takeover as the "man of the house" or "hippo" in the cell and a "politician" in the prison. By the end, having beaten up and possibly raped

Rocky, Smitty has become the wise guy who knows how to use the system to his advantage. He has become "Baldy's boy" and now enjoys the protection of the highest-up prisoner in the system. Smitty's better education and slightly higher social status on the outside translate into advantages over the others on the inside; he learns the ropes fast and realizes that the system favors the few who ruthlessly dominate the many.

In spite of his full embrace of this prison machismo system, Smitty is intrigued by gentle and bookish Mona, who at first gives him friendly advice but later rejects his sexual advances once he offers him protection as an "old man." As an effeminate-looking man, Mona is referred to by guards and inmates as "it" and seems to be the lowest on the prison's social totem pole. As such he ends up a victim of frequent gang rapes. He is a "punk," not a man, is considered to be as low as a woman, and is frequently referred to as "bitch." Jack Henry Abbott, a lifelong prisoner and self-taught writer, describes punks in *The Belly of the Beast* (1981) a decade after Baldwin's production of Herbert's play in Turkey: "In prison, if I take a punk, *she is mine*. He is like a slave, a chattel slave. . . . Anything I tell him to do, he must do—exactly the way a wife is perceived in some marriages even today. But I can sell her or lend her out or give her away at any time. Another prisoner can take her from me if he can dominate me" (80).[36] Abbott's reading of the punk's sexual subordination through the racial metaphor of chattel slavery echoes Baldwin's views on racism and sexual oppression as being inextricably connected. It highlights the homosocial bartering in which gender and race, or traffic in women and slaves, are at the center of the economy of male dominance both on the inside and outside of the prison.

Despite being feminized and racialized by his predicament as a punk, Mona nevertheless survives his situation by "disconnecting" his body and mind from the abuses he suffers as an "independent" inmate. Paradoxically, he is thus able to preserve his dignity and integrity in the midst of the power struggles and sexual violence that are the modus operandi in a male prison. Mona's plight, Herbert seems to suggest, is a synecdoche for the plight of excluded minorities in a world overrun by power-obsessed men who destroy one another in their mad race for dominance. Mona's ability to survive and retain a degree of humanity that others do not have attracts Smitty, who reveals to him his need for love and ability to feel pain, in short, his endangered humanity.

The play ends with Mona and Smitty sharing a brief moment of understanding, compassion, and caring that seems to be close to the kind of brotherly love that was Baldwin's ideal. They resolve their argument about

Smitty's advances and Mona's rejection by reading together and laughing over Shakespeare's Sonnet 29, which gave Herbert's play its title. Their platonic exchange — "For thy sweet love remember'd such wealth brings, / That then I scorn to change my state with kings" — is the only tender moment in the play and is brutally interrupted by Rocky and Queenie. A fight erupts as they proceed to hit Mona, who is then dragged off to a beating by the guard. It is clear that Mona may not survive his punishment, though Smitty pleads with the guards that it was he who has made the "pass" of which Rocky and Queenie accuse Mona. Smitty's final lesson is that as a "sissy," or an unmanly male worse than a woman or a person of color, Mona has been designated a scapegoat and victim by the social forces both within and without the prison.[37] Nevertheless he has had the most resilience — or, ironically, has been the most "manly" and human of them all — as he has survived with his sense of self and ability to love and feel compassion intact. That was what attracted Smitty, but also what spelled Mona's demise.

The end of act 3 is both "traumatic" and "constricting," as described in Baldwin's notes to *Düşenin Dostu*, as it features Smitty's transformation into a hard-faced incarnation of revenge. Using his knowledge of the guard's misdemeanor (which Rocky has revealed to him) to his advantage, Smitty brutalizes Rocky and Queenie and pronounces his superiority to them as a "hippo" who is well connected with the all-powerful and mysterious guy "on top," Baldy. Herbert seems to suggest that now that Smitty has been deprived of his last chance for love and attachment, he has been thrust for good in the violent embrace of hegemonic masculinity that runs the world. But while he is the man in charge in his cell, like a punk and a slave, he is also Baldy's "boy" outside the cell. His power over Rocky and Queenie, in other words, comes from his having been dominated by Baldy. It is not clear whether or not Smitty realizes this as the play ends. As he is listening to Mona's distant cries of pain during a beating, his last line expresses the brutal economics of masculine power in the loveless world in which you either dominate, or are destroyed by, others: "I'll pay you all back" (Herbert, *Fortune*, 96).

Herbert's play allowed Baldwin to explore further the interplay between race and sex, especially between race and homosexuality, that he made central to *Another Country* and suggested as important even to the deep-southern context of *Blues for Mister Charlie*. While *Blues* centered on the white-black male power struggles and the intransigence of southern racists' viewpoints, it also gestured at the necessity of mending homosocial relations between black and white men, as well as fear of miscegenation and homosexual panic as the flip sides of racism and sexual violence.[38] By having made sexual violence central among the other interlocking systems of oppression—racism, sexism, misogyny, xenophobia—Herbert's *Fortune* privileges male gender and homosexuality and reveals them as embroiled with racism. This kind of focus resembles Baldwin's focus in *Giovanni's Room* and certainly inspired his interpretation of Herbert's play.[39] Baldwin's subsequent works *No Name in the Street*, *If Beale Street Could Talk*, and *The Evidence of Things Not Seen* owe much to his intense involvement with *Düşenin Dostu* in Istanbul. They further his dramatic explorations of the male prison-house motif in Herbert's play as they engage domestic and generational conflicts in the black family, the impact of the ghetto and urban segregation on American youth, and the rise of the industrial prison complex.

Open to the newest innovations in the art world, Turkish theater of the 1960s was more radical in many ways than American theater, at least in Baldwin's eyes. While he admitted that he had seen only several plays and had only a vague notion about Turkey's long theatrical history, he was certain that American theatrical history was lacking. He told Poyrazoğlu: "It is very difficult to talk about American theater. There is no such thing as American theatrical tradition. . . . There is off Broadway. . . . There are very noble projects and research there." Expressing "hopes for the future of the American theater," Baldwin meant that he was waiting for that central institution in the nation's culture to embrace and acknowledge all members of American society, including people of color; the tradition that reigned then was exclusively white. And if he could not contribute to that effort in the United States in the way he wanted, he was only too happy to do so between home and exile in Turkey.

According to Kenton Keith, the African American cultural attaché in Istanbul who was a frequent guest at Baldwin's house, Turkey was ready for Baldwin and needed his message. It was "bursting at the seams with cultural fervor. . . . There was music, there was jazz, there was theater," and to a Western observer, the scene was "much less Islamic then than now," with "people having non-traditional relationships all over the place . . . and the tradition [was] to bring a good Turkish wine as a gift."[40] Having moved in similar circles to Baldwin's and often in the same ones with him, Keith stressed that the educated Turks he knew were not religious; they "were entertainers . . . loved scotch and didn't have to hide it . . . [just as] they felt free to express their views and way of life." Istanbul was an Islamic city, with hundreds of mosques calling people to prayer. And yet while some people "carried on the basic rites and rituals," many, especially the educated elite, lived secular lives surrounded by cultural "Islam that lay very lightly on [their] shoulders."[41] In such a climate, Keith thought that Gülriz's and Engin's decision to have Baldwin direct the play for their theater was "brilliant"; like them, he saw his compatriot's abilities quite differently from how they were perceived in the United States. To Keith, by 1969 Baldwin "was at the height of his powers. . . . He was an important American figure. . . . The whole thing was exciting . . . [because] at that time you have to say that Istanbul was ready for that type of a play. . . . The theater world was wonderful; there was no TV then [and] there were seven to nine separate stages of the Turkish Municipal Theater [and State Theater] . . . plus all the private theaters."[42] Oktay Balamir similarly saw Baldwin become a star of Turkish culture overnight: "[He was] the sensational director of Düşenin Dostu; everybody wanted to be able to say, 'Oh, by the way, and James Baldwin came by . . .'"[43] "You should understand," Kenton Keith told me in our interview, "the rock stars of that day were actors and directors."[44] Baldwin as a rock star? He must have found that comparison amusing. But looking at some of his photographs in the Turkish press, he seems to enjoy being in the spotlight and rocking the house.

Engin Cezzar explained his choice of Herbert's play in his memoir as a consequence of his taste for troublesome productions, given that the play had been "igniting events and was being censored in every country it was staged in." He also liked the setting: "A play that takes place in a penitentiary and tells about how juvenile prisoners were tortured and raped. I have never seen such language." He was convinced that it was "a terrific play," and his love of "such bold projects" and of taking "great risks" made him invite Baldwin to direct it. Cezzar was aware of Baldwin's considerable theatrical experience and especially his earlier collaboration with Elia Kazan. He simply "wrote him a letter and invited him. He came immediately" (121). While he was sure that his blood brother would jump at the project, Engin worried that Gülriz would not like Herbert's play, so he read Fortune in English and translated it for her as he went along, trying to convince her that they should produce it. She was skeptical at first, just as he had feared, given the play's theme, setting, and explicit language, but then saw the production as an opportunity to target an important social issue in Turkey that was kept invisible and considered unspeakable. In the end, she writes in her memoir, "we got seduced by the play," thus confirming the workings of literary erotics, even in a text as traumatizing and brutal as Fortune:

25. James Baldwin, Gülriz Sururi, Bülent Erbaşar, and Oktay Balamir at a party, 1970. Private collection of Zeynep Oral.

I'nde davetliler eğlenirken ile eşi Tolga Aşkıner de tebrikleri kabul ediyordu.

Böyle yerlerde hiç görünmeyen Avni Dilligil o gece Mustafa Değhan'la Galata Kulesi'nde uzun uzun arkadaşlık etti.

lukların en neşeli erkeklerir.den t Boralı, oyun arkadaşı Suzan yeni bir kadın arkadaşıyla... Bu teyi sonuna kadar bozulmadı.

Yine beraberler. Gülriz, Engin ve zenci yazar James Baldwin Kule'de de birbirlerinden hiç ayrılmadılar. Kokteylin en neşeli simalarıydılar...

26. James Baldwin and *Düşenin Dostu* theater troupe at cocktails. *Ses*, 1970.

When Engin first read me *Düşenin Dostu* . . . my first reaction was "this play cannot be staged in Turkey." I could not sleep that night, I was so impressed by the play. Even though I was aware of the facts [it dealt with], I was disturbed. . . . Next morning, as soon as I woke up, I asked Engin to read the play to me once more. In this second reading, I understood at once why I was disturbed. It reminded me of one of Halit Çapın's interviews displaying the painful truth about the street kids [in Turkey]. . . . I concluded that many would be disturbed just like I was as they watched this play, but would wake up like me, seeing that closing their eyes to the truth would not do. They would start to think and perhaps would begin looking for solutions to the problem. At a certain level, they would find themselves among those responsible for the youth whom we push aside, calling them "Thief! Fag!" Up until today, we had employed examples from all walks of human life in our theater. We decided to focus on the problems of a group in our country that could not be underestimated. One had to think cool-headedly how the people in this play had come to be where they were. It is a fact that realities disturb people. We would be disturbed while watching the tragedy of the victims, and while watching their efforts to go beyond the point where we thought they deserved to be. We would not like to believe in the reality we saw. (Kıldan İnce, 428)

The play's extreme realism and the level of its engagement with social issues that in their eyes transcended national and ethnic boundaries appealed to Gülriz and Engin, whose theater worked hard to offer a combination of a lighter repertoire that ensured good attendance and a favorable response from the authorities, and more serious pieces like *Düşenin Dostu*. Sururi was especially concerned with the links between social justice and sexual exploitation and saw the brutalities depicted in the play as reflecting the lives of the Turkish poor, especially the street kids of Istanbul, who were fair game for gangs, prostitution, and other forms of crime.

Following this line of thinking, like many other Turkish intellectuals of her generation, Sururi focused emphatically on class issues rather than individualism of desire, choice of partners, and sexual identity. At the time, while gender and sexual revolutions were going on elsewhere, there were no official gay or lesbian organizations in Turkey, and homosexuality, although very much present and accepted, was treated as something everyone knew existed but never spoke about.[45] Despite this silence, there was a flourishing gay life at the time, Poyrazoğlu told me: "There were parks, you could hustle in the streets, there were clubs." Like Engin and others, Poyrazoğlu

27. Zeki Müren with statue in the Canary Islands. *Ses*, 1969.

28. Zeki Müren onstage. *Ses*, 1969.

confirmed that Ottoman culture had accepted homoerotic desire and what we now call homosexual sex acts, but they were not spoken about or named the way they have been in American culture, especially after Stonewall.[46] Indeed, from what many of my interviewees told me, it was a kind of love and lifestyle that "had no name" in the Turkish "street"; it was treated as invisible and unspeakable, at the same time as, for example, some excessively visible pop-culture stars of the sixties and seventies, such as Zeki Müren, were clearly queer and routinely and flamboyantly challenged accepted gender norms and sexual conduct.[47] This paradox made it possible for the more conservative, straight-laced older generation to enjoy and respect someone like Müren as long as his or her sexual identity and lifestyle were not named and made an issue in public. I would later learn from Oktay Balamir that Baldwin knew well and liked Zeki Müren and was much aware of the political dimension of homosexuality in Turkey, "which was a fact of life in a male-centered culture" of that country.[48]

Gülriz's memoir is perceptive about homosexuality being the elephant in the bourgeois living room; she names things for what they are. She realized that what was at stake in *Düşenin Dostu* as directed by Baldwin, as well as in Turkish society at the time, was very complicated. By referring to class, she targeted issues of social welfare and linked them with the issues of individual desire by referring to freedom of sexual preference. This approach motivated her to support the play, in hopes that it would make a political statement and achieve didactic goals. She had social responsibility in mind, and in her memoir emphasizes the role of theater in fostering activist attitudes:

> A person should be able to choose his [or her] own sexual life. In Düşenin Dostu this was not the case. In our prisons, the backstreets and outskirts of the big cities, this was not the case. [People lived] without any right to choose [how to live]; they lived not by free will, but by force and violence. Indeed, the rules of life struggle were harsh in our country. Besides, how were the families, the parents treating their children? How should they? I wanted mothers, who knew no responsibility other than the clothing and feeding of their children, to see this play. (Kıldan İnce, 429)

Sururi is speaking of serious problems—homophobia, male rape, violence, child prostitution, and child abuse. She also refers to the indifference of wealthy liberals and the lack of serious and open discussion about these issues. Set up in the Turkish context in terms of its idiom and local references throughout, the play thus echoed these issues, especially the suffering of socially invisible young queer people. Another point that Gülriz as the producer hoped to drive home was the interlinked issue of class and parental negligence, as all the inmates in Düşenin Dostu are hurt beyond repair and turn to the life of crime because of their parents' abandonment or criminal activities, which are often caused by poverty.

Abbott mentions exactly the same social causes of juvenile delinquency in his prison autobiography In the Belly of the Beast, where he describes himself as a "state-raised convict." Like Rocky in Fortune, Abbott became hardened and embraced violence precisely because he was neglected as a child and had to accept the prison modus operandi as the only way to survive in the so-called institutions of correction and resocialization. The Canadian account of Herbert and the American account of Abbott correspond to a certain degree with the realities of Turkish prisons of the late 1960s. But, as Oktay Balamir told me, we should be cautious about overgeneralizing about Turkey as the locus of graphic brutality and male-on-male sexual violence. In the early 1970s, Turkish prisons were harshly criticized in the West, and so we should remember that "staging such a play . . . [showed the West] that your prisons . . . [were] no better than ours." Balamir also mentioned Alan Parker's well-known film Midnight Express (1978), which he considered offensive, an "extremely distorted" cinematic production "based on a true story" of an American tourist who ended up in a brutal Turkish prison for an attempt to smuggle hashish.[49] Irvin Schick, who was among the crowds picketing the film when it opened in Boston, objected to its racist depictions of the Turks, although he agreed that its depiction of prison rape was "most certainly realistic."[50]

The explicit sexual content and violence portrayed in the play Baldwin directed were shocking to Turkish audiences and its language and setting in a prison seemed to be as much of a tough sell. But this was true only at the beginning, and only for some of those who saw Düşenin Dostu. Balamir explained that the theatergoers at the time were mostly the educated elite, "not the ordinary people," and that, despite its shock value, "for them this [play] was revolutionary and they [soon] liked that." He laughed, too, at what seemed to be the bourgeoisie and pseudo-intellectuals getting their kicks from high culture at the same time: "They subconsciously mastur-bated at seeing such a play; [they were] telling others that such plays could be done in Turkey." Yet some of my other interlocutors emphasized that it was in fact "everybody," including the "ordinary people" who went to see the play; there were, after all, enough kinds of theater in Istanbul to serve every taste, from vaudeville, to Turkish plays, to the classics of the European masters.[51] The producers, and even Baldwin in his interview with Poyrazoğlu, anticipated that the play might end up banned on the grounds of linguistic obscenity and disturbing content. As Engin told me, chuckling at the memory, he himself was a magnet for bans but had decided to stage the play nevertheless. Perhaps the company hoped, too, that having Bald-win direct the performance would give it legitimacy and attract attention to it, as well as protecting it from governmental intervention.

When Baldwin was looking for a translator to navigate the Turkish ver-sion of Fortune and Men's Eyes, he asked for someone not only fluent in Eng-lish but also possessing literary skills and a familiarity with the theater, so that he could understand and contextualize Balamir's and Poyrazoğlu's rendering of the play's text in Turkish, their cuts and substitutions and ref-erences to the local scene. Zeynep Oral, a young journalist and drama critic, agreed to became Baldwin's assistant. She is important in the constellation of Baldwin's Turkish friends, as she not only was at his side every day dur-ing rehearsals but also became his close friend. I met her for an interview in 2001 at her beautifully designed modern apartment with the requisite view of the Bosporus. Engin Cezzar, who simply picked up the phone and made an appointment for me to meet Oral on my last day in Istanbul, told me that she was "one of the most important people who can talk about the play." Oral is a feminist and a well-known and well-respected journalist with intimidating credentials who has interviewed the likes of Leyla Gencer and Salvador Dalí. During our interview, however, she was informal, direct, open, warm, and friendly; I felt as if I had known her for years. Oral started by telling me that when she and Baldwin first discussed their possible collaboration, Baldwin assuaged her doubts that she could do a good job by saying, with his usual charm and just a touch of fibbing: "Oh, at least you know something about theater and directing, being a critic and all that. Me, I know nothing!"[52] She had met Baldwin for the first time a couple of years before, when she interviewed him at his Pasha's Library house in Rumeli Hisarı for an article that she was writing for Yeni Gazete in 1966. There is an interesting story attached to her second meeting with Baldwin, on the evening of the very same day.

Soon after their interview, she had the misfortune of becoming an object of Baldwin's angry drunken harangue when they met by chance in a nightclub. She related the story with a big smile, although I was sure she must have been shocked and angry when it took place. When she entered the club, she saw Baldwin sitting with Engin and Gülriz at a bar, listening to a Turkish performer singing jazz. When Oral joined them and remarked politely that the music was "nice," Jimmy went off screaming at her that it was an insult and that the singer was "butchering his culture."[53] He also forbade her to "publish one word about me!" Oral remembered that there was quite a scene, and people around them commented that the "Arap went mad." She was deeply offended by the unexpected outburst and also terrified at what Baldwin might do next, as she had already submitted her copy of the interview, and it was to appear in the paper the next day. The worst was that here was the same man who had charmed her with his manners and intellect earlier that same day, and now he seemed to have become a monster. Oral eventually accepted Baldwin's sincere apology and a bunch of roses the morning after. A couple of years later, having become his assistant on the set of Düşenin Dostu, she also became the critic who wrote the most, and perhaps most movingly and astutely, about Baldwin in Turkey.[54]

Oral told me that one of the most important parts of the process of Baldwin's production of Fortune was the virtually familial emotional closeness that evolved between the actors and their director. She stressed that her own relationship with Baldwin soon became intimate and passionate while still platonic and that it transcended race, gender, sex, and sexuality: "We used to cry and laugh together. And I don't cry with my other male friends!" Like

29. James Baldwin, Zeynep Oral, and the *Düşenin Dostu* troupe
at a party, 1970. Collection of Zeynep Oral.

Gülriz, Zeynep bonded with Jimmy instantly and understood his attractiveness for other women, some of whom would develop crushes on him. She
soon became his confidante; "we had no inhibitions." They often "talked
the womanly talk" about kids, pregnancy, and heartbreaks, as he had much
experience in each area, given his turbulent love life and apprenticeship as
his mother's right-hand man, helping her to raise his eight siblings.[55] Oral
remembered fondly how caring Baldwin was during her pregnancy, and how
marvelous he was with her kids once they were born. She knew well Jimmy's
younger brother David and admired their closeness and support of each
other; she was struck by their loving, "almost erotic" relationship: "They
would speak the same words at the same time. Then they'd laugh, hug, and
give each other a high five. I've never seen brothers so caring and tender
with each other." She recalled Jimmy's French boyfriend, Alain, and many
occasions on which he was a source of both intense happiness and misery
to Baldwin during his visits in Istanbul. She echoed Engin: "[Baldwin] used
to cry on my shoulder a lot!"

Oral loved working with Baldwin as his right-hand woman and stressed
that his being the play's director was the main attraction of that demanding

job. In an article she published on February 5, 1970, in the Turkish news-paper *Milliyet*, she emphasized her own learning process: "He was telling me about the anxiety [about the play] he felt in the first couple of days." She quoted Baldwin as saying, "I hated, hated Engin Cezzar in every sense of the word. You cannot imagine how I hated him when he asked me if I would like to stage the play. . . . However, it was too late and there was no turning back. It was not like I did not want to do it. . . . Besides I have never done anything like this till today." As Oral described her reaction to this tirade: "By that time I had learned that 'hated' meant 'getting highly excited' in Baldwin's vocabulary."[56] She also got along with him because she deeply admired his works, especially *The Fire Next Time*, and dated the birth of her racial consciousness, her discovery of her "whiteness," to reading that book.[57] She stressed several times what was important to her about their relation-ship: as an intellectual and apprentice, she followed Baldwin as if he were a prophet of a new way of thinking about the world, and she "internalized the kind of responsibility that he advocated." She also loved him for being a fighter and resister, for being a dissenter who would not compromise. She told me that she was aware that she idealized his struggle for racial justice in the United States. But she never saw him as merely American. To her, Bald-win was part of a "universal" struggle for a better world, the struggle that she and other Turkish intellectuals saw as part of their own as they opposed American imperialism and promoted leftist or Marxist approaches to solv-ing issues of domestic politics. Baldwin, she felt, enabled her to voice her own political views. She saw herself echoing the national situation and need in her response to him: "We *really* needed his kind of thinking in Turkey in the 1970s."

Staging the shocking play directed by Baldwin was a prime opportunity to promote this new way of thinking about individual freedom and the re-sponsibility of the state for its subjects. But even Oral, in her inconspicuous job as the director's assistant, drew criticism and was aware that her in-volvement meant taking a certain intellectual and social risk. She illustrated this with an anecdote that rendered the problem in micro scale. Apparently, her conservative, "old money" in-laws were scandalized by the fact that she was involved in the production of *Düşenin Dostu* — "such an immoral play" — and that her married name would appear on the theatrical posters. To mark her outrage at this form of intrafamilial censorship, Zeynep ostentatiously signed her writings about the play and Baldwin with her maiden name, Birsel, instead of Oral. Still, she appeared with her married name in *Tiyatro Dergisi*. Being associated with the play, she was branded as partaking in the scandalous goings-on depicted in it. Still, she stressed that her rebellion against the mind-set of the bourgeoisie was not "so much" about sexual freedom. The problem as she saw it had to do with the issues of form and representation, on the one hand, and content and ideology, on the other. Her rebellion was intended as an affirmation of the play's extremely realist mode of presentation, its right to be located in a prison, its right to use the foul language of the inmates, and its right to engage reality "as it was." It didn't "matter what it was really about. . . . The point was to speak up for a human rights issue."

This insistence on splitting form from content seems an interesting maneuver, a rhetorical device to allow for a covert discussion of the unspeakable center—homosexuality—of the play. Considering Sururi's writings on the subject, it is thus easier to understand the complexity of the Turkish cultural climate in 1969 and 1970. The play's rawness and explicitness, its prison setting, and its reliance on "dirty" language—Zeynep told me she could not bring herself to repeat some of the words even years later when we talked—were all inseparable, of course.[58] But at the time, the setting alone was enough of an issue and enough of a scandal. And "Nobody talked about homosexuality then!" "Look at me," she said at one point, "I was a married woman, pregnant with my second child, who went back home after her day of work on the play. . . . You have to understand. A lot of intellectuals then were quite conservative, quite ordinary; just married folks with kids." I respected Oral's honesty and admired her protectiveness of her privacy, as well as that of her friends and Baldwin. I sensed that she was simply trying to explain the actions of her younger self. She told me later that there was no organized response to the play from any groups of sexual minorities; she was certain that there would be today. "You know, that was the way then: nobody called out that the emperor was naked although *everyone* knew it and saw it!"

The nakedness of the emperor in matters sexual is one of the issues that plagued Baldwin throughout his life; it is one of the larger subjects in his works. When I asked Oral about how Baldwin was perceived as a gay or bisexual or queer artist, she said that his sexuality was "never talked about," either. I was stunned, because Baldwin never hid his lifestyle and confided in her regarding his French lover from Martinique, Alain. We ended up discussing language and discursive representations, rather than analyzing reactions and perceptions. Oral told me that, yes, they went out to bars and nightclubs and had lots of fun and good food together. She remembered that Jimmy loved to dance and was really good at it. He would often sing for his friends and perform a routine with a top hat and silk scarf, but she did not see him as enacting campy or queer spectacles. She had no idea if there were gay hangouts in the city and how he "conducted that part of his life." At the same time, she resented the assumption that Baldwin came to Turkey for sex; she repeated several times throughout our conversations and added with vehemence: "I don't think he even set his foot in a hamam! . . . I am sure he'd ask me for a recommendation before going."

Like his sexuality, Baldwin's race was both excessively visible and invisible; it was the first thing people noticed that made him an "Arap," but it was not talked about and thus "did not matter." Oral smiled her knowing smile and told me that, of course, Baldwin was noticed and exoticized, being as he was one of the few black men around. I learned later that one of the women who had a crush on him made a sketch of Baldwin's close-up photograph in profile that appeared on the back cover of the Sururi-Cezzar theater company's newsletter and wrote a poem to him to accompany the image. The poem is not a masterpiece, as Balamir, to whom Baldwin gave it, describes it. But it talks about the writer's tragic blackness and extols his adopted Turkishness, which is proof of how beloved and welcome he was in Istanbul:

> Your skin wouldn't be black,
> Were you not born there.
> That ill fate on your forehead
> Wouldn't be written.
> You wouldn't have seen
> The dark gaze of pain
> In those eyes that look at you
> F[uck] the homeland
> Recognizing human rights
> Not recognizing you.
> You are ours, one of us.
> Your past may be there
> But from now on, your future is with us.
> You are in our hearts.[59]

The author of this poem expressed the feelings of many Turks toward Baldwin; she framed the page with the drawing and the text and gave it to Baldwin as a gift. He was thrilled to receive it but later left it with Balamir, who has ever since displayed it in his apartment in Ankara. Like others, Oral agreed that Baldwin enjoyed his popularity in Turkey, and she emphasized

Doğmasaydın orada
Olmazdı derin siyah
Yazılmazdı alnına
O simsiyah yazılar
Sana bakan gözlerde
Görmezdin acıların
Kara bakışlarını
İnsan hakkı tanıyan
Sizleri tanımayan
Memleketin içine...
Sen bizimsin bizdensin
Mazin olsa da orda
Artık atin bizimle
Kalbimizde sen varsın

TÜRKÂN AYDERE

30. Sketch and poem by Baldwin's female admirer, 1970.
Reproduced by permission of Oktay Balamir.

that his visibility or exoticism as a black man did not invite discrimination and alienation but rather cultivated celebrity and admiration. It seemed to her that Baldwin enjoyed his campy minstrelsy and stardom as Turkey's resident "Arap." She knew that others called him Yamyam; she thought that, away from the home scene in the United States, he embraced opportunities to be subversive and performative, and most of all he embraced his notoriety in Turkish culture as the star director of *Düşenin Dostu*.

Like many other Turkish intellectuals of her generation and class in the late 1960s, Oral thought that racial issues were located in the United States, not in her own backyard. "The 'Kurdish problem' did not exist as a racial issue when Baldwin was here," she told me. She thought that attributing the statement "The Kurds are the Niggers of Turkey" to Baldwin was absurd. As with homosexuality, "nobody talked about Kurds in terms of race." They were instead seen as a geographically located group: "The people in Eastern Turkey were very poor and lived in caves; they needed water and health care; class issues were what mattered."[60] Oral's insistence on being a participant in the "universal" struggle for human rights at the time made it clear that—perhaps similarly to her class-conscious American counterparts whom Baldwin branded "white liberals" and sometimes essentialized and misunderstood—she was taking a more global view of her position and her country rather than only looking on the ground at the local issues.[61] This way of thinking seemed to me to tie back to her evocative conundrum of the "emperor's clothes." While it may be impossible to name things for what they are and admit a crisis at home for its theorizers, at least some of Düşenin Dostu's audience could see the social issues at stake when they attended the play, even if they did not openly discuss them. The passion that Baldwin put into staging the performance would thus bear fruit even if not many spectators would dare to give the specific crisis that the play addressed its proper name.

The Director as Lover

In act 1 of John Herbert's *Fortune and Men's Eyes*, the hard-nosed Rocky and flamboyant Queenie compete to impress the new arrival, Smitty, while trading put-downs in prison slang. Androgynous Mona, or Jan, remains on the sidelines, interjecting once in a while as an impromptu guide to "another country" of the correctional facility where Smitty is to serve his six-month sentence:

Rocky: Cripes! You'll never forget you played Sally Ann to me once. When you sobered up and felt like a little fun, did you miss me?

Queenie: . . . Yeah—also my marble clock, my garnet ring, and eleven dollars.

Rocky (*laughing*):   Oh jeez, I wish I coulda seen your face. Was your mascara running?

Queenie: He's having such a good time, I hate to tell him I like Bob Hope better. So where did you come from Smitty . . . the big corner?

Mona: That means the city . . . it's a slang term. You'll get used to them.

Smitty: I feel like I'm in another country.

Rocky: What's your ambition kid? You wanna be Square John . . . a
           brown nose?
Queenie: Ignore the ignoramus. He loves to play the wise guy.
Smitty: I'm willing to catch on.

Baldwin impressed his cast and collaborators with his "natural" way of directing, and Engin and Zeynep confirmed independently of each other "that Baldwin . . . made an exceptional theater director" (J. Campbell, *Talking* 234). Oktay Balamir, an experienced theater journalist, agreed with this opinion and added that Baldwin's astute descriptions of Leo Proudhammer in *Train* proved his closeness to the theater and his sensitivity about the craft of acting. "He would have made a good actor," Balamir told me, especially a "film actor . . . who would be chosen for certain parts . . . [like] being angry; he acted that out perfectly." To Balamir, Baldwin's anger and rage were both genuine and artful; he understood that at times he had to engage in public performances of these emotions when provoked on issues that he cared about.

All the Turkish actors who worked with Baldwin on *Düşenin Dostu* agreed that his technique of directing "from the inside" was new and sometimes disturbing to them. Leeming notes that one of them felt that working with the black gay American writer helped him to come out because the director "was able to ease him away from self-consciousness to a position from which he could not only channel his dilemma into the character he was playing but change his own life" (*James Baldwin*, 307). Baldwin's charisma, charm, and indeed seductiveness as an artist and mentor were also confirmed by another actor, who was initially troubled by Baldwin's erotic persona and by having to act in a play that dealt with homosexuality. Thanks to Baldwin's patience and dedication, the actor experienced a total conversion in the process of rehearsing and ended up playing his role with "genuine feeling, because he thought of his director 'almost as if he were a lover'" (307).

This is how Zeynep Oral remembers their first working sessions:

During the first rehearsal . . . everybody sat around the table and read the play, just like they would do for any other play. On the second day it was read a second time; on the third day, a third time. Sixth, seventh, eighth day, they were still reading. Day fifteen, day sixteen, the same thing. . . . During these readings, Baldwin was . . . getting into a deep analysis of the characters. As days passed, each of the five prisoners (including the

31. Baldwin and friends reading the play around the table before rehearsals. Collection of Zeynep Oral. Reproduced by permission of Akçura and Yapı Kredi.

guardian, who is also in a way imprisoned) reached gigantic proportions in our eyes, gained different subjectivities, and became one of us. On the twentieth day, the play was still being read. (Akçura, *Engin Cezzar Kitabı*, 139)

Soon the actors complained because they felt they were wasting time reading and analyzing literature instead of doing the real work of rehearsing onstage. But when Baldwin finally asked them to act out what they had been discussing, Oral observed a "miracle": everyone was in control of his role and understood his character as deeply "as if they had been rehearsing onstage all this time" (139). Before the miracle took place, however, Bald-

32. Cast of *Düşenin Dostu*, Oral, and Baldwin preparing the play for rehearsals. Collection of Zeynep Oral. Reproduced by permission of Akçura and Yapı Kredi.

win had his own share of anxiety and doubt that he revealed only to Oral: "I wanted to try myself out, but I was scared. In the end there was that possibility that I might have to admit to myself that I blew it" (139).

The cast who threw in their lot with their unorthodox director consisted of Cezzar as Smitty, Ali Poyrazoğlu as Queenie, Erdem Alkal as Rocky, Aydemir Akbaş as the Guard, and Bülent Erbaşar as Mona Lisa. The last character was the most difficult to cast, as Baldwin wanted someone who had the natural looks and androgynous energy of Mona. As Balamir remembers, the actor they found was so good that he simply "stole the show," even though Cezzar's Smitty was the de facto protagonist of the play.[62] In her memoir, Gülriz remembers that she came across a suitable actor to play Mona completely by chance:

> Jimmy used to say to me, "Find a Mona Lisa like I want, and don't worry about the rest." One day I had invited Bülent Erbaşar to my house to talk about the décor for the play. Bülent Erbaşar had done the interior decoration of Kenter Theater and prepared the stage sets for many plays. He was a very valuable set designer, who had worked with us in "Nikâh Kâğıdı" and "Haftada Bir Gün." He had a law degree and had also acted

33. Mona, Rocky, and Guard in *Düşenin Dostu*: behind bars. *Tiyatro*, 1969.

34. Smitty and Queenie in *Düşenin Dostu*: behind bars. *Tiyatro*, 1969.

35. Bülent Erbaşar as Mona/Jan, January 1969.
Collection of Zeynep Oral.

in the Municipal Theaters for a period of time. While we were talking, I remember myself suddenly jumping to my feet and shouting "I found him!" Bülent was going to play Mona Lisa. I found Mona Lisa on earth, while I was looking for him in the sky. (Kıldan İnce, 429)[63]

After Sururi told Erbaşar, "I must introduce you to Jimmy immediately!" she took him to see Baldwin, who "gave a cannibal cry, 'Wav!' as soon as he saw Bülent." The trouble with this character was that even though Mona/Jan did not have as many lines as other characters, his presence was key to the dynamics between the others. In the fragment from act 1 quoted at the beginning of this section, Mona serves as a translator and buffer between Smitty and the brutal world he has just entered. Mona is also the quintessential queer in the play, straddling the boundaries of gender, sexuality, and class, and the ultimate other; someone that Baldwin could perhaps relate to. In the final scene, when Smitty and Mona bond for a moment, Mona delivers some of the most important lines of the play about love, dignity, and respect, which sound eerily like Baldwin's own mantra of brotherly love.

Bülent Erbaşar's performance was so poised and delivered with such feeling that it eclipsed all the others. Sururi describes Erbaşar's presence onstage in her memoir: "Bülent used to smile with his pearly white teeth, slanted eyes, as he was looking at you with an incredible sadness in his young, delicate face surrounded with his brown hair that was mixed with some grey . . . Bülent read this Shakespeare sonnet [29] with Engin onstage every night with such simplicity and sincerity that I cried each time I listened to it" (430). Zeynep Oral remembers that when Baldwin was explaining how to play the character of Mona to Bülent, he stressed his softness and sensitivity, subtlety, and difference from the other men. As Oral was trying to translate this for the actor, who knew some English, and for the others who did not, Bülent touched her lightly and said softly: "Don't worry, I am like that anyway." (This was an oblique confession, and this is as close as we came to outing anyone in our interview.)[64]

Other characters in the play included the prison guard Holy Face, played by Aydemir Akbaş, to whom Baldwin explained, as Poyrazoğlu recalled, "You are a lifer here—the prisoners come and go, but you remain here!" Oktay Balamir remembers that Akbaş "was extremely good, especially because people were accustomed to seeing him in comedies and here he was a tough guard." Balamir commented as well on the actors' age, as all of them, except for the guard, who was to be past middle age, were playing very young men, in their late teens like Smitty and Mona, or early twenties like Queenie and Rocky. "It was perfect casting for Mona," no matter Erbaşar's "more advanced age" (the actor was in his thirties then) because of his "fragile looks . . . [that made] the audience pity him more than the others." Balamir saw Ali Poyrazoğlu and his drag performance as "a hit, a shocking hit," even though he found his blond wig "irritating." A theatrical purist, Balamir could not understand "why Ali simply did not dye his hair just as the actual character did in the play." Erdem Alkan, who played Rocky, was a new face on the Turkish stage, and Balamir could not recall much about him except that he "did his job." Engin, who began losing hair at the time, had to use a wig to look younger. Balamir thought that because of the wig he "did not look the part as it was intended in the West," although he did well.

Gülriz remembers the process of producing the play in her memoir—she was the female producer with the all-male cast, and Zeynep Oral the only other woman on the set: "I used to watch the rehearsals without getting bored. While Engin was helping with the mise-en-scène, however, Jimmy proved that he was indeed a very powerful interpreter. Everybody acted very well" (Kıldan İnce, 430). Engin recalled especially fondly the long discussions à la literary seminar that proceeded stage rehearsals as Jimmy's Turkish "welcome table": "By the time we went on, we were living our parts" (J. Campbell, Talking, 234). Baldwin wanted to make sure that all the actors were comfortable with their roles and understood their characters' motivations and circumstances of personal pain.[65] As if to facilitate that, he also took a paternal approach to the actors, whom he literally called "children," using one of the few Turkish expressions he knew. Oral recalled his words in her account for Milliyet: "Waiting for the players to arrive, [he would be] calling 'Çocuklaaa . . . [Kiiids!]' . . . Where are these çocuklaa? It does not work this way, don't they know? At this time the only reason they live should be this play. Maybe Aydemir's arrived, but is sleeping somewhere. Let's look for him.' 'This time I am serious. I'll show them! I am getting angry!' Nevertheless, a couple of minutes later when they showed up saying, 'Arap, sorry, last night . . . overslept,' that angry man's dark black face used to illuminate, and with a big child-like smile the 'culprits' were forgiven" (Akçura, Engin Cezzar Kitabı, 139).[66] Oral also writes about the director sharing his actors' "joys and sorrows," as one night Ali had to "go on stage the night his father passed away"; Baldwin "tried to show him the compassion of a [surrogate] father" (140).

Always a writer, Baldwin penned a brief explanation of the play that was given to the actors and also published as program notes in the company's newsletter, Tiyatro Dergisi.[67] Always an inquiring reader, he was at the time studying Tyrone Guthrie's notes on directing Chekhov, as he felt that there were similarities between Chekhov's use of symbols and Herbert's in Fortune and Men's Eyes.[68] Baldwin refers to The Cherry Orchard as a framework and frame of reference to understanding the functioning of homosexuality as a symbol in Herbert's play: "Fortune and Men's Eyes is concerned with prison homosexuality in precisely the same sense that Chekhov's The Cherry Orchard is concerned with cherry orchards. As Chekhov's play ends, we hear, from far away, the sound of the axe beginning the destruction of the trees—the destruction of a human possibility doomed by human folly. The boys in Fortune and Men's Eyes are, like those trees, cut down, and, in this case, before our eyes. The play, then, confronts us with the question of how people treat each other, and especially with the question of how we treat our children" (Tiyatro Dergisi, no. 13, n.p.).[69]

As in his other plays, Baldwin was concerned with "keeping the faith" between the actors and the audience, between the director and the actors, and between himself as an interpreter and everyone else involved in the process. Poyrazoğlu remembers that Baldwin insisted that everyone understand and embrace the mission statement of sorts that his notes articulated. Jimmy was emphatic that his interpretation of the play transcend geographic and national borders: "The four prisoners in this play—or, rather four of the five prisoners in this play, for the Guard is a prisoner, too—are scarcely more than children, and the play could very well be taking place in an orphanage, a boarding house, a school, a coffee house, or West Point. The play is taking place, in fact, wherever society's victims are thrown together, and the action of the play is really, at bottom, the effort of our victims to become something more than the numbers we stamp on their carte d'identite, or on their flesh" (*Tiyatro Dergisi*, no. 13, n.p.). Baldwin admitted that the sexual content of *Düşenin Dostu* was "shocking . . . only because it so ruthlessly conveys to us the effect of human institutions on human beings." Homosexuality was nothing new, especially in male prisons: "No one, after all, can take it as a revelation that incarcerated males, in prisons as in monasteries, turn for release and affection toward each other." He also targeted the prudishness and intolerance of homophobic audiences: "Nor can anyone seriously claim to be shocked by being informed that love between men is among the many human possibilities." Weatherby's biography quotes Baldwin saying that he directed the play as a "'twentieth century morality play,' a 'modern *Oliver Twist*'" (*Artist on Fire*, 302).

The last lines of the director's statement emphasize Baldwin's well-known message of human kinship: "It is absolutely and eternally true that all men are brothers, and that what happens to one of us, happens to all of us." He also points at "the play's tremendous, really wondrous compassion and precision," as well as its didactic appeal and social currency: "We have endeavored to be faithful to the play—which is exactly the same thing as saying that we have endeavored to be truthful with you. To begin to think seriously on what has brought the people in the play into their hideous situation is to begin to reflect on what has brought us into our own hideous situation: if we can face it, then we can change it, and set our children free" (*Tiyatro Dergisi*, no. 13, n.p.). In 2001, Engin Cezzar showed me the original pages of the director's statement, which Baldwin had typed on onionskin paper and signed "JB Nov. 22, Istanbul [1969]."

The rehearsals had a ritualistic character, with Jimmy presiding like a high priest, smoking incessantly, drinking, taking in every word. Oral remembers him sitting on a tall chair near the stage, always holding a cigarette, intensely focused. Ali Poyrazoğlu smiled at a similar memory of Jimmy "perched on a stool like a rooster." As a director, he said, Baldwin was always professional, "calm, not interfering, not overtly outspoken," but at the same time able "to communicate his ideas with an amazing economy of words." He tried to make the actors understand that the play emphasized the power of experience, that "life on the inside of the prison was not much different from the life outside."

«Düşenin Dostu...» oyunun provalarından bir sahne. Solda oyunun yöneticisi James Baldwin. Fotoğraf Amerikalı gazeteci Angelo Castrillon tarafından çekilmiştir.

Bütün İnsanlar Kardeştir

James BALDWIN

Chekhov'un VİŞNE BAHÇESİ'nin vişne ağaçları ile ilgisi neyse, DÜŞENİN DOS-TU'nun hapishanelerde homoseksüel ilişkilerle ilgisi odur. Chekhov'un oyunu sona ererken uzaktan bir balta sesi duyarız. Bu ağaç kesiminin başlangıcı - insan olanaklarının insan budalalığı ve vurdumduymazlığı ile yokedilmesidir. Düşenin Dostu'ndaki çocuklarda bu ağaçlar gibidir. Yalnız bu kere onların kesilişini gözlerimizle görürüz. Öyleyse oyun bizi şu incelemeye zorluyor. İn-

36. Baldwin's statement appears in *Tiyatro Dergisi*, no. 13, under a black-and-white photograph of Baldwin at rehearsal with Cezzar and Poyrazoğlu performing onstage, 1969.

The message from the director and his background as a black American political activist resonated with the revolutionary cultural moment in Turkey at the end of the 1960s, when leftist student unrest and anti–Vietnam War protests were common occurrences. The cultural attaché Kenton Keith stressed in our recent interview that the anti-American sentiment in Turkey at the time "was very complicated." In addition to the protests against the U.S. involvement in Vietnam, Turkish students, intellectuals, and artists were upset by what they considered the threatening, offensive, and patronizing style and tone of the so-called Johnson letter from their NATO ally, which has been an iconic example of U.S. imperialism to the Turks ever since.[70] The letter from U.S. president Lyndon Johnson, which was leaked to the press, addressed the Turkish and Greek governments on the subject of the precarious situation on Cyprus in 1967. In the aftermath there was unrest in Istanbul, where crowds pushed some marines of the U.S. Sixth Fleet into the Bosporus; in the capital city of Ankara, demonstrators overturned and burned a car of the U.S. ambassador Robert Komer when it became known that he was involved in the CIA's Phoenix Program for the "strategic neutralizing" of members of the Viet Cong. At the same time, Keith stressed, all these actions were tempered by "a real pro-American system of intellectual connections with the U.S. . . . People went to school there . . . [and] everybody had an uncle who served in Korea."[71]

While all this was going on, Baldwin was immersed in directing the play. He told Oral, "My mind and soul are so preoccupied with this play that I cannot work on my book. Man is not a robot that can switch from one job to another" (Akçura, *Engin Cezzar Kitabı*, 140). The written instructions that he gave to the individual players were intended to help them understand and inhabit their characters onstage. Poyrazoğlu felt that Baldwin was both directing a play and "writing orally a novel for [its] characters." For example, to Engin he drove home the idea that the whole play "stands or falls on Smitty's journey" from innocence to corruption as a young man: "To have seen love fail—twice—and to have seen how the world destroys love—or how one's father is willing to destroy his son—is to have a lot to 'pay back.' People who reach this point become saints or tyrants or poets" (J. Campbell, *Talking*, 235). In light of Baldwin's message in the program notes, this semiautobiographical and self-reflexive comment made a lot of sense. Once again, here was a character whose relationship with his father echoed Baldwin's own past. And there was Baldwin, now an elder to a new generation of "children"—from his nephew for whom he wrote "My Dungeon Shook," to the Turkish "çocuklaa" in Düşenin Dostu, to the many Black Power models for Black Christopher in Train—whom he was trying to reach with his work.

The character of Smitty in Fortune also helped Baldwin to contextualize and revisit his struggles with the fathers of his earlier fictional characters: John Grimes from Go Tell It on the Mountain, David from Giovanni's Room, Richard from The Amen Corner, the other Richard from Blues for Mister Charlie, and even the white racist Jessie from the short story "Going to Meet the Man," whose father's abuse makes him into a racist, rapist, and murderer. Comparing Fortune to Chekhov's The Cherry Orchard, Baldwin pitched against each other the realistic depictions of "fortune" (money, politics, class, fate) and "men's eyes" (the regimes of representation and self-fashioning) that besiege the play's male characters. His concern that the spectators in Istanbul recognize the collective social responsibility for the corruption of the young resonated with Sururi's and Oral's concern for the city's street children and spoke to the progressive Turkish audiences invested in exposing social problems such as poverty, abuse of minors, and prostitution. Baldwin's play ends with the deafening sound of the iron bars that separate the stage from the audience being slammed shut, thus sealing the fate of the children imprisoned behind them, "cut down . . . before our eyes."

Baldwin made the massive iron bars an integral part of the play and was involved in designing the stage set, which had to be redone several times to meet his specifications. He also paid extremely close attention to lighting and music, which was composed especially for the play by Don Cherry, who happened to be passing through Istanbul at the time.[72] Cezzar, in his recent memoir, remembers signing up Cherry to compose the soundtrack:

One day, coming back from a rehearsal, on Gümüşsuyu in front of the German Embassy [close to Baldwin's apartment at the time], we saw a black family sitting on a carpet stretched on the pavement: a weird-looking black man wearing colorful clothes, a very blonde woman, and two children. Jimmy saw them and stopped dead in his tracks and said, "It can't be."

"What is it? It is just the hippies. Do you think the hippies only exist in America? This is Istanbul. The road to Katmandu passes through here" [said Engin].

"But this is Don Cherry, man."

"Who the hell is he?"

"You don't know him? The famous jazz virtuoso. This is good luck. I

37. Cherry, Baldwin, and Cezzar with a copy of Herbert's play *Fortune and Men's Eyes*. Reproduced by permission of Akçura and Yapı Kredi.

38. Cherry, Baldwin, and Cezzar recording soundtrack to *Düşenin Dostu*. Reproduced by permission of Akçura and Yapı Kredi.

was wondering what we would do with the music. That's it. We've found who is going to do the music."

The man on the pavement was indeed Don Cherry. And Don Cherry was indeed a great musician. We took them from the pavement into the house, ate and drank together, and worked for fifteen days. He created wonderful music with a piano and a small trumpet. (121)

Cherry was on his way back from Africa, at the moment in his career when he was involved with world music and collaborating with musicians from different countries. In Istanbul he hooked up with the famous jazz percussionist Okay Temiz, who, as Cezzar described, "joined the group . . . and we went into the studio. Okay brought all his stuff [instruments]. For one and a half hour nonstop, they made a wonderful recording. We used most of it during the play" (121–22).

Oral confirmed that sound was very important to Jimmy, and besides working with Cherry to get the original soundtrack right, Baldwin manipulated the stage design and props to juxtapose silence and noise. For example, he would have the actors bang on and shake the heavy iron bars that separated the length of the stage from the audience, or the guard would run his stick over the bars or hit them violently. Zeynep was impressed with how, in their roundtables, Baldwin would move in and out of the play to contextualize the characters and their actions; she also observed how hard he tried to envision and locate it in Turkey, even in specific spots of Istanbul to help everybody imagine it. She also recalled that although he obviously did not speak Turkish, he would use both the English text and the Turkish translation during rehearsals and follow both closely: "It was amazing to see that he would always be in the same spot on the page as the actors were in their Turkish version. . . . He had an amazing grasp of what exactly was happening on the stage; he knew and felt it." She saw it as "communal and confessional experience." Baldwin's copious notes in the typescript of the play and on pieces of paper attached to it made that clear. Poyrazoğlu, who has this copy of the play and has considered restaging it after over three and a half decades, is convinced that he could re-create it now the way Baldwin directed it on the basis of these detailed comments. "It was a cult classic, you know," he told me, and said he regretted that he could no longer play Queenie and would have to find "a very young cast."

The local cultural politics must have been somewhat bizarre for someone from the West like Baldwin, who, having heard that the play might cause trouble with the authorities, worried that Gülriz and Engin would lose money or have their reputations damaged. Given the content of Düşenin Dostu, there was wild anticipation in the media already during the rehearsal period, building the suspense right up to opening night. Weeks before the premiere, the journal Ses commented on the daring of the whole enterprise, calling it the first Turkish production in the "new genre of theater . . . called 'Theater of Horror' . . . [that] is currently sweeping all of Europe."[73] A brief note in the subsequent issue of the same journal warned that viewers younger than eighteen would not be allowed to see the production, which, it taunted, "for people who have never seen a prison before, will open a window to a different world."[74] The theater critic Refik Erduran reported in his review for Variety that at first Baldwin himself had worried about what this might mean to his reputation; he called directing Herbert's play "an odd endeavor" and confirmed that some of his advisors told him that it was an "invitation to disaster" or that he was only going to "make a fool of himself" (91).

The success of Baldwin's method of directing was proved by the explosive reception of Düşenin Dostu, which ran into the spring of 1970 and played for 103 performances. "It was the hit of the year," Balamir confirmed, "a milestone in the history of Turkish theater." Zeynep Oral reported: "On the opening night I looked at Baldwin when a deafening applause filled the theater at the end of the performance. Was he crying? . . . All I could see were shining eyes and the whitest of teeth chattering with excitement. I said, 'You did it.' 'No, I did not, they, we, all of us did it. Our audience asked for it and so it happened,' he said" (Akçura, *Engin Cezzar Kitabı*, 139). Leeming recalls that Baldwin was "ecstatic about *Fortune*'s success," along with the cast, who held an "elaborate party" for him on December 23, 1969, a "Baldwin Christmas" that included decorating him with a replica of a medal "given by Ottoman sultans to honor great deeds." The medal made him into a "pasha," or, as he wrote to his brother David, knighted him as "Sir James Baldwin" (*James Baldwin*, 308). Sick in bed on a visit to New York in January 1970—he had to leave soon after the opening—Baldwin wrote in an enthusiastic letter to Engin that he was happy that the play continued to be a hit. He was impatient to get back to Istanbul to "see it again" and was thinking "seriously" about staging *Blues* next. He was sure that they had done an extraordinary thing and that it would be "madness" not to continue. He was disappointed that the New York press did not report on the play, but mentioned that many of his friends had somehow heard of its success.[75]

The play went on a national tour, to Izmir and Ankara and many other places, among them the small mining town of Zonguldak on the east coast of the Black Sea. Its success in "proletarian locations, very leftist, and working-class," such as Zonguldak, as Poyrazoğlu classified them, was a particularly significant achievement. Poyrazoğlu thought that the play received positive reception in those unlikely places because people understood Baldwin's message that "the prison could be anywhere," that it was about men and their "own culture of violence." In a review published soon after opening night in the newspaper *Son Havadis* (December 25, 1969), the critic Hikmet Saim explained the attraction of the play that later helped it to be received so well all over Turkey: "*Düşenin Dostu* is a 'naked' play but never obscene. Calling *Düşenin Dostu* obscene is no different than admiring the sculpture of Venus for its nudity rather than for its aesthetic value. Sexuality in this play is as carefully calibrated as poison is calibrated to yield medicine. The author knows the essence of lust and where art ends and obscenity begins very well" (Akçura, *Engin Cezzar Kitabı*, 131). Balamir explained to me that the play's reception reflected regional differences, often subtle. For example, the city of Izmir "greeted [it] warmly, being a more 'permissive' city to gay issues," whereas the Turkish capital, Ankara, was rather "stunned" by it.[76] Still, the "conservative capital," where audiences were "generally accustomed to watching the 'master works of classical theatre' staged by the

Scenes from *Düşenin Dostu*.
Reproduced by permission of
Akçura and Yapı Kredi.

39. Cezzar as Smitty in
monologue.

40. Cezzar as Smitty and Erbaşar
as Mona have a "talk."

41. Cezzar as Smitty and Alkal as
Rocky fight it out.

Turkish State Theatre," embraced Baldwin's message, and so the play ended up performed in a "huge movie house to packed audiences."[77]

Soon after *Düşenin Dostu* opened on December 23, 1969, to a "gala night audience . . . a mixture of society people and left-wing intellectuals," the play became a notorious political scandal (Erduran, "Shock Sensation," 91). That it stirred the city officials' suspicions was somewhat welcome news to the company; this helped to generate interest in the play and secure its important position in Turkish theatrical history. The play was indeed banned by the governor, Vefa Poyraz, albeit briefly, and only after so many people had seen it that the officials backed off quickly.[78] The details of the case are difficult to understand to non-Turks, I was told, but reflected clearly both the unprecedented freedom of speech in Turkey at the time and the exciting climate that the play generated. The district attorney's report filed after the play had been investigated by officially appointed "experts" reacted to the charges that *Düşenin Dostu* "hurt the public sense of propriety and modesty" (Akçura, *Engin Cezzar Kitabı*, 129).[79] But the experts' report reaffirmed the play's rights as an artistic production, and quoted the twenty-first article of the Turkish republic's constitution — "Everyone has the right to learn, teach, express, propagate and explore arts and sciences" — in its defense. It also referred to the Turkish Supreme Court ruling that stated the "obligation of artists to critically expose false and immoral perceptions by exhibiting them." The play, the report concluded, was "oriented toward a positive goal in terms of its main argument and ending" and thus fully appropriate to be performed (129–30).

Engin's memoir includes a colorful account of the police intervention in the aftermath of the ban, which also demonstrates the interest in the play on the part of state officials: "I reopened the theater. We perform and the governor sends his men to shut it down. We object that the governor has no authority to shut down the theater, and it reopens. . . . Every day there are policemen at the door, waiting. One day, they begged at the ticket window to see the play. They must have wondered what had been banned. The audience was very engaged; there were no empty seats. I said they should find a place for themselves at the back. Suddenly there emerged a wall of policemen at the very back. We performed under these circumstances that night." Cezzar also includes an anecdote related to the civil suit he had to deal with in the aftermath of the police intervention and his arrest for resisting them, or for the "obstruction of justice": "My lawyer was Orhan Apaydın. In the last trial I was scared out of my wits. . . . We entered into a crowded hall [at the courthouse]. For some reason most of the audience

42. Scenes from the play: Ali (Queenie) and Bülent (Mona) in drag, rehearsing for their Christmas performance. Reproduced by permission of Akçura and Yapı Kredi.

seats were filled with nice looking women, many fully made up, and dressed up. Orhan told me what to say and not to be afraid, as he was certain that I would be acquitted. I did what he said."[80] After the judge declared Cezzar acquitted, there was an explosive reaction from the audience, who all stood up and cheered: "'Engin, long live, brother!' The ones who cheered were women, but the sound that came out of them was of men's voices," Cezzar was stunned to discover. "I realized that they were all transvestites. They were the ones who claimed the play and supported it: the friends of the 'Friend of the Fallen'" (122). This show of transgender support for the play proved its importance to different constituencies of Istanbul who resisted cultural censorship of sexual and artistic freedom. The theatrics of local drag queens in the municipal court also confirmed that Baldwin's play helped to legitimize displays of gender performance in the public sphere and state-controlled spaces.

It also impressed Charles Adelsen, who came to see the play as part of his research for a report on Baldwin in Istanbul for Ebony magazine. Adelsen's description sounds tongue-tied when he writes about the outcome of the play without dwelling on its contentious subject. In Adelsen's eyes, Baldwin "turned the topical into the timeless" (40).[81] Kenton Keith liked the play quite a bit and proclaimed it a "triumph" and a revolutionary contribution to Turkish culture, although he did not go into detail about its breaking of sexual taboos either: it was a "very, very graphic and very stirring portrayal. . . . Everybody was believable. . . . And it was fascinating that it *could* happen in Turkey." Balamir, who has been the most forthcoming of my interviewees in matters of gender and sexuality, put it more plainly: "The play was a success because it was a revolutionary play for the Turkish audience. Although they were aware of homosexuality in Turkish prisons, and in prisons all over the world, this was the first time homosexuality was vividly being shown [in the theater]." He mentioned that in the 1950s there was a performance of *Tea and Sympathy*, a play with implicit homoerotic themes, which was a big hit.[82] "But that was just an opening of a door," he stressed, "whereas in *Düşenin Dostu* we were talking about screaming queens on the stage," which was very new. Baldwin relished all of that, Oktay said in our interview; he "enjoyed himself immensely and had great big fun" with the play's success. But when it was banned, Baldwin was scared and worried: "I still remember his face. . . . He took it very seriously. It *was* a serious thing, but we Turks, we can always find a way," Oktay said with a laugh.

Reviews in the Turkish news media were enthusiastic, with some mixed and negative responses issued by more conservative publications. In the Armenian newspaper *Jamanak*, A. Yerag wrote: "I heard from many that the play is immoral; many complained about its obscene language. However, we say that the play is realist and moral in its essence and the rest is just details. How can one deny the facts [of life]?"[83] Reporting for *Ses* magazine again after the premiere, Sezai Solelli emphasized the powerful and contentious effects of Baldwin's production on the audience, who either loved or hated it. Solelli encouraged his readers to see the production for themselves rather than forming judgments or yielding to prejudgments and to "have the courage" to do so. He placed his own impressions in the context of the polar responses he witnessed among the spectators: "If you ask me, you should listen neither to your friend who represents the whole thing as a horrible boogey, avoiding to confess that she actually liked the play because she is oppressed by the rules of morality; nor should you listen to those who feverishly recommend it, despite the discomfort they felt as they were watching the play, because they don't want to be called backward minded. Don't try to find anyone with a sincere opinion."

Solelli praises Herbert's veracity and realism, his autobiographical "insight and feeling," and admires Baldwin's impressive "ability . . . to stage the play with the intended level of feeling," as well as his talent at "communicating" with the audience. Most important, he praises the collective courage of Baldwin's team "to stage such a play in Istanbul" and their honesty in facing "sex in its stark nakedness" at a time when the subject was shunned and marginalized in Turkey. His conclusion sums up Baldwin's success: "*Düşenin Dostu* is the most daring, most painful and the most blunt play I have ever seen."[84]

Like Balamir and others I talked to in Turkey, Poyrazoğlu assured me that Baldwin's readers in the United States had no idea what a feat he had accomplished with the staging of Herbert's play. This accomplishment was confirmed in the rave review in *Her Gün* by Hilmi Kulturu, who praises Baldwin's masterful balancing act between melodrama and "horror play" that Herbert's text might have devolved into in the hands of a lesser director (Akçura, *Engin Cezzar Kitabı*, 133). Like many others, this review stresses Baldwin's artistry and experience and implicitly credits some of the play's success to his fame. This view is echoed in the American theater journal *Variety*, where the Turkish playwright and journalist Refik Erduran commented: "If Baldwin had not lent his name and skills to this production, it would have been ignored by Istanbul's mass audience and instantly denounced by the left as another example of Western decadence." Instead the play "provided the first occasion . . . [that] brought together the city's theatrical factions on a middle ground" (91). Erduran's review appeared under the title "Shock Sensation in Istanbul as Homo Play on Prisons Directed by Baldwin" and quipped that "while Ottoman history hardly evidences an excessive devotion to heterosexuality, the modern Turkish theater has so far maintained what is considered decorum on the subject." At the same time, despite the play's "uncompromising" Turkish translation that sounded more "abrasive" than the original and the fact that throughout the performance "shock followed shock," the audience's mood "seemed to shift from discomfiture to fascination, to compassion" (91). The reviewer Rauf Mutluay agreed, calling Baldwin's play "marvelous" and "very powerful," and focused on theater as a mirror to society. Baldwin's rendering of the play "reflect[ed] the truth. Who says that the truth is always soft, nice and funny? In the face of truth, at times you feel pitiful, uneasy at every word of it, and if you have tears, you shed them." What was at stake, then, was the political role of the Turkish theater at a specific moment in national history and the play's ability to shock but also provide a safe space for catharsis, what Mutluay called its "mission": "If you would like to laugh without thinking, there are many cheap stages around you. But come here to be a little disturbed, please."[85]

Gülriz Sururi rhapsodizes about their collective success in her autobiography:

The play attracted much reaction. It was just as we wanted, the audience leaving the theater in tears, then coming back and buying new tickets, saying that they want to send it to their sons, to this person and to that person. There were many who saw the play three or four times. . . . The press found our choice to be right on and celebrated our theater for drawing attention to such a (social) wound. However, some conservative circles said, "Turkish audience is not ready for such a shock!" Thus, on our gala night, a celebrated novelist who had been in prison for many years left the theater and protested against *Düşenin Dostu* with this behavior. This author was Kemal Tahir. (*Kıldan İnce*, 430–31)[86]

Sururi's memoir includes as well some of the reactions to the play by members of the audience, as the company planned and conducted a survey to obtain some solid data on how the spectacle was received. They did so in case they were threatened with a shutdown by the government. "Ninety percent of the thousands of replies we received were for the continuation of the play." A person who signed only his or her initials wrote, "The play must go on. It is absolute reality without any hint of invention. I know this well, because I have been in prison for three and a half months.— T.B." "A scientist," who identified himself or herself as "Psychologist K.O.," stressed the necessity to open up painful subjects: "Open wounds do not kill" (*Kıldan İnce*, 432). Other responses include a student who wrote for a group of young men sharing a dorm who came to see the play together: "If revealing the malfunctioning of society should be banned, this would only show the weakness of the responsible people, those who are supposed to give direction to society, and instruct us in living up to the highest expectations. We would like to let you know that we stand by you in solidarity as we congratulate you for your courage, and for the positive influence you made in this society, and for your success in staging the play. Sincerely,—K.C., on behalf of the students at Cağaloğlu Boys Dormitory." As Gülriz wrote simply: "*Düşenin Dostu* sits at a corner of my memory as one of the best and most daring choices made in Turkish Theater."

Despite these positive reactions, Zahir Güvemli's article for *Yeni Gazete*, which combines a review of the performance with an interview with its director, criticizes the play for its "disturbing content." Güvemli echoes to a degree Mutluay's concern with theater as a tool of social change but is disturbed by *Fortune*'s frank treatment of homosexuality and violence among men. Assuming that it must have been the flamboyant black American director who was responsible for the play's selection, Güvemli asks Baldwin why he had to choose "this [particular] play to show the misery of humanity." Baldwin replies that it was not he but Cezzar who chose *Fortune*. The journalist then presses Baldwin into a declaration concerning the "formal rules of morality." When Baldwin responds that he does not "believe in the theoretical rules of morality, but in morality reflected in practice," Güvemli voices his discomfort with the play's production in an exchange that is clearly indicative of the reaction of a large part of the audience who criticized *Düşenin Dostu* but came in droves to see it. This would be the ambivalent crowd that Balamir described as "subconsciously masturbating" at what they saw:

ZG: In this play, first the words and the language, and second the events, are disturbing to me. It will surely disturb others like me. Is this the purpose of theater?

JB: Did this play disturb you?

ZG: Yes, very much.

JB: Then the purpose has been fulfilled. The purpose of this play, if not the whole theater, is to disturb people.

Güvemli avoids referring directly to the homosexuality, violence, and profanity that bother him, using instead vague references to "morality" to get Baldwin to comment on his intentions. Baldwin, typically, upholds his stance that the artist must be "a disturber of the peace." Güvemli continues to press Baldwin further about the choice of the play, as if he had not heard Baldwin's reply that Cezzar was the one who selected it. What seems to be at stake here is the expectation that art not evoke strong feelings, alienate anybody, or challenge institutions:

ZG: In your essay in the bulletin [director's notes in *Tiyatro Dergisi*], you say that all humans are brothers and you show how this is actually not the case in life. There are lots of plays that have the same subject matter. Why did you not direct one of them?

JB: As I said, the choice was not mine.

ZG: But haven't you thought that this play would be met with resistance and the audience might reject it?

JB: In my opinion, the right thing to do is not to reject but rather accept the play. If the audience rejects this performance, then this means that they accept the situation as it is. Unless the society and the audience feel disturbed by this play, they won't try to correct the situations displayed there.[87]

Güvemli's article thus sets itself up in opposition to Baldwin and his play. It targets the play's foul language, "which is not legally allowed to appear in print here," and designates the role played by Poyrazoğlu (Queenie) as that of a "pervert." The photograph that accompanies the text shows the scene in which Mona and Queenie appear in drag in the prison's annual Christmas performance—Mona rehearsing to play Portia from *The Merchant of Venice* and Queenie appearing as a blonde bombshell lounge singer à la Mae West. The interview is preceded by a brief, dramatic description of Baldwin's appearance that seems to tie him to his subjects on the stage: "At the top of the Galata Tower, we are interviewing the black American playwright and novelist James Baldwin, who has been living in our city for some time and who has directed *Düşenin Dostu*. The author is very charming with his lace shirt and dark red jacket. He is wearing a medal of Sultan Abdülaziz, which Gülriz Sururi wore last night."

Although informed by the "genteel" homophobia common among theatergoing and literary conservatives in practically any culture, such commentary may not have seemed entirely hostile to the Turkish readers of *Yeni Gazete*. Perhaps by that time Baldwin was becoming a kind of a "resident alien," a literary-theatrical version of Zeki Müren, and so Güvemli's descriptions of his wardrobe and habits of sharing adornments with famous female actors were expected and welcomed; or maybe they would not have been a big deal. On the other hand, like the other ambivalent representations of Baldwin the Arap, Baldwin the Lion, and Baldwin the Yamyam, this one contains a disturbing element that seems not to have been lost on Baldwin given his bristling responses in the interview.

Quite a different focus on Baldwin's appearance and effectiveness as the director of *Düşenin Dostu* can be found in Charles Adelsen's "A Love Affair: James Baldwin and Istanbul." A journalist who lived in Istanbul, Adelsen reported on the play for *Ebony* in March 1970. He attended rehearsals and performances of *Düşenin Dostu* and described Baldwin for the magazine's American audience with the flair of someone who wanted to play up the outlandishness of his Turkish location:

Baldwin the director: a Turkish Maltepe cigarette at his lips, a simple bronze ring on a finger of his musically-eloquent hands . . . on the other side of the ocean, at the edge of the Orient, an orange and black mini-scarf loosely tied around his neck, looking up at the bright stage lights. As though tethered to the small, cluttered table before him—it is rehearsal—he takes one, two, three steps to the left, four, five, six steps to the right. The fingertips, like a pianist's, rest lightly on the edge of the stage. (42–44)

Adelsen's piece is much more generous toward the play and its director than Güvemli's but conspicuously avoids mentioning homosexuality in the play and in connection with its director or his location. Unlike Güvemli, who reads Baldwin *through* the play and its "scandalizing" and "immoral" content, Adelsen uses the performance as a background to emphasize Baldwin's celebrity and mystique as an African American artist in the Orientalized setting of Turkey. His article begins with a detailed description of the production's opening scene that gives us his impressions of Baldwin's vision of how *Fortune* and its characters should first be encountered by the audience:

Several hundred people sit in the warm darkness of a theater and wait. The house lights have been killed; not even an exit light lessens the inky darkness. Then jangling bells, a nervous drumming, sounds too loud to be heard comfortably scratch at nerve endings.

No ordinary curtain exists between the audience and the actors in this play. Across the length of the stage are bars; iron, well-made harsh and unpainted bars, the soon-to-rust bars of a reformatory for men; young men being punished by a righteous society.

At stage right, a light gleams through a tiny window, barred of course; gleams, is gone and gleams again. Overhead spotlights pick out forlorn figures on stage. The light at the window—Hope?—gleams, dies, gleams once more. (40)

In Adelsen's reading, *Fortune and Men's Eyes* reveals Baldwin reflecting on social issues that cut across national borders, as his interpretation seems to respond to the famous sentence from Dostoyevsky's "The House of the Dead": "The degree of civilization in a society can be judged by entering its prisons."[88] On the other hand, the play is also part of the larger seductive and exotic scene in Istanbul, which Baldwin inhabits and co-creates. While listing the minutiae of Baldwin's dress, manners, and body language, Adelsen links the writer's persona to his living space, his "crowded" flat located "on one of Istanbul's many San Francisco–like hills": "A housekeeper goes in and out of rooms, a child at her skirts; jazz musician Don

Cherry—dressed in a crazy-quilt costume as for some never-ending harle-quinade—sits on the sofa talking about the music he has composed for the play. . . . Engin Cezzar pouts through the pages of the book *Fortune and Men's Eyes*. . . . The two Cherry children are moving about in circles around the table" (44).

Adelsen gestures at the exotic, even implicitly homoerotic, while refer-encing it with the familiar and heteroerotic—Istanbul is very much like San Francisco geographically, but then Baldwin is having a "love affair" with the "strange, so strangely beautiful, city" (46) that is famous for its "bewitch-ery," "earth smell and water smell . . . [and] green hillsides" (42). As part of that city, Baldwin's apartment has "something of the atmosphere of a *retreat* about it—the sort of place to which one goes, shutting the door behind him, to do a little looking at that curious thing, one's soul. And that tells much about James Baldwin, and says much about Istanbul" (44). By emphasiz-ing Baldwin's celebrity and Istanbul's Oriental seductiveness, but also his "soulful" preoccupations and peaceful abode there, Adelsen effectively, if not entirely intentionally, camouflages Baldwin's homosexuality. This lets him divert his readers' attention from the assumptions of sex tourism con-cerning Baldwin's Turkish exile; at the same time, Adelsen spices up his text with references to San Francisco, at the time proclaimed the gay capital of the world. The reasons for such an approach are obvious: the black queer artist needs to be made palatable to the average readership of the strongly heteronormative *Ebony*.

A sensitive reader of bodies on location, Adelsen also stresses that Bald-win loves Istanbul because he is at his "creative best" there (46). At the same time, Adelsen uses the city to frame his vision of Baldwin in a series of often self-contradictory refractions. To Adelsen, cast against the dramati-cally different and foreign backdrops of ancient Constantinople, Baldwin appears as

> a carefree singer-dancer one used to find in those films made long ago in a never-was-carefree time . . . [a] little-boy-up-after-dark, little-boy-allowed-to-play-in-the-rain . . . a Baldwin infinitely older than *anyone* else one knows . . . very gentleman-of-the-world . . . immensely sadder than one would ever want James Baldwin . . . to be . . . sitting almost child-small on a high stool with the hubbub persiflage attending the opening of a posh new boutique (blue velvet walls, gaunt women in floppy white hats and *fashionable* beads bearing down on one) . . . a man-very-far-away-from-home . . . in a room where Japanese lanterns almost touch

the Turkish carpets, a room with books all over the walls . . . a man, in that moment, awash in a special sort of aloneness out of which the great eyes look past strangers for someone he *knows*, toward a friendship tried and trusted where he can anchor his soul for a while, keep himself from drifting further into the stream of loneliness. (46)

This mosaic portrait of Baldwin as an eroticized and Orientalized man-child-sage is very helpful to understanding some of the impact that *Fortune* and Istanbul could have had on the ways Baldwin was received as a black queer writer at home, especially by the African American popular readership. This audience was largely hostile to his sexual persona, and such feelings clearly dictated how Adelsen wrote his piece for *Ebony*. While the most extreme expressions of anti-Baldwin attitudes found their way into Cleaver's *Soul on Ice*, and some of the statements by LeRoi Jones (Amiri Baraka) and Ishmael Reed,[89] the middlebrow public, black and white, somewhat resembled the Turks on the subject of homosexuality. That is, the general public knew all about homosexuality but was not ready to accept Baldwin's message that the struggle for sexual liberation was equally as important as the struggle against racism and economic inequity. It was therefore quite a feat to place Baldwin in Turkey, on the "erotic margin" of the world, while writing for a popular, image-shaping black magazine, and Adelsen's account elicits our admiration for how well he manages to do his job *and* pay homage to Baldwin at the same time.[90]

By 1974, Baldwin would remark that he felt that, to some of his black friends and audience at home, he was no more than a sensationalist image akin to the one Adelsen paints, an "aging, lonely, sexually dubious, politically outrageous, unspeakably erratic freak," as he describes himself in *No Name in the Street* (1972).[91] His fourth volume of essays, *No Name in the Street* was a product of this period and closes his Turkish decade, at the same time as it opens up new thematic and formal doorways onto Baldwin's oeuvre. His observation about his perceived "freakishness" as an artist signals his awareness that the kind of work he was doing was increasingly opaque to readers who did not want their notions of race, gender, and sex disturbed or mixed up and queered, for that matter. Many among his American audience and critics would never understand that while allowing him relative freedom from racial discrimination and offering venues to explore new formal approaches in his works, Baldwin's Turkish decade helped him to explore, expand, and indeed explode his earlier approaches to gender and sexuality.

43. James Baldwin, close-up with cigarette, circa 1969–70. Collection of Zeynep Oral.

44. James Baldwin and his actors with Zeynep Oral in front of
Sururi-Cezzar Theater, 1969. Collection of Zeynep Oral.

Between *Düşenin Dostu* and *No Name in the Street*, Baldwin would theorize,
rehearse, and stage Americanness as always and everywhere racialized and
sexualized. He saw the erotic as part of art and also as part of language.
In his 1986 interview with David Leeming, Baldwin explicitly compared
writing to making love, even though—or perhaps because—the interview's main subject was Henry James and the entrapments of the American
Dream: "Writing is a private endeavor—a little bit like making love. But like
making love, it has repercussions. You avoid the journey at your peril; you
seal yourself off and do something much worse to yourself than the world
can do to you" ("An Interview," 51). In one of his letters to Leeming, Baldwin
also stressed that one's work and performance in public always reflect one's
honesty in the bedroom.

Baldwin's Turkish sojourn, or his love affair with Istanbul, to echo Adelsen's title, made possible the groundbreaking design and content of *No Name in the Street*, which was for the most part misread, misunderstood, and underappreciated when it came out in 1972. In the next chapter, I read it closely as the key work among Baldwin's writings that describe his trips to the American South. As a safe space where he could confront his most disturbing memories of the South, Turkey helped Baldwin to take on the contentious issues concerning urban space, black masculinity, and homosexuality, as well as allowing him to craft a statement of literary purpose to which he would hold true until his death. As an artist trapped between international exile and home in the United States, which, by the end of the decade, was rapidly becoming a "house of bondage," Baldwin faced the condition of his biblical outcast hero, Job, whose story inspired the title and epigraph of his fourth book of essays: "His remembrance shall perish from the earth and He shall have no name in the street. He shall be driven from light into darkness, and chased out of the world" (Job 18:17–18).[92]

FOUR

EAST TO SOUTH

Homosexual Panic, the Old Country,

and No Name in the Street

I think that there's something similar about all people who stand in relation to a major culture in a kind of disadvantaged way. . . . Watching people on the streets of Turkey and dealing with some of the people who I know here, one's aware of a certain kind of uneasiness in them, in relation to the western world, a certain kind of angle (anger?) to their relation to it. Which echoes something in me . . . because of our own peculiar relationship to the west. It really isn't a good comparison, I suppose, to be a Turk and to be a Black, but in both cases I think that one is forced to examine some things by oneself, outside the context of which one is born, the context of what one's taught.

—JAMES BALDWIN, interview with Sedat Pakay, May 9–10, 1970

When Charles Adelsen described Baldwin's "love affair with Istanbul" in his article on *Fortune and Men's Eyes / Düşenin Dostu* for the March 1970 issue of *Ebony*, he reported that the writer was "at his creative best" in Turkey and placed his comment alongside a photograph of a smiling Jimmy (46). But the cover of that issue of *Ebony* featured quite another kind of black celebrity: the "Star Couple," or the Afro-sporting "Mod Squad's Clarence Williams III" and "wife, Gloria Foster," who "boast brilliant acting careers." The hierarchical positioning of the glamorous African American man and woman in the photograph — he looking sternly into the camera from behind his dark shades, she reverently looking up at him with a hint of a smile — reflected acceptable gender and sexual conduct for Blacks at the time. Almost a decade later, Michelle Wallace echoed some of these hierarchies in the title of her groundbreaking study *Black Macho and the Myth of the Superwoman*. The image of the black man as larger than life, powerful, and virile and the black woman as his self-abnegating helpmeet and backbone of the community informed the appeals of Afrocentrism and Black Power that came to dominate black popular culture and its representations nationwide following the mid-1960s.

Such a cultural and political climate was also shaped by the rise of women's and gay liberation movements. Negative reactions to feminism and to the coming out of men and women who declared their sexual identity to be a public as much as a private issue contributed to the rise of homophobia among African Americans, a sentiment that reflected all too well the prevailing attitude among all Americans at the time. The attendant sharpening of demands for "true manhood," and not only among Blacks, might have been the reason why Adelsen cautiously mentioned homosexuality only once in his piece on Baldwin, when referring to the subject of Herbert's play, and why he refrained from commenting on Baldwin's erotic relationships. The love that had "dared not speak its name" was considered a "white" issue among the majority of African Americans.[1] It was literally glossed over by *Ebony*'s cover photo, which reinforced the only kind of erotic union that was to be named and embraced by the magazine's audience, many of whom would have been uneasy about Baldwin's private life, not to mention his involvement in Herbert's play and his habitation in an Eastern city filled with homoerotic "Turkish baths."[2] *Ebony*'s rendering or "covering" of Baldwin as a queer man exemplified some of the gentler approaches of the so-called black community to their lesbian, gay, bisexual, transsexual, and transgender brothers and sisters.[3] Like other black queers at the time, Baldwin was sensitive to such exclusions from the "race" and by the end of the decade began exploring them in the pages of a new book of essays he was writing in Istanbul, *No Name in the Street* (1972). As he described himself in its pages, he realized that in the eyes of the young militants he was an odd figure and a disturbing image of blackness that they wanted nothing to do with: the "aging, lonely, sexually dubious, politically outrageous, unspeakably erratic freak."[4]

A black writer who became an iconic symbol in the early sixties, Baldwin suffered from what Maurice Wallace calls an "aggrieved socio-visibility."[5] Baldwin was an irresistible figuration of blackness, a curious hybrid of racialized and seemingly incompatible cultural symbols for Whites, many of whom saw in him the metaphorical miscegenation of funky Harlem and the intellectual Europe of Henry James. Fern Marja Eckman, the author of a celebrity biography of Baldwin published in 1966, described him as an enchanting piece of racialized architecture: "Jagged as a sliver. . . . He looks like a wood carving in a Gothic cathedral (not Notre Dame, which he doesn't care for, but perhaps Chartres, which he loves). He is economically built, even stingily, tiny and narrow, so thin it is hard to believe he casts a shadow . . . like a flickering light" (Furious Passage, 12–13).[6] When his famous face appeared on the cover of Time magazine against a jaggedly split white-and-black background in 1963, he seemed larger than life. Still, the unattributed text inside described him in unmistakably sissy terms: "He is a nervous, slight, almost fragile figure, filled with frets and fears . . . effeminate in manner."[7] To the writer of that article, one could not be a freedom fighter and a man when one was queer.[8]

Henry Louis Gates Jr., who met and interviewed Baldwin at the end of his life, stressed that "by the late sixties, Baldwin-bashing was almost a rite of initiation" among black militants.[9] Eldridge Cleaver's infamous Soul on Ice (1968), which does to Baldwin what it accuses Baldwin of having done to the "stud" writer Richard Wright, demonstrated that this bashing had also a lot to do with a species of homosexual panic that spread on both sides of the color line. Cleaver condemned Baldwin's homosexuality as a "racial death wish" and an expression of the desire to be no less than a woman, and a raped black woman at that, that is, to have a baby by a white man. A misogynist, self-acknowledged rapist, and bombastically anxious heterosexist whose sexual ambivalences have been probed by many critics, Cleaver "lusted" after Baldwin's books in Soul on Ice, on the one hand, and reduced him to his "little jive ass," a despised fag's body, on the other.[10] Amiri Baraka, who struggled with his own sexual identification, and undoubtedly many of Cleaver's Black Power peers similarly defined their aggressively heterosexist, homophobic, and inevitably misogynistic masculinity against Baldwin's much more complex figurations of gender, race, sexuality, class, and power.[11] When Quincy Troupe interviewed Baldwin shortly before his death and asked him who had hurt him "the most recently," he replied by adding one more name to the ranks of black men who had despised and disowned him: "Ishmael Reed . . . [who] ignored me for so long and then he called me a cocksucker" (202).[12]

In a curious twist, as Baldwin was losing audiences among mainstream Whites and radical Blacks, by the end of the decade he was embraced by a camp whose members tended to be upper-middle-class white men mostly familiar with his "white" homosexual romance *Giovanni's Room* and the transgressive loves of *Another Country*. Baldwin was perhaps the only black queer who appealed to the post-Stonewall gay crowd who, while often resorting to comparisons of their plight with that of African Americans, created and inhabited an exclusively white "queer space."[13] Between overall American homophobia and what Delroy Constantine-Simms calls the "greatest taboo" in the so-called black community, the British filmmaker Isaac Julien found in Baldwin a misunderstood ancestor for black gay men on both sides of the Atlantic.[14] In Julien's groundbreaking film *Looking for Langston*, Baldwin survives as an image; we see his expressive face carried on a poster; he is an icon, sign, and father figure.[15] As Gates observed, "We like our heroes dead" (in Suleiman, 319). It can certainly be said that, in the United States, Baldwin was buried by many of his compatriots well before his death.[16]

A painful sense of himself as a political and sexual misfit and outcast, as well as someone who was trapped by racial and sexual stereotypes and who became passé in his home country, would last throughout his later career. In his interview with Quincy Troupe in 1987, Baldwin summed up his place in American letters: "It's unbearable, the way the world treats you . . . if you're black. . . . because time is passing and you are not your legend, but you're trapped in it." On New Year's Day, 1978, he recorded in his diary that he felt caught in a trap that was "cunning" and "merciless."[17] Some fifteen years earlier in *The Fire Next Time*, he wrote about being imprisoned between the "white fantasy" and "black fantasy" (Leeming, *James Baldwin*, 316). He was writing about the Civil Rights Movement and the racial hierarchies that locked all Americans in an international spectacle: "And here we are, at the center of the arc, trapped in the gaudiest, most valuable, and most improbable water wheel the world has ever seen" (141). In 1957, when he first visited the American South as a northern "foreigner" and confronted the workings of segregation, he felt threatened, violated, and trapped in national "history's ass-pocket," as he recalled in *No Name in the Street* (NNS, 61).

Baldwin expresses his feelings of entrapment in charged metaphors that suggest an interesting spatial conundrum. When he revisits his first southern trip in No Name in the Street, a decade and a half after it took place, he describes his inability to "find a resting place, reconciliation, in the world where I was born" (126). This statement on the inevitability of exile, so that he could "walk and talk . . . [and] live without the stifling mask" (126), is also related to the ways in which his larger artistic and social project on race and sexuality brings together American and international locations, especially the American South and Turkey, where No Name in the Street was written. Deeply hurt by the young black militants' vision of him as a traitor to the race, Baldwin undertook in this book a careful analysis of black masculinity in relationship to homophobia on both sides of the color line. He also set out to recast his vocation as a transnational black queer artist who challenged the notions of black authenticity, and especially authentic black masculinity, that left no place for someone like him in the imagined black community, and that, as Kendall Thomas wrote two decades later, "have now become unwitting traps" (66–67). Writing about the legacy of the decade in Sister Outsider (1984), the black lesbian poet Audre Lorde expressed astutely the situation in which Baldwin also found himself by the end of the sixties: "I learned that if I didn't define myself for myself, I would be crunched into other people's fantasies for me and eaten alive."[18]

This chapter traces Baldwin's process of self-definition and unmasking through reflections on race, gender, sexuality, and segregation in the two-essay book No Name in the Street. The first part recounts the circumstances of the book's writing in Turkey and introduces its structure, contents, and context in Baldwin's oeuvre. While Turkey does not feature in the book explicitly, No Name in the Street arose from Baldwin's experience in the theater and his contacts with the culture of Istanbul at the end of his Turkish decade. The second part reads the first essay, Baldwin's account of the traumatic experience of his first tour of the American South in 1957, and focuses on his representations of black and white masculinity in the region as being dependent on a homosexual panic that reflects and dictates specific practices of segregation. The third part briefly considers Baldwin's advocacy on behalf of his imprisoned friend Tony Maynard in the second essay and approaches it as a reflection and extension of the first essay. Maynard's case serves as a springboard for Baldwin's astute critique of transatlantic systems of oppression, which globalize the regional racism and sexual violence that Baldwin encountered in the South.

Baldwin's memories of what he called the Southland could not be fully unlocked and written down until he composed *No Name in the Street* in Istanbul, thus amplifying the importance of this locale to shaping this specific text, as well as his further writing career. Against its generally negative reception by critics, I read this work as a seminal text that links race and gender relations between North and South to what I call "regional homosexual panic" that entered the American literary imagination in the turbulent 1950s and the 1960s. Baldwin's engagement with Turkish culture and politics at the time of its writing and his advocacy on behalf of political prisoners at home and abroad provide rich contexts for his autobiographical encounters with intimate family settings, urban segregation, and racist and sexual violence in the United States. Written during his Turkish exile, *No Name in the Street* provided a safe space for Baldwin to reassess his role as a black queer writer at the close of the 1960s. In its attention to gender and sexuality, it continued the focus of his interpretation of *Düşenin Dostu* and foreshadowed his later, little-discussed novels *If Beale Street Could Talk* and *Just above My Head.*

No Name in the Street reveals the systems of gender, sex, and sexuality as processes rather than fixed definitions and theories and shows them as central to Baldwin's reevaluation of the Civil Rights Movement and to his response to the rise of Black Power and its specific model of masculinity. In 1970 Baldwin told John Hall, "For the past year I've been in Istanbul, writing, as you know, a long essay on the life and death of what we call the civil rights movement" (*Conversations*, 102). It is from Turkey, looking back from the East to the American South and the ubiquitous West, that *No Name in the Street* explicitly links this death to the redrawing of racialized gender and sex divisions between white and black men regionally, nationally, and internationally. It predates important discussions on gender and can be seen as anticipating Judith Butler's statement that "no simple definition of gender will suffice, and that more important than coming up with a strict and applicable definition is the ability to track the travels of the term through public culture."[19] *No Name in the Street* is a traveling text that engages public and private cultures, and its hybrid genre—part confession and diary, part political essay, and part a mock picaresque—lends itself to the kind of literary improvisations on boundary-crossing American identity that preoccupied Baldwin in his later career.

Writing No Name in the Street in Turkey

In the same year that *Ebony* carried Adelsen's article about Baldwin's love for Istanbul, Sedat Pakay shot his short film about Baldwin as a transient resident and temporary exile in the Turkish metropolis. Unlike *Ebony*, which seemed to "cover" or take attention away from the writer's sexual identity while simultaneously Orientalizing him and his Eastern location, Pakay's *James Baldwin: From Another Place* placed him and his black queer body squarely at its center. The film's viewers could see what many in Baldwin's American audiences were not ready to face: at the close of the sixties, while many of his domestic critics and black militants were proclaiming his artistic demise, Baldwin was quietly employing the free spaces of Turkey to generate new work. Shot while *Düşenin Dostu* was playing to full houses, Pakay's film also visually highlighted Baldwin's fascination with men's culture and homosociality by interspersing many scenes of the writer interacting with groups of males in the streets of Istanbul. The scene in his writing studio, inside Baldwin's apartment, also glimpses an issue of *Life* magazine open to the mug shots of several Black Panthers. It is as if they, Cleaver, and his cohorts were not just on Baldwin's mind but metaphorically present in the room with him in 1970 as he was writing *No Name in the Street*.

A long interview and outtakes that Pakay recorded with Baldwin as they were making the film attest as well to the writer's preoccupation with national and international identity at the time when he was composing *No Name in the Street*. All his Turkish friends I spoke to stressed that he was highly critical of American foreign policy; we can hear this in the soundtrack when he mentions the "human hope" invested in America and its record of "bloodguiltiness," ignorance, and "wickedness" as "the most powerful country in the world," which deserves to be compared to fascist and totalitarian regimes elsewhere. He spoke of "a new kind of totalitarianism" and "a kind of color wheel" of American and European racism that echoed the imagery of *The Fire Next Time* and anticipated the international focus of *No Name in the Street*.

By 1970, Baldwin was not only more critical than ever of his home country but also ready to speak of Turkey with more understanding. He told Pakay that uneasy comparisons between the Turkish and black American conditions helped him to redefine his vocation as a transnational writer:

> I think that Turkish people—that is to say, the level of Turkish people with whom I can deal, because I don't know the people in the villages,

46. Sedat Pakay, "James Baldwin at Taksim Square, August 31, 1965."

and I don't really know the anonymous millions of people who walk up and down these streets—I think that it is difficult to move in some way out of the memory of a very glorious past into whatever is demanded now. I must say that, speaking as an outsider, there is something very moving and very exciting about that, something very affirmative. I sense a kind of energy here which may have tremendous repercussions on this part of the world, and even the disadvantage of having had an empire which is gone may prove to be an advantage in some time to come, because something is left to that, to that way of dealing with the world.

What Turkey could teach America, he insisted idealistically, was "a kind of sense of other people and how to deal with other people" that it learned after having ceased to be an empire, a sense that the United States could not yet attain, bent as it was on building its own.[20] As he told Ida Lewis, Turkey also enabled him to find his "master stone . . . [and] to find a way of chiseling out what I *see*" (*Conversations*, 87; italics mine). The new vision on his mind had to do with *No Name in the Street*. He had trouble finishing it, much as he did *Another Country*; and like his third novel, he substantially wrote and finished the book in Turkey.

In "The Price May Be Too High" (1969), an article published in the *New York Times* while he was working on *No Name in the Street*, Baldwin described the precarious situation of the black artist in the United States, where "things are more important than people . . . [and where] incorporating the black face into the national fantasy" can be done only in "such a way that the fantasy will be left unchanged and the social structure left untouched." But the part of American social structure that interested Baldwin had to do with more than politics, culture, and representation. Rather, it had to do with their underlying dimension, that is, the material ways in which the state exerted control over urban space. Specifically, Baldwin was concerned with new legislation directed at the inner cities, the so-called Safe Streets Act which was passed by Congress and partially inspired the title of his book.[21] Having come from and written about the ghetto, Baldwin "fully expected that this act and others like it would be used to suppress justifiable black anger rather than to improve life in the cities" (Leeming, *James Baldwin*, 303). The imprisonment of black activists and the police brutality that followed seemed to prove him right.

While Turkey enabled Baldwin to embrace his queerness, find new modes of writing about it, and to pursue his notions of transient domesticity in a new social and cultural setting, it also helped him to engage a new interest in the architectural and ideological opposite of domesticity—prisons and incarceration.[22] It can be said that he went to Istanbul desperately looking for domesticity and ended up directing a play and writing much about incarceration in what by 1970 became a sort of ambivalent creative freespace in the East.[23] Against the backdrop of the war in Vietnam and the "war at home," the Cold War, the Algerian war, the social unrest in Turkey (parts of which involved the Kurdish minority), not to mention the race riots in many American cities that he virtually prophesied in *The Fire Next Time*, Baldwin wrote surrounded and besieged by militaristic and violent imagery, idiom, and stories everywhere he went. It was not surprising to those who knew him, then, that by 1971—the year when Turkey experienced yet another military coup[24]—he left Istanbul for good and would soon be living in Saint-Paul de Vence, a small, laid-back village in the South of France, which would become his semipermanent home until his death.

A survivor of the ghetto and of police brutality in Harlem, young Jimmy grew up vulnerable not only because of his skin color but also because of his sissy looks, a way of walking with a definite "switch" that was caused by scoliosis, and sexuality that he never hid.[25] Like all minorities of color, he was profoundly shaped by his experience of American social space and by having to negotiate the color lines dividing neighborhoods, restaurants, and workplaces; he saw himself as scarred and wounded multiple times in literal and metaphorical street wars.[26] His essay "A Report from Occupied Territory" presents American inner-city streets as a war zone: "I . . . know, in my own flesh . . . in the scars borne by many of those dearest to me, the thunder and fire of the billy club, the paralyzing shock of spittle in the face; and I know what it is to find oneself blinded, on one's hands and knees, at the bottom of the flight of steps down which one has just been hurled" (*Collected Essays*, 731).[27] Being black in America meant being marked for violence, even as a writer and a dissident, and this connection was clearly understood by Baldwin's friends and admirers in Istanbul, who saw his blackness in the context of U.S. civil rights violations against African Americans. Zeynep Oral emphasized that Turkish intellectuals sought to learn from his works, as they felt that Turkey needed to embrace Baldwin's vantage point at a time when their country was beginning to deal with its own religious, ethnic, and often racialized class issues.

When the journalist Tektaş Ağaoğlu asked Baldwin about his "serious, mature, fluent, and classical style" and its links with his "blackness" in a 1964 interview for the journal *Yeni Dergi*, Baldwin openly linked his writing with the violence that affected both individuals and the whole of U.S. society: "I never spend any effort on my style" (16), he said, "it was important to me to reach a strong and clear opinion on how I behave toward myself. . . . [My] anger became harmful to me. I had to get rid of it . . . to understand what I really felt and find a form to express what my real feelings were." Writing was a form of channeling anger and a form of survival, because "being an African American author puts one in a situation of war," that is, "[the war that] takes place between the social reality and the purely aesthetic interests of the author" (15).[28] While in Turkey and in transit between his many travel destinations during the 1960s and beyond, Baldwin produced what can be classified as antiviolence literature by combining his talents as an essayist, poet, and investigative journalist. This genre of war-zone prose—for example, "White Man's Guilt," "Going to Meet the Man" (1965), "Negroes Are Anti-Semitic Because They Are Anti-White" (1967), "White Racism or World Community" (1968), *The Devil Finds Work* (1976), "An Open Letter to Mr. Carter" (1977), "Notes on the House of Bondage" (1980), "Dark Days" (1980)—combined literary aesthetics with Baldwin's public activism by bringing together oral histories, political commentary, and autobiography.[29]

Despite its focus on masculinity and violence, the very process of writing *No Name in the Street* was rather peaceful; perhaps that peacefulness made the book possible in the first place. Baldwin began *No Name in the Street* in

47. Sedat Pakay and James Baldwin at Baldwin's apartment while shooting
From Another Place, 1970. Photo by Sedat Pakay.

his house in Bebek and continued in the apartment across from the German Embassy in the Taksim Square area. Pakay's film shows a view of Taksim Square from the balcony of that apartment; Baldwin's smiling face is framed with trees, cars, and the urban landscape of the street he is looking at. Brenda Rein, a young African American woman who was then married to the U.S. cultural attaché in Istanbul, Kenton Keith, helped Baldwin to type the manuscript of *No Name in the Street.* He was suffering from hepatitis and could not manage the pace of writing, editing, and typing the final draft, so that he kept missing his publisher's deadline. Rein stepped in as a personal assistant to the writer, a task that had until then been performed by Baldwin's sister, Gloria, who had just gotten married and needed time for her new family. As Rein remembers, after the play opened, Baldwin was in demand socially: "I was busy shutting the door and telling people they couldn't see him. . . . There were not many telephones, so people just kept coming by and knocking at his door." Baldwin, who "was in a weakened condition" and spent a lot of time wrapped up in a blanket in his chair, needed someone to make sure he delivered his work. Telling him, "Let's get the show on the road!" Rein would go to the small, bare back room that was Jimmy's study (which we glimpse in Pakay's film) and type up the pages

48. Brenda Rein mimicking Baldwin's "thinking
expression," Oakland, 2006. Photo by author.

Baldwin had written in longhand. "I was typing so fast that I can't even remember what it was all about," she confessed, laughing apologetically, in
our interview.

Their rigorous labor would last from early morning until afternoon, when
what Rein called "King Jimmy's lunch salon" would begin in the "nice, large
living room." Baldwin would stop working and entertain "his court"—the
people who came by to see him—over food. He had a maid and a cook and
"loved Turkish cooking." He would have company until late and then would
often return to writing; Rein worked for him only in the mornings because
she had two small children at home who were taken care of by a Turkish
housekeeper.[30] If he was not entertaining, Brenda and Kenton would sometimes invite Baldwin over for dinner at their house in Balmumcu, where
he would "treat us like we were his children . . . and he loved our little
kids [Pamela and Vincent]." Rein remembers that Baldwin was sharing the
apartment with Alain, his lover from Martinique, who "was very good looking" and was "very nice" to her; Alain was also trying his hand at writing.
Jimmy and Alain usually spoke French together and were "not very demon-
strative." She stressed that Baldwin's sexuality was not a public issue in his
Turkish milieu: "You see, Jimmy was never, you know, a 'flaming fag,' and
was very private about his life."

Ali Poyrazoğlu agreed and emphasized that Baldwin had a "certain dignity" that kept him away from most undignified forms of gay life in Istanbul. Like Rein, Poyrazoğlu also knew and liked Alain but wondered at how

he and Baldwin managed to keep at peace given that they both had to write; he suggested that perhaps sometimes they did not: "Can you imagine two typewriters going in the same house?" Baldwin supported Alain's efforts and helped him financially; in his letters to Engin, Baldwin refers to Alain as the "child" and asks his friend to look out for him. Baldwin snatched bits and pieces of domestic bliss whenever he could; often he confessed to difficulties with his lover to Engin and Zeynep. Alain would soon leave Baldwin, who would be left to finish *No Name in the Street* ill and heartbroken. His solitude and illness made him despondent and prompted a suspicion that he would not, in all likelihood, ever realize his dream of having a long-term, marriage-like relationship; in his writing, then, he also pondered the feasibility of same-sex unions between men and the social and political reasons that made them difficult and dangerous in his home country.

When Baldwin mentioned working on *No Name in the Street* to the *New York Post*'s Nick Ludington, who came to Istanbul to interview him in 1969, he called this book "a new civil rights analysis." But in the same interview, he also claimed from his Turkish exile that "what we called the civil rights struggle can be said to have been buried with Martin Luther King."[31] While it would not be until the 1980s that he began to express his views on sexuality more directly in essays and interviews—what he had been exploring freely in his novels—the issue of erotic liberation and the ways in which racism and homophobia were inextricably connected took center stage in the discussions on civil rights in *No Name in the Street*. This two-essay volume echoed in its structure *The Fire Next Time* and appeared four years after Baldwin's erotically charged and critically dismissed fourth novel, *Tell Me How Long the Train's Been Gone*, which featured a love affair between an older and a younger man, both of them black. It also marked the end of his regular and prolonged stays in Turkey.[32]

Published a decade after *Another Country*, and like it largely written on the "erotic margin" of the mythical Orient, *No Name in the Street* took further that novel's explorations of racialized queer identity at a time when visual representations of blackness fit the image on that cover of *Ebony* in 1970. It was a reply of sorts to Cleaver's *Soul on Ice*, whose focus on masculinity and power and whose attack on Baldwin betrayed a great anxiety about race and the erotic. As E. Patrick Johnson poignantly puts it, at that time, "reinscribing black masculinity as the site of authentic blackness in the name of protecting and liberating the 'race' . . . [amounted to] making the black thang a dick thang." With the publication of his fourth book of essays, Baldwin was targeting "the dick thang" of all hues.[33]

It is important, however, to note Baldwin's reluctance to link his explorations of racialized sexuality to organized activism and political movements. As much as he had championed erotic liberation since the late 1940s with the publication of his early essays "The Preservation of Innocence" and "Gide as Husband and Homosexual" (otherwise known by the telling title "The Male Prison"), Baldwin resisted the term "gay." He was aware of the exclusion of people of color from the same-sex rights political movements that emerged in the wake of the famed Stonewall riot of 1969, but he never joined a gay organization. As he told Richard Goldstein in an interview for the *Village Voice* in 1984, "I am not a member of anything. I joined the Church when I was very, very young, and haven't joined anything since, except for a brief stint in the Socialist Party." He explained his outsiderism as a personal quirk, "I'm a maverick, you know," but also stressed solidarity with the struggle against heterosexist oppression and segregation: "That doesn't mean I don't feel very strongly for my brothers and sisters."[34]

With the publication of *No Name in the Street* in 1972, Baldwin expressed that solidarity in literary terms and demonstrated his commitment to queering blackness in his later essays as much as in his fiction. His last novel, *Just above My Head* (1979), would not only have a black gay artist as its main character but also feature a whole gallery of queers of all hues. He put his sentiments about sexual otherness rather directly in *The Devil Finds Work* (1976), a provocative reading of American movie classics whose genesis also dates back to Turkey. Writing about the film *Home of the Brave* (1949), which told the story of a friendship between a black and a white soldier, Baldwin admonished in his preacher-of-Eros style:

> And, let's face it, kids, men suffer from penis envy on quite another level than women do, a crucial matter if yours is black and mine is white: furthermore, no matter what Saint Paul may thunder, love is where you find it. A man can fall in love with a man: incarceration, torture, fire, and death, and still more, the threat of these, have not been able to prevent it, and never will. It became a grave, a tragic matter, on the North American continent, where white power became indistinguishable from the question of sexual dominance. But the question of sexual dominance can exist only in the nightmare of that soul which has armed itself, totally, against the possibility of the changing motion of conquest and surrender, which is love. (82)

Love always went hand in hand with work for Baldwin. At another point in *The Devil Finds Work*, which directly continues some of the thematic threads of *No Name in the Street*, he comments on himself as an artist, and therefore an "artificer" in the marketplace of American culture, who was facing "a heavy question": "I loved my country, but I could not respect it. . . . I loved my work, had great respect for the craft which I was compelled to study, and wanted it to have some human use." To Baldwin, being a writer was not compatible with being a patriot if his country was not following a course he could support. He realized that "these two loves might, never in my life, be reconciled: no man can serve two masters" (111).

As with *Another Country*, while writing *No Name in the Street* Baldwin also wrestled with the deep conviction that his life, and certainly his sanity and survival, depended on the successful completion of his works. He hit a low point in 1970. While the crew at Gülriz's and Engin's theater were running full-house performances of *Düşenin Dostu*, Baldwin was recovering from a breakup with Alain and fighting an acute case of hepatitis that required that he give up drinking and smoking and follow a strict diet. As Kenton Keith remembers, it was hard for Jimmy to stick to this routine; more than once he did not follow the doctor's orders. Ironically enough, Baldwin contracted the disease from his close friend Zeynep Oral, who had been his assistant during the production of the play. When Jimmy had found out that she was sick and miserable, he and Ali Poyrazoğlu visited her and brought her flowers; before long, Jimmy caught the virus, too, and his face and eyes turned yellow like Oral's. It was a small consolation to Baldwin that he had a friend who was suffering from the same disease. He was irked by his condition and felt depressed. It was as if Istanbul was losing its magical powers to heal and nurture him. He wrote his brother David about his work in progress in a manner similar to how he had once written Engin Cezzar about *Another Country*: "I just can't finish this book. I don't know what to do with it" (Weatherby, *Artist on Fire*, 305).

Oktay Balamir, who agreed to share Baldwin's apartment across from the German Embassy after Alain had left, took care of the ailing toast of the town and kept him company. Despite Baldwin's popularity among Istanbul's high society after *Fortune*'s opening, "Jim was very lonely. . . . [He] was weak and lazy . . . [and] had lost weight." Most important, he "was not concentrating on his work . . . [and] was slowly abandoned by his friends," who were busy with the play and the profits that it quickly brought the theater company. While Balamir and occasionally Poyrazoğlu took Baldwin out to the famous Club 12 in the Taksim area, where his entrance would be celebrated with a ritualistic performance of the song "Oh, Happy Days," he was mostly convalescing in solitude and worrying about his writer's block.[35] "He

49. James Baldwin with Oktay Balamir, and (across) Mordo Dinar, the Chilean ambassador, with friends (the general manager of Air France and his unnamed girlfriend), Istanbul, 1970. Collection of Oktay Balamir.

was not working at all," Balamir said. To cheer him up, his friends would sometimes take Baldwin to dine in Çiçek Pasajı, or the Arcade of Flowers in Balık Pazarı, a famous street overflowing with restaurants and wineries not far from Jimmy's apartment. They would sit in curbside taverns known as *meyhanes*, where many regulars knew and liked Baldwin and would often buy him drinks. There was the "Armenian lady accordionist" who "adored Jim" and played special tunes for him; on another occasion, a woman wrote a poem and sketched a portrait inspired by his photograph on the playbill for *Düşenin Dostu*, which he later received as a framed gift. Balamir felt truly sorry that Baldwin had difficulty writing. He compared Baldwin's ability to Dostoyevsky's and regretted that Baldwin did not manage to "write the great works he could have written." He would have, Balamir assured me, had he lived longer and been liberated from the American burdens of race. Now married for over thirty-five years and a grandfather of a Turkish American girl, Balamir told me that he cherished his time with Baldwin, whom he considered a genius. He felt that he benefited for life from their friendship and literary conversations: "During those days we used to talk about world literature . . . Charles Dickens . . . and he was reading the book given to him by Hilary Sumner-Boyd [of Robert College], *The Idiot* by Dostoyevsky."[36]

Finding himself confined in his ailing body and trapped in his writer's block somewhat like Dostoyevsky's protagonist in his sanitarium, Baldwin could not finish No Name in the Street the way he would have liked. He saw it as a pivotal work in his career and as being of a genre that defied completion. In the epilogue, he wrote about it as a kind of legacy he was leaving to the younger generation: "This book is not finished—can never be finished, by me" (196). He was so reluctant to let go of the manuscript that his brother David had to wrestle it from him and send it to Dial Press, which had been waiting to publish it for quite some time. Don Hutter, who edited the book, told Weatherby, however, that "there was not a great deal . . . in the way of revisions, just fine-tuning," and that Baldwin was "very easy to work with" (Artist on Fire, 305). But the book had been far more difficult to write than may have seemed to those reading it, and for Baldwin it marked a turning point similar to the one that Another Country had marked ten years earlier. As if echoing Eldridge Cleaver's worst fears about his person, and in terms that resound with those Baldwin had once used to describe the birth pains of his third novel, he explained his condition regarding No Name in the Street: "He was pregnant by the 'Mighty Mother Fucker' and there was nothing he could do but push the book out, however painful the process might be" (Leeming, James Baldwin, 309). More than his other works, this one employed feminine and maternal metaphors and signaled his interest in transgender narrative vantage points, or in taking on a female narrative voice and persona that he would embrace in If Beale Street Could Talk and in The Welcome Table. Baldwin dedicated the volume to his mother, Berdis Baldwin, and to Beauford Delaney, as well as two freedom fighters from the South, Rudy Lombard and Jerome Smith.[37]

Like Another Country, No Name in the Street focuses on the complex intersections of race, gender, sex, and nationality and uses improvisational narrative techniques to illustrate them. Campbell disliked the book precisely for those of its features that seemed to reflect Baldwin's efforts at transgression and innovation, its "tone of a notebook or diary" and "lack of design and chronology," qualities often associated with women's writing; he nevertheless admitted that it contained "many pages of mesmerizing prose" (Talking, 244). No Name in the Street is considered Baldwin's fourth essay collection but actually does not fit any specific genre of nonfiction prose.[38] Given his Protestant prophetic rhetoric and the resonance of his style, imagery, and approach to the American self with the works of Emerson, Whitman, Douglass, and Du Bois, however, the book can be considered a uniquely Baldwinian, black queer variation on what Sacvan Bercovitch has termed the "auto-American-biography."[39] In an interview with the *Chicago Tribune's* Robert Cromie recorded in 1969, when he was in the early stages of writing *No Name in the Street*, Baldwin defined himself in terms reminiscent of Flaubert while discussing his relationship to *Tell Me How Long the Train's Been Gone*: "I am all the characters in the novel."[40] He also stressed his commitment to self-reflexive writing: "Autobiography is not simply what you see. . . . It's happening all the time. . . . [It is] the truth about the person. . . . There is not a way for a person *not* to make a confession in everything he does."[41]

In terms of the book's subject matter, Baldwin's inclusion of homosexuality in the discussions on civil rights, especially in a book that "was a long essay about people like the Black Panthers,"[42] verged on speaking the unspeakable and violating a communal taboo; it was a sacrilegious transgression into a territory whose provenance was black, male, and straight. Apart from the biblical reference to Job and a nod toward his own transgressive lifestyle, the title of *No Name* suggested that "the love that dare not speak its name" should concern African Americans all over the nation. Like his first two collections of essays, *Notes of a Native Son* and *Nobody Knows My Name*, *No Name in the Streets* relied on its author's identity as both representative and anomalous. It echoed his position as the nameless bastard son of slave owners, the anonymous black American citizen of the ghetto, the native son who was identified as "Negro" rather than by his or her proper name in the streets of the nation, but also as the singular poet and prophet, the exilic black intellectual and celebrated transatlantic author who was queer.

As was the case with *Another Country*, the genesis of *No Name in the Street* had something to do with gendered performance, Engin Cezzar, and Istanbul. It opens with the story of a suit that Baldwin mentioned in a letter written to his "dear brother" from New York in 1968: "Between 2&3 weeks ago, I had to fly from Hollywood to N.Y. to do a benefit with Martin at Carnegie Hall. I didn't have a suit, and had one fitted for me that after-noon. I wore the same suit at his funeral."[43] The suit was the required manly piece of apparel at official functions and is the "particular" that appears early in the first essay of *No Name in the Street*, "Take Me to the Water," only to become a larger symbol of the "rupture" that Baldwin underwent at the time. Caused partially by his shock at King's murder, that rapture "was exceedingly brutal and . . . involved . . . the deliberate repudiation of everything and everyone that had given me an identity until that moment" (NNS, 13). After King's funeral, Baldwin mentioned his suit to an interviewer, saying "melodramatically" that he could never wear it again.

It then became a reason to visit, at his sister Gloria's urgent prompting, an old friend from junior high school in Harlem who, having heard that Baldwin had a suit to spare, invited him to dinner and asked that the suit be given to him. "He was just my size," Baldwin confirmed, but that was the only thing the two men, who had not seen each other in thirty years, had in common, as the pleasant visit soon deteriorated into disagreements about Vietnam. The friend's mother watched them in silence, having her "sourest suspicions confirmed" (NNS, 21); as Cheryl A. Wall emphasizes, this scene illustrates the total "failure of language," as "nothing Baldwin says reaches his friends."[44] Thus rendered mute, Baldwin also felt that he was seen by his hosts—and thus by a large segment of the black public—as a traitor to the race and his people. He felt that he appeared to them as someone who was famous partly because he held "difficult opinions" and engaged in activism merely to "sell [his] books" (20). At the same time, he also knew that his churchgoing and war-supporting former friends saw him as a hard-drinking and, again, "sexually dubious . . . freak" (18), and that this unspoken difficulty and his queer identity created perhaps the most insurmountable divide between them.

No Name in the Street met with mixed critical responses in the United States. Mel Watkins's review in the New York Times was largely positive and praised the evolution of Baldwin's rhetorical style, which Watkins saw as having inspired the New Journalism. Most of all, Watkins embraced Baldwin's unique "black preacher's style" that shaped the text. Yet he ignored its preoccupation with sexuality and gender.[45] In a more recent, and much more reactionary, critique, Brooke Allen accused Baldwin of having undergone a "transformation from a thinking, reflecting human being to . . . a sort of Charlie McCarthy dummy who could be relied upon to spew out whatever fashionable radical opinion was currently most fashionable and most radical." Linking homosexuality with mental disorders, Allen blamed Baldwin's lifestyle, his "entourage of acolytes and gigolos," for the deterioration of his writing, for his having gone "mad" on the pages of No Name in the Street.[46] Baldwin's attacks on white liberals in the book have clearly not lost much of their punch, whereas his focus on the interconnectedness of race and sexuality may seem radical or exaggerated to some readers even today.[47]

Leeming explains that by the late 1960s, "White Americans were complaining of Baldwin's 'ingratitude,' and the black militants appeared to assume that he was playing up to them so as to be welcomed 'home.'" Baldwin, who felt that he was doing neither, asked his brother David, "Have you ever known me to kiss ass?" (Leeming, *James Baldwin*, 316). This question is significant, as it echoes, however trivially in its use of common profanity, the focus of the first part of *No Name in the Street*, in which Baldwin remembers his first visit to the American South in 1957, when both his sexuality and race were on the line. Recalling this visit is crucial to his reevaluation of the national and international political situation in the book, but most of all to the reevaluation of his own work at a critical historical juncture. It took fifteen years and the remote, liminal location of Istanbul before Baldwin could face writing about some of the instances of racist violence, sexual desperation, and poverty of spirit that he witnessed and experienced in the Southland, what in *No Name in the Street* became the charged space of the South as "American history's ass-pocket."

The profound intertwining of racism and homophobia that he encountered as he traveled the segregated region signaled a kind of spatially contingent homosexual panic among its population that is the central focus of my reading of *No Name in the Street*. Eve Sedgwick explains that "since the eighteenth century in England and America, the continuum of male homosocial bonds has been brutally structured by a secularized and psychologized homophobia" that has been at play "in the complex web of male power over the production, reproduction, and exchange of goods, persons, and meanings."[48] Baldwin's works since *Giovanni's Room* show how clearly this coupling of hegemonic masculinity—or male power—and hatred of same-sex unions, especially those between men, has also been inextricably involved with race.[49] In "The Preservation of Innocence" (1949), an essay that clearly anticipated Sedgwick's argument, Baldwin described a "panic which is close to madness . . . [and is] concerned . . . with the ever-present danger of sexual activity among men" (*Collected Essays*, 599). In this essay, Baldwin commented on the fear of homoeroticism that pervaded the early post–World War II books featuring same-sex attachments; his remarks were as applicable to what he witnessed in the South in the late 1950s and throughout the 1960s.

No Name in the Street should be read as a climactic text in Baldwin's ongoing project of demonstrating the intertwining of race and sex, and specifically its importance to the manifestations of white supremacist masculinity as based in homophobia. At the same time, it also takes on homophobia among Blacks, as Baldwin tries to situate himself, not always gracefully, vis-à-vis prominent figures of the younger generation such as Cleaver, who reviled him, but also those who were sexually ambivalent like Malcolm X, as well as Huey Newton, who supported Baldwin and spoke against black ostracism of homosexuals.[50] Same-sex love was a difficult and contentious topic politically and also one that posed formal challenges, with which Baldwin dealt by employing the jazzlike genre improvisation that he began to embrace when he wrote *Another Country*. Echoing *The Fire Next Time*, *No Name in the Street* consists of two essays, but this is where the two books' structural similarities end.

The first part, "Take Me to the Water," resembles a retrospective auto-biographical narrative rather than a classic essay. It is introduced with a quotation from a slave song based on the story of Samson and Delilah that became a blues classic popular in the 1960s, an invocation to "tear this building down."[51] Beginning with vivid memories of Berdis, Jimmy's mother, and his paternal grandmother, Barbara (a former slave), the essay progresses somewhat similarly to Baldwin's famous confessional "Notes of a Native Son." Baldwin's narrator also reminisces about his siblings and childhood, triangulating among the American North, France, and the American South between the late 1950s and early 1970s and finally moving toward a climactic section that involves a series of shocking encounters with whites and segregation during his first southern trip in 1957. The pre-occupation of "Take Me to the Water" with the origins of black American identity in the region, the South–North migrations, the architectonics of specific locations, and the body politic that shape the "mind as a strange and terrible vehicle" of memory (10) shifts in the second part.

"To Be Baptized," introduced by a proverb — "I told Jesus it would be all right / If He changed my name" — Baldwin moves in increasingly widening concentric circles from the individual, local-national, and collective lens of the South to a more global perspective on the United States as part of the Western world, which is approaching a fin de siècle.[52] Between the two parts, a careful reading discloses a logical progression of the narrative per-spective from the intimate and intranational to the more general and inter-national focus that helps to place Baldwin's southern journey in the context of his transnational passages. Among other issues, he comments on Frantz Fanon and postcoloniality, relates his experience of writing a screenplay based on Alex Haley's *The Autobiography of Malcolm X* for Hollywood, and protests against the incarceration of black activists in the United States. At the center of this part stands his long-term involvement in the case of his unjustly imprisoned black friend Tony Maynard and his shock at the murders of the Civil Rights Movement leaders, the trinity of martyred black men whom Baldwin so often invoked: "Medgar, Malcolm, Martin." As his own world widens, Baldwin's narrator becomes more aware of the chains of racism binding Europe, Africa, and both Americas, and the prisons that Western civilization has built as much on several continents as in the minds of both its victims and perpetrators and beneficiaries.

Istanbul was the lens and location that enabled that discovery and its articulation, and the city is present in No Name in the Street in similar ways to how it functions in Another Country. It was the nurturing authorial lair where Baldwin could exorcise and embrace his traumatizing material from a safe distance. It was the invisible city that provided a vantage point from which to revision the past and face the repressed memories of the American South that he describes in the first part of No Name in the Street. It was a freespace where he considered his efforts to free Maynard and to speak on behalf of Angela Davis and the Black Panthers, all subjects that echoed in his letters to Cezzar. "To Be Baptized" also reflects the profound impact of the sexual, gendered, and spatial metaphorics of the prison house of hegemonic masculinity that Baldwin explored in his interpretation of Düşenin Dostu. Its openness and, at times, boldness reflect the freedom from public scrutiny and condemnation that Baldwin felt in Istanbul as a queer. As Oktay Balamir said in our interview, "This may sound surprising to you, but Jim's homosexuality was never apparent in Turkey. None of the Turks took him as a 'gay writer.' He met all the top authors of Turkey, including Yaşar Kemal. . . . People just knew but didn't care about it. . . . It was just a marginal issue."

But writing is also a kind of performance, of staging feelings and analyzing anxieties. It is, as Baldwin observed, always about autobiography and self-scrutiny; it is a one-man show. Structurally, No Name in the Street works somewhat like the stage set design that Baldwin insisted on for Düşenin Dostu. That design took time before Baldwin approved it, as he wanted a specific effect of both pulling together and separating the audience and the actors by means of thick steel prison bars that stretched across the stage. By the play's end, no one was sure on which side of the bars he or she belonged—the final curtain was replaced by the deafening noise of the bars slamming shut in the darkness that enveloped the theater. It can be said that Baldwin designed the two parts of No Name in the Street to do something similar to its readers. More than in any of his earlier essays, he was intent on showing that where and how we live matters, that the planned organization of our communities goes hand in hand with the segregation of our bodies, minds, and desires, and that this in turn enforces a national system of racist and heterosexist prohibitions.

No Name in the Street is equally preoccupied with the metaphorical and material aspects of the built environment. Baldwin's literary representation of
the South especially maps out a new way of approaching social space which
the feminist geographer and theorist of visual culture Irit Rogoff defines
as "always differentiated . . . sexual or racial . . . always constituted out of
circulating capital . . . always subject to the invisible boundary lines which
determine inclusions and exclusions" (Terra Infirma, 35).[53] While the South
seems to Baldwin to be virtually "another country" within the borders of
the United States before he goes there, upon his return North it becomes
both a rich source of artistic representations of place and a representational
space that helps him to communicate his vision of the nation. Baldwin's
autobiographical and fictional depictions of the South as a racist hell go
hand in hand with his symbolic reading of the region as a synecdoche for
America, or as the "nation's soul." Metaphors related to place, space, travel,
and architecture inflect his literary imagination throughout the text.[54]

No Name in the Street highlights the vital role of space and place in shaping society and culture, or what the French philosopher Henri Lefebvre
defines as social space that "signifies power at the same time as it enacts
prohibitions and commands bodies" (The Production of Space, 142–43). Baldwin does not so much discover in the South, as comes to see it confirmed
and amplified, that the American built environment has been designed to
maintain racial hierarchies and that these hierarchies also arise from racialized sexual hierarchies nationwide. As Lefebvre suggests, the making of
nationhood through architecture "implies violence . . . of the state" (112).
In the South, segregated buses, public facilities, and racial directives such
as "whites only" emphasize that each race must know its "proper place."
The nation's turbulent history has proved, and sometimes proves still, that
expectations of place must be maintained with violence—bombings, lynchings, Klan raids, and police brutality—as well as with the more insidious
forms of political, psychological, and intellectual control and surveillance.
But Baldwin's confrontation with the southern landscape and built environment does not reveal only the predictable architecture of racism enacted
by segregation and the omnipresent fear of miscegenation. It also reveals
a kind of racialized "homosexual panic" among the men in power, a panic
that dictates specific spatial practices and representations of the black male
body not only for the region but also for the whole nation.

A child of displaced southerners, Baldwin did not visit the American South until 1957, nearly a decade after his flight from New York to Paris. He went there as a returned black immigrant of sorts and wrote in the essay "A Fly in Buttermilk": "If I had not lived in France for so long I would never have found it necessary—or possible—to visit the American South" (Price of the Ticket, 161). Baldwin had described the region before he went there, in an early essay, "A Journey to Atlanta" (1948), which relates his younger brother's visit with a church choir, as well as in the short story "Sonny's Blues" (1957), which has at its center a man's death at the hands of southern racists. After his first trip and numerous other visits, the South features prominently in Baldwin's other works, such as the essay collections Nobody Knows My Name: More Notes of a Native Son and No Name in the Street, the novels Another Country and Just above My Head, the play Blues for Mister Charlie, several essays gathered in The Price of the Ticket, and the short story collection Going to Meet the Man.

The familial themes of works such as "Journey to Atlanta" and "Sonny's Blues" confirm that Baldwin's interest in exploring the region was certainly personal—to confront his ancestral land, as he was "but one generation removed from the South" (Collected Essays, 199).[55] He also had political motivations—to "pay his dues" and witness historic events there—and artistic plans to juxtapose northern myths and his own fears with the experience and perception of actual places and flesh-and-blood people in order to become a better writer. To Ida Lewis, he mentioned feeling ashamed of "sitting in cafes in Paris and explaining Little Rock and Tennessee" while the fight was going on at home and the Algerian war began claiming his friends in Paris, many of whom were Arabs and Africans and "began to disappear one by one" while "my green American passport saved me" (Conversations, 84).[56] Baldwin also went south in a somewhat commercial capacity as a reporter hired by Harper's Magazine and Partisan Review, which paid his expenses as he collected material for essays that they would publish with a view that accounts by a rising "Negro" writer would appeal to their readers.[57] His works by 1957 showed a versatility and talent for capturing the issues of race through diverse genres; by that point he had published two major novels, a groundbreaking book of essays, a play, and numerous articles and book reviews.

Like other writers of color, Baldwin had been aware of his assigned "place in the white republic," if not on the American literary totem pole; he knew that he "was expected to write diminishing versions of *Go Tell It on the Mountain* forever" (Baldwin's introduction to *The Amen Corner*, xv).[58] He felt "painted into a corner" (*Conversations*, 285). As "a Negro writer," Baldwin was presumed to possess expertise on matters southern—that is, racial— by virtue of his ancestry *and* skin color. But his trip to the post-plantation South also implied confronting unspeakable sexual things in the "nether" (so to speak) region of the country scarred by slavery, rapes, lynchings, and recent violence in the wake of the Civil Rights Movement. His racialization as a "Northern Negro" emissary went hand in hand with his sexualization after the recent publication of *Giovanni's Room* in 1956. That is, we could say that already by the late 1950s, Baldwin was understood in the United States to exist within the geography of (racialized) sexual perversion,[59] and this fact said not as much about him as about the ways in which Americans saw themselves as a nation constructed in between the dichotomous visions of North and South, white and black, and hetero- and homosexuality.[60] Baldwin used this knowledge in *No Name in the Street*, which should be read as one of the key accounts of the national psychosexual and racial drama at the heart of that historical moment.

Baldwin grew up in Harlem among African American migrants from the South. His first contact with white southerners took place in the North, too, in the 1940s, when he worked a menial job in New Jersey, otherwise known as "New Georgia," or "what I will always remember as one of the lowest and most obscene circles of Hell" (*Price of the Ticket*, xi). Although the white southerners he encountered there made him feel rage so murderous that he feared for his actions and safety, he wanted to probe their racist hatred and would soon begin to claim that it was destroying both its victims and perpetrators. When Baldwin visited the South a decade later, he felt that he had unlearned how to "act black" while living abroad, that his cosmo- politan manner, northern accent, and moderate celebrity would be liabili- ties and even make him a target. Terrified of the real threat of bodily, and specifically sexual, harm, he saw violence as written into the landscape of the region. Upon first glimpsing the "rust-red earth of Georgia" from his plane, he wrote in *Nobody Knows My Name*, "I could not suppress the thought that this earth had acquired its color from the blood that had dripped down from these trees" (87). The nightmarish image of the lynching tree and "a black man, younger than I, perhaps, or my own age, hanging from a tree, while white men watched him and cut his sex from him with a knife" (87), persists in Baldwin's works following 1957.

But while Baldwin stresses violence and segregation as key factors shaping southern social relations, he also makes the everyday heroism of Blacks crucial to understanding the workings of racialized homosociality at the core of American history.⁶¹ By closely reading several pivotal scenes from "Take Me to the Water," the first part of *No Name in the Street*, let us see how Baldwin, though paralyzed by fear, in fact confirms his agency as a black, male, and queer artist *through* his encounters with and by narrating the racist and homophobic spaces of the South.⁶²

Writing *No Name in the Street* in Turkey a decade and a half *after* his first visit to the American South in 1957, Baldwin recalls his return to New York from that maiden voyage as having resulted in a kind of a nervous breakdown. His reaction reflects the book's focus on repressed memories and illustrates its reliance on writing that imitates theatrical and cinematic flashback techniques to convey what amounts to an oblique confession:

> I collapsed in the home of a friend . . . and, re-living my trip, surrendered to my nightmares, and, as far as the city was concerned, vanished. I could not take it on. . . . While in the South I had suppressed my terror well enough . . . to function; but when the pressure came off, a kind of wonder of terror overcame me, making me as useless as a snapped rubber band. . . . I sensed in it a pattern which I was never, in fact, thoroughly to overcome. (NNS, 56–57)⁶³

Baldwin relates his psychosomatic reaction to the terror of his southern memories while back in his familiar territory, while "in hiding" in New York. His recounting of the events, places, people, and experiences causes him a sensation of having been displaced and erased, of having "vanished" into a dreamscape of nightmares. It is only in between the conscious and unconscious mind, inside the in-between, split-screen-like liminal location between memory and writing, as an "invisible man" of sorts, that he can recount what has caused the terror.

No Name in the Street offers a threefold layering of memories and locations, and this quotation helps to illustrate its workings. First, there is the frame of the story, or the events that took place on Baldwin's first trip in 1957, which are conveyed by means of vivid descriptions of people and places in the newly discovered South. Second, there is the narrative framework for the somewhat repressed and self-conscious recollections of these events that emerges following what amounts to the narrator's nervous breakdown upon his return to New York. Third, there is the place where the process of writing and composing parts of the text unfolds, or the unlikely locale of

Turkey a decade and a half after the events described took place. It is this freespace authorial location so far removed from both the South and the North in the United States that makes possible recalling the most frightening experiences. In such a context, the passage describing the narrator's collapse signals a complex and deliberate design at work in the text.

Baldwin's narrator, who has escaped the southern terror with a suitcase "full of contraband" (NNS, 56), is also a kind of "contraband" himself. During the Civil War, escaped and former slaves were referred to by that term, and Baldwin plays on it to elucidate the complexity of his situation as a northern black writer who must go back to the Old Country like an immigrant to rewrite his people's history. All throughout *No Name in the Street*, he interweaves similar—sometimes mentioned only in passing, sometimes clearly explained—multilayered cross-references and moments of retrospection and introspection that bind his individual story to African American history. This narrative "pattern," which, he admits, he was never to "thoroughly overcome," twists with kaleidoscopic symmetries; at times this technique seems more novelistic than essayistic, with part 1, which describes the past, being reflected and refracted by part 2, which is set in a more contemporary moment. *No Name in the Street* is a hybrid and transnational genre all of its own and, as James McIntosh remarks, "autobiographical in a special way" by means of allowing Baldwin to "imagine what his own place is (racially and culturally and sexually if you will) in the contemporary black and American scene."[64] It recounts the unpacking of Baldwin's repressed memories of the South—that "suitcase of contraband"—and his reflections on the present political situation in the safe space of Turkey. It also conveys his confrontation with himself as a black queer artist entering a new decade and answering his own call to "set your house in order." Baldwin forces himself to account for what he has previously and deliberately withheld from his readers, what he has kept behind his mask as a writer "painted into a corner": "The mind is a strange and terrible vehicle, moving according to rigorous rules of its own; and my own mind . . . began to move backward in time, to places, people, and events I thought I had forgotten" (NNS, 10).

I agree with David Leeming that *No Name in the Street* is "one of . . . [Baldwin's] most original works" and that its originality might be precisely the reason why it has been one of his least appreciated and most misunderstood books (*James Baldwin*, 313). As Baldwin characterized some of the prospective readers of this work to John Hall of the *Transatlantic Review* in

1970, "The very people who clamor for new forms are also people who do not recognize them when they come. Since this is so, the only thing I can do is to work, and see where my experiments lead me" (*Conversations*, 104). When Hall asked him about his "formative influences" as a writer, Baldwin mentioned in one breath three disparate sources: "my father, the church, and Charles Dickens" (102). In another interview after the book's publication, he characterized *No Name in the Street* as heralding a "holocaust coming . . . the story of the civil rights movement up to the death of Martin Luther King." At the same time, he made it clear that "it's not a documentary. It's a personal book—my own testimony" (111–12). Add to this that the work was largely created in Turkey and that Baldwin felt that he had to go east to write openly about the American South, and the reasons for his readers' and critics' confusion, not to mention hostility and unwillingness to do more work than usual to deal with this text, should be clear. As Campbell states, Baldwin attempted to "forge a new idiom" and a "new morality," as the two meant the same to him (*Talking*, 270); this was not, however, what his readers at home expected.

Regardless of the confusion that Baldwin's narrative strategies caused for American readers, his tampering with chronology and sequences of cause and effect, his veiled references to history, and his autobiographical openness that so disturbed some critics of the book should be seen as part of a deliberate pattern.[65] Most significant to my reading, *No Name in the Street* targets the unspoken and unspeakable sexual experiences that Baldwin went through in the South as a black queer and that he had to confront and write about to remain true to his prophetic mission as an artist. For example, the description of the narrator's collapse in New York upon his return from the South is immediately followed by a passage that explains the peculiar way in which blacks and whites communicate:

> My terror involved my realization of the nature of the heathen. I did not meet any of my official murderers, not during that first journey. I met the Negro's friends. Thus, I was forced to recognize that, so long as your friend thinks of you as a Negro, you do not have a friend, and neither does he—your friend. You have become accomplices. Everything between you depends on what he cannot say to you, and what you will not say to him. And one of you is listening. If one of you is listening, to all those things, precisely, which are not being said, the intensity of this attention can scarcely be described as the attention one friend brings to another. (NNS, 61)

The "things that are not being said" signal a kind of social game between men across the color line, a homosocial dynamic that keeps them on guard and makes them afraid of each other at the same time as their relationship may have the appearance of cross-racial friendship. Baldwin describes this as one of the central issues in *No Name in the Street*, which has to do with a pivotal moment in the text, a moment whose importance has virtually been overlooked by critics.[66] It takes place early in the book's first part and catches the reader by surprise as Baldwin confesses to what he has omitted in his earlier works:

I have never, for example, written about my unbelieving shock when I realized that I was being groped by one of the most powerful men in one of the states I visited. He had got himself sweating drunk in order to arrive at this despairing titillation. With his wet eyes staring up at my face, and his wet hands groping for my cock, we were both, abruptly, *in history's ass-pocket*. . . . This man, with a phone call, could prevent or provoke a lynching. . . . Therefore, one had to be friendly: but the price of this was your cock. (61–62)

The sexual and political "things unsaid" between men in this passage are narrated so briskly, with such efficiency, that it could be overlooked in a casual reading. Upon closer scrutiny, however, it is clear that the scene has been carefully, albeit subtly, foregrounded. The narrator's confession of his nervous breakdown and the "contraband," "nightmares," "vanishing," and "terror" that precede it signal that something important and traumatizing is about to be revealed, something that was in fact so traumatizing that it had to be repressed for a long time.

Although Baldwin admits that he "has written elsewhere about those early days in the South, from a *distance* more or less *impersonal*" (61), it is only at a safe remove from the time and place of the event, that is, from Turkey, that he can bring himself to tell this story. Up close and personal, this loaded scene recalls the fears of racist violence that he expressed in earlier works, especially the essay collection *Nobody Knows My Name*, which features several pieces on the South. But what Baldwin describes here for the first time is "the things not being said" between the black and white men in the region. It recounts a private white attempt at *sexual* violation of Baldwin's public black male body. This attempt by a powerful white politician to sexually subjugate a powerless black queer writer echoes the brutal history of the relationships between masters and slaves. The scene is overshadowed by what both men know about but do not mention, that is, the threat of public castration at the hands of a lynch mob should the narrator fail to be "friendly." Baldwin does not tell us exactly how the scene ended, so we do not find out exactly what being "friendly" meant in that situation. We can only speculate about how he got out of it and by what means: By feigning a gentle refusal? By joking about and thus erasing the intention of the gesture? By pretending the whole thing was a misunderstanding? Or, what is scarier to contemplate, by letting the man have some kind of satisfaction? Whatever happened, Baldwin's text makes it clear that a certain degree of complicity, or unspeaking friendliness, had to be carefully calculated into the situation so that the white man would be left undisturbed and the black man safe.[67]

The groping scene clearly indicates that the kinds of knowledge that Baldwin's narrator has gained about the South reveal a closely guarded psychosexual secret behind whiteness and patriarchal masculinity. While confronting his fears as a black queer at the mercy of white power, he becomes increasingly aware of the fear and sexual longing that are the price that white men pay for holding on to power in the region, and not only there. Marlon Ross's theory of "race rape," which explains how powerful white men "enforced their rule [by] castrating, raping, and committing other forms of racial-sexual violence against others as proper objects of violent subordination," is helpful for explaining the larger historical context of this encounter ("Race, Rape, Castration," 312–13). Ross claims that the history of the systematic extermination of black male bodies by white lynch mobs revealed a codependence of racism and homophobia, as it demonstrated an "ironic" instance of homosexual or "penetration panic." That is, lynchings were not simply about race, that is, the blackness of African American bodies, but also about the gender and sexuality of both black and white men, as "race rape . . . *implicitly* insinuates within the normal desire for masculine control through penetration a *normalizing fear* of being penetrated by other, lesser men."

Let us analyze Ross's statement in relationship to the groping scene in *No Name in the Street*. In a patriarchal society, such as the American South with its history of slavery and chivalric masculinity, white heterosexual men maintain their dominance over women by possessing them sexually and by having agency politically while limiting or denying the agency of white women and Blacks. In sexual terms, the men in power associate being penetrated with being feminine or with being unmasculine and nonwhite, that is, with being an object, and hence powerless and insignificant. For this hierarchy to hold true for the few chosen men in power, however, not only women and slaves or former slaves but also other men, some of them white, are necessary. Michelle Wallace explains that "in a male chauvinist society each man is somewhat threatened by every other man's virility" (Black Macho, 71). Wallace's comment refers to the "black macho" type of masculinity but also suggests that all masculinity's hegemonic forms share similar sex and power dynamics.

According to those dynamics, subjugating, emasculating, and making into an "other" some men, such as gays or "nigger lovers," for example, are necessary to creating, justifying, and maintaining the superiority of the few men in power. Hence in the extreme instance of a lynching, destroying a man's sexual equipment destroys him as a threat to one's power as a male and as a potential source of attraction to women, on whose possession and "trafficking" the powerful men base their comparative worth.[68] But the act also destroys the other man as a potential source of attraction and thus a threat to the heterosexually defined men in power, whose sense of their own sexual superiority derives from homophobia combined with racism. Echoing Robyn Wiegman's rendering of a similar theme, Ross stresses the flip side of this power dynamic, or the repression of "the desire to be penetrated . . . [or] the likelihood that just on the other side of aversion is the lure of the forbidden" (315).[69] Having just worked on the Istanbul production of Düşenin Dostu, in which exactly the same mechanism dominated all the relationships between the inmates, Baldwin was able to restage, as it were, a crucial encounter from his own past in No Name in the Street.[70]

Baldwin anticipates this kind of reasoning already in his short story "Going to Meet the Man" (1965), in which a public lynching, castration, and race rape become a formative moment for the self-hating, sexually ambivalent, white racist narrator, who was forced to witness this horror as a small child.[71] Having grown up, the narrator, Jesse, becomes a policeman but, as a victim of racist and sexual abuse, becomes a victimizer and abuser of black bodies of both sexes. Race rape becomes the necessary condition for both his whiteness and official heterosexuality; the story takes place in his bed, when he is not able to have intercourse with his wife until he summons the memories of castration that he witnessed at that "picnic" as a child. On a larger scale, Jesse's story, like David's in Giovanni's Room, symbolizes the individual enactment and tragic consequences of the national myth of the white heteronormative pursuit of happiness. Like Jesse in "Going to Meet the Man," the dirty old white politician that Baldwin encountered in the "history's ass-pocket" in No Name in the Street is a product of this myth at the core of white American manhood. He is the Man, or Mister Charlie, who, regardless of his power, is pathetic and doomed in his desperate attempt to reach out to his black other in order to admit to his humanity and vulnerability, to break through the "things that are not being said." Baldwin never lets us forget that white masculinity thus constructed and enacted is a trap and a murderous weapon: "When the loveless come to power, or when sexual despair comes to power, the sexuality of the object is either a threat or a fantasy" (NNS, 63). This is yet another instance in his works that makes it abundantly clear that artists often "get it" much sooner than critics and theorists. By revealing that the flip side of heteronormative national whiteness is racialized "homosexual panic," a panic shot through with interracial homoerotic longing, Baldwin foregrounds and anticipates Ross's and Wiegman's claims about race rape, white desire for blackness, and the fear of same-sex love.[72] Baldwin also shows how the kind of black masculinity that the Black Power movement embraced and promoted responds to and partially replicates this model in its exclusion of someone like himself.

Baldwin's psychosexual representations of the South in *No Name in the Street* construct it as a geographic synecdoche for America, a special place where national manhood takes on "the spirit" of the nation. His narrator discovers this from a precarious, back-entry, segregated position in which he finds himself when he first arrives in the region. He faces there his somewhat privileged position as a black northerner visiting the South—his relatively better social position than that of most southern Blacks and many Whites—and his fear of being discovered as a Yankee "foreigner" as soon as he begins to speak or fails to observe the unwritten color lines of the towns and neighborhoods he visits.[73] His first encounter with the Southland is described by means of mixing seductive descriptions of the region as pastoral and enchanting with the terrifying images it evokes given its brutal history of race relations, urban blight, and poverty:

> There was more than enough to fascinate. . . . The great, vast, brooding, welcoming and bloodstained land, beautiful enough to astonish and break the heart. The land seems nearly to weep beneath the burden of this civilization's un-nameable excrescences. The people and the children wander blindly through their forest of billboards, antennae, Coca-Cola bottles, gas stations, drive-ins, motels, beer cans . . . stilted wooden porches, snapping fans, aggressively blue-jeaned buttocks, strutting crotches, pint bottles, condoms in the weeds, rotting automo-

bile corpses, brown as beetles. . . . Over all there seems to hang a miasma of lust and longing and rage. (NNS, 68)

Baldwin's narrator confronts his ancestral roots in what he calls the Old Country of the South, the land that he has known only from reading and family stories. But he realizes that as such it is also a source for his version of the national story.[74] He finds himself in a "territory absolutely hostile and exceedingly strange" (67), but he also feels "lucky" to have been "out of the country for so long" and, in effect, for having arrived in the South as "simply, helplessly, nakedly an odd kind of foreigner . . . [who was] more fascinated than frightened" (68).[75] While affording him a privileged vantage point, his nakedness and foreignness also provoke the groping incident and his first encounter with the segregated urban space in the region.

During his first visit to Montgomery, Alabama, Baldwin's narrator discovers that "the racial dividing lines of Southern towns are baffling and treacherous for a stranger, for they are not as clearly marked as in the North."[76] Upon entering a restaurant that he presumes to be a black establishment, he is rendered speechless once again by an instance of "things not being said":

I will never forget it. I don't know if I can describe it. Everything abruptly froze into what, even at that moment, struck me as a kind of Marx Brothers parody of horror. Every white face turned to stone: the arrival of the messenger of death could not have had a more devastating effect. . . . They stared at me, I stared at them.

The spell was broken by one of those women, produced, I hope, only in the South, with a face like a rusty hatchet, and eyes like two rusty nails—nails left over from the Crucifixion. She rushed at me as though to club me down, and she barked—for it was not a human sound: "What you want, boy? What you want in here?" . . . "Right around there, boy," said a voice behind me. A white man had appeared out of nowhere. . . . I stared at him blankly. He watched me steadily, with a kind of suspended menace. . . . He was pointing to the colored entrance. And this was a dreadful moment—as brief as lightning, and far more illuminating. . . . I found myself in a small cubicle, with one electric light. (71–73)[77]

This near-slapstick encounter with what Craig E. Barton terms "America's dual racial landscape" depicts Baldwin's "foreign" narrator negotiating southern segregated urban space.[78] It describes a transition from a moment of danger, when Baldwin trespasses into the forbidden white space, to a moment of suspended menace and relative safety, as he is rendered invisible at the back of the restaurant, where Blacks belong. On another level, however, the scene's preoccupation with architectonics, its placement immediately after a passage describing the "unspeakable, despairing, captive avidity" of inmates in an "asylum" for "mad women" (69), invites a spatial reading of the racialized "dividing lines" of gender and sex.

Dell Upton, a historian and theorist of architecture and the urban environment, explains that the built environment and its various forms serve as registers of national identity: "Architecture is an art of social story-telling, a means for shaping American society and culture and for 'annotating' social actions by creating appropriate settings for it."[79] As an "appropriate setting" for enforcing racism, the segregated public spaces in the South prevent proximity between bodies that have been color-coded as different. Segregation was set up to ostensibly maintain the myth of white heterosexual homogeneity and purity, that is, to prevent socializing across the color lines and thus to prevent miscegenation, otherwise known in Thomas Jefferson's hypocritical pre–Civil War idiom as racial "amalgamation." But given the rich spectrum of mixed-race people he encounters, Baldwin indicates that the threat of interracial romance is only a pretense, a smokescreen for the real reason for segregation: "Because the South is . . . so closed a community . . . the prohibition, precisely, of the social mingling revealed the extent of the sexual amalgamation" (79). The other reason for the existence of back entries to restaurants, waiting rooms, and restrooms, for having whites-only drinking fountains and other strictly divided and policed public facilities, is the unspeakable threat of what cannot be controlled and eradicated. He discovers that just as the fear of miscegenation has to do with the fear of blackness and the erotic, so does the fear of homosexual desire. Homoerotic desire and same-sex love between men, including love between white and black men, are the unnameable and the unspoken, the ultimate assault on male whiteness and nationhood.

As John Howard Griffin reports in his troubling account of passing as an African American in Black like Me (1960), segregated facilities in the South were routinely used to frame and entrap as "perverts" and thus expose, compromise, and render useless many civil rights activists. But this tyranny of social space and sex spilled over into the ranks of the movement's activists. Baldwin, who was known as "Martin Luther Queen" and regarded with caution by the main leaders and organizers of the civil rights events, including King himself, was not asked to speak during the march on Washington in 1963. It says something about the segregation of homosexuals on both sides of the color line, too, that the march was organized by another black queer man, Bayard Rustin, who was asked to keep his identity hidden and was prevented from taking credit for his hard work.[80] As if echoing this discovery of the closet in which both black and white men have locked themselves for fear of their brothers, and foremost for fear of themselves as erotic beings, the black gay poet Essex Hemphill stated two decades after *No Name in the Street* was published: "I discovered any man can be seduced — even if the price is humiliation or death for the seducer" (*Brother to Brother*, xxviii).

Let us return to the restaurant scene, where Baldwin sketches a loaded picture of segregation by means of architectonic descriptions that juxtapose not only black and white bodies but also compulsory heterosexuality and forbidden homoerotic desire. The man who directs Baldwin to the restaurant's back entrance with all the kindness "expected from a guide in hell" cannot follow him there, just as Baldwin's frightened narrator cannot enter the man's white space (72). The white man cannot be kinder to the black man, no matter how much he might have wanted to be, because their public relationship is defined by the "suspended menace" of racism and homophobia. This means that any attempt at more intimate contact or closeness between men's bodies is impossible; the only closeness takes place through acts of violence, acts that in his essay on black writing ("Alas, Poor Richard," 1961) Baldwin sees as standing in for sex. Strict segregation breeds near madness, as Baldwin demonstrates in his powerful depiction of sexual abuse and confusion experienced by Jesse, the white racist deputy in "Going to Meet the Man."

Marlon Ross's theory of "race rape" as an unspeakable condition of American homosociality helps once again to demonstrate the workings of the strict grid of gendered, sexual, and racial symmetries operating here: "The male who fears beating up a faggot cannot be truly masculine, must be a faggot himself. The man who fears lynching the black man risks being identified with the black man" ("Race, Rape, Castration," 315). When in *Soul on Ice* Eldridge Cleaver comments on Richard Wright's descriptions of "the practice by Negro youths of going 'punk-hunting'" — a practice that echoes similar pursuits by Vivaldo and his peers in *Another Country* — he admits that it seemed "not unrelated . . . to the ritualistic lynchings and castrations inflicted on Southern blacks by Southern whites" (105). This comment, and a French kiss Cleaver shared with Baldwin at a party where Huey Newton saw them, were perhaps among the reasons that made Baldwin treat Cleaver in surprisingly kind and generous ways when he wrote about him in *No Name* in the Street (170–72).[81] Rather than taking his revenge on Cleaver, Baldwin called him "valuable and rare," perhaps because he understood the contradictions and pain behind Cleaver's assault; Baldwin knew, perhaps, that in assaulting him, the older black male artist, the angry young man was also assaulting a part of himself.

While No Name in the Street reveals a homosexual panic at the heart of white masculinity, it also suggests that in their violent, racist-homophobic paranoia, the fraternity of white men precludes any real male friendships based on emotional and bodily closeness among themselves. This is the price for keeping alive their outspoken bond of presumed superiority over Blacks, gays, and women. The restaurant scene suggests also that although the black man remains the haunted victim of such a dysfunctional model American manhood, he is nevertheless endowed with superior powers of vision and self-knowledge. This is so because of his positioning as a victim and survivor of this social order, as someone who, by knowing more and having learned from the tragedy of his origins, ends up seeing and understanding more, being more masculine and, in effect, more American, in Baldwin's eyes.

What I am suggesting here is that Baldwin scripts a curious reversal of gender, race, and sex hierarchies in No Name in the Street and that he does so by means of carefully orchestrated settings in which black and white men come into contact. In the scene in the restaurant, Baldwin's narrator emerges unscathed from his first encounter with southern segregation because he allows the dynamics of space to take precedence over speech. He is in fact rendered mute by the encounter with the "hatchet face" and the "guide in hell"; he says nothing in self-defense, as he fears recognition and retribution as a regional trespasser, or a northerner whose speech and manner would immediately give him away. He is then relegated to an inferior space in the back, where he passes through the "colored entrance." The backside of the building, literally the rear or posterior part of the place whose front door services white men, contains a "small cubicle, with one electric light, and a counter, with, perhaps, four or five stools" (73). Still silent and intent on looking, the narrator finds this place a surprisingly advantageous if traumatizing vantage point. Now he can see the whites' separate room very well; he is "close enough to touch them . . . close enough to kill them all."[82]

Seen through a window covered with "cage-wire mesh" (73), the white men in the frontal space of the restaurant appear to be creatures on display locked in perpetual, self-conscious competition with each other. They seem condemned to what amounts to a closet, with the "hatchet-face" server—Baldwin's grotesque specimen of white southern womanhood in distress—overseeing the slow annihilation of their manhood. Ostensibly put in place to prevent Blacks from having access to Whites, and *not* vice versa given the national history of its violent enforcement, segregation works rather more complexly as a set of spatial practices, that is, on the level of how bodies interact with and negotiate social space around them. What Baldwin's narrator is able to glimpse from his backroom vantage point is that racial segregation keeps whites locked up, too.[83] They become their own jailers because maintaining white heterosexist patriarchal superiority can be enforced only by denying their own humanity as much as that of the Blacks. They end up imprisoned in their own "malevolent poverty of spirit" (78).

In its oblique celebration of the charged "backside" vantage point on race, sex, and social space, Baldwin's text gestures toward reading it within the field of explorations of the homoerotic possibilities and locations—discursive and anatomical—in the work of queer studies scholars in the early modern era.[84] While an exposition that would do justice to the fascinating arguments on the historical instances and literary employments of the notion of the "posterior," gender inversion, social order, servitude, mastery, and transgender performance is well outside the scope of this study, I would nevertheless like to pause momentarily at this unexpected critical juncture.[85] Baldwin's rich and underexplored politics and poetics of place and space invite approaching his works as compelling "occasions of criticism"—to use Ken Warren's term—across academic disciplines.[86] As a writer who pioneered theorizing sexuality in terms that have by now become familiar to scholars and students of queer studies, Baldwin was aware of the profound links between historical periods and literary traditions that shaped the American regional and national imaginary of race and sex.[87]

Therefore it is important to point out certain obvious historical and discursive links between the early modern notions of power, self, enslavement, and sexual conduct and those that English Protestant immigrants brought to, and transformed in, the New World in the seventeenth, eighteenth, and nineteenth centuries. As the works of historians and literary scholars of American sexuality and gender demonstrate, the historical imprint of the ideologies of conduct in early modern English culture was carried and adapted through the centuries in the colonies and then throughout the United States. It survived and evolved into the nineteenth- and twentieth-century period that witnessed not only the end of slavery, Reconstruction, and its blood-soaked aftermath in the time of Ku Klux Klan raids and widespread lynching but also the birth of heterosexuality and homosexuality as definable practices, as the followers of Michel Foucault have demonstrated. Hence the landscape of power and desire that Baldwin encountered in the Southland in No Name in the Street reflected the topographies of what the early modern studies scholar Nicholas F. Radel terms the crossbreeding of the "discourses of erotic behavior with ideologies of social control" ("Can the Sodomite Speak?" 151).[88] Given the impact of race on the historical, literary, and popular representations of American identity, Baldwin's transgressive vantage point at the rear of that segregated restaurant in Montgomery enabled a compelling diagnosis of its psychosexual underpinnings in the 1950s.

Baldwin's notion in No Name in the Street that the South is the nation's "asspocket" echoes the early modern notion of "ass" in terms of the politics of location and body politic. That is, "ass" signifies both geographic location and narrative vantage in No Name in the Street as a text that privileges a gay and queer perspective of color. As Mario DiGangi explains, "'Ass' can signify at once the beast of burden and the bodily locus of disciplinary/sexual subordination: a convergence of servitude and eroticism that becomes particularly meaningful within early modern discourse of male service" (Homoerotics, 65). Baldwin's penetrating insights on white masculinity are based precisely in his postslavery, contraband status and segregated location as a black man. His "expertise" on race and sexuality and his exposure of the homosexual panic in the midst of white supremacy constitute a clear violation or inversion of the existing social order. That is, as a black queer artist, he is the "black boy," mule-man-slave, "beast of burden," and contraband who has upstaged, if not threatened, his victimizer with metaphorical penetration. In an act of preposterous literary inversion, he has usurped, albeit only momentarily, the position of power that has been reserved for "the Man."[89]

But this position is an ambivalent one. Later, when Baldwin describes his arrival at the Montgomery airport during his first southern trip, he experiences another instance of this kind of marked and privileged "back-entry" vision. He describes becoming a "marked man in the South—all you have to do, in fact, is go there" (NNS, 76), by virtue of entering that geographic location, when he is confronted "on the morning of [his] first arrival, by three more or less senior citizens, metallic of color and decidedly sparing of speech" (77). Being the "only thing, of any color, to descend from that plane," he relates being watched by them:

It was eerie and instructive to realize that, though these were human beings like myself, I could not expect them to respond to any human request from me. There was nothing but space behind me, and those three men before me: I could do nothing but walk toward them. Three grown men: and what was the point of this pathetic, boys-together, John Wayne stance? . . . The plane had landed and here I was—and what did they suppose they could do about it now? short, of course, of murdering every black passenger who arrived, or bombing the airport. . . . They watching me all the while, the MIA car drove up. And if the eyes of those men had had the power to pulverize that car, it would have been done, exactly as, in the Bible, the wicked city is leveled. (77–78)

As in the restaurant scene, being a "marked" man implies for the narrator the obvious dangers of bodily harm and sexual violence at the same time as it connotes advantageous vision and superior ability to negotiate and read segregated social space and national history. But the price for such an ocular, spatial, and ontological advantage is terror: "I was carrying my typewriter, which suddenly seemed very heavy. I was frightened. The way they watched me frightened me. Their silence frightened me" (77). Unlike in the restaurant scene, in Montgomery, "the cradle of the Confederacy, the whitest town this side of Casablanca, and one of the most wretched on the face of the earth" (78), the narrator cannot pass for a black southerner who has stumbled toward the white entry by mistake. Contextualized within telling references to the biblical Sodom—"the wicked city"—the narrator's arrival in the South is narrated as almost comical and seems like a scene from a 1950s Cold War western. We behold little Baldwin stumbling under the weight of his typewriter in a mock walk down toward the John Wayne–like white men. Clearly auto-ironic, the passage renders white men as inanimate objects, metallic robots, and mindless weapons of the Man. This allows Baldwin's black queer narrator to assert his manhood, albeit momentarily, at the same time as it reveals the absurdity of this gendered and racialized construction.

When Baldwin's writer-cum-warrior looks at the white men at the airport, he reads their faces as "an exact indication of how matters were with them below the belt."[90] By thus enacting a fantasy penis-envy revenge, by emasculating the men who frightened him, he assigns true manhood to nonheterosexist bodies of color and what amounts to abnormal sexuality, impotence, and, alas, in a misogynist-ageist slip, effeminacy and decrepitude, to those aspiring to whiteness: "It began to seem to me . . . that the only thing which prevented the South from being an absolutely homosexual community was, precisely, the reverberating absence of men" (65). By making it an anomaly, by aligning whiteness with the qualities commonly used in homophobic descriptions of gay and impotent straight men, Baldwin suggests that true manhood is contingent on an ability to accept and embrace homoerotic desire and the back entry vantage point. Conversely, queer men of color are the ones who possess the secret of the "human touch," redeeming "love," and are able to "say 'yes' to life." (Why else would powerful southerners worship at their feet or be scared of them?) Baldwin might be gesturing toward strategic essentialism about sexuality and race here, but he needs to do so to demonstrate that white racist hysteria and homosexual panic make southern males, in fact all males in the country, captives of a sexual fantasy that perpetually emasculates them all, even though its deadly exorcisms target black bodies: "It is absolutely certain that white men, who invented the nigger's big black prick, are still at the mercy of this nightmare, and are still . . . doomed . . . to attempt to make this prick their own: so much for the progress which the Christian world has made from that jungle in which it is their clear intention to keep black men treed forever" (63).

Like the restaurant encounter, the airport scene marks another moment of transition from danger to safety inside the Southland. The narrator's intense airport confrontation comes right before he turns to describing the black people he met on his first trip. Baldwin now seems to be looking into a mirror of animated phenotypes. The South is to northern Blacks their Old Country, and to the whole nation a womb and cradle from which its rich human mix seems to have sprung. Spatially segregated by color lines written into the land, towns, and cityscapes, black bodies bear the marks of racial mixing, marks that demonstrate the instability of these lines. The colors of their bodies and textures of their hair in Baldwin's account take on the hues and tectonic variety of the shapes and surfaces in the region, but also of the human types that Baldwin had encountered outside the United States (79). Such phenotypic richness is a result of sexual violence, suffering, and tragic familial ties across the color line between black and white; sometimes it is a witness to love that dared defy the laws of the land. It also attests to the deeper self-knowledge and the mixed-race victims' ability to survive violation, race rape, and segregation with their humanity intact. No wonder that Blacks could thus with their very existence defy the Whites and produce their queer writer-warrior in Baldwin's narrator, "knowing what they knew. And white men couldn't bear it—knowing that they knew" (80).

The Kingdom's Decline

In "To Be Baptized," the second part of *No Name in the Street*, Baldwin demonstrates that the divisions of sex and race that he finds in the South reflect similar divisions on the national and international levels. Baldwin's strategic recollections of his first confrontation with the South move in the second part to an account of his advocacy on behalf of his imprisoned friend Tony Maynard and to an indictment of "all of the Western nations . . . caught in a lie, the lie of their pretended humanism" in the context of imperialism and colonialism (85). As we recall, the epigraph of the first part, "Take Me to the Water" evokes the roots of *No Name in the Street* in African American folk expressive culture—"If I had-a-my way / I'd tear this building down." The epigraph for the second part echoes black spirituals and biblical and Protestant imagery of baptism, naming, and religious communion—"It would be all right / If He changed my name." Both play with the literal and symbolic meanings of creation and destruction, regeneration and redemption. Like the title, which comes from the book of Job—"His remembrance shall perish from the earth and He shall have no name in the street. He shall be driven from light into darkness, and chased out of the world" (Job 18:17–18)—these references confirm the importance of religious connotations to the message and structure of *No Name in the Street*.

This does not mean that in this book Baldwin simply went back to his roots in the black church but suggests that he reevaluated his approach to Christianity, especially given his contacts with the Muslim world while in Turkey. In an interview with David Frost in 1970, Baldwin reveals how he felt about organized religion and spirituality decades after his early days as a teenage preacher in the pulpits of Harlem:

Frost: Are you Christian or Muslim?
Baldwin: (*Laughing*) I was born a Baptist.
Frost: It's not *that* funny!
Baldwin: It is to me.
Frost: And what are you now?
Baldwin: I am trying to become a human being.
Frost: And what does one know when one's reached that stage?
Baldwin: I don't think you ever do. You work at it, you know. You take it as it comes. You try not to tell too many lies. You try to love other people and hope that you'll be loved. (*Conversations*, 93)

This exchange emphasizes Baldwin's ability to find his situation—as a black queer who used to be a preacher and now resides in a Muslim country—comical at times. He tries to define his multiple allegiances and to challenge binary notions of identity, especially religious identity in a world historically defined by strife between Judaism, Islam, and Christianity. The publication of The Fire Next Time in 1963 confirmed that Baldwin's artistic project was not to be defined by a narrow religious or ideological creed but was a humanistic endeavor that emphasized identity as process and shedding of established labels and notions as key to attaining awareness and selfhood. At the same time as he proclaimed in that work that it was time "we got rid of" God, he used religious culture as one of the frameworks indispensable to understanding the ways in which race and sex functioned in his country on the level of individual experience and as systems of social control and cultural representation that inevitably shaped that experience.[91]

In The Devil Finds Work (1976), an evocative essay (some of whose early parts can be traced to Turkey) on the American twentieth-century cinema, Baldwin discusses the ways in which the performance of faith in the church and the leap of faith experienced in the theater are deeply intertwined:[92]

> We are all each other's flesh and blood.
>
> This is the truth which it is very difficult for the theater to deny, and when it attempts to do so the same thing happens to the theater as happens to the church: it becomes sterile and irrelevant, a blasphemy, and the true believer goes elsewhere—carrying, as it happens, the church and the theater with him, and leaving the form behind. For, the church and the theater are carried within us and it is we who create them, out of our need and out of an impulse more mysterious than our desire. (36)

Echoing his statement to Frost, as well as what he wrote in the director's notes to Düşenin Dostu, that "all men are brothers," Baldwin separates the institution of the church and its performances of ritual from true faith and its reliance on intimate human bonds. Like spectators in the theater, in the church, believers "create" their "flesh and blood" humanity by means of passion and desire, without which they cannot connect with each other and cannot obtain self-knowledge. That is why Baldwin told Frost that he was not trying to be a Christian or Muslim in Turkey but aspired simply to become a human being. His prolonged stays in the East helped him to embrace such a vantage point and influenced how he structured religious references in No Name in the Street.

Baldwin's references to the black church provide an interesting context for the more panoramic and international vantage point in the second part of *No Name in the Street*. While keeping that in mind, however, I would like to focus on the ways in which they provide an important and unexpected framework for the profane undercurrent in the book's second part, or the places where it echoes the instances of "homosexual panic" from "Take Me to the Water."[93] "To Be Baptized" is dominated by a narrative of the case of Tony Maynard, Baldwin's former "bodyguard and chauffeur and man Friday" (100), and Baldwin's attempts to free him first from a German prison and then from several American prisons. Maynard's story serves as a logical extension, in a northern and transatlantic context, of Baldwin's encounter with the South. Read in such a symmetrical manner, the two parts of *No Name in the Street* offer parallel intra- and international contexts for reading the ways in which white males exercise their power through spatial practices of segregation and incarceration of people of color, what Baldwin terms "a formula for a nation's or a kingdom's decline" and "seas of blood" (88, 89). Structurally and tectonically, Baldwin's description of his arrival in Germany to visit his friend and the account of the case as centering on unspoken and unspeakable sexual allegations closely mirror his focus on the groping, restaurant, and airport scenes in "Take Me to the Water."[94]

When first confronting the prison in Hamburg where Maynard is being held, Baldwin feels "frightened in a way very hard to describe" and analyzes his fear in the context of both post–World War II history and specific dangers facing Blacks that he is familiar with as an American: "The fact that this was the fabled Germany of the Third Reich, and this was a German prison, certainly had something to do with . . . [this fear]" (104). When he is about to see Maynard, Baldwin recounts another instance of menaced vision and empowered insight: "I was not so much afraid to *see* him as I was afraid of what might have happened to him" (104). As if battling the violent images of lynching and "strange fruit" that had pursued him while in the American South, Baldwin's narrator fears for his friend's safety in a German prison but also links his fear as much to Maynard's blackness as to an "indecent proposal" at the core of the criminal case against him (105). The crime Tony is accused of took place in 1967 and involved the murder of a white marine in Greenwich Village. The white marine intervened in a disagreement between three other men: one white and one black, who were together, and a "young [presumably white] sailor." As a result of the marine's intervention in defense of the sailor, he was shot and killed by the black man, allegedly "because the black man had made an indecent proposal to the sailor" (105). The black man and his white sidekick fled the scene after the murder; the sailor disappeared, too. Maynard, who had a criminal record—some of it incurred as a demonstrator in the South—and the common misfortune of being black in the wrong place at the wrong time, was arrested and then released for lack of evidence. Fearing police brutality, he fled to Germany, where he was tracked down by the FBI. Although there was hardly any evidence against him at the time Baldwin found him in the Hamburg prison, Maynard faced extradition to the United States, which he saw as tantamount to a death sentence.

In another risky, ambivalent rhetorical twist that brings together homophobia and black male solidarity, but also a homosocial-homophobic bonding of black men against white men, Baldwin shows his narrator sympathizing with Maynard. Upon seeing Baldwin during the first prison visit, Tony spews out his loathing for gay men and asserts his aggressive black heterosexuality as chief proof of his innocence in the case involving alleged homosexual advances: "'Can you *see* me doing that?' Tony asked. His face was extraordinarily vivid with the scorn he felt for so much of the human race. 'Since when have I even *talked*'—his face convulsed as though he were vomiting—'to punks like that?'" (105; first italics mine).[95] As he says this, however, he is talking to and looking at Baldwin, who as a black man and his friend is his mirror but is also gay and part of "so much of the human race" that Maynard reviles. In a surprising twist, Baldwin's narrator seems to play along in narrating this uncomfortable exchange and by agreeing that homoerotic behavior would be completely atypical of Tony, who is big and black and could not possibly have been caught in a situation like that unless he were "mad."

Given Tony's appearance, no sailor—that ubiquitous target of (white and black) homoerotic desire in popular representations[96]—"would have accosted him," given that "Tony looks dangerous" (106).[97] That Tony would have accosted a handsome sailor is out of the question, too; his only reaction to a sight of such a "sailor" would be "a curse" (106). Having thus presented his friend as an icon of stereotypical aggressive black masculinity, Baldwin proclaims Tony innocent while commenting on the American judicial system as invested in producing fictions of black male identity: "In order to believe any of this, it would be necessary to invent a Tony whom no one knew. But that, of course, would pose no difficulty for the police or the jury or the judge" (106).[98] Paradoxically, then, Baldwin has to strategically uphold his friend's image as a black macho to prove his innocence in a case built on homosexual panic. This is because the person who is the suspect here, "the Tony that no one knew," appears to be someone like Baldwin, a black queer who is seen as a menace to white men in both the United States and Germany.

Just as in "Take Me to the Water," in "To Be Baptized" Baldwin uses himself as a character in his own story to show the reader the inevitability of the trap of racialist and homophobic thinking. When Baldwin sees Tony again, it is after Tony has been "beaten, and beaten very hard," by his German prison guards. Maynard looks almost like a body that has been cut off a lynching tree: "cheekbones . . . disappeared and one of his eyes was crooked; he looked swollen above the neck . . . swelling on his shoulders" (115). This scene fulfills Baldwin's initial premonition regarding German Nazi violence against non-Nordics as an extension and reflection of what he has just witnessed, heard about, felt threatened by, and imagined in his nightmares about the South. In the eyes of American police and to the German guards, Tony's race marks him as guilty, that is, guilty of both an alleged murder and a sexual misconduct, regardless of how "mad" these accusations are and regardless of how Tony identifies himself sexually. No matter where he finds himself in his black body, in the West dominated by white supremacist ideologies, Tony's sexual self-identification is irrelevant, precisely because he is not in control of his identity. Like Baldwin, who was a target of police attacks even as a child—"small black boys have the advantage of being able to curl themselves into knots, and roll with the kicks and the punches" (108–9)—Maynard ends up being beaten and threatened with death for being black and male and thus sexual, *both as*, and no matter whether, straight and gay or both. Paradoxically, then, he ends up being like Baldwin, or is taken for a black sexual outlaw,[99] because in the eyes of the white "police or the jury or the judge," in the eyes of the West, his race marks anything he does as a sexual perversion. We can read Baldwin's shift of action from the South to Nordic Western Europe in the second part of *No Name in the Street* as an attempt to trace sexual and racial symmetries in the social spaces of the South, in the nation at large, and in the wider Western world.[100]

No Name in the Street engages black and white masculinity and homophobia in subsequent parts of the text, where Malcolm X's death and the suicide of Baldwin's friend Eugene or Gene are mentioned (117–18).[101] We have glimpsed some of what the book develops in more abstract language already in *Another Country*, where white southerner Eric's desire for black LeRoy in Alabama has "no name, no name for him anyway" (*Another Country*,

203). As I show in chapter 2, Eric, who leaves the South for the North to escape his family and then emigrates to France, embodies white Western masculinity and aligns homoerotic desire, love, and human warmth with black male bodies. He is certain, that is, that his longing had "dreadful names" for other people, but for him "it had only a shape and the shape was LeRoy and LeRoy contained the mystery which had him by the throat" (204). LeRoy is Eric's first lover; he is older and a flesh-and-blood signifier of the unnameable because of his race and sexuality; he does not seem gay at all but simply knows what to do as someone who possesses greater erotic knowledge. The consummation of their desire—or white male desire for black maleness as signifying transgressive racialized sexuality—takes place in the charged backwoods space of their segregated Alabama town, by the "railroad tracks and the warehouse" or "the town's *dividing line*," that is, the color line. Eric proclaims, having heard from LeRoy what the town thinks, and thinks it already knows, about their relationship: "If we've *got the name*, we might as well have the *game*" (205; italics mine). But Eric needs to learn that such a "game" of interracial homo-love and sex carries with it a risk of death for *both* men, as LeRoy tells the "poor rich white boy": "You *better* get out of this town. Declare, they going to lynch you before they get around to me" (206). It is only by accepting this kind of threat hanging over a white gay man, like a lyncher's noose over a black one, as the price for being who and what he is that Eric is able to take in the "eternal and healing transformation" that his dystopian encounter with LeRoy works in him as a sexual being.[102]

Not by accident, then, does Baldwin have this scene in *Another Country* precede the one in which we encounter Eric and Yves in their utopian house of love, sea, and summer in southern France—a scene, as I have shown, also shot through with references to the exoticized and homoeroticized East. In a long retrospective passage, Eric remembers *both* his first sexual encounter with black LeRoy in Alabama and his first time making love with his white French lover, a former street hustler biblically named Yves. Unlike Eric and LeRoy, who hide in nature, Eric and Yves consummate their love in a hotel room in the shadow of the spire of the Chartres Cathedral, that phallic monument to the power and might of Christianity and the cult of the Virgin (207–23). Although the reader does not know what became of LeRoy after Eric's flight from the South, the suicidal death of his other black lover in New York—Rufus—stands at the center of *Another Country*'s narrative. Eric's erotic history implies that the price of the ticket to white male sexual safety and satisfaction involves negotiations and perils of interracial homosociality. I recall this moment from *Another Country* once again, and in a rather different context, to emphasize that the stories of black men and women like Rufus and his sister Ida, and like Baldwin, like Tony Maynard, and even like Eldridge Cleaver in *No Name in the Street*, make it clear that they pay a much greater price for sexual freedom.[103]

No Name in the Street echoes as well some of the complex stories of racial and sexual violence in *Going to Meet the Man*, especially the title story, "The Outing," "Previous Condition," and "Come Out the Wilderness." Its focus on space and place invokes the careful blueprinting of segregation and sexual violence in the play *Blues for Mister Charlie*, where the churches, private homes, town, and courtroom are all starkly divided into black and white, as much as is the speech, imagination, and every aspect of life in that symbolic southern town. The fault lines of Whitetown and Blacktown from *Blues for Mister Charlie* seem to be imprinted on Baldwin's memory when in the course of *No Name in the Street* he finds himself in Hollywood to write a screenplay for a movie about Malcolm X and soon begins to feel as if he were playing a part in a "cheap drama" (123). In Los Angeles, segregation, racism, and his own story come together as he imagines his black body stretching to the breaking point between the boundaries dividing Watts and Beverly Hills (124, 126–27).

In *The Evidence of Things Not Seen* (1985), a late essay on the serial murders of black children in Atlanta, Baldwin discusses his memory of the South in terms of a complex design of remembering and forgetting: "From afar, one may imagine that one perceives the pattern. . . . But, as one is not challenged—or, more precisely menaced—by the details, the pattern may be nothing more than something one imagines oneself to be able to remember. . . . [But] terror cannot be remembered. One blots it out. The organism—the human being—blots it out" (xiii).[104] It seems that to Baldwin, imagination and memory conspire with the body, or the "organism—the human being," to suppress the most painful and terrifying aspects of past experience. At the same time, he stresses that this is a coping strategy, which, to a writer, has to do with constructing and perceiving patterns or arranging bits and pieces of experience, perception, and literary imagination into designs and models for safe textual display.

In such a context, Baldwin's post-1957 conviction that segregation had disastrous effects on the minds, bodies, desires, and sexual identities of Whites, too, gives this system of racist spatial control a quasi-religious dimension. The betrayal of the Blacks by the Whites gains a nearly biblical weight in Baldwin's rhetoric—it is a tragic denial of love for their brothers and sisters and thus for themselves that necessitates a palpable personal crisis of near-metaphysical dimensions. Carol Polsgrove's study of the Civil Rights Movement, *Divided Minds*, stresses instances of such a crisis in case studies of white intellectuals who were blind to the suffering of Blacks who lived next door to them; despite progressive politics and excellent education, they were completely unaware of "the fact of American life."[105] Baldwin's explanation for this situation is directly related to the effects of spatial divisions between bodies designated as black and white: "Segregation has worked brilliantly in the South, and . . . [in] the nation. . . . It has allowed white people, with scarcely any pangs of conscience whatever, to create, in every generation, only the Negro they wished to see. As the walls come down they will be forced to take another, harder look at the shiftless and the menial and will be forced into a wonder concerning them which cannot fail to be agonizing" (NNS, 84).

To Baldwin, any change in race relations must bring about a reorganization of social space and the ways we think. When at the end of *No Name in the Street* Baldwin boards a bus after a boycott and observes the silence around him, he thinks of a deep and painful connection between black and white southerners, and, in effect, all Americans. The people he observes on the scene, he reflects, "made me think of nothing so much as the silence which follows a lovers' quarrel," as he realizes that the Whites seemed to have been actually hurt and felt "beneath their cold hostility . . . betrayed by the Negroes, not merely because the Negroes had declined to remain in their 'place' but because the Negroes had refused to be controlled by the town's image of them" (144). Confirming yet again the links between spatial politics, constructions of the self, and imagination, Baldwin links the Blacks' rejection of their place in a white supremacist society to their resistance to having their self-image controlled by the Whites. The white identity vanishes once it is no longer anchored in its flip side—the "Negro" whose image has been emplaced at the core of their tormented selves.

In its focus on the homosexual panic underlying whiteness, *No Name in the Street* implies that male nonreproductive homosexuality is a threat to the white hegemony in the West, a crime that has "no name" in any street, on any continent, one that in the eyes of the world deserves the ultimate punishment of death. In this context, *No Name in the Street* seems to be engaged in post-Stonewall discourses on gay liberation and the ways in which homohatred is linked to racism.[106] At the same time, it recounts Baldwin's search for his place as a black queer writer in American and African American culture. The two parts of the book complement each other as much as the accounts of his past and present development, as much as treatises on the inseparability of racism and homophobia. Their titles also add up to a complete line from a spiritual — "Take Me to the Water to Be Baptized"[107] — that links naming to "going home" and foreshadows the confrontation between the elder black queer writer and the Black Power generation that is at the core of No Name in the Street. The lesson that men could and did desire and love successfully one another intra- and interracially, as Baldwin experienced in his own life, may be left unspoken in No Name in the Street, but it is explored as a reality in his later works, especially Just above My Head and the unpublished play The Welcome Table.[108] The final lines of "Take Me to the Water," as sung by the queer diva Nina Simone, who was Baldwin's friend, suggest imminent departure and desire for a renaming at home: "Can't stay here no longer . . . I'm going back home to be baptized." While these lines echo Baldwin's farewell to Istanbul, where he embraced his black queerness, they do not prophesy a return home to the United States. Rather, they foreshadow his transition to a home of his own in the unlikely location of Saint-Paul de Vence in the south of France.

While Baldwin's southern texts shuttle back and forth along the north-south trajectory and represent national identity through the metonymic lens of the segregated, homophobic South, they also participate in a larger project of redeploying the erotic for critiques of white supremacy in the West. If, following Julia Kristeva, we take for granted that classical Western thought locates the origins of Eros in ancient Greece and homosexuality, then there is no possibility of erotic desire without a homoerotic component. As Kristeva claims in Tales of Love, "any eroticized desire (male or female) for the other is a mania for joying in a fellow-being under the illusory presence of a superior" (62).[109] Kristeva's notion of homologation reverberates in the context of Judith Butler's more recent discussion of "melancholy gender": "the more hyperbolic and defensive a masculine identification, the more fierce the ungrieved homosexual cathexis" (Psychic Life of Power, 135, 139). Butler stresses what I hope we have already seen in Baldwin; in fact, reading her through him as someone who theorized black queerness decades before it became an academic term opens up another avenue for using Baldwin's theories of identity today.

Baldwin states in No Name in the Street: "I recognized that the South was a riddle which could be read only in the light, or the darkness, of the unbelievable disasters which had overtaken the private life" (478). This is Baldwin as the Emersonian intellectual, the writer of the auto-American-biography of the decade whose end he encapsulated in the closing pages of No Name in the

Street. The answer to the riddle of the South to the black queer writer shaped by the 1960s is the answer to the national "problem" that he embodies:

> I say "riddle": not the riddle of what this unhappy people claim, madly enough, as their "folk" ways. I had been a nigger for a long time. I was not struck by their wickedness, for that wickedness was but the spirit and the history of America. What struck me was the unbelievable dimension of their sorrow. I felt as though I had wandered into hell. (478)

As Baldwin told Sedat Pakay in Istanbul in 1970, while still struggling with the manuscript of *No Name in the Street*, "In America . . . the eccentric, the visionary . . . the prophet, the rebel, in politics as in art . . . has always been despised . . . so that people hesitate to think their own thoughts." And what is most significant about this inability to transcend "total mediocrity" is that thinking on one's own does *not* mean being "stoned or driven from the village" but only that "no one will talk to [you]; because the great crime in America is to become an oddball, to be different from the people around you." Echoing the slamming of the prison bars at the end of *Düşenin Dostu*, Baldwin points to the ways in which what Americans consider democracy ends up cutting them off from their humanity. The fear of difference, of being an outsider, or a queer, is "much more tyrannical than the fear of the lash or the fear of some physical punishment, because it operates from the inside and it makes you your own prisoner. It gives you the key and you lock the gate on yourself."[110] And so at the end of the play, both the actors and the audience end up staring at the iron bars, mesmerized by their mutual imprisonment.

But Baldwin does not leave us without hope, as he insists to the young Turkish artist that they both have much to do: "What one has to do is try to work on the consciousness of the people. . . . I believe that people can be better than they are . . . that the effect of some people has been quite incalculable." He quotes Malcolm X as someone who "changed the minds of a great many people, and not only black people and not only in America," and mentions a "kind of seed, a kind of depth charge," as what we need to strive for to change our consciousness. In *No Name in the Street*, Baldwin states something extremely interesting about Malcolm, too, something that shows once more how attuned he was to the ways in which gender, race, and sexuality inflect national stories: "There is, since his death, a Malcolm, virtually, for every persuasion" (119).[111] And this Malcolm is in Baldwin's eyes a curious hero in a curious hagiography; he is like the famous European Catholic female virgin warrior, Saint Joan, easy enough to "claim" for all

of us (120, 119). But as such he is also a transgender figure, a hybrid symbol "filtered through the complex screen of one's limitations" (120). And
as such, celebrated and queered, he takes his place at Baldwin's spacious
"welcome table," a meeting space for those who transcend boundaries and
divisions of identity. That space and that meeting, as well as Baldwin's last
play, The Welcome Table, are the subject of the conclusion of this book.

CONCLUSION

Welcome Tables East and West

When you're writing, you're trying to find out something which you don't know . . .
what you don't want to find out. But something forces you to anyway.
—**JAMES BALDWIN**, interview with Jordan Elgrably and George Plimpton, 1984

Baldwin's Turkish experience enabled him to frame the antiracist and anti-homophobic message of No Name in the Street, but it is little known that this book and the specific circumstances of its writing followed him to the south of France, where, between travels and visits to the United States, he spent the last sixteen years of his life. His third play and last completed work, The Welcome Table (1987), originally designed and begun in Istanbul around 1967, was set and written two decades later in his ancient sprawling house in Saint-Paul de Vence. Baldwin drafted the early parts of The Welcome Table soon after the staging of Fortune and Men's Eyes/Düşenin Dostu and the completion of No Name in the Street. Both the play he directed and the book of essays he wrote in Istanbul, as well as his letters to Cezzar in which he rehearsed many ideas and phrases that later appeared in his works, echo in the characters and dialogues of The Welcome Table. The play was later resurrected and finished in collaboration with the African American theater director Walter Dallas, who now heads the Freedom Repertory Theater in Philadelphia. Dallas dates the beginning of their working relationship to 1983, when they attended a party at Coretta Scott King's house in Atlanta, after which Baldwin read to him from the first act of the play.[1] Cezzar, who followed the writing process of *The Welcome Table* over the years, claims emphatically that the play's genesis goes back to the lively gatherings that Jimmy and his Turkish friends held throughout the 1960s, especially during the production of *Düşenin Dostu* and their last sojourn in Bodrum in 1981: "Jimmy *always* had a welcome table in Turkey!"[2]

The rich transnational contexts of Baldwin's last work help to recast the trajectory of his authorship today, the trajectory that many critics have represented in the all-too-familiar terms of ascendancy and decline, or before and after the 1963 caesura of *The Fire Next Time*. Never content with being pigeonholed, whether according to literary critical fashion, or to his race, gender, or sexuality, Baldwin provides the best key to reading his oeuvre in a letter to Cezzar dated in late 1958, which has recently been published in Turkish translation in the volume entitled *Dost Mektupları* (Letters from a Friend, 2007): "I know I don't really need to say it, but I was very sad after our last conversation. Remember what you told me about the water wheel; and think back, friend, think back. We may seem to be moving slowly but the point is, we're moving (And that doesn't say it very well, either, but you know what I mean."[3] Like the ebb and flow of conversation, the changing shades of meaning, and the often unspeakable feelings that pass between interlocutors, letter writers, and readers, Baldwin's works emerging from his Turkish decade resist linear representation. Like the water wheel, they have their own rhythm and demand that we appreciate its jazzy turns and eerie revolutions, that we follow the complex curves of their author's creative process rather than trying to pin that process down to an easy formula.

I focus this concluding chapter on *The Welcome Table* and *No Name in the Street*—strange bedfellows at first sight, to be sure—because putting these works in conversation helps to bring back full circle the explorations of key themes that have inspired my project. Baldwin saw his last play from the start as being about "'exiles and alienation'"; like *No Name in the Street*, it came out of his need to witness history but also to "'get away from . . . the horror of our time . . . to ventilate, to look at the horror from some other point of view'" (Leeming, *James Baldwin*, 373–74). At the same time, he placed erotic attraction, sexual desire, and gendered performance at the center of *The Welcome Table*, aiming it, like *No Name in the Street*, at the "children of our era" who must learn that "love is where you find it."[4] In *The Welcome Table* he wrote against what Joseph Beam termed the "nationalistic heterosexism" embraced by many black writers of his time.[5] Baldwin dramatized in that play the bold creed on androgyny and representation with which he closed his 1985 essay, "Freaks and the American Ideal of Manhood," first published in *Playboy* and later retitled "Here Be Dragons" in *The Price of the Ticket*:

> We are rarely what we appear to be. We are, for the most part, visibly male or female, our social roles defined by our sexual equipment. But we are all androgynous, not only because we are all born of a woman impregnated by the seed of a man but because each of us, helplessly and forever, contains the other—male in female, female in male, white in black and black in white. We are a part of each other. Many of my countrymen appear to find this fact exceedingly inconvenient and even unfair, and so, very often, do I. But none of us can do anything about it." (689–90)

It is in light of this reevaluation of the politics of identity, desire, and representation that Baldwin undertook late in his career, the reevaluation whose deep roots I have traced to his Turkish decade, that we must approach this writer's works as "ripe for reassessment" today, to borrow a phrase from Henry Louis Gates Jr.'s critique of Baldwin's sentimental streak. Gates sees Baldwin as forever split as either an essayist or a novelist, as looking in the "mirror of literary antecedents" and seeing, "to his horror . . . Harriet Beecher Stowe in blackface"; he had become her "true 20th-century literary heir" ("Cabin Fever," 31). But I propose that we reassess this writer's complex authorial ancestry through the lens and locations of *The Welcome Table* and *No Name in the Street*. Like "Here Be Dragons," these works were written by a black queer writer, one who was ahead of rather than behind his time.

Edith, C'est Moi

The action of *The Welcome Table* takes place during one day, from early morning until "round around midnight," in a large Provençal house in the south of France. The play's Turkish and transnational roots can be seen in its cast of main characters, all of them female and, as Leeming notes in his biography, all deliberate self-portraits of the author who by the 1980s "had long since . . . assumed a more feminine character" (376). The protagonist, Edith Hemings, is an intriguing transgender figuration of Baldwin, a veritable hybrid of the charismatic artists he knew and admired in Turkey, the United States, and France: Gülriz Sururi, Eartha Kitt, Bertice Redding, Josephine Baker, and Nina Simone.[6] Given that Baldwin was working on the early sketches of this play around the same time he was finishing *No Name in the Street*, Edith, the famous aging Creole actress-singer from New Orleans, may also have been foreshadowed in its opening and closing pages that are devoted to his female ancestors.[7]

The Welcome Table also features Regina, Edith's old friend who has recently been widowed and drinks heavily (modeled on Baldwin's friend, Mary Painter), and Laverne, Edith's cousin who also runs her household (partially inspired by Bernard Hassell, the choreographer friend and manager of Baldwin's house). Other characters include an Algerian gardener, Mohammed, who was to be the hero of Baldwin's unrealized novel *No Papers for Mohammed*; Rob, who is Edith's "protégé and lover"; and Mark, a Jewish man who is also Rob's lover. There is the elderly Mlle Lafarge, a "pied noir" or a French woman exiled from Algeria, inspired by Jeanne Faure, whose house Baldwin bought in Saint-Paul de Vence;[8] Daniel, a former Black Panther who is trying to become a playwright; Terry, a photographer; and Peter Davis, a black American journalist who is clearly modeled on Henry Louis Gates Jr. (Gates, "The Welcome Table," 318). The dramatis personae section ends with an interesting note on the identity of the characters, which specifies that Regina, Mark, and Rob are "in appearance" and "legally" white, as is, with "something of a difference," Mlle Lafarge. Terry's character is completely open to interpretation: male or female, black or white.

The play's action revolves around Peter Davis's interview with Edith on the day when the household is celebrating Mlle Lafarge's birthday. As we progress toward the birthday party and the late night interview that follows it, we glimpse complex relationships and erotic entanglements among the characters, who participate in various encounters, conflicts, and conversations. As Dallas assured me, Baldwin and he aimed at a more "Chekhovian" than "Baldwinian" approach in the play, by which he meant that *The Welcome Table* shares virtually nothing with *The Amen Corner* and *Blues for Mister Charlie*, which Dallas classified as "folk drama." In its form, flow, and mood *The Welcome Table* owes much to Baldwin's love for *The Cherry Orchard*, as well as to his engagement with Tyrone Guthrie's adaptations and explications of Chekhov's play which Baldwin was reading while directing *Düşenin Dostu*. *The Welcome Table* represents "slice-of-life" theater, dependent on the "Chekhovian innuendos, on "the subtext, the unspoken"; it was meant to show "history happening" (Leeming, *James Baldwin*, 373, 374). But while the play definitely echoed the "biracial, bisexual, confessional milieu" of the "scene" at Baldwin's house in Saint-Paul de Vence (374), it also grew out of and reflected the gender-bending social scene that he was a part of in Turkey.

So...nothing is resolved in the play. The play is simply a question posed – to all of us – 'how are we going to live; how are we going to live in this world with a vocabulary which is useless?' ...orays, frontiers, and flags are useless. Nobody can go home anymore. I can't go back to Greece or back to Africa. I can't even go back to the Bronx, you know. But that is what the play is about. It's not intended to resolve anything."

James Baldwin on The Welcome Table

51. Playbill for performance of *The Welcome Table* at the Academy of the Arts in Philadelphia, directed by Walter Dallas, 1990–91. Collection of Walter Dallas.

In its explorations of how gender roles and the bipolar notions of sexuality imprint and imprison men and women, it took further the focus of Düşenin Dostu on the conflict between love and power, as well as the focus of Another Country and No Name in the Street on interracial and transgender romance and representations of black and white masculinities.

Like the texts framing his Turkish decade, *The Welcome Table* marked a new turn in Baldwin's writing as his time in the East was coming to a close. He was "terrified" of this play, as Walter Dallas told me in a recent interview, because he was trying "new things" in it both as a playwright and as an intellectual.[9] In an unpublished letter to Dallas written on August 18, 1983, Jimmy apologized for a long silence and reported with characteristic hyperbolic flair that he was living under "unmentionable" stress

52. Walter Dallas, Freedom Theater, Philadelphia, 2006. Photo by author.

and was struggling in a "sea of troubles" so vast that he feared drowning; still, he was eager to collaborate on their project. In a note dated March 20, 1984, he asked Dallas to take over the revisions, as he had "nothing to say about it." Almost four years later, just months before his death, he wrote about putting the finishing touches on *The Welcome Table* and cutting it by "about twenty pages." He felt he was done with it at that point and wanted Dallas to "take it over."[10] The letter also dwells on Baldwin's efforts to concentrate on the "coherence" and "precision" of the characters he calls "my people." Baldwin explains that Daniel, for example, was originally modeled on "a couple of Black Panthers," specifically Huey Newton and Bobby Seale, who had clearly been among the inspirations and audience he had in mind while writing *No Name in the Street*. But by that time he had revised his view of the masculine dilemmas in the play—what he calls "our troubles" certainly "didn't begin" and "haven't ended" with the Panthers model; the "ball is in your court," Baldwin concluded. Dallas, who had his own Black Panthers period as he told me, understood well that the dilemma of the play's black male characters existed "outside politics," and he welcomed the opportunity to refine Daniel and Peter in his own way.

The most intriguing part of Baldwin's letter to Dallas is the moment when Baldwin refrains from discussing the play's main female characters because "losing [his friend, the actress] Gerry Page was such a blow." Page was the same age as Baldwin when she died. When he wrote Dallas, Baldwin had already been diagnosed with cancer and may have sensed that he was not going to recover. Focusing on the vicissitudes of his "convalescing" and on how "everything is new," but also "old" and "frightening" when one's body "refuses to be taken for granted," the last part of the letter makes it clear in powerful and moving ways that, apart from a new genre of theater, Baldwin was embarking in *The Welcome Table* on "a kind of self-examination he was not quite ready to attempt" (Leeming, *James Baldwin*, 356). Given the play's physical setting in a house that was a virtual carbon copy of Baldwin's sprawling abode in Saint-Paul de Vence, where he died on November 30, 1987, and the fact that he was working on its manuscript until the last days of his life, *The Welcome Table* can be read not only as a coda to his Turkish experience but also as his artistic last testament.

Henry Louis Gates Jr. describes the welcome table at Baldwin's house in Saint-Paul de Vence in a series of essays based on his 1973 interview with Baldwin and Josephine Baker, which Gates conducted as a young reporter for *Time* magazine.[11] The specific piece of furniture that Gates refers to is the "long welcome table under the arbor, [where] the wine flowed, food was served and taken away, and James Baldwin and Josephine Baker traded sorties, gossiped . . . and remembered their lives" ("The Welcome Table," 306). Nicholas Delbanco, a frequent guest in 1971 and 1973, remembers the Baldwin entourage at his "Provençal court": "a chauffeur large enough to double as a bodyguard, a cook, a companion named Philippe . . . a dancer or painter in attendance—old lovers or associates from some project . . . [who] came from Italy, America, Algeria, Tunisia, Finland. Brothers and nephews passed through" (*Anywhere Out of the World*, 29). As Leeming notes in the biography, the "house itself is a metaphor for his mind, for his many selves" (*James Baldwin*, 376). Baldwin's stage directions for the play link the outdoor and indoor spaces and state that the rooms in Edith's abode exist "by suggestion," with the main one appearing as a "combination" of a dining room and office by virtue of a "prominent," large wooden table that holds the tools of the trade of the author: a typewriter, paper, and books. This could be a frame from Sedat Pakay's film depicting Baldwin's apartment near Taksim Square. As in Turkey, in *The Welcome Table* the space of writing is also the space where social gatherings take place, where the words typed on the page echo the conversations uttered among friends, and vice versa.

Zeynep Oral remembers another gathering at another welcome table in her essay, "James Baldwin: Bir Gün Mutlaka mı?" (Definitely One Day?), which recounts her visit in 1981 with Engin, Gülriz, Jimmy, and his brother David, who were all vacationing in the Anatolian coastal resort of Bodrum:

Silence. Nobody was talking any more. Night was falling over the small cove. The sun was already down and the thousand-year old olive trees were submerged in the darkness. My eyes wandered over the papers at the top of the table that we were sitting around. On the open page of the book the Turkish shepherd was asking the Greek fisherman: "The earth is full of creatures, but they fight with each other. . . . But . . . who turned off the full moon?" I looked at the sky. (Did I wait for light from above?) There was no full moon in sight. Then I turned to the dark black face of James Baldwin, who had started to type again: it was full of such light! (281)[12]

This description bridges the early and late Turkish inspirations for *The Welcome Table*, the vibrant metropolis of Istanbul and the sleepy fishing village of Bodrum. Oral's account depicts Baldwin deep in work; he seems to be a mythical artist demigod lost in time and space. The work he is writing is a screenplay based on Osman Necmi Gürmen's Turkish-French novel *L'Espadon*, or *The Swordfish*, on which Baldwin and Cezzar collaborated that summer. It was the last project on which they worked together; but Baldwin continued toiling, on and off, on *The Welcome Table*, the project that precipitated their falling out soon after its completion.

Cezzar wrote to Baldwin about the screenplay for *L'Espadon* in a letter dated November 13, 1979, where he rushes his blood brother to work and mentions the intended time for shooting the film as July-August 1980; the location was to be Bodrum and vicinity. Cezzar's "director of photography" in Sweden and coproducer were breathing down his neck; eager to land the project and afraid that it might not fly without Jimmy, he blamed the delay on "Mr. Baldwin's work rhythm" (Cezzar, *Dost Mektupları*, 154). Engin begs his "dear Arap" to return to the "old world" at once, or else he would drag him back in person. The book that is the subject of the letter, *L'Espadon*, or *The Swordfish*, centers on what Baldwin had been interested in since writing *No Name in the Street*: relationships between men and how ethnicity, race, and the erotic shape those relationships in international contexts. The novel recounts the friendship of a fisherman and a shepherd, one of them a Turk and the other a Greek. It was published in French as *L'Espadon* (Gallimard, 1978), with an introduction by the Greek author Vassilis Vassilikos. Oral relates that Engin and Jimmy had a clear idea who would direct the film — they thought that Constantinos Gavras, who was Cezzar's friend and also knew Baldwin, would be "ideal," and he agreed enthusiastically. Costa-Gavras was happy about the choice of James Baldwin as the author of the screenplay. He said to Engin: "You and I are so close to the subject matter that we might fall into traps even if we don't want to. Baldwin, on the other hand, can look at the events from the outside. Furthermore he has been through the issues of racism" (Oral, *Bir Gün*, 273). As usual, the friendship, the aura of the place and its peace, worked for Baldwin: "After Mediterranean's smell, taste, the silence of the Torba Cove, and three months of work, the scenario was finished" (Çalışlar, *Engin Cezzar'ı Takdimimdir*, 96).

When the script was completed and Baldwin left Bodrum, Cezzar took it to Costa-Gavras. Baldwin hoped that they would start shooting the film soon afterward, but it turned out that the script had to be seriously reworked. In his memoir *Engin Cezzar'ı Takdimimdir*, Cezzar describes what happened next:

> I took [the script] back to Paris, to Costa. He read it with excitement and called me the day after.
>
> "The story is good, Engin, but the scenario is not good."
>
> I was destroyed. . . . Jimmy's lawyers are expecting advance payment from the producer. I cannot say to Jimmy that [Costa] did not like it and wants to re-handle the script. My situation was worse than the political situation of Cyprus. . . .
>
> I knew Jimmy well. He would be furious if I told him that Costa had not liked his scenario, that he failed and that I would do it. I asked Costa to call him and explain why he had not liked it, so that I would not be caught in the middle. . . . [Then] I called Jimmy. Before I could say hello, he started to shout at me.
>
> "How could you change my script? Where is my money? Where is the producer you promised?"
>
> . . . This was my last conversation with him. After this, we did not talk to each other again. . . . If we could see each other again, we would have made up somehow. We could not. Jimmy was gone. My blood brother and I parted badly. . . . As it coincided with a weekend, no matter how much I begged the American Consulate, I could not get a visa to go to his funeral. (96–97)

Despite this falling out between the Turkish blood brothers, Baldwin retained fond memories of Cezzar and asked Leeming to read to him from their screenplay of *L'Espadon* just days before he died. The publication of the aforementioned volume of Engin's and Jimmy's letters, *Dost Mektupları* (Letters from a Friend), with Cezzar's annotations and many photographs documenting their time together, marked the first appearance of Baldwin's correspondence in print. As Cezzar emphasizes in his introduction, the volume honored the twentieth anniversary of Baldwin's death: "These letters have been burning my hands for years. Saying to myself that it was either too early or too late, I delayed sharing them with readers. . . . [Finally,] I created a book of comradeship and friendship" (7).

The letters Cezzar made available only in Turkish provide an indispensable epistolary record of their extraordinary relationship, and an intimate portrait of Baldwin, who at times appears in them as the restless writer who could not find his place in the world and, at others, as a vulnerable lover who often did not place his affections and desires wisely. In some letters, he is an imperious diva whose personality could test the best of friends; in others, he is a haunted witness of his time, constantly metamorphosing, constantly in flight, constantly unable to keep up with himself.[13] The multifaceted-performer character of Edith in *The Welcome Table* seems to arise from the pages of these epistolary missives; but she also resonates with the persona of Cezzar, who was happy to take on several gender-bending roles throughout his career. By no means a simple sublimation of the two men, however, Edith is a complex transgender character who refracts Baldwin's hybridized Turkish "family" — the threesome of Engin, Gülriz, and Jimmy holding hands on the Galata Bridge — captured so well in the photograph that Charles Adelsen included in his *Ebony* spread about the writer's "love affair" with Istanbul. Part-Jimmy, part-Engin, part-Gülriz, Edith and the play at whose center she stands take us back full circle to the working table on which *No Name in the Street* was written, thus marking the end of Baldwin's Turkish decade.

Black Velvet Revolution

When Brenda Rein was in her twenties and married to the cultural attaché Kenton Keith, she helped Baldwin type up the manuscript of *No Name in the Street* in 1969–70 and frequently shared with him her thoughts on the militaristic stance of her generation. Baldwin, who abhorred violence, would respond with characteristic subtlety to the black nationalists' call to "drive all the white devils into the sea": "First of all, we don't have enough guns!"[14] Rein's and Baldwin's impassioned discussions echoed the themes of *No Name in the Street* and often ended in observations about American ignorance of national history. "Jimmy told me," she said in our 2006 interview, "that Americans cannot think beyond one generation!" Multilingual and well traveled, Rein recently surprised a customs official in Istanbul — where

Americans are not always greeted with a happy smile these days—with her fluent Turkish. To this day, even when she canvasses for Barack Obama's campaign, she channels her friend's rage about his compatriots' lack of self-knowledge and familiarity with other cultures: "You can quote me on this: Americans in general are politically the most ignorant people—the most misdirected and indoctrinated people in the world."

Having fought against ignorance of all kinds throughout his life, Baldwin saw himself as a misunderstood "revolutionary artist," one whom the younger generation of Blacks needed to embrace and learn from, no matter that many of its members repudiated and even despised him. Aware that he was "an odd quantity," he cautioned, "so is Eldridge; so are we all."[15] When he referred to Cleaver and his homophobic attack in No Name in the Street, Baldwin not only was very gracious and generous toward his younger adversary but also explained the generational tension between the dramatically different types of black masculinity that he and Cleaver represented by juxtaposing "the odd and disreputable artist and the odd and disreputable revolutionary" (172). These two types of black leaders "seem to stand forever at an odd and rather uncomfortable angle to each other, and . . . at a sharp and not always comfortable angle to the people they both . . . hope to serve" (172). Baldwin's intervention was to overcome this split by educating his audience, especially the younger generation, about the ways in which ideas about gender and race, or rigid notions of masculinity and blackness, were its cause. As he made clear as late as 1986, in his introduction to Michael Thelwell's Duties, Pleasures, and Conflicts, Baldwin had once been labeled an "angry young man" himself but had learned that his commitment was to making black manhood part of a larger picture—"the power and the glory and the limitless potential of every human being in the world" (xx, xxii).

Almost a decade after Baldwin published his account of meeting Elijah Mohammed in The Fire Next Time, he exhorted his younger brothers: "We need each other, and have much to learn from each other, and, more than ever, now" (NNS, 173). But when he described his experience of writing a screenplay about Malcolm X's life, he compared it to Bernard Shaw's experience of writing a play about Joan of Arc: "It is easy to claim [Malcolm] now, just as it was easy for the church to claim St. Joan" (119–20). By drawing irreverent parallels between the lives, cults, and institutional appropriations of the martyred Black Muslim leader and the martyred French Catholic saint, Baldwin transgressed the boundaries of race and gender, boundaries that were especially sharply drawn in the late 1960s and early 1970s. Like Malcolm X and Joan of Arc, Malcolm X and James Baldwin may have seemed strange bedfellows. Still, Malcolm X, who read and admired Baldwin's works, saw clearly that they needed each other, too: he as a "warrior" and Baldwin as a "poet" of the movement (Thelwell, *Duties, Pleasures, and Conflicts*, 93).

No Name in the Street, written when *The Welcome Table* was first taking shape as an idea and then a sketchy draft, pioneers feminist and queer approaches to identity by embracing autobiography and combining transgressively what Thelwell called Baldwin's experience of blackness underwriting his art (92), and what bell hooks has termed the rhetoric of "talking back."[16] Baldwin's transgender approach may not be apparent, given the book's overall focus on masculinity, but the first sentences of "Take Me to the Water" are proof enough. They offer evocative recollections of Baldwin's mother, Berdis, whom he associates with creativity and manual labor: "'That is a good idea,' I heard my mother say. She was staring at a wad of black velvet, which she held in her hand, and she carefully placed this bit of cloth in a closet. We can guess how old I must have been from the fact that for years afterward I thought that an 'idea' was a piece of black velvet" (NNS, 3). Not only does Berdis Baldwin introduce her firstborn to the power of figurative language but she also emerges as an oppositional figure to his authoritarian stepfather: "It did not take me long, nor did the children, as they came tumbling into this world, take long to discover that our mother paid an immense price for standing between us and our father" (NNS 3, 5).[17]

In this context of gendered power struggle, it is significant that, having examined it, the mother places the "idea" ("black velvet") in a closet. This symbolic gesture signals what her son learned quickly from his stepfather: that intellectual pursuits and alternative ideas were not considered manly or godly and that they had to be kept secret. Because this brief scene opens *No Name in the Street*, it foreshadows and frames Jimmy's subsequent struggles to embrace his authorship and identity as a black and queer male in the remainder of "Take Me to the Water." It also provides a provocative context for his musings on black masculinity in "To Be Baptized" and is echoed in the epilogue, where Baldwin calls on his generation to be the "midwives" of a new world order (NNS, 196).[18]

While eliciting the powerful influence of Berdis Baldwin on her son, the opening of *No Name in the Street* also glimpses Baldwin's paternal grandmother in New Orleans. Grandma Barbara, a former slave who bore children to both white and black men and stayed with the family in Harlem until her death, emerges as another important ancestor responsible for Baldwin's first lessons in figurative meaning. On her deathbed, Barbara gave young

Jimmy "one of those old, round, metal boxes, usually with a floral design, used for candy. *She* thought it was full of candy and *I* thought it was full of candy, but it wasn't. . . . It was full of needles and thread" (4). The contents of the box suggest Baldwin's transgender inheritance; they are a kind of Pandora's box for the black queer artist he was to become. Baldwin employs these tools of the undervalued feminine trade to stitch together new literary patterns of "black velvet," to mend the tears in the crazy quilt of American identity.[19]

Whether or not Baldwin the revolutionary artist thus parades in *No Name in the Street* in drag as a mythical seamstress or weaver—Arachne, Penelope, or Circe—is not as important as the fact that it is Baldwin's female ancestors who pave his passage into a queer or "quare" (to echo E. Patrick Johnson's playful recasting of this term) identity and authorship.[20] As Leeming recalls his talks with Baldwin over nearly three decades, the writer often insisted that his "first and most important [influence] . . . was his mother . . . a consistent source of strength and self-esteem." Berdis remained her son's staunchest supporter throughout his life, and "in letters and at Sunday dinners, and any way she could, she preached the doctrine of love to her son. . . . [She] taught him that racism and hatred hurt the racist and hater as much as the racism's victim."[21] Jimmy's homage to his mother and grandmother as his first guides in the world of human relationships, as well as in the world of literary art, echoes and anticipates the focus on the black family in his subsequent and unjustly undervalued works: *If Beale Street Could Talk*, *Just Above My Head*, and *The Evidence of Things Not Seen*.

Baldwin's homage to black women in these works echoes the slave narratives of Frederick Douglass and Harriet Jacobs, in which mothers and grandmothers stand as central forces of strength, resilience, and love. It reminds us of the novels of Zora Neale Hurston and Nella Larsen, in which race, sex, and gender are inextricably connected in women's life stories of empowerment and loss. It also anticipates the works that bridge cultural, literary, and autobiographical approaches, from Alice Walker's "In Search of Our Mother's Gardens" (1974), with its affirmation of female creativity ("and yet, artists we will be" [237]), through Audre Lorde's *Zami: A New Spelling of My Name* (1982), with its affirmation of racialized and sexualized "biomythography," to Michael Awkward's *Scenes of Instruction* (1999), with its admonition against patriarchy and violent machismo: "Don't be like your father" (37).[22] Baldwin's underappreciated *No Name in the Street* and the works that followed it fall under Nellie McKay's typological statement that autobiography is "the genre of preference in the development of black literary culture."[23] A seminal work in the Baldwin canon that both reflects and forecasts the development of African American literature and criticism on the cusp of the twentieth century, No Name in the Street also anticipates the rhetoric of "personal criticism" embraced by the second wave of feminist theory. In the vein of the third wave and beyond, it dares to queer not only race, sex, and gender but also national authorship.

In an interview with Robert Cromie of the Chicago Tribune, Baldwin paid homage to Turkey and to the Turkish men and women who helped him make the best of his exile in the East. He told Cromie that writing Tell Me How Long the Train's Been Gone in Istanbul taught him that "it's very frightening to be a writer . . . and especially an American writer . . . and an American success."[24] A Turkish proverb that someone, possibly Cezzar, translated assisted Baldwin as he dealt with the predicament of losing his young black audience at home. "The great trick is not to be deluded by your obscurity or by your fame," he told Cromie. "A Turk . . . told me when I was living in Turkey, an old Turkish proverb, I gather. It's a water wheel, by which he meant life. You know, the trick is to hold your nose when you're under and not get dizzy when you're up." The water wheel is a recurring metaphor in Baldwin's works and in his letters to Cezzar. Having recently heard from Sedat Pakay another version of a proverb that uses this metaphor, "Değirmen iki taştan, muhabbet iki baştan" ("The water mill needs two stones, love needs two beings"),[25] I now know why the image of the "gaudiest, most valuable, and most improbable water wheel the world has ever seen" dominates the jeremiad at the close of The Fire Next Time. This is a Turkish imprint on that text that I did not discover until concluding the revolutions of my own project.

During a recent visit with Sedat Pakay, I heard another example of Turkish folk wisdom. When we discussed the reasons why Baldwin loved Turkey, Pakay suddenly laughed and told me that it was probably because Turkey was deve kuşu or like an ostrich. In Turkish devekuşu means literally "camel bird" or "neither a camel nor a bird"; a queer creature, indeed.[26] On the day we spoke, I was also fortunate to view the unused footage from the reels that Pakay shot while making James Baldwin: From Another Place in 1970. The sequence I saw did not have a soundtrack, which I had to read from a transcript. The experience of watching Baldwin's animated face without being able to hear his voice was a little disturbing. But then there were several compelling moments when the silence was welcome, when Cengiz Tacer's camera lingered on Baldwin's features while he was resting, eating bread dripping with honey, interacting with his Turkish cook, leisurely feeding pigeons by the Spice Bazaar, watching men in the streets play games, or

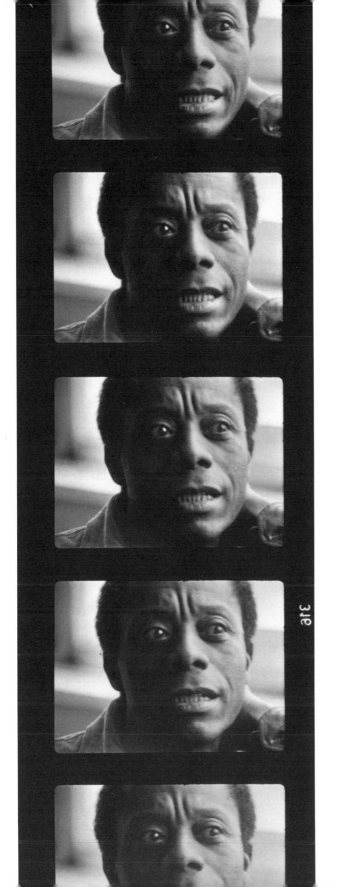

53. Sedat Pakay, *From Another Place*. James Baldwin in close-up talking, 1970.

walking with Pakay. These moments showed a man who was at peace, who savored life's every moment by living in it, and who was both in and out of place, no matter how strange or unexpected that place might seem to him.

Before my trips to Turkey, I had seen Baldwin's house in Saint-Paul de Vence, touched the weathered surface of the welcome table where he talked to Josephine Baker and Henry Louis Gates Jr., and lingered too long in the room where he died. Although I will never forget my visit to that first and most personal of all the Baldwin spaces I have seen, it is Pakay's film and photographs that capture Jimmy's presence in ways that no leftover object, vacated space, or preserved setting can. Let me stop here with the images of Baldwin's face seen through the lens of Sedat Pakay's camera, especially with the moving close-up of his brooding sideways expression.

I am profoundly grateful to all the remarkable people whom I have met around Baldwin's welcome tables east and west. I arrived as a belated guest, who missed the opportunity granted to many who benefited from Baldwin's immediate presence and closeness. Still, as a scholar and someone whose life has been touched and changed by his works, I have been treated to a feast.

NOTES

Preface

1. On the application of Bakhtin's theory to reading African American literature, see also Henderson, "Speaking in Tongues"; Gates, *The Signifying Monkey*; Peterson, *Up from Bondage* and "Response and Call"; and Hale, "Bakhtin in African American Literary Theory."

2. In an interview in the *Black Scholar* in 1973, Baldwin acknowledges his Native American heritage, too: "I'm part Indian" (Standley and Pratt, *Conversations*, 148).

3. Mae G. Henderson, "Speaking in Tongues," 352.

4. Gates, "The 'Blackness of Blackness,'" 698.

5. The voice-over narration is a cheaper technique than dubbing and still widely used in Polish television and on DVDs and VHS tapes. It is an edited translation of the transcribed soundtrack that is read in Polish with the original soundtrack vaguely audible.

6. This material may have come from the English filmmaker Dick Fontaine's and his African American codirector Pat Hartley's documentary *I Heard It through the Grapevine*. It shows Baldwin revisiting the South in 1980 and includes his commentary and meetings with local civil rights activists. David Leeming reports in his authorized biography of Baldwin that Fontaine's documentary was presented on "prime-time television in England" in 1982 (*James Baldwin: A Biography*, 353), so it is possible that TV Poland could have obtained clips of it around the same time.

7. My teacher and graduate advisor at Warsaw University was Professor Zbigniew Lewicki, to whom I am grateful for early guidance and encouragement as I was trying to decide whether or not I was cut out for academic work. Unlike today, when it seems to be the fastest-growing field within American cultural studies,

in the Poland of the 1980s, African American literature was not taught as a subject in its own right.

8. John Grimes's experience with the church and sexuality confused me at first reading, while the beauty and complexity of Baldwin's prose challenged my language skills. Thanks to my invaluable mentor and dissertation advisor, Joseph Hynes, I was soon hooked. Hynes guided me toward Baldwin with patience and grace and helped me to see that the unfamiliar was good, that following literature to unexpected places was every reader's and critic's duty. I later cotaught a class on gender and sexuality with a brilliant colleague and mentor, Nicholas F. Radel, who first encouraged me to read *Giovanni's Room*.

9. Regenia Gatewood and Susan Freeman were among the brave students who stunned the class with their daring readings.

10. Exploring a new field meant coming to terms with identity politics, with how I saw and positioned myself as a white-looking academic, no matter that I was a citizen of another country, one that was historically largely Slavic and Jewish and contained a rich spectrum of other ethnic groups, a country that definitely did not see itself as part of the West. Michael Awkward's "Negotiations of Power" was among the readings I perused then while asking myself where immigrant critics and international scholars fit in his picture. See also the comprehensive collection on this issue edited by Lisa A. Long, *White Scholars/African American Texts*.

11. In *The Erotic Margin*, Schick quotes Hamilton Fish Armstrong's *Where the East Begins* (New York: Harper and Brothers, 1929): "In the nineteenth century, [the Orient] was sometimes held to begin at the river Leitha, a small tributary of the Danube just downstream of Vienna" (66). For other accounts of Eastern European Orientalism, see Zaborowska et al., *Over the Wall/After the Fall*.

12. Standley and Pratt, *Conversations*, 87. The interview was with Ida Lewis for *Essence*.

13. Ibid., 106. Interview with John Hall for *Transatlantic Review*.

14. For a reading of Bakhtin and Du Bois, see Hale, "Bakhtin in African American Literary Theory." See also Peterson, *Up from Bondage*.

15. Said, *The Edward Said Reader*, 380.

16. I am indebted to my colleague Professor James McIntosh for encouraging me to pursue this genre connection, as well as to Bercovitch's "Emerson the Prophet."

17. Issues of "personal criticism" have been thoroughly engaged by feminist theorists in the late 1980s and throughout the 1990s. To recall Sidonie Smith and Julia Watson, "personal criticism attentive to the norms of narrative self-disclosure may enable a more nuanced space for writing the self" (introduction to *Women, Autobiography, Theory*, 33). For the sake of clarity and brevity, I am compelled to restate that the personal is political to my subject, James Baldwin, and it is equally so to me as an international and immigrant feminist scholar writing about him. My project plays on the borders of literature, history, and American and Afri-

can American transnational cultural studies. These are, in my view, the fields of knowledge and the academic disciplines that have been asking tough and important questions about authority and authenticity vis-à-vis identity politics and self-positioning of diverse gendered and racialized scholarly subjects.

18. Though I am sure that some readers will disagree with my choices in this regard, I consider such disagreements as a legitimate—and, indeed, important—part of academic discourse. My own position is that I would be remiss—and my work would lack an important dimension—if I did not attempt to engage these issues in a balanced way, not only in terms of the analysis but also in terms of my own textual production. In this I echo the approach of Baldwin's biographers David Leeming and Fern Marja Eckman, at the same time that I also heed Stuart Hall's call for scholars in cultural studies to "touch on questions larger than our own personal experience, while never letting go of the subjective dimension" (*Critical Dialogues*, 402). Critics in African American studies who have been my inspirations—bell hooks, Michael Awkward, Henry Louis Gates Jr., Nellie McKay, Robert Reid-Pharr, and Cornel West—continue to productively implicate themselves in their works, and I have looked to their writings as models while writing my book.

19. The only comprehensive study of the works published beyond 1963 is Lynn Orilla Scott's *James Baldwin's Later Fiction*; Trudier Harris's *Black Women in the Fiction of James Baldwin* offers important readings of *If Beale Street Could Talk* and *Just above My Head*.

20. This field emerged with Paul Gilroy's magisterial *The Black Atlantic* and encompasses the work of historians, literary critics, and scholars in cultural studies who pursue African American international projects: among others, Penny Von Eschen, Kevin Gaines, Nikhil Singh, Tyler Stovall, Michelle Wright, Brent Hayes Edwards, and Dale Peterson.

21. Lorde, *Uses of the Erotic*, n.p. Lorde's definition addresses feminist and black feminist and lesbian issues "in the face of a racist, patriarchal, and anti-erotic society." This seems to echo directly Baldwin's statement in *The Fire Next Time*, where, like Lorde, he links white Protestant culture's shunning of sensuality and eroticism to its exclusionary politics, as well as in his late essay "Here Be Dragons" (1985), where he proposes an androgynous approach to identity.

22. To a degree, in its focus on location and setting, my project echoes the focus on "thematic orientation" or on "making one variable, [Turkey,] the constant that is complemented by an investigation of further recurrences" that Werner Sollors defines in *Neither Black nor White yet Both* (30, 26–27). Like Sollors's work, mine stresses that we must study non-English-speaking literary traditions as part of the greater landscape of American letters. I hope to show here that we must also include material "about and for" American, and especially African American, writers in studying them within and without their national locations. That is why I include at the core of my study oral histories and biographical, journalistic, and literary critical accounts of Baldwin produced by his Turkish friends.

23. I use the term "literary imagination" in its commonsense usage but also in the racially loaded sense that Toni Morrison defines in *Playing in the Dark*. That is, I want to pause and note the obvious fact that there is no such thing as an innocent, neutral, or unaffected literary imagination; that "nothing is just what it is" without having been inflected by race and sexuality and the relationships of power that have created them; there are no innocent fairy tales. To return to Morrison's *Playing in the Dark*, Baldwin's influence on this work is profound, and somewhat unacknowledged, and in this sense, via Morrison, I am referring back to Baldwin's own theorizations of the literary imagination in essays such as "As Much Truth as One Can Bear," "The New Lost Generation," "Notes for a Hypothetical Novel," and "The Creative Process." An excellent collection of essays, King's and Scott's *James Baldwin and Toni Morrison*, takes on comparisons and dialogues, as well as contentions, between these writers.

24. From the essay "Many Thousands Gone" (1951), through the short story "This Morning, This Evening, So Soon" (1965), to his late autobiographical piece "The Price of the Ticket," Baldwin daringly combined elements of immigrant narrative and the rhetoric of the Middle Passage. I discuss this in the essay "'In the Same Boat': James Baldwin and the Other Atlantic," in *Historical Guide to James Baldwin*, ed. Douglas Field (Oxford: Oxford University Press, 2009).

Introduction

1. For a concise biography of Baldwin, see Zaborowska, *The Literary Encyclopedia*, http://www.litencyc.com/.

2. Baldwin did not find out about his illegitimacy until he was in his teens and overheard a conversation between his parents, who meant to keep it a secret. He depicts a situation that comments on his "bastardly" condition as a writer in a compelling scene in *Go Tell It on the Mountain*, where he aligns being a writer with being cast out from multiple communities. Fourteen-year-old John Grimes is at school, writing on the blackboard the letters of the alphabet that the children have memorized that day, when the school principal, "a woman with white hair and an iron face" "of whom everyone was terrified," enters the room and points at the blackboard, at John's letters, asking whose writing that is. "The possibility of being distinguished by her notice did not enter John's mind . . . [so he thought] it was he who was selected for punishment" (22). When the principal praises him, telling him that he is "a very bright boy," the experience turns from terror to empowerment: "That moment gave him, for the first time if not a weapon at least a shield; he apprehended totally, without belief or understanding, that he had in himself a power that other people lacked; that he could use this to save himself, to raise himself; and that, perhaps, with this power he might one day win that love which he so longed for" (22).

3. Another important factor in Baldwin's coming-of-age and career track as a black writer was the changing character of his city at a time when, as Kenneth Warren

stresses, the "emergence of the metropolis, not merely as the locus for trade but as the psychic map for renegotiating personal and group identity," brought about the "rewriting of points of origin—whether African homeland or rural small town—in terms of a telos of urbanization." See K. Warren, "Appeals for (Mis)recognition," 397–98.

4. Sorting out the terms that would describe that identity is a precarious enterprise, and Baldwin has been referred to as gay, homosexual, queer, and bisexual by various constituencies. In "Here Be Dragons," he explains: "The condition that is now called gay was then called queer. The operative word was faggot and, later, pussy, but those epithets really had nothing to do with the question of sexual preference: You were being told simply that you had no balls" (Price of the Ticket, 681). E. Patrick Johnson's and Mae G. Henderson's "Introduction: Queering Black Studies / 'Quaring' Queer Studies," in the field-defining volume Black Queer Studies: A Critical Anthology (Durham, N.C.: Duke University Press, 2005), offers an excellent preview of the issues involved in the semantics of these terms, especially "queer," also as paired with those that connote race and blackness for African American subjects. For my purposes, I will refer to Baldwin as a black queer writer, echoing sometimes Johnson's vernacular term "quare," which is especially applicable to the chapter on No Name in the Street. I will at times use the other terms as well, given their currency in specific historical contexts and Baldwin's own usage, while, as Johnson's and Henderson's introduction puts it, "throw[ing] shade on [their] meaning in the spirit of extending [their] service to 'blackness'" (7).

5. Leeming, James Baldwin, 27. Wilmer Stone, "a radical southerner who preached socialism in his classroom," was the advisor to the editorial board of the journal.

6. David Baldwin's death meant that his stepson could not go to college because he had to work to support his family.

7. Norse, Memoirs, 12. Robert Reid-Pharr's important essay "Tearing the Goat's Flesh" stresses the shift in the post–World War II articulation and actualization of sexual desire. Baldwin moved from Harlem to the Village, via the Bronx, at the time when this shift was taking place. See also Dievler, "Sexual Exiles," on the "heightened fixing of identity categories, sexual and otherwise" in the postwar Village (165).

8. In his preface to Norse's memoirs, written when they were both much older, Baldwin echoes his sense of alienation by aligning himself with poets, whom he sees as society's outlaws who must remain in exile until all people are "able to love one another and learn to live in peace" (10). By hinting at the utopian and naive nature of this poetic project, however, Baldwin subtly but surely returns Norse's racializing gaze. He positions Norse among the ambivalent white liberals, on the one hand, and affirms their affinity as poets in exile "who prayed for each other," addressing their own "peculiar gods," on the other.

9. Their relationship included a brief affair, as Norse confirms.

10. Herb Boyd's important new biography of the writer and his birthplace, *Baldwin's Harlem*, gives a detailed picture of the teachers and writers who influenced young Jimmy, especially the poets Countee Cullen and Langston Hughes, as well as Gertrude Ayer and Orilla "Bill" Miller, who were his elementary school principal and teacher.

11. Baldwin's first professionally published work was a review of the socialist realist writer Maxim Gorky's *Best Short Stories* in the *Nation*, April 12, 1947.

12. Baldwin stresses the importance of his other leftist friends, however, who "it is not too much to say . . . helped to save my life" (834): Saul Levitas of the *New Leader*, Randal Jarrell of the *Nation*, Elliott Cohen and Robert Warshow of *Commentary*, and Philip Rahv of *Partisan Review*. He also mentions Bill Cole of Knopf, without identifying his political leanings; Cole was the editor who "saved" *Go Tell It on the Mountain*.

13. See Baldwin's "The Discovery of What It Means to Be an American."

14. Miller's important essay "The Discovery of What It Means to Be a Witness" follows Baldwin's evolution as a witness after Richard Wright's death in 1960. While I agree with much of what Miller says, I do not agree with his opening claim that this is a crucial moment that makes Baldwin reject the term "exile" as "a description of his position as an African American writer living predominantly in Europe" (331). It is true that Baldwin embarked on "searing criticism of exile as a simplified 'way out' of complex conflicts of nationality and sexuality" (333), and we can see this especially clearly in his literary manifesto "As Much Truth as One Can Bear," but this does preclude the fact that he also embraced that condition while living in Turkey. Miller's astute reading of Baldwin demonstrates the difficulties that arise when Turkey is excluded from the map of the writer's life: it makes more coherent criticism easier, but at the price of focusing Baldwin's world on the Franco-American binary, or the West.

15. In addition to critical texts, Baldwin's French connection features in two volumes of autobiography and travel writing by Nicholas Delbanco: *Running in Place: Scenes from the South of France* (1989) and *Anywhere Out of the World: Essays on Travel, Writing, Death* (2005), and a novel-in-progress by the Congolese writer Alain Mabanckou.

16. See also Walters, *At Home in Diaspora*; Nwankwo, *Black Cosmopolitanism*; and Appiah, *Cosmopolitanism*; as well as volumes focusing on race and sexuality in an international context: Glave, *Words to Our Now*; Luibhéid and Cantú, *Queer Migrations*; and Cruz-Malavé and Manalausan, *Queer Globalizations*.

17. Edwards echoes here similar statements made by Werner Sollors on American literary history in general. Sollors's works on multilingual American literature and its contexts have been an important inspiration for my scholarship and for this project.

18. See Johnson and Henderson, *Black Queer Studies*; as well as Ferguson, *Aberrations in Black*; and Ross, *Manning the Race*. I am especially indebted to Marlon Ross, Robert Reid-Pharr, Dwight McBride, and Maurice Wallace, whose essays on Bald-

win guided me through the theoretical challenges of the early stages of this project.

19. Like many scholars, I agree that the definitions of the "East" and the "Orient" imply "ideological rather than geographical associations." I use the terms interchangeably while being equally aware of their loaded connotations and the fact that I cannot begin to address them all in this project on Baldwin. See Obeidat, *American Literature and Orientalism*, which also defines the "Muslim East" as the "area from Turkey on the Black Sea southward through Syria, Jordan, Saudi Arabia, and Egypt back along the coastal lands of North Africa and up through Muslim Spain" (35).

20. Irvin Cemil Schick's *The Erotic Margin* offers perhaps the most theoretically and historically comprehensive introduction to this theme. What Schick calls the theme of "oriental sexuality . . . gained a significant place in European visual and verbal artistic production beginning in the eighteenth century" (1), and by being associated with the constructions of the Orient illustrates the Foucauldian links between space and power. For references on location, national culture, and homosexuality, see Schick's chapter "The Homosocial/Sexual Business of Empire" (158–61).

21. Turkey is important to consider on its own terms, given its importance in twentieth-century American policy—for example, as a NATO ally in the Korean War. See also Reina Lewis, who observes that "although Turkey and the Ottoman Empire feature large in representations associated with Orientalism, little attention has been paid to the case of Turkey . . . [which] provide[s] another paradigm for the analysis of competing colonial powers and the political and cultural effects of Euro-American cultural policy" in that region (*Rethinking Orientalism*, 4). For example, Said's *Orientalism* conspicuously elides discussions of Turkey, despite its prominence in the representations of the Orient in the literature of Western Europe. For the history of foreign relations between the United States and Turkey following World War II, see G. Harris, *Troubled Alliance*.

22. The Baldwin-Cezzar letters are identified by the number and date listed on them. Among my scholarly inspirations are Mullen's *Afro-Orientalism*, Von Eschen's *Satchmo Blows Up the World*, Ross's *Manning the Race*, Edwards's *The Practice of Diaspora*, Appiah's *Cosmopolitanism*, Nwankwo's *Black Cosmopolitans*, Gunning's *Dialogues of Dispersal*, Hernandez's *Blackening Europe*, and others.

23. I pun here on the title of Philip Deloria's important recent volume on Native American cultural history, *Indians in Unexpected Places*.

24. Leeming, e-mail correspondence with author.

25. These editions are *Kara Yabancı*, translated by Tanju Kurtarel and published by Ağaoğlu Yayınevi in 1970, and *Bir Başka Ülke*, translated by Çiğdem Öztekin and published by Yapı Kredi Yayınları in 2005. *Bundan Sonrası Ateş*, the Turkish edition of *The Fire Next Time*, was translated by Kıvanç Güney and released in January 2006 by Yapı Kredi Yayınları. The same publisher issued Çiğdem Öztekin's translation of *Giovanni's Room* in the summer of 2006.

26. The cover of *The Five* features Baldwin holding a small black child, a picture taken during one of his early trips to the South (most likely in Louisiana). This is somewhat out of context for the predominantly northern locations of *The Fire Next Time*, or Harlem and Chicago's South Side.

27. He may also have worked there on the early drafts of the film criticism that makes up *The Devil Finds Work* (1976).

28. Leeming, interview with author; Cezzar, interview with author; Standley and Pratt, *Conversations*, the Baldwin-Cezzar letters.

29. Interview with author, Istanbul, September 2005.

30. Americans had been living in Istanbul and Turkey and visiting there for a long time before Baldwin "discovered" it. The establishment of Robert College, for example, a missionary school that became what is now Boğaziçi Üniversitesi (Bosphorus University) and Robert Koleji (high school), created a colony of United States citizens beginning in the latter half of the nineteenth century. See also Fortuny, *American Writers in Istanbul*.

31. Happersberger told me that he could not recall much of his stay in Istanbul at the time. He went there "to get divorced" and would often hang out with "a friend of Engin's who was a theater designer" and had lots of money from a stipend, "a big, tall, strong guy . . . [with whom he] simply drank morning to night" to forget his trouble. Interview with author in Switzerland, June 2005.

32. Interview with author, June 2001. See also J. Campbell, *Talking*, in which he emphasizes that "between the end of 1964 and the middle of 1967, Baldwin was semi-resident in Turkey" (209).

33. They now hang at Engin Cezzar's apartment.

34. Keith was the cultural attaché in Turkey at the time and arranged for Baldwin to give a talk to an invited audience at the American Cultural Center in Istanbul. Keith does not recall the exact date, only some time in 1969–70. Baldwin told him, "I won't embarrass you," knowing well that Keith's boss was apprehensive about the event given the black writer's antigovernment and anti–Vietnam War reputation. Interview with author, April 10, 2006.

35. Cherry brought his Swedish wife, Maki, and children, Nenah and Eagle Eye, who are now well-known musicians.

36. I could not confirm whether or not Kitt and Baldwin ever met in Istanbul. Kitt's song "Üsküdar'a Gider iken" describes wealthy Turkish women who fantasize about and flirt with young male clerks (katib). The lyrics can also be interpreted as implying a possibility of illicit erotic encounters that would titillate Western listeners. The song's Orientalizing images have little to do with women's fashions or for that matter with sexual conduct in modern Turkey in the late 1960s. They exoticize and misread women of higher social standing living in Istanbul at the time. These women had not been covering their faces since Atatürk's introduction of the secular state in the 1920s.

37. Information provided by Kenton Keith. Interview with author, April 10, 2006. I have recently had a very interesting conversation about race, sexuality, and living

and teaching American literature in Turkey with Terence Powers, an African American who has taught at one of Istanbul's Islamic universities and claims to have experienced more racist and homophobic reactions from Americans living in Turkey than from the Turks (e-mail exchange on homophobia with Collegium for African American Research listserv on October 27, 2006).

38. As Campbell and Leeming explain, *No Papers for Mohammed* was never completed and remains in a twenty-some-page manuscript among Baldwin's papers. Leeming reports that it was "based on Baldwin's own recent scare with the French immigration authorities and on the case of an Arab friend who had been deported to Algeria." It was to focus on Muslim themes; the title character was based on a gardener named Mohammed who worked for Baldwin in Saint-Paul de Vence (Leeming, *James Baldwin*, 314). When interviewing Baldwin about it, J. Campbell felt that the novel would surely be completed, as its theme addressed the writer's "personal conundrum" related to the fact that Baldwin's residency in Turkey coincided with the "first waves of Turkish immigrant workers flooding into Germany and Switzerland." Baldwin sympathized with them as "an outcast of a different continent," but later, when employing an Algerian man as a gardener in Saint-Paul de Vence, he felt that the man saw him "as the master of the plantation." Campbell also cites an interview in French from 1974, in which Baldwin said, "I have seen in Mohammed, in his eyes, his voice, his actions, myself; and at that moment, I became the oppressor" (*Talking*, 271). Leeming also notes that Baldwin made an agreement with the publishing house Lippincott for the project in the early 1970s and used the advance for the down payment when buying his house in Saint-Paul de Vence. He also bought the "long dreamed-of car, a Mercedes. . . . And even went so far as to take driving lessons, but after a potentially disastrous although minor wreck, he hired a young chauffeur who later absconded with the car" (*James Baldwin*, 314, 376).

39. Leeming notes that Baldwin was in fact so upset by his experience with Hollywood, which coincided with a fight with a lover, that he attempted suicide by swallowing a large dose of sleeping pills; like before, he was discovered in time to be rushed to the emergency room. Leeming also notes Spike Lee's reliance on Baldwin's scenario for his film on Malcolm X, as well as that the version of the script rewritten by Arnold Pearl was eventually made into a docudrama by Warner Brothers but was not distributed because it was considered too "inflammatory" (*James Baldwin*, 301).

40. See also Leeming on the scenario for *Inheritance* (*James Baldwin*, 316–17).

41. Oktay Balamir shared with me a copy of a dramatization of this novel, whose copyright is dated 1964. It is impossible to discern whether this is a copy of the theatrical rendering that Baldwin wrote with Cezzar in 1956 or a different version intended for the screen. More recently, Douglas Field Jr. confirmed the existence of a screenplay written by Michael Raeburn and Baldwin "in the 1980s . . . in France" (e-mail correspondence with author, January 14, 2008).

42. For more detail, see Leeming, *James Baldwin*, 357–58. The only work by Baldwin

that was ever made into a film was Go Tell It on the Mountain, produced for American Playhouse on PBS in 1984.

43. I was not able to ascertain whether the screenplay of The Sacrifice was completed in the written format. Leeming comments that Baldwin "had not liked it. But he thought he saw possibilities in it as a film and once more gave in to his movie-making obsession"; Leeming mentions that Baldwin and Cezzar asked Costa-Gavras to consider the project (358). I have been able to locate a treatment of this play, a dense single-page description in Baldwin's handwriting, at the archives at the Schomburg.

44. See Cezzar and Çalışlar, Engin Cezzar, 96.

45. There is some confusion as to what exactly Cezzar and Baldwin worked on and finished that summer. Leeming claims that The Swordfish was also known as The Sacrifice, which would have been the play based on Dilmen's Kurban (James Baldwin, 357–58). Cezzar stressed that the story of The Swordfish is one of the "things we lived together and nobody knows about it or has written about it" in his memoir (95). He explains, "I found . . . a novel called Kılıç Uykuda Vurulur (Sword Falls, While Asleep) by a very interesting author, Osman Necmi Gürmen. He is from Siverek, a member of the Bucak Tribe, and graduated from Sorbonne. I met with the author in Bodrum and we got on quite well. He was living in France at the time. He had written the novel in French with the title L'Espadon (The Sword-fish). It was a remarkable story of the friendship and the separation of a Turkish shepherd and a Greek fishing family in Cyprus" (95–96). Cezzar also talks about proposing this project to Costa-Gavras.

46. Leeming mentions this only in passing in his text. When I interviewed him, he explained that there was little similarity between the two cities.

47. The ethnic and linguistic diversity of the Harlem that Baldwin grew up in during the 1930s would have prepared him for some of Istanbul's mixes. Chester Himes confirms this in A Rage in Harlem with references to the many languages spoken there.

48. Leeming states: "According to his [Baldwin's] instructions, I wrote to Howard Dodson at the Schomburg Center in New York agreeing that his 'papers' should be deposited there" (382). He confirmed it to me in our interview on June 30, 2003. The papers are now kept by Baldwin's sister, Gloria Smart, the executor of the Baldwin estate. Smart has not allowed scholarly access to them since her brother's death but has made exceptions for Engin Cezzar, who quotes one of Jimmy's letters and has recently published their collection in Turkish as Dost Mektupları (Letters from a Friend, 2007), and for Sol Stein, who includes large portions of previously unpublished material in his Native Sons.

49. Germaner's and İnankur's Orientalism and Turkey reproduces several paintings that hang in the Dolmabahçe Palace in Istanbul and represent the Arab peoples as darker-skinned: Gustave Boulanger's "Bedouins at the Oasis," Alfred de Dreux's "Prancing Horse," Victor Huguet's "Bedouins in the Desert," and Adolf Schreyer's "Arab Horseman" (98, 108, 126, 146).

50. Avni Bey—I use his nickname at his insistence—was very aware of race issues in the United States, although he never traveled there, and remembered watching *Roots* on Turkish television around 1980 or 1981.

51. Campbell highlights the Western cliché about the erotically charged East that Baldwin himself must have recognized as a new arrival. Because, as a writer, he "carried his personal geography with him" when he came to Turkey, Baldwin seems to have found in Istanbul a place where his own "natural" foreignness, migrancy, and sexual outsiderism could flourish (*Talking*, 212).

52. Also see Kenneth B. Clark, *King, Malcolm, Baldwin*.

53. After Baldwin had sent him a telegram concerning the dramatic situation in the South, Attorney General Robert Kennedy met with him on May 23. On May 24, Baldwin brought several other prominent African Americans for another meeting. Ironically, Baldwin's political importance as a black intellectual and leader was later confirmed by Kennedy's orders to have him followed by the FBI. See also Kenneth B. Clark, *King, Malcolm, Baldwin*.

54. Interview with Ida Lewis for *Essence*.

55. Pakay, *From Another Place* (film and outtakes).

56. I conducted these interviews in 2001 and in 2004. The 2004 interview took place long-distance, via e-mail and a list of questions, as well as in person with the invaluable assistance from Aslı Gür, a Ph.D. candidate in the University of Michigan Department of Sociology, who has served as my research assistant and translator on this project.

57. This term appears in the essay "The New Lost Generation" (1961), at the time of Baldwin's transition to Turkey (*Price of the Ticket*, 309).

58. See Baldwin's musings on a similar theme in the essay "Princes and Powers" (1956), in *Nobody Knows My Name*, where he contemplates Du Bois's inability to attend the Conference of Negro-African Writers and Artists at the Sorbonne University in Paris.

59. Leeming stresses that Baldwin's fear intensified as he received repeated proof that he was being followed and that his phone was bugged (*James Baldwin*, 225–26). Given the emergence under the Freedom of Information Act of his hefty FBI file, it is clear that Baldwin escaped to Turkey for both political and personal safety reasons. (See also Wallace's chapter on Baldwin and the FBI in *Constructing the Black Masculine*, and J. Campbell, *Talking*, 167–75.)

60. Soundtrack to *From Another Place*.

61. West, *Democracy Matters*, 79.

62. On various forms of Cold War Orientalism, see also my introduction to *Over the Wall / After the Fall*; as well as C. Klein, *Cold War Orientalism*; and Castillo, "Soviet Orientalism."

63. Hidden beyond the evocative partitions of the Berlin Wall and the Iron Curtain, Eastern Europe was demonized as the Evil Empire in various forms of discourse, such as political speeches, cartoons and jokes, and literature, cinema, and other forms of art. It was used as a negative example of "not-like-us" to glorify the

superiority of American economy, culture, and politics. Such a myopic focus vilified the Soviet Union and Russia but also stripped the representations of its neighboring countries, known as "satellites" rather than by their proper names, of their individual national identities, specific locations, and unique cultures. See the introduction to Zaborowska et al., *Over the Wall | After the Fall*.

64. C. Klein, *Cold War Orientalism*, 114. Klein quotes from an editorial that mentions Turkey along with "the Soviet Union, Egypt . . . Israel, India, Pakistan, Afghanistan, and Indonesia" (114).

65. A recent example of women's travel writing that both debunks and perpetuates this model is Ashman and Gökmen, *Tales from the Expat Harem*.

66. See also McAlister's reference to Baldwin's essay on the affinities between Blacks and Jews as the chosen people (*Epic Encounters*, 87).

67. Dwight McBride's essay "Straight Black Studies" says very well what I originally wanted to say here, as it situates the issue in terms of disciplinary discourses on race and sexuality, or the reluctance of many African Americanists to embrace queer topics or even talk about race and sexuality in the same breath. McBride foregrounds some of the important debates on this theme, such as the black queer studies debate and the diaspora versus domestic studies debate.

68. Citing an extensive list of works that deal with this topic is well outside the scope of this project. The most important titles for this study include Irvin Schick's *The Erotic Margin*, Said's *Orientalism*, Boyd and Freely's *Strolling through Istanbul*, Freely's *Stamboul Sketches* and *Inside the Seraglio*, and Pamuk's *Istanbul*, as well as fiction such as Maureen Freely's *The Life of the Party* and Elif Şafak's *The Saint of Incipient Insanities*.

69. See Carol Polsgrove's *Divided Minds* and the essays by Kendall Thomas, McBride, and Wallace in *Black Queer Studies*.

70. I am aware that some of these approaches reflect and echo Baldwin's own ambivalence concerning his racial and sexual identity, especially in the early, formative period in the Village in the late 1940s. Leeming discusses the "demons" that the budding writer struggled with, as well as his initial resistance to his role as an essayist and desire to be predominantly a novelist (*James Baldwin*, 52–53).

71. Despite the overwhelming riches of theory in cultural studies, it is not easy to talk about sex and race in the same breath even these days. On the one hand, there is the need to present Baldwin's complex vision in, let's say, more straightforward terms for those concerned with racial justice; on the other hand, there is the desire to enlist his works in the politics of gay liberation for those who may leave other aspects of identity—race, class, and nonbinary sexualities—out of the picture.

72. Deloria's work comes in handy again with its emphasis on how even the very naming of "an anomaly simultaneously re-creates and empowers the very same categories that it escapes" (5). By suggesting Baldwin's erotic attachment to Turkey, Adelsen hints at his anomalous identity, or homoerotic proclivities,

without having to name them. As Robert Aldrich demonstrates in *Colonialism and Homosexuality*, "By the late nineteenth century, a widespread belief circulated in Europe that homosexuality (and other sexual deviance) was endemic in the non-European world" (5), a belief that would have been largely shared in the United States. Aldrich also calls attention to Said's reluctance to discuss homosexuality in *Orientalism*, to having created what Joseph Boone terms the "conspicuously heterosexual interpretive framework" (7).

73. Said's comments on the ways in which American Orientalism, in its greater "social sciences" focus, differed from European Orientalism, with its philological focus, are important to note for their subtle and not-so-subtle distinctions between Western approaches: "Cultural isolatos like Melville were interested in it; cynics like Mark Twain visited and wrote about it; the American Transcendentalists saw affinities between Indian thought and their own. . . . But there was no deeply invested tradition of Orientalism, and consequently in the United States knowledge of the Orient never passed through the refining and reticulating and reconstructing processes, whose beginning was in philological study, that it went through in Europe" (*Orientalism*, 290).

74. I am concerned here not as much with disproving or proving that any instances of what might pass today for "sex tourism" did or did not occur for Baldwin as with demonstrating the pervasiveness of stereotypes about his life and Turkey as a location.

75. See, for example, Polsgrove, *Divided Minds*; and reviews by Dupee, Roth, and Bigsby in Bloom's *Modern Critical Views: James Baldwin*. Nelson's "Critical Deviance" offers a comprehensive review of the homophobic reception of Baldwin's works.

76. See also Adams, "Giovanni's Room," which lists many examples of such approaches.

77. "The Preservation of Innocence" anticipates the much later essay "Here Be Dragons." Lawrie Balfour also mentions this connection between Baldwin's early and later essays in *The Evidence of Things Not Said*.

78. "Go the Way Your Blood Beats," 178.

79. I base this observation on having read the letters that are available at the Schomburg Center at the New York Public Library, the letters from Baldwin to Cezzar that Mrs. Gloria Smart, the executor of the Baldwin Estate, kindly agreed to let me see, and my interviews with David Leeming, who told me about having organized Baldwin's papers after his death but not being permitted to quote from them in his biography.

80. Like Campbell, I have been heartened by the publication of Sol Stein's *Native Sons* (2004), which contains facsimiles of about a dozen letters between Baldwin and Stein, as well as the story "Dark Runner" and the play *Equal in Paris*, both based on the essay that Baldwin published under the title "Equal in Paris" in his seminal volume *Notes of a Native Son* (1955).

81. This may be seen as somewhat relevant to the homemaking strategies described by the Norwegian American Orm Øverland in *Immigrant Minds, American Identities*.

82. Writing about his disgust at the McCarthy era and the "impotence and narcissism of so many of the people . . . I respected," Baldwin condemned both the man behind the scourges but also those who even stooped to debate whether or not McCarthy was indeed "an enemy of domestic liberties" (*No Name in the Street*, 33).

83. See also a discussion on this piece in Porter, *Stealing the Fire* (125–26) and Bryan R. Washington's discussion of Baldwin's rewriting of white canonical exile in *The Politics of Exile*.

84. "Baldwin, in Istanbul, Denies, He's Given Up the Struggle," interview by Nick Ludington, *New York Post*, December, 12, 1969.

85. West embraces Baldwin as a prophet who wanted to inspire "an America caught in the web of self-deception and self-celebration . . . by tapping into . . . black resources" (*Democracy Matters*, 84).

86. Essex Hemphill puts this evocatively in "Living the World / Looking for Home": "I don't have a sense of a singular home any longer. I need to reclaim my sense of someplace singular. A lot of times, for me, writing is retrieval" (310). See also Reid-Pharr on the "backhanded treatment" and homophobia Baldwin encountered despite of, and often because of, his celebrity, regardless of the profound lesson of his works: "The privacy and sacredness of the individual and the individual's body must be maintained even and especially at the moment at which that individual offers up his own life story as a potent metaphor for the reality and the promise of the human condition" (*Once You Go Black*, 114–15).

87. The title of this section deliberately echoes the title of the excellent collection of essays edited by Dwight McBride, which is one of the key inspirations for this project.

88. Michael Thelwell insists that in the 1960s, "history and politics and literature . . . [were] inextricably intertwined" and that "Jimmy Baldwin . . . [was] the defining voice" (in Chametzky, ed., *Black Writers Redefine the Struggle: A Tribute to James Baldwin*, 2). This collection originated in a conference, "Black Writers Redefine the Struggle: A Tribute to James Baldwin," at the University of Massachusetts, Amherst, April 22–23, 1988.

89. Missing completely Baldwin's point about the racialization of American masculinities in *Blues for Mister Charlie*, Philip Roth criticizes him for stereotyping black sexuality in terms that reveal more about Roth's own approach to race and sex than Baldwin's: "It is soap opera designed to illustrate the superiority of blacks over whites. . . . Negroes . . . make love better. They dance better. And they cook better. And their penises are longer, or stiffer" (Roth, "Blues for Mr. Charlie," 41).

90. Lynn Orilla Scott's *James Baldwin's Later Fiction* is the only book wholly committed to recovering and giving justice to the late Baldwin. Of note are the relatively

recent literary critiques by Nicholas Boggs, who analyzes Baldwin's little known children's story "Little Man, Little Man" ("Of Mimicry and [*Little Man Little*] Man"); and by Warren J. Carson, who reads *Just above My Head* ("Manhood, Musicality, and Male Bonding," 215–32). Lawrie Balfour's *The Evidence of Things Not Said* makes a persuasive case for "the rhetorical force of his later work," although it does not engage Baldwin's fiction, only his essays (13). Edited volumes by Trudier Harris (*New Essays*), D. Quentin Miller (*Re-Viewing*), and Dwight McBride (*James Baldwin Now*), as well as Melvin Dixon's *Ride Out the Wilderness* and Keith Clark's *Black Manhood*, have also been turning the tide. Gates mentions *Tell Me How Long the Train's Been Gone* in his essay "The 'Blackness of Blackness.' " See also José Esteban Muñoz's *Disidentifications* for references to *Just above My Head*; and Reid-Pharr's excellent treatment of that novel in *Once You Go Black*.

91. *Early Novels and Stories* includes *Go Tell It on the Mountain, Giovanni's Room, Another Country*, and the short story collection *Going to Meet the Man*.

92. In this I echo David Leeming's work on Baldwin, as well as that of several scholars who appear in references throughout this book, especially Lynn Orilla Scott, D. Quentin Miller, Dwight McBride, Robert Reid-Pharr, and Lawrie Balfour. A full discussion of the conflicting views on Baldwin is well beyond the scope of this project, as it would necessitate, in my mind at least, a thorough evaluation of the complicated history of scholarship on the writer and a close reading of all his works—a subject for quite another book. That is why I mention only a few representative approaches in the introduction and deal with select others in subsequent chapters. For an example of a full-length study on Baldwin's divided career, see Horace Porter (*Stealing the Fire*), who not only agrees with Albert Murray's opinion that after the publication of *Another Country* and *The Fire Next Time* Baldwin stopped producing good literature but also claims, "None of Baldwin's later novels or essays rivals the narrative ingenuity and rhetorical power of *Go Tell It on the Mountain* and *Notes of a Native Son*" (160). Although we may not want to dispute literary tastes, Leeming's readings, as well as the exciting new scholarship on Baldwin's later works, prove that this is not true.

93. Lamming, *The Pleasures of Exile*, 56. Copyrighted in 1960, this work appeared at the time when Baldwin was plotting his trip to Turkey.

ONE Between Friends

The chapter epigraph is quoted from Sedat Pakay's statement accompanying the portfolio of photos published with Nkosi's "The Mountain," *Transition: An International Review*, no. 79 (1999): 124.

1. Pakay's film was shot in May 1970 and released in New York in 1973. Thorsen's film was released by California Newsreel in 1989.

2. I want to thank the Danish students who took that class for their insights and inspiration as we read Baldwin together. Klaus Dik Nielsen went on to write a compelling master's thesis on gay identity and race in *Another Country*.

3. Thorsen's montage consists of excerpts from the opening scene in Baldwin's bedroom, of Baldwin in the streets of Istanbul, and of his studio monologue on his sex life and American homophobia. More quotations from Pakay's film follow in the next chapter.

4. Sedat Pakay delivered an inspiring talk at the University of Michigan, "Knowing Jimmy," at the symposium "Covering the U.S. Empire," January 8, 2004. It included all these elements, as well as an anecdote about how Columbia Pictures supposedly considered casting Charlton Heston as Malcolm X in the movie for which Baldwin was hired to write a script in the late 1960s. The script was never filmed, but Baldwin completed and published it as *One Day When I Was Lost*. It served as an important inspiration and resource for Spike Lee's film.

5. With the exception of Rosa Bobia's *The Critical Reception of James Baldwin in France* (New York: Grove/Atlantic, 1998).

6. *Tespih* is a singular noun in Turkish, like "rosary," although it translates as plural, "worry beads."

7. Pakay confirms that the opening scene was influenced by *Giovanni's Room*. Interview with author, June 2005.

8. I thank my students in AC 699, "James Baldwin and the Black Novel, 1950–1990," which I taught for the Program in American Culture and Center for Afroamerican and African Studies at the University of Michigan, for their stimulating comments on Baldwin's works and their great company during the semester when this book was taking its final shape. I especially cherish Tayana Hardin's poignant comment on the impact of the bedroom scene: "I'm not faking my funk. Here I am in my drawers. What you see is what you get." Dale Veregge called my attention to Jimmy's "obvious switch," and Anya Cobbler to his "hyperawareness of himself" and ability to make us feel "like he is looking at *you*." I also thank Ebony Thomas, Tim Pruzinsky, Craig Derbenwick, Aymar Jean, and Sean Field for their stimulating presentations and feedback throughout the semester.

9. It may not be clear from the brief glimpse of the ship onscreen that it is indeed an American warship, but I have it on the authority of the filmmaker that it is so.

10. Soundtrack to Sedat Pakay, *James Baldwin: From Another Place.*

11. See also Campbell, *Talking*, 252.

12. In this letter, Baldwin is also describing his reluctance to face a return to New York.

13. Cezzar told me in one of our interviews, "Jimmy stopped writing letters in the 1970s." Their correspondence clearly tapered off then, but Baldwin did not stop writing letters to others. It will take a thorough study of Baldwin's papers, once they have become available, to trace the patterns of his epistolary relationships. Cezzar and Baldwin had a falling out over a movie script that they wrote together in 1981, and this is probably what contributed to the waning of their correspondence (see conclusion). Baldwin's unpublished letters to Engin Cezzar are kept by the Baldwin Estate. They have been published in Turkish translation, with

Engin Cezzar's notes, as *Dost Mektupları*. For more information, see J. Campbell, "Room in the East."

14. For details, see Leeming, *James Baldwin*, 284.

15. Thelwell, Introduction, in Chametzky, *Black Writers Redefine the Struggle*, 2.

16. Noting the importance of artists' homes to their works, Bożena Mądra-Shallcross writes: "The situation of 'dwelling in' is an existential necessity that grows out of the need for shelter or even camouflage for newly emerging intimacy and its secrets, which allow the budding of the first marks of individuality" (*Dom romantycznego artysty*, 13). Echoing Gaston Bachelard, David Kranes defines home as a space of safety and creativity: "Home is what, at heart, we always hope to get-away to. We are all seeking to inhabit that space that most empowers us, which feels most rewarding, most secure, most natural, most intimate" ("Play Grounds," 93). Elizabeth Grosz, on the other hand, emphasizes the importance of urban space to dwelling: "The city is one of the crucial factors in the social production of (sexed) corporeality. . . . [It] has become the defining term in constructing the image of the land and the landscape, as well as the point of reference, the centerpiece of a notion of economic/social/political/cultural exchange" ("Bodies-Cities," 242–43). Stressing the links between place and dwelling spaces, the cultural critic Irit Rogoff claims that "geographies have . . . become a great deal more than the scientific location and articulation of the natural world; they are now also a euphemism for concepts of 'home,' 'emplaced culture,' and 'embodied identity'" ("Other's Others," 193).

17. Fuss, *The Sense of an Interior*, 1. Fuss targets disciplinary approaches to spaces of writing: "If architectural historians treat the domestic interior more literally than figuratively, ignoring the metaphorical in favor of the functional, literary critics, for their part, tend to treat the domestic interior as pure figuration" (3). Like Fuss, I am trying to put the two in dialogue, by emphasizing his unorthodox modes of dwelling, and to show how Baldwin resists and problematizes their separation.

18. Fuss writes about Emily Dickinson, Sigmund Freud, Helen Keller, and Marcel Proust. She mentions in passing that waiting for other scholars is the great project of writing about Frederick Douglass's house in Washington, D.C.

19. There are no easy answers to this question. Although he distanced himself from the great American writers of the past in essays such as "Everybody's Protest Novel" (1949) and "As Much Truth as One Can Bear" (1962), Baldwin was well aware that his economic success was making him closer, in terms of class, to the bourgeoisie that he disdained. I am also grateful to my colleague James MacIntosh for reminding me that even the white "bourgeois" writers like Hawthorne, James, Hemingway, Bishop, and Lowell were often unsettled.

20. Øverland focuses on the late-nineteenth- and early-twentieth-century depictions of non-Anglo-American immigrants, or "foreigners."

21. Here is a comment from an e-mail I received from Irvin Schick that describes an

exilic situation of a writer who, as a young child, was part of the Baldwin circle in Istanbul: "It may interest you to know that Şavkar Altınel, an old friend of mine (also from Robert College) who now lives in England, wrote in his review of one of Maureen Freely's novels, something like: 'Exile is a country in itself, and those who have lived in it once will never be able to leave it.' Maureen [Freely] grew up in Turkey and Greece and lives in England, and her novels (and translations) are very much shaped by her experience as triple expatriate." E-mail correspondence with author, April 9, 2007.

22. Irvin Schick kindly explained to me the rich context behind the title of Sururi's memoir: "The entire title . . . [refers to] the way mystical poets described the bridge of Sırat-ı Müstakim, which must supposedly be crossed by every soul after death. It is thinner than a hair and more trenchant than a sword, and those who fail fall down into the fires of hell. Those who succeed reach God on the other side. . . . The word 'al-sırat al-müstaqim' in Arabic is a Qur'anic phrase that occurs in the first chapter of the Qur'an and elsewhere, and means literally 'the straight path.' It is interpreted as the true faith, i.e., Islam. But the mystics viewed it as this bridge that souls cross in the afterlife. [A] poem by Yunus Emre . . . [also] sheds light on Gülriz Sururi's thinking: 'Sırat kıldan incedür kılıçdan keskincedür / Varup anun üstüne evler yapasım gelür' (the Sırat [bridge] is thinner than a hair and more trenchant than a sword / I feel like going and building houses upon it.' This displays the tremendous self-confidence that a Sufi like Yunus Emre felt, regarding his love for God and the favored status he believed he would occupy with God because of it. Not only does he think he could easily cross the bridge, he thinks he could build houses upon it! It may or may not be that Sururi felt that her life had been as tough to navigate as the Sırat bridge, but that she had been able to deal with it well enough that she can now build houses upon it. Who knows?" E-mail correspondence with author, April 9, 2007.

23. Interview with author, May 30, 2001.

24. Interview with author, September 10, 2005.

25. The exact meaning in Turkish is actually "the tenth member of the family," but given that there were nine siblings including Jimmy, "sibling" sounds right, too.

26. Interview with author, May 23, 2001. James Campbell mentions Paul Newman and Montgomery Clift as possible leads; his "Room in the East" gives more detail about Engin and Jimmy's attempts to turn *Giovanni's Room* into a play. In the letter from July 29, 1958 (letter 5), Baldwin writes about Josh Logan, the theater director, missing the novel's focus on homosexuality and comments on Logan's rejection letter: "He [Logan] feels 'let down' by the play, does not find the 'electricity of the novel' in it, does not 'care at all about the boy and girl.' . . . It sounds as though he has rather misread the play" (4). In the letter Baldwin also mentions other directors, Gadg (Elia Kazan), Audrey Wood, Frank Corsaro, Eli Rill (who ended up directing the Actors Studio workshop production in the spring of 1958), and Bobby Lewis. He chuckles about Marlon Brando as a pos-

sible lead: "'One good thing, we're not likely to get a rejection from Brando, simply because he never answers anybody'" (4). In a letter of May 14, 1959, he mentions Philip Rose and Lloyd Richards, who produced and directed Lorraine Hansberry's *Raisin in the Sun*, as "hot about *Giovanni*" (letter 14).

27. Leeming emphasizes Cezzar's trustworthiness and stability as a friend (*James Baldwin*, 263).

28. This is not, however, confirmed or mentioned anywhere in Cezzar's autobiography.

29. Leeming describes an incident in which Baldwin was enraged by a sociologist who dared to refer to his close friends, whom Baldwin considered brothers, as "siblings" (247).

30. The other reassurances about the platonic nature of Baldwin's friendships with his male Turkish friends I encountered often sounded as if they were instances of self-censorship for the benefit of the "American academic."

31. Aldrich offers an interesting reading of blood brotherhood rituals across races and nationalities in his analysis of Henry Morton Stanley's novel *My Kalulu* (1873) (*Colonialism and Homosexuality*, 38–39). He also discusses Stanley's "affair with Africa," pointing at the gendered and homoerotic connotations of colonial relationships (47).

32. Quoted from J. Campbell, "Room in the East," 5.

33. I have been allowed to glimpse the letters in the form of photocopied originals by the Baldwin Estate in 2004. As the Baldwin papers are not available to scholars, I regret that I cannot provide quotations, and have had to drastically limit my discussion of the epistolary friendship between Cezzar and Baldwin. Hilton Als writes passionately about the need to publish "one great Baldwin masterpiece," or his letters. He explains that they have not been published yet because the family "felt he shed a negative light on them, particularly on David Baldwin, who was their father, and not his. And they were uncomfortable with his homosexuality." Hilton Als, "Family Secrets," in "James Baldwin's Grand Tour," PEN America: A Journal for Writers and Readers 1.2 (2001): 28.

34. Thanks to Fatma Müge Göçek and Ayşe Öncü for helping me establish contact with Engin Cezzar, as well as Aslı Gür.

35. The term "autoethnography" has a long history in anthropology and is treated at length in Reed-Danahay, *Auto/Ethnography*. See also Roth, *Auto/Biography and Auto/Ethnography*; and Mary Louise Pratt, *Imperial Eyes*.

36. Cezzar also worked in communist Czechoslovakia, where he staged a Turkish musical in the 1970s. As in Turkey, with his knack for interweaving current political events into his theater, he was threatened with being shut down unless he complied with local censorship. As Engin told me, he had no choice but to change some things. Paradoxically, and in ways that reminded me of the rather similar conditions in which the best Polish theater I saw as a student in the 1980s was created, this fact actually helped him make the staging of the play more powerful and poignant. "I should have thanked those guys for forcing me to

do that!" he concluded. (In letter 50, dated September 27, 1974, Baldwin writes from Saint-Paul de Vence asking Engin to come visit him "from Poland.")

37. As I later found out from Sedat Pakay, the Park Hotel, which contained one of Jimmy's favorite bars, used to stand there. I later met the aged bartender, who used to run another bar, at the Divan Hotel, and liked to call himself Avni Bey, or Mister Avni. He told me that Jimmy would always have a blast at the Divan bar: "And he always, always had a drink in his hand," Avni told me with a wink. The Divan Hotel was a favorite hangout for Leeming, too. Avni Bey is Afro-Turkish, or looks black, according to American epidermal classifications. He speaks very good English and spent hours telling me about how proud he was to be able to talk to Baldwin and entertain him. Avni retired some years ago, having opened and then sold Avni's Pub, which still stands across the street from the disturbingly ugly Hilton. We met and chatted in his pub on my last day in Istanbul, September 10, 2005. Avni Bey was clearly revered by the young men who run the place now, who refer to him affectionately as "the Old Man." I left with a recipe for çoban salatası. Interview with author, September 10, 2005.

38. More stories about that period follow in chapter 4.

39. He would be given a "pasha's medal" by the crew of *Fortune and Men's Eyes*, which he directed a couple of years later. As he wrote to his brother, David: "he was now 'Sir James Baldwin'" (Leeming, *James Baldwin*, 308). This was the only "knighthood" he received.

40. Leo's assistant, Pete, has an "Oriental face" that reappears throughout the narrative and suggests a vague connection to the East that I explore further in chapter 3.

41. That is how Engin and Gülriz preferred she be referred to. I use both forms.

42. I am basing this judgment on the translations into English by Aslı Gür.

43. Cezzar assures me that this photograph was taken at their house. Leeming dates it 1966 but does not specify the location.

44. I would like to acknowledge once again David Leeming's help, as he agreed to be interviewed about my many questions. I am also grateful for his scrupulous account of names and places in the biography, which has helped me to confirm many of my claims and sustain many of my hypotheses.

45. The memoirs were published in two volumes. The first, *Kıldan İnce Kılıçtan Keskince* (Istanbul: Milliyet Yayınları, 1978), covers the years from her birth to 1977; the second, *Bir An Gelir* (There Comes a Moment) (Istanbul: Doğan Kitap, 2003), covers 1980 to 2002.

46. Antep is a city in southwestern Turkey famous for its cuisine, especially the best red pepper kebab in the country.

47. I later learned from other Turkish friends of Baldwin's that the picture Sururi painted for me in our interview was perhaps rosier than reality—at least in comparison to what those other friends remembered.

48. On the "chuckle," see Deloria, *Indians in Unexpected Places*.

49. Interview with author, September 2005.

50. Aslı Gür, who as my research assistant and translator became my linguistic tie to Turkey in the process of writing this book, told me that she thought that by referring to meat eating and culinary delights, the term *yamyam* might also connote a person who was ravenous and passionate about life. Irvin Schick wrote me: "It is clear in my mind that Baldwin was only given this nickname because he was black, and that it was a racist reference. Not racist in the sense of KKK-type hatred, but racist in the sense of a totalizing, race-based characterization. . . . If a Turk called me çıfıt, for example, which is an ethnic slur for 'Jew,' I can't imagine any circumstance in which this might be 'harmless banter.' Racial slurs are racial slurs, and while Turkey does, indeed, not have the racial history and legacy of the Atlantic slave trade, Turks were black slave owners as well, and skin color has always been a measure of a person's 'quality' in Turkey." E-mail correspondence with the author, April 9, 2007.

51. Thanks to my colleague Kirsten Gomard of Aarhus University for sharing this with me. Julian Tuwim's poem, whose title translates much in the way that the Danish one does, ends with a line that expresses patronizing regret at "nice little Bambo's" inability to attend a Polish school with Polish children; it was taught as part of the communist multicultural agenda. The original source for both poems, I believe, was one of the early-twentieth-century American examples of racist rhymes that feature prominently in Marlon Riggs's documentary *Ethnic Notions.* That the Polish curriculum still uses "Murzynek Bambo" can be seen at the website of Ogniskowiec (Śląski Publikator Internetowy), which presents a lesson plan (konspekt) built around the poem and other racialized rhymes featuring "Eskimos" and "the Chinese." I have yet to come across a culture where there is not some form of the "Africanist persona" used to scare children or amuse them in rhymes about stereotypically named "dark friends" in Africa. The infamous "Jolly Nigger Money Bank" that Ralph Ellison has his invisible man try to destroy seems to have circumnavigated the globe: my partner bought one in a seaside store in Skagen, Denmark, and then I heard from a Belarusian friend that she had seen them sold in postcommunist Moscow, too.

52. James Baldwin, interview with Henry Lyman, "Poems to a Listener" series, WFCR, Amherst, Mass. Aired on *All Things Considered,* National Public Radio, April 8, 2007.

53. In a letter from 1962, Baldwin described the process of filming a TV documentary based on this essay, "a *court metrage*" of about forty-five minutes that he could not "imagine" ever being shown on American TV. The shoot took "four *long* days" and featured Baldwin's narration in French and English; he felt "by way of being the star" and was glad to have gotten the "*feel* of the medium" (letter 28; emphasized words in original are underlined).

54. In *Troubled Alliance,* George S. Harris reproduces cartoons that illustrate "race prejudice in service of anti-Americanism" and may shed some additional light on the paradoxical ways in which race was seen and articulated in Turkey at the time (136–37). The first cartoon was published in 1966 (*Cumhuriyet,* February

19), when there were widespread protests against the U.S. military presence in Turkey, and depicts the hunched, Sambo-like figure of a black serviceman with grotesque facial features. The serviceman is looking up at a white military court official who is positioned high above him on a lectern. The caption reads: "Yes, sir, I seduced her, but I was on duty." Another cartoon, from *Milliyet*, June 16, 1968, depicts a monstrous "Octopus America" in a stars-and-stripes hat whose tentacles are strangling various ethnically and racially marked national representatives, including one who could be a Turk. While the first cartoon is clearly racist in its fixation on black sexuality and its sympathy for the plight of white officers commanding black troops in Turkey, the second uses the same style of racist representation to protest U.S. imperialism all over the world. In both, however, the black body is the most marked and possesses the most exaggerated stereotypical facial features.

55. This brought back memories to me, too, as this was a familiar practice in Poland under martial law. In Polish the word for moonshine is the somewhat explosive sounding *bimber*.

56. Here is my invaluable source, Irvin Schick, on the medal: "In the Mevlevi context, *sikke* (as in *Mevlevi sikkesi*) refers to the headdress of this dervish order, resembling a truncated cone. I would suppose that Cezzar and Sururi had pendants shaped like the Mevlevi headdress hanging from their necks, perhaps with calligraphy." E-mail correspondence with the author, April 9, 2007.

57. Some copies of Engin's letters survive and are reproduced in *Dost Mektupları*. On their falling out, see the conclusion in this volume.

58. Cezzar stresses that addressing his black friends with the term "nigger" was mutually agreed upon. When he describes his collaboration on *Hair* with Bernard Hassell: "And baby, he was the proudest, happiest nigger I've ever seen in my life. Excuse me, I call these friends of mine that unused word. That's the way we do it."

59. I realize that I am providing somewhat conflicting reports here about the place where the novel was actually finished and Baldwin inscribed "Istanbul" on its last page. Both Cezzar and Çapan claim that it was in their respective spaces, but in this matter I trust Leeming's account, which confirms Çapan's apartment in Bebek as the definitive location.

60. I realize this narrative was most likely rehearsed repeatedly before I recorded it; there is the instance of Thorsen's film, for example. Still, it seems that, in a similar fashion to his stance on writing, Cezzar may have been approaching his performances as onetime, unrepeatable events, too.

61. The actor Engin refers to was probably Şirin Devrim, a woman who later lived in the United States and wrote *A Turkish Tapestry: The Shakirs of Istanbul* (London: Quartet, 1994). I omit Cezzar's use of the n-word, which he employed a couple of times but then abandoned, perhaps seeing my discomfort.

62. See also John Freely, *Stamboul Sketches*.

63. In a letter dated March 21, 1960, Baldwin writes about his efforts to help Engin

"out of [his] country," and explains his difficulties with securing a permit for him by referring to the exoticization of Turkey as a homoerotically charged location. Apparently any "mention" of Baldwin's "male friends" brings to the minds of those "not-quite best of men" he has been dealing with an "endless series" of "Turkish (forgive me) baths" (letter 21).

64. Leeming explained to me that this was a "long-term love affair," which seem to undermine Cezzar's statement. Refutations of erotic connections often tell us much about those who make them.

65. Nigel Hatton (Ph.D. candidate from Stanford University) presented a Kierke-gaardian reading of *Another Country* at the "James Baldwin Anniversary Conference," University of London, Queen Mary's College, June 2007.

66. I first noted the last sentence in Kazan's *A Life* (43). I thank Werner Sollors for alerting me to the blurb; e-mail to author, November 6, 2006.

67. Kazan, *A Life*, 705, 704.

68. Just as Baldwin was afraid of losing his passport, so Gabriel García Márquez could not get a visa to the United States for years. See also Kevin Gaines, *American Africans in Ghana: Black Expatriates and the Civil Rights Era* (Chapel Hill: University of North Carolina Press, 2007).

69. *Kurban* was originally published in 1967. The title could also be translated as "victim." Most likely Baldwin and Cezzar worked on it both some time in 1974 and in 1981 in Bodrum. I say more about this in the conclusion.

70. The events in Greece that Cezzar is referring to took place in 1974, when a new government came to power after Turkey had invaded Cyprus and caused many civilian deaths. The United States tried to broker a peace agreement, with no success. In 1975 the Turks announced the formation of the Turkish Federated State of Cyprus; the Turkish Cypriot leader Rauf Denktaş became president. In 1983 the Turkish Cypriots declared themselves an independent state, which is recognized solely by Turkey.

71. Despite his promises, Cezzar did not share the scripts of *The Sacrifice* or *The Swordfish* with me. I was able to obtain a copy of the treatment of *The Sacrifice*, an eight-page summary in three acts in Baldwin's handwriting, from the Schomburg Center for African American Research in New York. This document does not contain dates or place names, so it is impossible to locate it in Baldwin's trajectory or in the chronology of his friendship with Cezzar.

72. See, for example, Bernard Lewis, *Race and Slavery in the Middle East*; and Siegal, *Islam's Black Slaves*. In "Room in the East," Campbell includes a longer anec-dote about Kemal's black cat, whose name was Jimmy, "'named after the other Jimmy'"; the succeeding generations of Kemal's cats bore that name, too (3).

73. David Leeming suggested in our interview that some of the impressions Cezzar had of Baldwin's actions and decisions should be taken with a grain a salt, espe-cially given Cezzar's own admissions that he did not remember everything very well. For example, Leeming recalls that Engin would repeatedly try to encour-age Jimmy to, as he put it in the interview, "buy [a house] in Turkey. . . . When

he said things like 'I should buy the Pasha's Library.'" It is not clear that, given Turkish real estate laws at the time, this would have been possible, however. Leeming told me that he saw Baldwin's buying the house in Saint-Paul de Vence as a good decision, especially financially, which would prove "valuable to the Baldwin Estate today if treated properly" (correspondence with author).

74. See also the poem by Czesław Miłosz, "My Faithful Mother Tongue," *The Separate Notebooks*, trans. Robert Hass and Robert Pinsky et al. (New York: Ecco Press, 1984), 193.

TWO Queer Orientalisms in *Another Country*

1. Baldwin-Cezzar letters, letter 7, August 9, 1958. Baldwin also writes that there "seems to" be no way of hiding "the truth" in this novel and reinforces this in a parenthetical sentence in French that he does not "stand a chance" to do so.

2. The letter also mentions a screenplay, which is coming slowly, on which Baldwin works before going to bed and hopes to finish by the weekend and send "down to the city."

3. Leeming's biography gives a series of references to this novel's inspirations and development that are worth looking at chronologically. He dates the genesis of the novel to Baldwin's early years in the Village, when he was trying to sort out his "confused sexuality" and channel some of his thinking into a novel under the working title *Ignorant Armies*. This project, whose characters would "suddenly stop . . . speaking" and make him lose "his sense of the novel's form," would later break into *Another Country* and *Giovanni's Room* (52–53). Leeming stresses that the Village years "had been traumatic . . . and . . . somewhat productive" and had made Baldwin realize that he had reached an impasse and needed to leave (53). In Paris, Baldwin was desperate for money and tried to work as a singer in "an Arab nightclub" (67); around 1951 he was working on another novel, *So Long at the Fair*, that would evolve into *Another Country* (68). While in New York in December 1954, Baldwin met his lover, the Swiss Lucien Happersberger, at the airport; that scene would later be reworked into the novel's conclusion featuring Yves's entry into the United States (99). In 1956, getting ready to leave France the following year, Baldwin was hoping to finish the novel and took a trip to Corsica to be able to focus on writing (118, 120). Once there, driven to despair by his current love affair and writing trouble, he considered suicide, but "the call to witness asserted itself at the last minute, and he stepped out of the sea and turned back to *Another Country*" and realized that "Eugene Worth . . . would be the primary instrument for a central portion of *Another Country*." At the same time, Baldwin also "spent a great deal of time wondering how he could best contribute to the American civil rights struggle. He was, of course, discovering what *Another Country* had to be about. And he was saving himself from despair" (132). Leeming also emphasizes that the writing of the novel that made Baldwin "face himself" was a reason for his return to the United

States to "avoid the arrogance that might come with isolation in his European tower" (133). See also references to the short story "Come Out the Wilderness" as "closely related to Ida and her dilemma" (149), Baldwin's trip back to Paris, where he was hoping yet again to finish the novel (151–53), which he was also working on while living on Horacio Street in the Village in 1959. In 1960 he published an excerpt, "Any Day Now," in the spring issue of *Partisan Review*. On the length of the process of writing *Another Country*, see also Dievler, "Sexual Exiles," 163.

4. Standley and Pratt, *Conversations*, 59.

5. Cezzar, interviewed in Karen Thorsen's documentary *James Baldwin: The Price of the Ticket* (1989); Leeming, *James Baldwin*, 263. Thorsen's film embellishes the familiar in Baldwin's connection to Turkey and thus domesticates the country as a location for a black gay writer. Baldwin's residence in Paris was never characterized in such terms; he himself stressed his reactions to the strangeness of the city and France in "Equal in Paris," "Encounter on the Seine," and "The Discovery of What It Means to Be an American."

6. Soundtrack to Thorsen's *James Baldwin: The Price of the Ticket*.

7. I refer to the "East," "Orient," and "Orientalism" somewhat interchangeably in the readings that follow and include some scholarly references to these terms. My intention in this chapter is to elucidate the "Orient" as part of the complex context for rereading Baldwin's *Another Country*, rather than to present an exhaustive study of the diverse and voluminous criticism and theory on the subject.

8. The complete sentence reads: "In his essays, since 'The Fire Next Time,' the lapse took the form of an anxious, almost epileptic compulsion to connect with the realities of a developing black America, to find a prophetic role while spending too much time in France and Turkey." While both locations, as European and foreign, are to blame, I focus only on Turkey. I also want to acknowledge this review's ambivalently positive reading of *Just above My Head*, in which, Leonard claims, Baldwin "recovers himself." This novel's "cage of bone" surrounds an "astonishing heart." John Leonard, review of *Just above My Head*, by James Baldwin, Books of the Times, *New York Times*, September 21, 1979, C25.

9. See Kim Fortuny's forthcoming work, *American Writers in Turkey: Melville to Baldwin*.

10. Dievler discusses Baldwin's "recognition of one's state of exile" through "the act of writing"; "only by actually emigrating was Baldwin able to come to terms with the fact that he was disconnected from his native culture—actual exile and its attending creative productivity enabled Baldwin to understand where he was from" ("Sexual Exiles," 165).

11. Interview with the author, June 2005.

12. Dwight A. McBride examines the same scene, albeit as excerpted in Thorsen's documentary, and without acknowledging Pakay's authorship of it, in "Can the Queen Speak?" 39–40. McBride's conclusion that the scene "undercuts the veracity of Baldwin's statement" (40) is supported by the tone of Thorsen's film,

but Pakay's complete cinematic statement makes it rather ambivalent. I agree with McBride's astute reading of the "narratives that African American intellectuals employ to qualify themselves in the terms of race discourse to speak for the race" and that Baldwin sometimes seems to fall prey to them (42).

13. Schick defines the title phrase of his study the *Erotic Margin* as bringing together notions of spatiality and sexuality to focus on the "erotic writings produced in Europe (and . . . North America), but staged in or otherwise related to the Middle East and particularly Turkey" (10). His notion of staging narratives depicting erotic fantasies in faraway lands in the East echoes Said's notion of representation as a theatrical idea that helps us to sort out the relationship between the East and the Orient: "The Orient is the stage on which the whole East is confined. . . . Not an unlimited extension beyond the familiar European world, but rather a closed field, a theatrical stage affixed to Europe." Schick's and Said's definitions are also helpful to my reading of all Western travelers as, to lesser or greater degree, "Orientalists" and thus exoticists focused on the erotic. As Said states, an "Orientalist is but the particular specialist in knowledge for which Europe at large is responsible, in the way that an audience is historically and culturally responsible for (and responsive to) dramas technically put together by the dramatist" (*Orientalism*, 63).

14. Lowe describes here the "junctures at which narratives of gendered, racial, national, and class differences complicate and interrupt the narrative of orientalism" (*Critical Terrains*, 5). This is precisely what Baldwin's black queer text does.

15. Darsey discusses Baldwin's Americanness and preoccupation with place ("Baldwin's Cosmopolitan Loneliness," 191).

16. Interview with author, September 2005, Ankara, Turkey.

17. Maureen Freely is the daughter of John Freely, who is the author of many books on Istanbul and a physics professor at Boğaziçi Üniversitesi. John also met Baldwin and has many fond memories of him. Maureen grew up with many of the colorful characters at Robert College in the 1960s. In our interview, John Freely assured me that her fictional descriptions of everyday life in Istanbul were realistic. At the same time, a casual perusal of popular publications from the era proves that, at least in the official media, women's bodies were as much on display and as uncovered in Turkey as they were in the West.

18. Graham-Brown, *Images of Women*, calls attention to the gendering of the region in images that take the "'Oriental woman' to represent the Orient itself" (7), as well as to the "fantasy of the Orient as the site of sexual freedom and experiment" (9). See also Christina Klein, *Cold War Orientalism*, which stresses both the similarities with, and differences of, specifically post–World War II American Orientalism from Said's model (10–11).

19. Like the works of these scholars, Reina Lewis's *Gendering Orientalism* draws close parallels between literary and visual culture (6) and pays attention to the importance of women and female sexuality as the "sign of the Orient's erotic and passionate potential" (173). See also Yeğenoğlu, *Colonial Fantasies*.

20. Schick's *The Erotic Margin* gives a detailed account of how this perspective developed in popular, and often prurient, travel writing during the eighteenth and nineteenth centuries. See also Germaner's and İnankur's *Orientalism and Turkey*, which emphasizes that "for Europeans experiencing the rapid changes of the Industrial Revolution the East seemed a picturesque world where nothing ever changed" (44).

21. See Von Eschen, *Satchmo Blows Up the World*, on the State Department–sponsored visits of jazz musicians to Istanbul (52–53). In a note to Cezzar written around 1970, Baldwin mentions Ken Keith, the Istanbul cultural attaché he was friends with in the late sixties. Keith was to be a liaison to promote an American-Turkish co-production of Shaw's *St. Joan* (1924) and Marlowe's *Tamburlaine the Great* (1587), the plays that Baldwin hoped to produce and direct with Engin and Gülriz in the 1970s (Baldwin-Cezzar letters, letter 54). While Baldwin agrees that his choice of these plays about a Catholic female saint and a Tartar conqueror was "outrageous," he argues for their cultural and artistic relevance to the specific political situation between East and West. I will return to the discussion of *St. Joan* and Baldwin's comparison of Shaw's heroine's fate with the fate of Malcolm X in chapter 4 and the Conclusion. On the Orientalism of *Tamburlaine*, see Obeidat, *American Literature and Orientalism*, 16–18, which claims that this play was written at the height of the perceptions of the "Turkish [Islamic] threat" in Europe (16).

22. Soundtrack to outtakes, *From Another Place*.

23. See also pp. 138–40 for a concise review of the historical and religious underpinnings of the "West–East global axis" as "a fundamentally racialized world social structure."

24. These two colorful characters, an Irish American and an Englishman, dedicated their book to "Three Who Loved Istanbul": Lee Fonger, Keith Greenwood, and David Garwood, all of whom Baldwin was likely to have met. Freely especially studied the area and later wrote numerous books about it and the neighboring regions. Like Boyd, Freely is a character worthy of a book of his own, an "irrepressible Irish storyteller," as Sedat Pakay told me (interview with author, June 2005). Freely's books were all published late during Baldwin's stays in Turkey or after he had left for France, so I am not sure he would have read them. See especially *Stamboul Sketches* (with Pakay's photographs) and *Inside the Seraglio*.

25. Soundtrack to outtakes, *From Another Place*.

26. See also other definitions in the works of Butler, Sedgwick, Stockton, Somerville (*Queering*, 142), Chauncey, Halberstam (*Queer Time and Place*), Ferguson, and E. Patrick Johnson. The closest to Baldwin's usage of the term is this observation from Sedgwick's *Tendencies*: "A lot of the most exciting recent work around 'queer' spins the term outward along dimensions that can't be subsumed under gender and sexuality at all: the ways that race, ethnicity, postcolonial nationality criss-cross with these *and other* identity-constructing, identity-fracturing discourses. . . . Intellectuals and artists of color whose sexual self-definition

includes 'queer' . . . are using the leverage of 'queer' to do a new kind of justice to the fractal intricacies of language, skin, migration, state. Thereby, the gravity (I mean the *gravitas*, the meaning, but also the *center* of gravity) of the term 'queer' itself deepens and shifts" (9).

27. Robert Reid-Pharr offers a compelling reading of Vivaldo Moore as an "optically white" and queer character ("Dinge," 84). See also Stockton's *Beautiful Bottom* on "the linguistic markers 'black' and 'queer' in the social field of signs" (27–33).

28. See also Nathaniel Deutsch, "The Asiatic Black Man: An African American Orientalism?" *Journal of Asian American Studies* 4.3 (2001): 193–20.

29. Interview with author, Istanbul, May 25, 2001.

30. Leeming interview with author, June 30, 2003.

31. Cezzar claims that Jimmy wrote "the last three parts" of the book at his house; this implies that Baldwin was mostly working on revisions while at Cevat's. Many years after their discussions, Çapan was unable to give me a detailed list of the specific editorial changes he suggested to Baldwin.

32. Interview with author, Istanbul, May 26, 2001.

33. Later Baldwin would travel back and forth between his house in the south of France and the United States to teach at the Five Colleges in Massachusetts in the 1970s and 1980s.

34. This was confirmed by Cevza Sevgen, now chair of the English Department at Boğaziçi Üniversitesi. As she told me, she was just "a little girl in the girls' high school" at the time. Sevgen remembers Baldwin's flamboyant clothing and mannerisms and how her class was overawed by his lectures (interview with author, September 2005).

35. Wallace's "On Being a Witness" takes on Baldwin's pedagogy (276–88).

36. Ağaoğlu, "James Baldwin'le Konuşma," 19; translated by Aslı Gür.

37. E. Lâle Demirtürk discusses a similar feeling of being an object of American cultural imperialism: "In fact, we Turks live in a country where we are constantly aware of the image-domination of the Western world, while witnessing Turkish stereotypes in movies or news in Western media as 'savage' non-persons. On Turkish TV we are bombarded by an abundance of American movies, some of which advertise either Middle Eastern or Turkish non-personhood. We are made into an audience (passive spectators) watching how we are caught up in the colonialist positionality, imposing its own 'construction of reality' . . . on and fixating its power relations with us." "Teaching African-American Literature in Turkey," 166. See also Reina Lewis, *Rethinking Orientalism*, for a historical perspective on how gender and specifically Western sexual curiosity about harem life were received by the Orientalized subjects (14–17).

38. In Thorsen's film, Kemal also argues for Baldwin's affinity with Dostoyevsky.

39. I would like to acknowledge my debt to Baldwin for showing me how to see, too. In this I echo the opening of Lawrie Balfour's *The Evidence of Things Not Said*, which was among the early inspirations for this book.

40. Baldwin was well aware of the racial coding reflected in Shakespeare's lines.

Scholars such as Kim F. Hall confirm that the "descriptions of dark and light . . . became in the early modern period the conduit through which the English began to formulate the notions of 'self' and 'other' so well known in Anglo-American racial discourse" (*Things of Darkness*, 2).

41. See Leeming, *Amazing Grace*, 166, 185.

42. Baldwin-Cezzar letters, letter 25, August 13, 1961.

43. Delaney visited Baldwin in Istanbul in 1967. Baldwin kept in close touch with him from the time they met until Delaney's death in 1979. Greenwich Village, where Delaney used to have a studio, provides one of the key settings in *Another Country*.

44. Other personal reasons had to do with Baldwin's attempts to win back Lucien Happersberger, the Swiss man with whom he had a deep love relationship when he first went to Paris, and who in part inspired the character of Giovanni in *Giovanni's Room*. As Baldwin was struggling with *Another Country*, Happersberger, with whom Baldwin had parted after two years of what he would refer to as "the love of my life" (Leeming, *James Baldwin*, 74–75), separated from his first wife and under Baldwin's pressure made vague promises that he might consider getting back together with him (154–55). The trip to Turkey, then, was an escape from that relationship, at the same time as, given Baldwin's unrealistic hopes for the reunion with his former lover, it meant a waiting period and transition into a new phase in Baldwin's erotic attachments. Happersberger visited Baldwin in Istanbul in 1962.

45. Baldwin's inability to escape New York is clearly linked to his inability to escape his racialization or his epidermal emplacement there, to his entrapment and alienation in this most populous city in the United States. Chinua Achebe praises Baldwin's architectonic vision of this entrapment in the 1960s American condition described in *The Fire Next Time*: "a tightly compressed image of the ghetto . . . as both a physical urban location and a metaphysical zone of the mind, bounded and policed by the language of tinted, selective information" (6).

46. Eckman, *Furious Passage*, 158–59.

47. Styron's and David Baldwin's comments come from Thorsen's documentary.

48. Perhaps in Turkey he could also get over Paris, the second most important metropolis in his life, which, as Michel Fabre says, "he had never wanted to call home" (213).

49. See Lebbeus Woods, *War and Architecture*. I find Woods's concept helpful here, though his definition does not take into consideration issues of race (rather remarkably, too, given that he is writing in the context of the war of so-called ethnic cleansing in the former Yugoslavia). Given that Baldwin was seeking refuge from racist violence in the United States, especially after his traumatizing involvement in the civil rights struggle in the South, Woods's "freespace" as a manifestation of healing agency, self-awareness, and antiwar protest seems pertinent (American racial unrest has been referred to as the "other Civil War").

50. Interview with Leeming in Thorsen's *James Baldwin: The Price of the Ticket*.

51. Irvin Schick articulates connections between place, meaning, and identity: the "ground we stand on becomes a mongrel hybrid of spatialities; at once a metaphor and a speaking position, a place of certainty and a burden of humility. . . . Understanding the social construction of place . . . means understanding the ways in which we construct our selves" (15–16). As John R. Stilgoe remarks about Gaston Bachelard's reading of the home, "Setting is more than scene in works of art. . . . It is often the armature around which the work revolves" (Stilgoe, introduction to *Poetics of Space*, x). Thus I argue for the impact of physical space and material culture — or the actual site of writing *Another Country* — on its final shape and its inner "armature" and on Baldwin's coming-of-age as a writer. I realize that Bachelard's theory privileges home and birthplace — "the house is one of the greatest powers of integration for the thoughts, memories and dreams of mankind" (*Poetics of Space*, 6). For writers like Baldwin, who have been homeless and displaced even in their home country, who live in exile and transit, this concept is still relevant but becomes radically revisioned through the lens of race, class, and sexuality.

52. See also Leeming on Baldwin's and Cezzar's beating (*James Baldwin*, 161).

53. Porter opens his chapter on Baldwin and Henry James with a discussion of this essay and reads it as Baldwin's acknowledgment of his debt to the Master. While I agree that like James, Baldwin struggled with "the conflicting demands of Art and life," I disagree that "Baldwin's personal life and literary career consistently mirror James's" (*Stealing the Fire*, 128). While the two writers were homosexuals, Baldwin was black and of lower-class origin, differences that he never forgot as an artist and political activist, and as an out black queer who fought for racial and sexual liberation at home and abroad.

54. Baldwin, "As Much Truth as One Can Bear," *New York Times*, January 14, 1962.

55. See Oates, "Tragic Rites."

56. Many contemporary critics tended to blame Baldwin for too much attention to sexuality, if not for obscenity and immorality, as evidenced, for example by the attempts to remove his books from libraries and school curricula in Louisiana and Montana, as well as Chicago. Emphasizing that the fact that "there are not even any Negroes" in *Giovanni's Room* makes him "a little uneasy," Leslie A. Fiedler criticizes Baldwin as immature for his exclusive focus on the "last stand of Puritanism as a defense of heterosexuality" ("A Homo Sexual Dilemma," 149). Joseph Featherstone complained that the stories collected in *Going to Meet the Man* (1965) show Baldwin having been driven by "the total hunger aching inside him . . . to invest certain aspects of secular life — notably sex — with a blasphemous grace" ("Blues for Mr. Baldwin," 153). More interestingly, Featherstone complains that in *Another Country* Baldwin's portrayal of "the redeeming majesty of the orgasm — multiracial, heterosexual, or homosexual" evidences not only a "lack of artistic control . . . [but] a loss of common sense" (154). Too much sex is madness, in short, especially across the color-coded lines of desire and middle-class propriety. For similar approaches to more recent critical and schol-

arly division of labor vis-à-vis identity politics, see also Ken Warren's comment on the "critical Academy's Tuskegee Machine. If you want to talk things black, you know which people to speak to" ("From under the Superscript," 100).

57. Baldwin-Cezzar letters, letter 30, August 1962.

58. This project never materialized.

59. This line comes from the chorus to "Yellow Dog Blues" (1912) and might also be a tribute to the father of the blues, who died in 1958.

60. Rufus introduces Vivaldo to Leona as "an Irish Wop" (24), and Ida talks about his "fine Italian hair" (308). This split immigrant identity may have been Baldwin's oversight, but it may also be deliberate, so as to show how European ethnic identities overlap and morph into whiteness.

61. On the other hand, Randall Kenan finds in *Another Country* a refraction of a larger American problem, a "configuration of interactions that encompass the full range of ways any two people can be together: a kind, on the personal level of complete social and sexual integration" (98).

62. See also Reid-Pharr, McBride, DeGout, Ross, Henderson.

63. I am indebted to multiple theorists for the definitions of queer, but Eve Sedgwick's classic statement theorizes most clearly what Baldwin arrived at in his writing three decades earlier, that is, the "open mesh of possibilities, gaps, overlaps, dissonances and resonances, lapses and excesses of meaning when the constituent elements of anyone's gender, of anyone's sexuality aren't made (or *can't* be made) to signify monolithically" (*Tendencies*, 8). By "queering," after Judith Butler, I mean a strategy and approach that engages "a discursive site," a "signal" linked to an inquiry into the historical "*formation of homosexualities*" that deploys its "deformative and misappropriative power" to challenge and complicate existing identity categories. As I will demonstrate in close readings of queer moments in *Another Country*, however, Baldwin shows the inherent racialization of the term. See Butler, *Bodies That Matter*, 229–30.

64. See Michelle Wright's treatment of the conflict between Wright and Baldwin in "Alas, Poor Richard!" and her evocative reading of Stowe's and Wright's "deadly embrace" (210–12).

65. At the beginning of the novel, when Rufus first meets Leona and has sex with her, she is referred to several times as "little Eva." The scene of their sexual encounter is a fantasy enactment of what would be unthinkable in Stowe's novel (and what is actually enacted on the body of a black woman in *Native Son*): the rape of Eva by Uncle Tom transformed by Baldwin into a likeness of Bigger Thomas.

66. In *A History of Gay Literature*, Gregory Woods marks the Orient as a queer location by quoting Said's statement about the Orient's becoming "a living tableau of queerness" (53).

67. Besides "The Price of the Ticket," Baldwin remembers Worth in "The New Lost Generation" (1961), where his friend chastises him: "You're a poet, and you don't believe in love" (*Price of the Ticket*, 306–7). Worth may also be related to other doomed black men in Baldwin's fiction, Richard from *Go Tell It on the Mountain*

and Fony in *If Beale Street Could Talk*. See also Leeming, *James Baldwin*, 201, which also links him to Arthur Montana in *Just above My Head*.

68. Eckman describes the structural challenge of *Another Country* by mixing metaphors related to procreation and architecture that echo Baldwin's own language from the letters to friends and family.

69. Baldwin's novel anticipates the triangles of desire in Girard's *Deceit, Desire, and the Novel*, and later in Sedgwick's *Between Men*.

70. Leeming, *James Baldwin*; Reid-Pharr, "Tearing the Goat's Flesh"; T. Harris, *Black Women in the Fiction of James Baldwin*. See also *JB Now*; Quentin Miller, *Re-viewing James Baldwin*; and Lynn Orilla Scott, *James Baldwin's Later Fiction*.

71. Katy Ryan's provocative reading of Rufus's suicide scene in the context of Larsen's *Passing* (1929) and McCarthy's *The Group* (1963) acknowledges Baldwin's artistic achievement in signaling "a revolutionary call to remember and restore the dead" and eloquently argues against reading his portrayal of Rufus as articulating the "victim ideology" ("Falling in Public," 114).

72. As with Delaney, the friendship with Painter dated from Baldwin's coming-of-age in the Village and survived until his death in 1987.

73. I am grateful to Bryan R. Washington's *The Politics of Exile* for pointing out the source of the epigraph for *Another Country*.

74. James's main character is the ambitious and wealthy American physician Jackson Lemon. While in London, he courts Lady Barbarina, who is not wealthy but of high social standing and a perfect embodiment of English "race" and femininity. (They marry and move to New York, where Lady Barbarina is miserable. Lemon's quest is to reproduce with someone who is racially pure and superior.) *Lady Barbarina*'s setting in New York and its focus on what James calls in the preface the "international relation . . . as a relation of intermarrying" (203) are transformed in Baldwin's radical preoccupation with the City as the site of interracial sex and queer transgressions in *Another Country*.

75. In *From Harlem to Paris*, Michel Fabre remarks that the "title of the novel *Another Country* may refer to France, to which Eric Jones, a white American actor, has escaped in order to forget a tragic love affair with Rufus, a young black jazz drummer" (211). James McIntosh also suggested to me that it might echo the title of Hemingway's short story "In Another Country."

76. I am grateful to Nicholas F. Radel for pointing out this connection to Marlowe's play. The same line from *The Jew of Malta* also opens T. S. Eliot's poem "The Portrait of a Lady," which echoes the title of Henry James's famous novel of Americans in Europe, *The Portrait of a Lady*.

77. Nicholas F. Radel, letter to author, March 25, 2006. See also Kim F. Hall's *Things of Darkness*, which discusses a convergence of issues akin to gender and race around blackness and Jewishness (39); G. Wood's chapter on Marlowe in *A History of Gay Literature*; and Obeidat's *American Literature and Orientalism*, especially the introduction, for a helpful summary of European and American literary approaches

to the Orient and the East. Also Bartels, *Spectacles of Strangeness*, for a close look at Christopher Marlowe's central reliance on the figure of a racialized other that emerged in the discourses on early modern identities that took place between the rhetoric of the state and popular culture, for example on the Elizabethan stage: "An important part of the support for English superiority and domination was the insistence on the otherness of the other and on what had been or were becoming stereotypical demonizations of such figures as the Turk, the Moor, or the Oriental barbarian" (xiii–xiv).

78. Said's analysis at that point in *Orientalism* of Flaubert's observances of various sexual grotesqueries does not ally itself theoretically with the meaning of "queer" that I have in mind. Nevertheless it reflects how the Orient has been represented as an excessive and transgressive location eroticized by Western writers.

79. Other "false faiths" included those of the Armenians, Maronites, and Orthodox Greeks. See also Little, *American Orientalism*, where he observes that even at the beginning of the twentieth century, Judaism and Jewishness were seen in a similar way in the New World: "As early as 1900 . . . U.S. policy makers tended to place Arabs and Jews near the bottom . . . of the hierarchy of races" (10). Little also observes that to John Quincy Adams, "the Jews [were] the worst" (11). By the late twentieth century, of course, Americans accepted the Israeli state as "more western than oriental" while continuing to regard the "children of Ishmael" as inferior and barbaric. See also pp. 11–24 for a useful review of the changing historical attitudes to Islam and Judaism. See also Said, *Orientalism*, 141, 145–46.

80. Back cover: James Baldwin, *Bir Başka Ülke*, trans. Çiğdem Öztekin (Istanbul: Yapı Kredi Yayınları, 2005). This description is paraphrased in another blurb about this volume in the journal *Radikal Kitap*, no. 238. An earlier issue, no. 236, introduces the blurb with the headline "The Other Voice of America: Exiled and Black" and extrapolates on the not-so-imaginative cover design, which features a blurry black man's head singing at a microphone: "All the characters in *Another Country* are looking for the same thing, which was the object of the search of their author: identity. The rhythm of this search is underwritten with jazz and blues. The music of guilty emotions, jazz is perhaps like another country that cannot be fully inhabited. A contemporary, genuine, and unforgettable masterpiece by Baldwin. *Another Country*, now in Turkish forty-three years after it was written." Blurb translated by Aslı Gür.

81. Dievler states that "almost all" characters in the novel are "artists . . . and their success or failure is tied to their ability to 'read or write' stories—their own and those of others" ("Sexual Exiles," 164).

82. Speaking of turning space into place, or giving meaning to locations, Schick reminds us: "Place is not merely the domain of thought, it is an integral part of political praxis, since people act less upon realities than upon their perceptions of those realities." In such a context, cultural production such as writing can be

seen as a form of praxis, so a novel, "like art, does not just mean, it also *does*" (234).

83. This section of the novel contains references to Vivaldo and Rufus sharing women for sex (134), and Vivaldo and a "colored buddy" of his in the army comparing penises in a Munich bar to show off in front of "a girl," but also "to each other" (134).

84. Vivaldo has used black women as a means of escape before. His guilty trips to Harlem in search of sex with black prostitutes and his involvement with Ida might also be read as linked to his desire to share blackness, and possibly queerness, with Rufus. On the other hand, they may suggest his homophobia and panic in the face of queer desire that Rufus made him feel. After all, he could not touch a black body unless he paid for sex, as he did with the prostitutes, or unless he used it as a means to escape American notions of race, as he does with Ida when they have sex for the first time.

85. See for example, what Trudier Harris calls the "bright plumage" of Helga Crane in Nella Larsen's *Passing*. See also Harris's chapter on *Another Country* in *Black Women*, and Germaner's and İnankur's *Orientalism and Turkey* for reproductions of socially marked and exoticized ("Arab") male and female bodies (146, 155). This scene is also a kind of replay of Rufus's and Leona's walk through the Village at the onset of their tormented interracial relationship, whose beginning and demise Vivaldo witnessed and perhaps unwittingly imitates, reveling in his power to draw admiration as a white man with an attractive black woman, rather than hostility as Rufus and Leona did.

86. See also Schick, *The Erotic Margin*; and G. Woods, "The Orient" (53–67), in *A History of Gay Literature*.

87. On Baldwin's exile from the sexual culture of New York, see also Dievler, "Sexual Exiles," 164–65.

88. The plagued city of the East that Eric sees in New York can also be read through the representation of the city of Oran in Albert Camus's *The Plague* (1947). By the time Baldwin was writing *Another Country*, he was familiar with Camus and the French approaches to Algeria. See also Baldwin's essay "The Male Prison" (first published as "Gide as Husband and Homosexual" in 1954), where he discusses André Gide's *Madeleine* and Gide's "fascination . . . for countries like North Africa" and the guiltless "sensuality" of its people (in *The Price of the Ticket*, 104).

89. In his introduction to *Four Plays*, by Christopher Marlowe, Havelock Ellis points out Marlowe's succumbing in the second part of the play to the "harsh and extravagant caricature [of the Jew]" (xi). Given Baldwin's title, then, this supports my reading of Steve Ellis as Jewish.

90. There is voluminous scholarship on this issue. See, for example, Jacobson, *Barbarian Virtues*; and Ramaswami Mahalingam, ed., *Cultural Psychology of Immigrants* (Mahwaw, N.J.: Lawrence Erlbaum, 2006).

91. The character of Ellis might be somewhat related to Norman Mailer, with whom

Baldwin had a falling out after Mailer's homophobic remarks about him in *Advertisements for Myself* (1960). Baldwin's essay "The Black Boy Looks at the White Boy," published as Baldwin was struggling with *Another Country* and right before he went to Turkey, portrays Mailer and his posturing as the "White Negro" as having much to do with American racialized and heteronormative notions of masculinity: "that myth of the sexuality of Negroes which Norman, like so many others, refuses to give up" (*Price of the Ticket*, 292).

92. See Sander Gilman on the stereotypes of avaricious and sexually greedy Jews in *The Jew's Body*. See also Zaborowska, "Americanization of a 'Queer Fellow.'"

93. See the works by Brodkin, Jacobson, Roediger, Michaels, and Lipsitz on the whitening of the ethnics after World War II.

94. The references to this trope are too numerous to list in one note. Within American studies, Henry Nash Smith's *Virgin Land* exploits it, and Annette Kolodny's *The Lay of the Land* provides its feminist revisionist reading. Andrea Smith's *Conquest: Sexual Violence and American Indian Genocide* (Cambridge, Mass.: South End Press, 2005) provides the indigenous perspective. Schick discusses it on pp. 1–10; see also the works of Reina Lewis; Nadine Naber; Linda Steet, *Veils and Daggers*, esp. 146–52; Meyna Yeğenoğlu; Lisa Lowe; and Matthew Bernstein and Gaylyn Studlar, among others. Some of these scholars, Schick, Lewis, and Lowe in particular, call attention to the picture being more problematic and complex in cases when the Western travelers to the East were women.

95. Germaner and İnankur emphasize the "mystique which surrounded [Eastern women] in the European mind and their inaccessibility to the European outsider." The "barbarity or eroticism which arose from the [European artist's] imagination" is mirrored in the image they reproduce, Jean-Jules-Antoine Lecompte de Nouÿ's "The White Slave" (1888) (*Orientalism and Turkey*, 42). This image, of a light-skinned nude houri smoking a cigarette and seated inside a Turkish bath on rich fabrics, with wine and food around her, provides an interesting visual context for my reading of the barbarity and eroticism of Vivaldo's fantasies. Along with the "white slave," the painting also features two black women, fully clad, who are clearly the servants to the houri. One of them is crouching over the water washing clothes, while the other, whose body is cut off by the edge of the picture so that only her left arm and leg are showing, is on her way out, carrying laundry. The interdependence between and hierarchy of the women's bodies could not be any clearer; it echoes Vivaldo's juggling act as he tries to position Ida in his imagining of their sexual encounter.

96. See McAlister; and Shohat and Stam.

97. Trudier Harris's *Black Women in the Fiction of James Baldwin* offers perhaps the fullest and most astute reading of Ida's complex position vis-à-vis the other characters in *Another Country*. My reading is indebted to Harris's statement that "Vivaldo has difficulty separating her from the . . . whores he has known. . . . [And he] still has at the back of his mind the mental trash that suggests that black women are un-

consciously free with their bodies" (119). There is also an interesting connection here to the escapade that Vivaldo recalls in detail, a confrontation with a pimp who threatens him with castration.

98. Naber presents contemporary female sexual stereotypes between East and West in "Arab American Femininities."

99. Schick's chapter "Gendered Geography, Sexualized Empire" (*The Erotic Margin*, 105–74) offers a rich review of literature on the subject of the West's relationship with xenotopia. See especially p. 114, where he links Freud to colonialism: "'The often-quoted 1926 statement by Freud that 'after all, the sexual life of adult women is a "dark continent" for psychology' is indicative of the connections between femininity, sexuality, and Europe's colonial relations with xenotopia." The way Vivaldo sees Ida clearly echoes this statement.

100. Baldwin may have read some of the accounts written about Ottoman women by Western female writers, such as Hester Donaldson Jenkins's *Behind Turkish Lattices*. Jenkins was an American teacher at the American College for Girls in Istanbul, then Constantinople, and wrote the book based on her research and experience of living among Turkish women. She includes a wedding scene description (54–67), complete with the removal of the veil by the groom and his first sighting of the bride (60), as well as accounts of young girls sold into slavery and trained to become wives and harem inhabitants. See also Mari Yoshihara, *Embracing the East*.

101. See Schick on the collective mass-body and mass-orgasm (202–5).

102. While we have no insight into Ida's mind in that scene, it is clear from her exchange with Cass later that she is profoundly aware of the complexity of her relationship with Vivaldo. Given her status as an avenging, Antigone-like figure, she is thus an example of what Sandra Gunning calls the "survival and defiance of white supremacist violence," as she enters in a "confrontation of internal cultural shifts . . . as African Americans appropriated and transformed white social codes of conduct" (*Race, Rape, and Lynching*, 139).

103. See also Ross, "Race, Rape, Castration."

104. See also Dyer's "A Passage to India." Writing about David Lean's film version of E. M. Forster's novel, he targets "white liberalism" and its "problem in dealing with black sexuality" in ways that are helpful for understanding Vivaldo's mental gymnastics and desire to de-racialize and re-virginize Ida: "So anxious are we not to be associated with this attitude [viewing black sexuality as dangerous, rampant, seething] . . . that we then fall back onto whitewashed images of black sexuality as almost non-existent in its innocence" (*The Matter of Images*, 122–23).

105. See also Zaborowska on Cahan's David Levinsky and his Americanization as heterosexualization (215–22). To this character, Gentile-looking and light-complexioned women, even Jewish women, imply white women, and thus his seduction of Vera is the ultimate Americanizing conquest as she is both white-looking and married.

106. Matthew Fry Jacobson's *Whiteness of a Different Color* and *Barbarian Virtues* exam-

ine in depth the racialization of the "white ethnics." Sander Gilman's work in *The Jew's Body* and *Disease and Representation* on the pathologization—racialization and oversexualization—of the Jewish body is instructive, too. See also Roediger; Waters; and Lipsitz on white and ethnic identities.

107. See also Keizer, *Black Subjects*; Connell's and Kimmel's works are helpful to defining and historicizing American masculinity.

108. As Robert Reid-Pharr remarks, erotic triangles and rectangles abound in this novel. I am aware of the charged geometric links between Vivaldo, Cass, and Richard—and to a degree Rufus, who is everywhere—but focus only on the relationships relevant to my immediate theme of Orientalism.

109. Vivaldo is also experimenting with weed at this moment, as he is hanging out with his friend Lorenzo and his crowd; he resists homoerotic advances from one of them in the course of the night.

110. When Vivaldo responds to Ida's question about his sexual history, specifically whether he has ever slept with black women, he tells her the truth about his trading in black flesh in the whorehouses of Harlem. Significantly, Ida is the one who has the courage to ask the question that he dares not ask of her upon discovering that she is not a virgin. As she does ask it, though, they are making love in the missionary position, and thus Vivaldo retains power and control over her body, although she may have the discursive upper hand. When Vivaldo tells Ida that he has paid black prostitutes for sex, their "struggle begins" as they labor through the intercourse but also initiate their history as an interracial couple that has to contend with the profound inequalities of power and twists and turns of desire and love that, as Baldwin stresses in Pakay's film, always "comes in strange packages."

111. See also links to the falls and jumps, some of which Ryan notes in "Falling in Public," such as Vivaldo taking the plunge into career and responsibility, "the only water there was" (a pathetic comparison with Rufus's suicide on p. 165); Eric has the same thought about his plunge into New York and his career there.

112. Given her full name, Clarissa, Cass and her feminine distaste for reality echoes Samuel Richardson's eighteenth-century heroine, a victim of rape, whose story contributed to the rise of the novel as a literary genre. So the names Cass and Richard might not be accidental and point to Baldwin's desire to locate his book in Anglo-American literary history.

113. Richard's implicit otherness as an ethnic is suggested during his final confrontation with Cass, as he aligns himself with Ellis (370).

114. This scene is a replay of another charged moment of arrival in New York in Baldwin's short story "This Morning, This Evening, So Soon," which was written at the time he was struggling with *Another Country*. See my forthcoming essay "'In the Same Boat.'"

115. This is how Oktay Balamir explains it: "It was him [Ali Poyrazoğlu] that named the play. . . . There is a common phrase in Turkey which . . . says, 'There would be no friend for the fallen one' or 'Once one falls down there won't be anyone

around to take him as a friend.' This bitter phrase is usually referred [to] during conversations for those that have gone bankrupt in business; or prostitutes; or prisoners." Letter to author, March 24, 2006.

THREE Staging Masculinity in *Düşenin Dostu*

The chapter epigraph is quoted from James Baldwin, "Bütün İnsanlar Kardeştir," *Tiyatro Dergisi*, no. 13 (1969). These notes were given to the actors and producers and appeared in the Sururi-Cezzar Theater's newsletter, translated into Turkish (most likely by Zeynep Oral). Parts have been reprinted in Campbell's biography. I also read a copy of Baldwin's original typed draft of these notes during my visit with Engin Cezzar in 2001. The Sururi-Cezzar Theater Company has closed down since then.

All translations from the Turkish are by Aslı Gür, unless noted otherwise.

1. In *Blues for Mister Charlie*, Baldwin responded to Elia Kazan's suggestion that he write a play inspired by the murder of Emmett Till in Mississippi in 1955. *Blues* was a work that Baldwin felt he "had to" write, and centers on the killing of a young black activist, Richard, by a small-town white racist, Lyle. It features the responses of the citizens of Whitetown and Blacktown—as the color-coded parts of the town are called—to the murder and the ensuing trial, which ends with Lyle's acquittal by an all-white, all-male jury. The play was performed by the Actors Studio and opened on Broadway on April 23, 1964, "to an audience of highly appreciative blacks and sometimes angry and often shocked whites" (Leeming, *James Baldwin*, 238). The production was contentious and fraught with emotional difficulties for Baldwin, who felt that Lee Strasberg and Cheryl Crawford did not understand his motives and were afraid to shock the white audience with the truths about racism that he tried to communicate: "The scenes that occurred . . . are now fixed in Broadway legend" (233). Because Baldwin insisted on a low admission price so that uptown audiences could see the play, the theater wanted to close it after a month, as it was not generating enough income. In an ironic twist, *Blues for Mister Charlie* was saved by a substantial donation from the Rockefeller sisters Ann Pierson and Mary Strawbridge that, in addition to a petition signed by famous actors and artists—Marlon Brando, Sidney Poitier, Lena Horne, Richard Avedon, Harry Belafonte, Sammy Davis Jr., and June Shagaloff—extended the run until late August. (See also the detailed account in Weatherby, *Artist on Fire*, 236–55.) When the truncated production was taken to London, Baldwin publicly protested the Actors Studio's handling of his material and later took up his disagreement with them in fictional form in *Tell Me How Long the Train's Been Gone*, which would be completed in 1967 in Istanbul.

2. The essay was originally published in *Esquire* in April 1960 and was later collected in *Nobody Knows My Name* and *The Price of the Ticket* as "The Northern Protestant" (*Price of the Ticket*, 171).

3. Baldwin's first play, *The Amen Corner* (1954), was a theatrical rendering of the

themes related to the black church and family life in Harlem that preoccupied him in his first novel. Sister Margaret, the Pentecostal minister of a small congregation, banishes sensuality and joy from her life, as they remind her of her estranged husband, a jazz musician. She demands that her congregation embrace similar "mortification of the flesh." Her world comes crashing down when her husband returns home ill to die, and their only son, whom Margaret has been grooming for the church, announces that he wants to leave home and pursue unholy music like his father. In the end, Margaret is demoted by scheming competitors in the congregation. But she triumphs spiritually in her final sermon, in which she embraces humanistic love and compassion that transcends religious creed and petty power struggles. Leeming suggests that the inspiration for her character was Mother Horn, "the minister who presided over Baldwin's own 'salvation'" (*James Baldwin*, 107). The play was first performed by the Howard University Players under the direction of Owen Dodson on May 11–14, 1955, and was attended by notables such as E. Franklin Frazier, Sterling Brown, and Alain Locke (107). The complete published version of *The Amen Corner* appeared in 1968 from Dial Press. For more detailed information, see Leeming, *James Baldwin*, 106–13 and 247–50.

4. Baldwin's other writings for the theater include a piece on Ray Charles that became a concert performance, *The Hallelujah Chorus's The Life and Times of Ray Charles, Written by James Baldwin and Performed by Ray Charles*, which was a major event at the 1973 Newport Jazz Festival in New York. George Wein, its producer, describes in his autobiography what it was like to work with two such strong personalities onstage: "At my request, Jimmy had visited Ray in California to discuss the program. I was prepared to put the show entirely in their hands. I had only one request as a producer. I wanted the concert to begin with Jimmy at the podium and Ray alone at the piano. . . . Ray Charles had a strong personality. . . . Ray would open with the band. That was that. Jimmy didn't press the issue. As a result, the concert fell short of my hopes. Jimmy read a lyrical passage at the beginning of the show, and later presented some material from his play, 'The Hallelujah Chorus,' with Cicely Tyson and other actors. Otherwise, it was a fairly standard Ray Charles show . . . a treat, but not the personal program that it could have been. . . . I never told him that I was disappointed with the concert" (Wein, *Myself Among Others*, 387–88). Leeming dates the Charles-Baldwin performance to July 1 at Carnegie Hall; he also includes David Baldwin and David Moses in the cast of actors who read from Baldwin's short story "Sonny's Blues," which contains one of the most moving passages on jazz performance ever written in English (*James Baldwin*, 319). Baldwin also collaborated on a play, *The Welcome Table* (1987), which was his last finished work, with Walter Dallas, an African American director and drama professor trained at the Yale Drama School. I discuss *The Welcome Table* in the conclusion.

5. Interview with author, Ankara, September 7, 2005.

6. Roth, "Blues for Mr. Charlie," 43; Howard Taubman, "Theater: 'Blues for Mister

Charlie,'" *New York Times*, April 24, 1964. Taubman's review is strongly racialized and, like Roth's, misses the key points that Baldwin's play makes about the stereotypes of gender and sexuality as inextricably intertwined with race. For example, Taubman writes that "Mr. Baldwin knows how the Negroes think and feel, but his inflexible, Negro-hating Southerners are stereotypes," at the same time as he waxes sentimental over Parnell's "tender and harrowing recollection of his love for a Negro girl of 17 when he was 18 and of the terrible moment when her mother, a servant in his house, discovered them," and considers these parts to have come from Baldwin "at the top of his form."

7. Letter 33, March 13, 1964. The Sururi-Cezzar Theater did not end up staging *Blues*. Baldwin also writes in the letter about the chilling of his friendship with Kazan: Baldwin had refused to allow Kazan to direct *Blues* at Lincoln Center, and he left conspicuously early from Kazan's production of Arthur's Miller's "opus-or opera," as he refers to the performance in the letter, a gala preview at the Center, where Baldwin had been invited as one of the "dignitaries." He emphasizes that he was "revolted" by the play and wanted to avoid having to talk to either Miller or Kazan at the reception afterward. (Baldwin may be referring here to the 1964 production of Arthur Miller's *After the Fall*, which opened at the American National Theater and Academy, at the time housed in temporary quarters in Washington Square Theater, on January 23.) In a letter (no. 48) of January 10, 1970, Baldwin revisits the idea of staging *Blues* in Turkey, encouraged by the tremendous popularity of *Fortune and Men's Eyes*, and is clearly excited about an abundance of other theater projects to do in Istanbul. He mentions having to finish the script for Moravia's *A Cultural Experiment* and considers as well staging *Slow Dance on the Killing Ground* with Sururi as the main character, a "desperate lady" in Brooklyn searching for an abortionist. Baldwin also mentions that Gülriz's not having been to America does not matter, that all she needs to know is that the American women's tragedy is that they never stop being girls.

8. According to Leeming, another of Baldwin's parable novels (280), *Train* was "painful" to write and carries a strong autobiographical message: "Leo Proudhammer is James Baldwin, complete with large eyes, 'pigeon toes,' and 'jiggling behind'" (*James Baldwin*, 278, 279).

9. Fremont-Smith, "Another Track," 27; Puzo, "His Cardboard Lovers," 155.

10. Baldwin was out of the country when Kazan testified in front of HUAC in 1952. Kazan was a member of the Communist Party between 1934 and 1936 but subsequently joined the witch hunts and decided to "name names," allegedly to protect his children (see Navasky, *Naming Names*, chap. 7). Kazan's compliance, however, was seen as an act of betrayal and cowardice; it ended his friendship with Arthur Miller and remained a stain on his reputation. There is no record I know of concerning Baldwin's take on this part of Kazan's history.

11. Kazan confesses, too, that the "merits of that play eluded me," no matter that it won the Pulitzer Prize (582). Interestingly, he also considers himself a kind of

immigrant "nigger" owing to his southern European origins and emphasizes that for that reason he and Baldwin got along well.

12. It was rather "uncharacteristic" of Baldwin "not [to] resist the urge for revenge in his treatment of Saul and Rags [stand-ins for Lee Strasberg and Cheryl Crawford], who are depicted [in *Train*] as arrogant, pedantic hypocrites—representatives of the white liberal establishment" (Leeming, *James Baldwin*, 279).

13. Campbell dates this letter February 1959, as does Cezzar in *Dost Mektupları*. I follow the date on the copy of letter 10 that I have read.

14. Lynn Orilla Scott's book provides a convincing analysis of the responses to *Train* that, she claims, were in "considerable degree homophobic," inadequate, and misguided, having missed "the extraordinary way that Baldwin's fourth novel engaged with and challenged the changing racial and sexual politics of the sixties" (23). She also cites Emmanuel S. Nelson's critique of homophobic reactions "from *Giovanni's Room* to *Just Above My Head* . . . [and his challenge to] the critical consensus that Baldwin was a better essay writer than fiction writer" (22). See Nelson, "Critical Deviance."

15. Letter to the author, July 22, 2006. In *Train* Baldwin notes that Leo's "dresser," Pete, has a face that is "dark, vaguely Oriental" (4). This comment calls attention to the blurring of racial boundaries in the novel, which continues *Another Country*'s preoccupation with queerness. A few years later, in an essay on Baldwin appended to his translation of *Tell Me How Long the Train's Been Gone* (1973), Balamir summarized how he felt about Baldwin as a Turkish intellectual, journalist, and critic. His statement explains the solidarity that progressive Turks felt with African Americans at the same time as they deplored U.S. foreign policy: "For [Baldwin], the existence of a man like Nixon in the White House is a disaster that needs to be remedied immediately. It is a disaster not only for blacks but also for whites. Baldwin ponders what the return home of the black kids who were sent to Vietnam, and what their having learnt there how to use guns might possibly lead to. White lies and black hopes. . . . How much longer will this disaster last?" Balamir ends with expressions of admiration for Baldwin's authorship and his mission to criticize his beloved country. Oktay Balamir, "James Baldwin Üzerine," *Ne Zaman Gitti Tren* (Istanbul: Sander Yayınları, 1973), 10. Trans. Aslı Gür.

16. Letter 39 from Cezzar to Baldwin, July 1968. (This is a transcript of a cable Cezzar sent to Baldwin.)

17. The scriptwriter was Arnold Pearl, whom Baldwin actually liked but could not dissociate from what he saw as Columbia's efforts to adulterate Malcolm's story and thus black American history (Leeming, *James Baldwin*, 299–93).

18. Letter 37 (1968); letter 38, April 12, 1968 (this is the famous letter about the deaths of "Medgar, Malcolm, Martin," from which Cezzar quotes in Thorsen's documentary; Engin published it in translation in his memoir by Çalışlar and recently published it as well in *Dost Mektupları*). See also letter 40, dated September 15, 1968.

19. Campbell quotes here from letter 37, dated 1968, that bears no day and month.
20. I mention this again because it was extremely upsetting to Baldwin, Pakay, and Leeming, while the Hollywood people at the time saw nothing wrong with such a racist proposition.
21. Leeming mentions that it was the Baldwin-Pearl script that Spike Lee used for his film. Warner Brothers bought the same script from Columbia and eventually made a film, which was screened "and soon buried . . . presumably because it was thought to be inflammatory"; Baldwin never saw it (*James Baldwin*, 301).
22. Zeynep Oral, untitled article, *Milliyet*, February 5, 1970; quoted in Akçura, *Engin Cezzar Kitabı*, 140.
23. Hilmi Kurtuluş, review of *Düşenin Dostu*, *Her Gün*, April 1970; quoted in Akçura, *Engin Cezzar Kitabı*, 133. Translated by Aslı Gür.
24. Schick explains: "There is a Turkish proverb that says *Düşenin dostu olmaz*, literally 'the friend of the fallen does not exist,' but more correctly 'the fallen has no friend.' As I mentioned earlier, I am quite certain that the name *Düşenin dostu* was selected consciously, as an implied negative, i.e., it refers to someone (the friend of the fallen) who does not exist." E-mail to author, April 9, 2007.
25. Ali Poyrazoğlu, "Interview with James Baldwin," *Tiyatro Dergisi*, no. 12 (October 1969): n.p. Translated by Aslı Gür.
26. For more information about the play and the author, see *Encyclopedia of Canadian Theater*, http//www.canadiantheatre.com. See also Tanya Talaga, "Obituary: John Herbert Turned Trauma into Acclaimed Theater Career," *Toronto Star*, June 25, 2001; and Dan Sullivan, "Theater: A Distressing *Fortune and Men's Eyes*," *New York Times*, February 24, 1967. See also Gertrude Samuels, "A New Lobby — Ex-Cons," *New York Times*, October 19, 1969, on the founding of the Fortune Society, an organization inspired by the play and run by ex-convicts with the goal of bettering prison conditions.
27. The "Male Prison" piece appears under this title in *The Price of the Ticket* but was originally published as "Gide as Husband and Homosexual" in the *New Leader* in 1954 and later collected in *Nobody Knows My Name*.
28. Oktay Balamir, interview with author, September 2005. Balamir confirmed that "the theater was raking in money from the play and did not pay [Baldwin], the director, a cent." According to Leeming, and as implied by Cezzar, this was perhaps the understanding from the beginning.
29. This came up several times as I talked with Poyrazoğlu in Bodrum, Turkey, on September 8, 2005. Like other Turkish intellectuals at the time, Poyrazoğlu was captivated by Baldwin's productivity, single-mindedness, and creative process at the same time as he was fascinated by his opposition to U.S. foreign policy. Poyrazoğlu applauded Baldwin's consistent commitment to fight against racism and appreciated his artistic shift in emphasis and form following the publication of *The Fire Next Time*: "Jimmy was constantly changing and developing"; he was "like a treasure case, full of jewelry and gold and diamonds," but only "if you

knew how to open it." This meant that it was hard to keep up with Baldwin as he searched for new ideas in what he wrote and read; he was a very "dynamic [writer] . . . always crossing borders . . . a restless voyager constantly on the road."

30. I have not been able to confirm whether or not Baldwin would have seen that performance. A brief history of *Fortune*'s performances: 1965, accepted for workshop production at the Stratford Festival Theatre (dir. Bruno Gerussi); 1966, second workshop production at New York's Actors Studio; 1967, opened in the Actors Playhouse, near Sheridan Square in New York City, ran there for a year, then toured in Canada (Toronto and Montreal) and across the United States to San Francisco; end of the year, opened at Charles Marowitz's Open Space Theatre in London and after nine months was moved to the Comedy Theatre in the West End by producer Michael White, where it played three months. Since 1967, *Fortune and Men's Eyes* has had more than four hundred productions in over one hundred countries and has been translated into almost every language used in the theater.

31. Interview with Aslı Gür, April 19, 2005. (This was a kind of second-degree interview, when I was unable to be in Turkey in person and so asked Aslı to carry my questions to Poyrazoğlu and record his answers. I then conducted a follow-up interview with Poyrazoğlu in September of the same year.)

32. Interview with author, September 2005.

33. Ibid.

34. Baldwin made his illegitimacy and abuse at his father's hands central to the larger landscape of his childhood in the Harlem ghetto, where he witnessed many of his peers' destruction by the "street"—which he describes in a vivid section of *The Fire Next Time*. This is also an interesting cross-textual link to Ann Petry's *The Street*.

35. Baldwin was in Istanbul at the time for an extended visit, and it is unlikely that he saw this performance, but he may have heard about it. The New York performances of the play included the Actors Studio workshop production in 1966, headed by Lee Strasberg, who had just worked with Baldwin on *Blues*; David Rothenberg and Mitchell Nestor produced and directed it off Broadway at the Actors Playhouse, where it premiered on February 23, 1967. The latter production starred Robert Christian as Mona, Victor Arnold as Rocky, Bil Moor as Queenie, Terry Kiser as Smitty, and Clifford Pellow as Guard.

36. See also Chester Himes's prison novel *Cast the First Stone*.

37. On the "sissification" of black male intellectuals, see Marlon Ross's "Beyond the Closet." Baldwin would certainly fall into Ross's category.

38. In the concluding moment in *Blues*, when Lyle is talking with Richard before he shoots him, the black man Richard taunts the white man Lyle about his possible attraction to the black male sexual apparatus. See act 3 (*Blues*, 120). I elaborate on this topic in the next chapter.

39. Herbert's text does mention race quite a bit, although there are no indications that any of the characters are nonwhite. The references that pop up in the dialogue are often racial slurs and insults paired with homo-hating speech. Queenie and Rocky use these a lot in reference to Native Americans (Iroquois), Asians, and African (North) Americans. On race and sexuality in *Giovanni's Room*, see Zaborowska, "Mapping Transcultural Masculinities."

40. The "much less Islamic" comment by Keith needs further explanation. As Irvin Schick explained to me: "The fact is that the vast masses were every bit as Islamic then as they are now. However, Islam was not as visible in the urban centers and elite circles then as it is now, mainly because of class differences and because of repression. Back then, 'Islamic intellectual' would have been considered an oxymoron. Today, Islamic intellectuals are visible, audible, and extremely well informed, and Islamic millionaires appear in the society pages." Correspondence with author, April 10, 2007.

41. Interview with author, April 10, 2006.

42. Both State and Municipal Theaters exist to this day.

43. Interview with author, September 2005.

44. This struck me as an important point that also reminded me of my own coming-of-age in Warsaw, Poland, where theater was the place to be for anyone who wanted to be close to cultural celebrities. As a first-year student, I went to a different theater every weekend and often saw two or three performances from Friday to Sunday night. As in Turkey a decade earlier, in Poland of the 1980s, state-controlled television did not matter much; in fact, you were considered rather uncool if you watched either of its two channels.

45. For background on gay, lesbian, transsexual, and transgender history and activism, see Bereket and Adam, "The Emergence of Gay Identities in Turkey"; Veli Duyan and Camur Duyan, "Gays and Lesbians' HIV/AIDS Knowledge"; Robert and Kandiyoti, "Photo Essay: Transsexuals and the Urban Landscape in Istanbul"; Drucker, "'In the Tropics There Is No Sin'"; and Petzen, "Home or Homelike?"

46. See Andrews and Kalpaklı, *The Age of Beloveds*; and Yüzgün, "Homosexuality and Police Terror."

47. A singer of popular Turkish music, Müren is said to have been the best-known star singer on the stage in the late sixties and early seventies, with continuing popularity until his death in the early nineties. Popular magazines in 1969 and 1970, just around the time when *Fortune* was being staged, closely followed his everyday life. His costumes, jewelry and accessories, hairstyles, travels in the country and abroad, et cetera, were all news. He had many fans from every walk of life and from every gender and age. His performances were found to be beautiful and artful, some of them in drag. In that respect Turks had no problem watching drag onstage in the clubs, on the one hand; but on the other, the media were silent about the lives of gays, lesbians, and transvestites who lived in the city of Istanbul. (Information gathered by Aslı Gür.) A noteworthy addition from

Schick: "Zeki Müren started with what was considered in the 1950s to be rather daring, such as wearing a purple tuxedo adorned with a single pearl, but it was many years later that he came on stage wearing a mini-skirt. . . . It was usually the 'high point' of the show when he made his appearance wearing some outrageous skirt covered with sequins. What is true is that he loved shocking people, and his audiences lapped it up. It was not only well known that he was homosexual, but often stated. He sang beautifully, and that is the main source of his success." Correspondence with author, April 10, 2007.

48. Interview with author, Ankara, Turkey, September 6–7, 2005.

49. Ibid.

50. He adds: "Every last Turk was portrayed as ugly, greasy—and, let us not forget, *dark*. . . . The fact that a statement like 'For a nation of pigs, it is surprising that you don't eat pork' (which is a total *non sequitur*, but let us set that aside!) could be uttered in a mainstream movie with no one criticising it. That is what had us angry." Correspondence with author, April 10, 2007.

51. Kenton Keith and Brenda Rein confirmed that in our interviews in 2005, as did Aslı Gür's research.

52. Interview with author, Istanbul, May 2001.

53. Leeming gives an account of this event in his biography (305–6).

54. In Oral's "Bir Gün Mutlaka mı?" (Definitely One Day?), she describes the night club incident on pp. 282–83.

55. Interview with author, Istanbul, May 2001.

56. Oral, quoted in Akçura, *Engin Cezzar Kitabı*, 138.

57. Phenotypically, Oral is fair; she is of the so-called Circassian descent, a phrase people frequently use to talk about a person who has actual ties to the Çerkez ethnic minority or about someone who is perceived to be very white. See also Schick on the "specific context of the European and Euro-American system of racialist thinking as refracted by art and literature," in "The Fair Circassian: Some Racial and Sexual Slippages of Orientalism" (unpublished paper, p. 36); the extended version of this article was published in Turkish as *Çerkes Güzeli* in 2004.

58. She is repeating a comment she made to Campbell, too: "In Turkish the play's obscenities were, for her, literally unspeakable—'Even now'" (*Talking*, 234).

59. Translated by Aslı Gür. Gür explained to me that "writing on one's forehead" is an expression for fate or destiny written on one's face; "black writing" means ill fate. Schick offers the following explanation for why Baldwin might have been embraced by the Turks: "There has always been a big difference in Turkey between foreigners (i.e., people from beyond the national borders) and local non-Muslims (Jews, Christians) in that the former were considered far preferable to the latter. . . . [For example,] I had a girlfriend in high school, whose parents were reasonably educated and had lived in Italy for some time. Nevertheless, they were very much opposed to their daughter dating me, a Jew. We eventually went our separate ways. . . . She subsequently married a Swede. . . . The point was that he was western, and therefore good; I was local and non-Muslim, and

therefore an embarrassment. Given this, I am actually not too surprised that Baldwin would be embraced by all these people." Correspondence with author, April 10, 2007.

60. Schick explains the paradox of forced assimilation by drawing on intersection-alities of ethnicity, race, and gender: "Hostility to Kurds is shaped by something other than racism pure and simple: if you are of Kurdish descent, you can rise to all sorts of high positions in Turkey (big businessmen, prime ministers, speakers of the house, etc., have been Kurds) provided that you are willing to renounce your heritage. If you insist on having a Kurdish identity, speaking Kurdish, etc., then you will be repressed. If you 'turn Turk,' however, no one will bother you. So racism is inappropriate as a category here. . . . In the 1960s, the pressing issue was class. Just as feminism was viewed as a bourgeois liberal deviation, since, after all, once the revolution comes, men and women will automatically be equal, likewise seeking cultural autonomy and identity for Kurds would have been viewed as irrelevant to 'the cause.'" He cautions, nevertheless, that "the Kurdish issue was very much on people's mind in the 1960s, though not always in the form of Turks oppressing Kurds. . . . Enlightened people, and people from that region (such as Yaşar Kemal) were well aware of the social and cultural oppression of Kurds by the state, as well as of past rebellions (e.g., 1928) that were put down in the most bloody fashion. Furthermore, the poorest laborers in Istanbul, such as porters or doormen or street sweepers, were often Kurdish immigrants. So it would be extremely reasonable for Baldwin to say that the Kurds are 'the niggers of Turkey,' whether or not he actually did say so" (cor-respondence with author, April 10, 2007). On race in Turkey, and especially the contentious issue of the ways in which the Armenian genocide and ethnic mi-norities, such as the Kurds, have been represented and treated, see also Akçam, *A Shameful Act*; and Maksudyan, "*The Turkish Review of Anthropology* and the Racist Face of Turkish Nationalism." Maksudyan documents the emergence of dis-course on the superiority of the "Turkish race" in the 1920s and 1930s, based on the "'minorities are other races' argument" and embroiled with the inter-actions "between the political elite and the scientific racist elite" (303). Martin van Bruinessen's "Race, Culture, Nation and Identity Politics in Turkey" quotes from the 1930 speech of the justice minister Mahmut Esat (Bozkurt), who ex-tolled the leading role of the Turks in nation building and clearly targeted the Kurds, the majority of whom hold the dirtiest menial jobs in Turkey to this day, as an inferior race: "It is my firm opinion, and let friend and foe hear it, that the lords of this country are the Turks. Those who are not real Turks (öz Türk) have only one right in the Turkish fatherland, and that is the right to be servants and slaves" (2). Esat's speech enraged public opinion at home and abroad, and he soon lost his job, but while the Kurds were officially defined as "real Turks" they remained subjected to "deliberate assimilation policies." Bruinessen's article can be found at the University of Utrecht website: http://www.let.uu.nl.

61. Oral's well-known book *Bir Ses* (A Voice, 1986) is, however, concerned with

local issues of incarceration and retells the prison experience of Reha İsvan and Ahmed İsvan, her husband and the former mayor of Istanbul, both of whom were imprisoned for many years by the military after the 1980 coup d'état.

62. This role earned Cezzar the Best Performance Award that year.

63. In Turkish: "to find someone in an unexpected place."

64. Erbaşar died young and gained an iconic status; all his friends cherish their memories of him as an unspoken queer. Oral referred to his queerness obliquely for that reason.

65. See also the accounts in Leeming, *James Baldwin* (306–8); Weatherby, *Artist on Fire*; and J. Campbell, *Talking*.

66. The correct form of "children" in Turkish is *çocuklar*; Oral is attempting here to reproduce Baldwin's accent and pronunciation.

67. *Tiyatro Dergisi*, no. 13 (1969): 2–3. This publication has since ceased to exist.

68. Sir William Tyrone Guthrie (1900–1971) was a British theatrical director. His approach to Shakespearean and modern drama, as well as publications such as *Theater Prospect* (1932) and *A Life in the Theater* (1960), influenced the revival of interest in traditional theater. See Guthrie, "Director's View."

69. I am quoting from the Turkish version; see also Campbell, *Talking*, 235.

70. Turkey signed the North Atlantic Treaty on February 18, 1952, along with Greece. Since then, as a congratulatory message on the NATO website posted on the fiftieth anniversary of their induction informs, they "have been 'key contributors' in promoting the security of the Euro-Atlantic area, and more specifically, NATO's Southern Flank." See http://www.nato.int/docu/update/2002/02-february/.

71. Keith also mentioned the paradoxical negotiation of protest against American foreign policy, on the one hand, and support for American culture, on the other, by using the example of the U.S. embassy library in Ankara, which would be "ransacked" by day by students and cleaned up at night by other students. "Now, however, you have a genuine anti-U.S. feeling throughout Turkey; even old allies" have turned against the United States, he stressed. Interview with author, April 10, 2006.

72. From Gülriz's memoir: "The play had breathtaking music. One of the notable figures of improvised music, Don Cherry, had come to Turkey with his friend Okay Temiz [a famous Turkish percussionist], his Swedish wife Maki and his two children, in order to study Turkish folklore. Okay had become one of the indispensable members of Don Cherry's group. Don Cherry had established an orchestra called Movement Incorporated by bringing famous jazz musicians of the world together. These days he has been lecturing on jazz in celebrated American universities and continues to give concerts. When he called Jimmy upon his arrival, he got into trouble, that is, we did not let him go before he composed music for the play. With Okay Temiz they composed wonderful music for *Düşenin Dostu*" (*Kıldan İnce*, 431). While the Cherry family has not received a copy of the music that Don Cherry composed for Baldwin's play, it may still be somewhere in the private archives of Cezzar or Poyrazoğlu, even though they were not "able

to find it as of yet." Okay Temiz developed a unique style, blending jazz, ethnic, and Sufi music. Besides traditional instruments, he plays percussive instruments of his own invention and making.

73. *Ses*, no. 47, November 15, 1969, n.p.

74. "Düşenin Dostu," *Ses*, no. 50, December 12, 1969, 21.

75. Letter 48, January 10, 1970. See also Erduran's review for *Variety* in January 1970.

76. Letter to author, e-mail, August 6, 2006.

77. Ibid.

78. Gülriz records in her memoir: "Just as the governor had the right to ban a play on the basis of Police Authority, we had the right to appeal to the Council of State and cancel the decision. And for the first time the governor, going beyond his power and against the constitution, acted to ban the play despite the prosecutor's decision that it did not constitute a case. We did not close our theater despite the governor's official order. We exercised our constitutional right to resist the ban. In the end, after the affirmative conclusion of the prosecution's expert report, the governor had to rescind his order. The events of the ban and its cancellation brought us great publicity. Newspapers wrote: 'This is a very daring project. We congratulate the troupe. *Düşenin Dostu* reveals a reality that turns one's world upside down'" (430).

79. I quote from the report as cited in Akçura: "By this office's initiative and according to Regulation 66/2, Prof. Sahir Erman, Prof. Ayhan Önder, and assistant Erol Cihan, from Istanbul University, Criminal Law and Procedural Law, were appointed as experts. This expert commission watched the 21:30 [9:30] p.m. performance of *Düşenin Dostu* on December 26, 1969. . . . In the report dated January 8, 1970, following the aforementioned observation, the commission states that there is nothing in the play that is in violation of the Turkish Criminal Law" (Akçura, *Engin Cezzar Kitabı*, 129).

80. Apaydın was a well-known lawyer, who defended human rights causes, including the former prime minister Adnan Menderes, toppled by the military in 1960 and subsequently hanged.

81. Oktay Balamir recalls meeting Adelsen, who then lived in Istanbul with his partner.

82. *Tea and Sympathy* is a stage play by Robert Anderson that was adapted by Vincente Minnelli into a movie (1956).

83. A. Yerag, review of *Düşenin Dostu*, *Jamanak*, April 10, 1970. Quoted in Akçura, *Engin Cezzar Kitabı*, 132.

84. Sezai Solelli, "Düşenin Dostu," *Ses*, no. 53, December 27, 1969. (Translated by Aslı Gür.)

85. Mutluay quoted in Sururi, *Kıldan İnce*, 432.

86. Kemal Tahir was a famous Turkish novelist, sometimes compared to Yaşar Kemal, though not as well known abroad. His novels are known for their criticism of Eurocentrism (and thus some parts of the Kemalist project), and he was known as a communist in the 1930s and 1940s, leading to his heavy persecution

alongside Nazım Hikmet and Yaşar Kemal. He spent fourteen years in jail. He was a "thought criminal," as these people were generally called in Turkey, that is, people jailed not on the basis of evidence proving their actions but on the basis of the texts they produced.

87. Güvemli, "Cezzars Are Staging a 'Daring' Play."

88. As the situation in American prisons worsened, as evidenced by the treatment of the Black Panthers, on whose behalf both Baldwin and the French playwright Jean Genet wrote much, Baldwin's works both echoed and anticipated what we today call the "industrial prison complex."

89. See Leeming, James Baldwin, 304; Weatherby, Artist on Fire, 290–93. See also Weatherby, p. 345, for a reunion with Baraka in the film I Heard It through the Grapevine. Baraka delivered a eulogy at Baldwin's funeral and is interviewed in Thorsen's film.

90. Nicholas Delbanco describes his first meeting with Baldwin in Istanbul and his attendance at the play in winter 1970 quite differently in his memoir, Anywhere Out of the World: "We had a drink together and went to Fortune and Men's Eyes, a play of his translated into Turkish. Not knowing Turkish, I was less than enthralled, and the meeting did not matter much and the evening was a blur" (28; Delbanco mistakes Baldwin's authorship of the play here). They became close friends later, however, after Baldwin had moved to Saint-Paul de Vence, where they were neighbors in 1971 and 1973.

91. Baldwin, No Name in the Street, 18; hereafter cited as NNS.

92. In "Intellectual Exile: Expatriates and Marginals," Edward Said describes exile as both an actual and metaphorical condition, akin to theatrical performance, especially for intellectuals who "remain outside the mainstream, unaccommodated, uncoopted, resistant" (The Edward Said Reader, 373). This description clearly relates to Baldwin's predicament in the 1960s as he lived in transition between the United States, Turkey, and Western Europe. Said stresses that for intellectuals who live abroad, as much as for some of those who remain home to transgress and challenge prevalent notions and mainstream values, restlessness and "even dissatisfaction bordering on . . . disagreeableness, can become . . . a style of thought, but also a new, if temporary habitation" (373): "The exilic intellectual does not respond to the logic of the conventional but to the audacity of daring, and to representing change, to moving on, not standing still" (381). Baldwin also fits the model of the transnational intellectual in Kwame Anthony Appiah's Cosmopolitanism.

FOUR East to South

1. This is a reference to the stormy love affair between Oscar Wilde and Alfred Douglas, immortalized in Douglas's poem "Two Loves" (1894). The last line, "I am the love that dare not speak its name," was echoed in Wilde's testimony during his trial in 1895.

2. Scholars like Marlon Ross, E. Patrick Johnson, Dwight McBride, and Robert Reid-Pharr point out the systematic efforts of some critics in African American studies to erase Baldwin's sexuality from discussions of his works and achievement.

3. Some critics have embraced Baldwin's appeals against essentialism. For example, see Lynn Orilla Scott's commentary on Baldwin's and Nikki Giovanni's *A Dialogue*, where he takes apart the phrase "Black is beautiful" (*James Baldwin's Later Fiction*, 74).

4. Baldwin, *No Name in the Street*, 18; hereafter cited as NNS.

5. *Constructing the Black Masculine*, 136. Wallace's chapter on Baldwin compares the official representations of him (such as Eckman's) with his depictions by the FBI in the copious file that was released under the Freedom of Information Act (133–46).

6. See also Darrieck Scott's reading of Cleaver's assault on Baldwin in "More Than You'll Ever Be."

7. *Time*, May 17, 1963, 26.

8. The article also states: "He is not by any stretch of the imagination a Negro leader. He tries no civil rights cases in the courts, preaches from no pulpit, devises no stratagems for sit-ins, Freedom Riders or street marchers. . . . Most Negroes still do not know his name" (26). Although the piece goes on to include some more nuanced information, including evocative quotations from Baldwin's interviews and works, it remains marred by its descriptions of the writer as a "sissy." See also Fields's "Looking for Jimmy Baldwin: Sex, Privacy, and Black Nationalist Fervor" on "evidence of Baldwin scapegoating" in the 1967 issue of *Black Panther Magazine*, where a cartoon pictures him subjacent to a black man licking Lyndon Johnson's cowboy boots; Baldwin is in the good company of King and Rustin. *Callaloo* 27.2 (2004): 463. A more recent piece by Michael Anderson in the *New York Times* echoes surprisingly similar sentiments as it presents Baldwin in updated visual and tectonic terms: "extremely odd-looking: small in stature, frog-eyed, oval-headed, he resembled an ebonite E.T." "Trapped Inside James Baldwin," *New York Times*, March 29, 1998, Book Review, 13. In the world post–Steven Spielberg, Baldwin has become a domesticated alien; like a favorite toy, he is familiar and comforting but cannot be taken seriously. Lewis Nkosi's piece in *Transitions* stresses that everyone remembers his or her first meeting with Baldwin as if he were an "augury," a religious revelation, a spiritual if not celestial visitation: "A man walking on sea shells, he wore a grin as wide as the moon." Nkosi, "The Mountain," *Transitions* 8.3 (1979): 123.

9. Gates, "The Welcome Table: James Baldwin in Exile," 312.

10. *Soul on Ice*, 100. See also the surrounding text: "It takes him a little longer each time to hustle back to the cover and camouflage of the perfumed smoke screen of his prose. Now and then we catch a glimpse of his little jive ass—his big eyes peering back over his shoulder in the mischievous retreat of a child sneak-thief from a cookie jar." The description of Baldwin as a retreating juvenile in this

quotation is interesting in its focus on Baldwin's posterior and in some ways strangely anticipates the vantage point from which his narrator sees the South in *No Name in the Street*. Hence Baldwin's bowing to the manly men of the second part, like Maynard and Cleaver himself, can be read as ironic and ambivalent. See also E. Patrick Johnson's reading of Cleaver's homoerotic confusions and Huey P. Newton's critique of his behavior in Johnson, *Appropriating Blackness*, 52–57, which was inspired by Robert Reid-Pharr's "Tearing the Goat's Flesh." Essex Hemphill mentions Cleaver's attack on Baldwin in the introduction to *Brother to Brother*, xxiii. On the other hand, reading Baldwin's public life as "generally secretive and closeted," Mark Lilly accuses him of homophobia, a "special and especially repellant kind . . . of which Baldwin is guilty time and again" (*Gay Men's Literature*, 144, 164–66).

11. Scholars of masculinity such as Robert Connell, Michael Kimmel, Marlon Ross, Brian Harper, and Sam Keen, among others, remind us that racism, xenophobia, and homophobia feed off each other. For a reading of Baraka's struggle with his sexual identity, see also Ron Simmons, "Some Thoughts on the Challenges Facing Black Gay Intellectuals," 217–21.

12. By the time Thorsen's documentary was made, Reed appeared to have changed his notions about Baldwin dramatically and appeared in the film as one of his ardent supporters. It is thus not clear if Baldwin's memory of Reed was based in fact or hearsay; still, I quote it after Troupe as it is partially confirmed by Leeming, who reports on an attack "attributed to (and later denied by) Ishmael Reed to the effect that [Baldwin] was 'a hustler who comes on like Job'" (*James Baldwin*, 304). Baraka appears in Thorsen's film, too. He delivered a eulogy at Baldwin's funeral that placed him firmly "in the tradition. . . . God's black revolutionary mouth" (Troupe, *The Legacy*, 134).'See Amiri Baraka, "Jimmy!" in Troupe, *The Legacy*, 127–34.

13. Betsky's *Queer Space* describes the seemingly socially unmarked realm of white urban males.

14. Constantine-Simms, *The Greatest Taboo*. See bell hooks's critique of the "black community" notion as essentializing and exclusionary in "Homophobia in Black Communities," in Constantine-Simms, *The Greatest Taboo*, 67–73.

15. See also Hemphill's "Undressing Icons" and "Living the Word/Looking for Home"; and Nero's "Re/Membering Langston" and "Fixing Ceremonies" on black homophobia and how two different versions of the film exist owing to the difficulties that the Hughes Estate made about Julien's outing of the poet. See also Gates's "An Interview with Josephine Baker and Baldwin (1973)," in Troupe, *The Legacy*, 161–72.

16. See also Kendall Thomas on the absence of the "other" Jimmy, or the gay Baldwin, from the speeches at his funeral and on the treatment of Baldwin by other black intellectuals who engaged "in a certain revisionist impeachment" after his death in "Ain't Nothing like the Real Thing," 55–57. See also Maria Diedrich, "JB: Obituaries for a Black Ishmael."

17. This entry can be found in the James Baldwin files at the Schomburg Center.

18. Lorde, *Sister Outsider*, 137. Baldwin echoed Lorde almost verbatim to Troupe when he mentioned having to "evolve a kind of mask, a kind of persona," to protect himself from "all these people who are carnivorous and . . . think you're help-less" (187). The mask is an interesting trope here, as it echoes not only Paul Lawrence Dunbar's famous poem "We Wear the Mask" but also foreshadows Essex Hemphill's use of this trope to describe homophobia and the disowning of black gay men and women by their community in *Brother to Brother*.

19. Judith Butler, *Undoing Gender* (New York: Routledge, 2004), 184. See also Cora Kaplan's reading of Baldwin's *Giovanni's Room* and *Another Country* in "A Cavern Opened in My Mind." I agree with Kaplan's claim that Baldwin's "strength . . . [is that] he identifies and theorizes the palimpsestic relationship of racial and psychosexual narratives" (39), and I am grateful for the inspiration that her essay has given to my thinking through this chapter.

20. For a brief discussion of Turkey's imperial history and post-Ottoman transformation, see Eissenstat, "Metaphors of Race and Discourse of Nation."

21. This was the Omnibus Crime Control and Safe Streets Act of 1968, passed by the Johnson administration.

22. As Leeming observes, "imprisonment continued to be an important leitmotif in Baldwin's thinking" into the 1980s (359).

23. It is important to remember his experience of the French justice and penal system described in the essay "Equal in Paris." Baldwin also intervened on behalf of Angela Davis, Huey Newton, Bobby Seale, the Harlem Six, Wayne Williams, and others. In letter 49 (May 15, 1970), he writes to Cezzar about "a [Greek] friend in trouble in Turkey" and asks for help with his legal status.

24. For an introduction to twentieth-century Turkish history, see, for example, Schick and Tonak, *Turkey in Transition*.

25. Leeming states that this "caused him to walk in a manner which people saw as effeminate" (45).

26. All biographers agree that Baldwin was terrified every time he went south. See, for example, Eckman's description of Baldwin's trip in early 1962, when he went to Mississippi to meet James Meredith and for the first time had an idea for the stage design for *Blues for Mister Charlie* (*Furious Passage*, 171–74). See also Nat Hentoff, "James Baldwin Gets Older and Sadder," *New York Times*, April 11, 1965, where Baldwin discusses the "war zones" of American inner cities and the "War on Poverty." See also James Baldwin et al., "Police Shooting of Oakland Negro," Letters to the Editor of the Times, *New York Times*, May 6, 1968.

27. This essay was published in the *Nation* on July 11, 1966, and interweaves Baldwin's experiences and impressions of racist violence in the context of the imprisonment and trial of the Harlem Six. The essay's scope ranges from the discussion of the larger social problem of ever-growing incarceration and criminalization of African American and Puerto Rican males, through summaries of participants'

accounts, to descriptions of wounds on a bystander's body, someone who was in the wrong place at the wrong time.

28. The quotation continues: "That social reality is both internal and external to the individual. In other words, as a black author, as soon as one opens one's eyes to this world, one finds a society threatening him. As one's comprehension develops, as one's life progresses, one sees the threat getting bigger and bigger, too. The outer world constantly demands one's attention, because one has to protect one's life, since this is a struggle for survival. There is also a bigger danger: As time goes by, the writer realizes that he starts to see himself as the others see him. When it comes to writing, he has to avoid social threats surrounding him, as if he were 'unburying' himself. He also has to reveal his real self that falls outside of and in opposition to the consciousness of the self the society inculcated in him. This is what I mean by war. . . . Because when a black person expresses his real identity without heeding what the whites say about it, then it means that he is attacking the whites' identity and their society. This is where the difficulty is" (Ağaoğlu, "James Baldwin'le Konuşma," 15). I am well aware that this begs the larger questions of violence, sex, and gender in relation to victimization and resilience in the face of institutionalized rape of black women. For the sake of clarity and brevity, and because there is much excellent work on this subject by critics such as Arlene Keizer, Farah Griffin, Sandra Gunning, Hannah Rosen, and others, I choose not to engage it at this point. I return to the importance of women in Baldwin's life in the conclusion.

29. Baldwin would have disagreed that he wrote in the "protest tradition" of which he accused Richard Wright in the essay "Everybody's Protest Novel" (1949). He later regretted his falling out with the elder writer, whom he had seen as his "idol." Still, in "Alas, Poor Richard," an essay written upon Wright's death, Baldwin objected to the "gratuitous and compulsive" descriptions of violence in the works of the author of Native Son (Price of the Ticket, 273). He wrote that in Wright's short stories "and most of the novels written by Negroes until today . . . there is a great space where sex ought to be; and what usually fills that space is violence." Baldwin's primary focus was the body and mind of the human being as the root and recipient of violence, the "rage, almost literally the howl, of a man who is being castrated" (273). In Native Son, he felt, instead of having the lurid details of "hacking a white woman to death" by the stereotypical black rapist and murderer, we should have been given a clearer justification for Bigger's humanity, his "terrible attempt to break out of a cage in which the American imagination has imprisoned him" (273). Cheryl A. Wall's Worrying the Line points at similar readings of Wright's works by Zora Neale Hurston, whose signifying on Uncle Tom's Children targeted the violent "fantasies of his black male readers, and/or the images of black men running through the minds of white readers" (221). Bigger Thomas, black men, and the whole American nation were locked in the "sexual myths . . . around the figure of the American Negro" and the "guilty imagina-

tion of the white people who invest him with their hates and longings," who make him the "target of their sexual paranoia" (*Price of the Ticket*, 273). Baldwin explored this "guilty imagination" with frightening efficiency in "Going to Meet the Man" (1965), a short story that features a white racist narrator, and made the sexual "hates and longings" of young white North American men central to his production of *Düşenin Dostu / Fortune and Men's Eyes*. With its characters caught up in a grotesque *danse macabre*, sex and violence dominated the play and would soon echo in the pages of Baldwin's fourth essay collection.

30. Interview with author, May 2006.

31. "Baldwin, in Istanbul, Denies He's Given Up the Struggle," interview with Nick Ludington, *New York Post*, December 12, 1969.

32. The issue of where the book was ultimately completed remains still a bit unclear, as Rein told me that she remembers typing up the whole manuscript and sending it off, completed, to the publisher, whereas Leeming quotes David Baldwin, who gives Saint-Paul de Vence as the location from which the book was sent in its final form. Leeming admitted, however, that the Baldwin brothers may have been confused about which book it was (interview with author, June 2006); Baldwin was also writing *The Devil Finds Work* as he was wrapping up *No Name in the Street*.

33. E. Patrick Johnson, *Appropriating Blackness*, 36.

34. "Go the Way Your Blood Beats," interview with Richard Goldstein, 175.

35. Today Club 12 has been replaced by She Bar at Sıraselviler Caddesi No 19/A in Sıraselviler-Taksim.

36. Interview with author, Ankara, Turkey, September 7, 2006.

37. Lombard was a student body president at Xavier University and became the chairman of CORE in New Orleans; he was one of the leading participants of the sit-ins at stores on Canal Street. Smith was a freedom rider who survived severe beatings during bus desegregation actions in the South; Baldwin invited him to participate in the meeting of black leaders with Attorney General Robert Kennedy on May 24, 1963. Smith's photograph would be included in the photo-text that Baldwin created and published with Richard Avedon in 1964, *Nothing Personal*. On this book, see Sara Blair, "Photo-Text Capital."

38. Cheryl A. Wall emphasizes that this book presents its two essays as "structurally innovative and intricately connected" and that Baldwin abandons in it his "strategic American exceptionalism" while preserving his sense of himself as a "moral agent." "Stranger at Home: James Baldwin on What It Means to Be an American," Zora Neale Hurston Lecture, Center for Afroamerican and African Studies, University of Michigan, April 3, 2008.

39. I am grateful to Jim McIntosh for pointing out this connection and encouraging me to think about it. See Bercovitch, "Emerson the Prophet." (Bercovitch's all-white model does not include Douglass or Du Bois, whom I add to the list because they seem to fit his theory and take its implications further in terms of Americanness being as contingent on race in interesting ways.) See also Carton, "The Politics of Selfhood."

40. I allude to Flaubert's famous statement about *Madame Bovary* and his authorial relationship to the novel's title character: "Madame Bovary, c'est moi."
41. Baldwin, "Authors and Their Books: James Baldwin Discusses *Tell Me How Long the Train's Been Gone* with Columnist Robert Cromie of *Chicago Tribune.*"
42. Ibid.
43. Letter 38, April 12, 1968. Quoted after Thorsen's *The Price of the Ticket.*
44. Wall, "Stranger at Home," lecture, University of Michigan, April 3, 2008.
45. Mel Watkins, "The Fire Next Time This Time." See also a detailed summary of the review in Weatherby, *Artist on Fire*, 308–13.
46. Allen, "The Better James Baldwin," 32, 33–34. Allen accuses Baldwin of racial essentialism in *Giovanni's Room*, whose white characters are "types, ideas rather than human beings," because Baldwin "has too little experience with the background, the class, the geographical rootedness he has imagined for them" (4).
47. See also Lynn Orilla Scott's perceptive critique of black approaches to Baldwin's later essays (72–74).
48. Sedgwick, *Epistemology of the Closet*, 185.
49. See also Mae G. Henderson's reading of the panic in *Giovanni's Room* as an extension of the "panic . . . [about] sexual activity between men" that Baldwin described in his early essay "The Preservation of Innocence" (1949), in Henderson, "James Baldwin, Expatriation, Homosexual Panic, and Men's Estate." I have written elsewhere (Zaborowska, "Mapping Transcultural Masculinities") that race may be implied in *Giovanni's Room* as well.
50. Newton's interview for *Playboy* in May 1973 is an interesting piece, as he openly supports Baldwin but uses the occasion to reassert his own heterosexual stance while questioning Cleaver's.
51. The song was known as "Samson and Delilah" and was popularized by the Reverend Gary Davis in the 1960s (album: *Gospel, Blues, and Street Songs*). It was recorded as "If I Had My Way I'd Tear This Building Down" by Blind Willie Johnson on December 3, 1927, in Dallas, Texas, and was originally released in 1928 by Columbia Records.
52. The title of the second part echoes another blues song, popularized under the same title by Roberta Flack. That Baldwin begins both books with musical epigraphs confirms his reliance on these black expressive forms as inspirations for the shape and form of his own improvisational, repetitive, and call-and-response narrative in *No Name in the Street.*
53. The richness of scholarship on social space makes it impossible to list all relevant references. In a recent review essay, Russ Castranovo discusses a return to formalism in American literary and cultural studies weary with discourses on identity, or a new tendency to put the study of race and genre together, as "race has always been entangled, often anxiously so, with form" (552). In its preoccupation with architecture and narrative form as markers and makers of Baldwin's sexualized and racialized (African) American self, this chapter nods in the direction of the "new formalisms" that Castranovo diagnoses. At the same time,

it locates itself in the critical terrain that claims material and social sources and consequences of both space and discourse. In employing geography to discuss Baldwin's locations and passages, I adapt spatial theory to literary and cultural study. My approach to Baldwin's literary contribution to our understanding of how spatiality works for race and sex and vice versa echoes as well René Girard's important claim that "great writers apprehend intuitively and concretely, through the medium of their art, if not *formally, the system in which they were first imprisoned together with their contemporaries*" (3). Unlike Girard, who does not venture outside the texts he analyzes, I link the literary and the literal, or the textual fault lines, shifts, and conflicts in Baldwin's texts, with actual sites of textual production, specimens of visual culture, and technologies of representation. In other words, even as I follow the movements of desire in narrative and visual triangulations resembling those famously designed by Girard, I place them in specific geographic locations and social circumstances within and without Baldwin's works. In full agreement, though, that "critical thought" has value only as long as it makes "literary substance" articulate (3), I demonstrate how the substance of Baldwin's works involves concrete instances of American spatiality, tectonic elements of narrative genres, and identity to construct a literary imagination invested in social change.

54. As we have emerged from what Michel Foucault identified as the century of space ("Of Other Spaces," 22), we seem to be even more mired and taunted by spatial considerations at the onset of the new millennium: continued segregation, New Urbanism's charades of "community" development, gentrification, ubiquitous globalization. Critics who link literature and architecture include, among others, Walter Benjamin, Fredric Jameson, Jennifer Bloomer, Catherine Ingraham, and Cornel West.

55. The South had always loomed to Baldwin like a foreign and mysterious land, although it was also a place of mythical familial origins that he was compelled to visit once he reconciled with his stepfather and decided to face the southern demons that had pursued and tormented Baldwin Senior. In "Journey to Atlanta," he imagines the region through a semipicaresque account of his younger brother David's trip there with a Harlem church choir, the Melodeers. The choir consists of several underage boys who have been invited on a concert tour of southern churches but upon their arrival in Atlanta end up being exploited as party canvassers and entertainers. Baldwin describes their treatment at the hands of their inept black manager and the rather white supremacist officials of the Progressive Party as indicative of the North-South schizophrenic mix of hypocrisy, piety, and self-aggrandizement. To his surprise, Baldwin's brother reports that "Negroes in the South [are not] different in any important respect from Negroes in the North" (*Price of the Ticket*, 24). However, he confirms what Baldwin has already guessed—that all American whites seem "all the same . . . [too] ain't none of 'em gonna do you no good; if you gonna be foolish enough to believe what they say, then it serves you good and right. Ain't none of 'em gonna do a thing for

me" (26). Baldwin paints a more vivid, albeit briefer, southern vignette in the short story "Sonny's Blues," which appeared just before he visited the region himself (1957). Sonny, an outlaw drug addict and jazz musician, and his nameless elder brother, a straight-laced and repressed member of the black middle class, demonstrate the importance of homosocial support among black men and of artistic expression for black families in the wake of the Great Migration. While celebrating the strength of family ties and the power of black music, the story emphasizes painful African American origins in the nightmarish, murderous South—a *place-wound*, where racists killed the young men's paternal uncle. Sonny's blues—while creating a space of its own in Baldwin's powerful rendering—carries and preserves the artistic expression of this painful legacy, linking the two regions and generations of victimized and surviving African Americans. Moved by Sonny's performance, if only for a fleeting moment, his emotionally blocked elder brother is able to embrace his family history and, at long last, face the unmourned death of his young daughter. Inside the "jazz space" of that cathartic instance, he also realizes the full impact of his mother's plea to take care of his brother, or to "be *there*" for him. Even though "you may not be able to stop nothing from happening" (119), she tells him, "you got to hold on to your brother . . . and don't let him fall, no matter what it looks like is happening to him and no matter how evil you gets with him. You going to be evil with him many a time. But don't you forget what I told you, you hear?" (*Going to Meet the Man*, 118). This moment highlights Baldwin's underappreciated respect for African American women's influence in shaping homosocial relations between black men. In another prophetic instance, "Sonny's Blues" seems to anticipate Baldwin's hurt by, and his response to, the post-1963 critiques of his works by his "younger brothers" of the Black Power movement. See also Griffin, *Who Set You Flowin.'* On Sonny, see Keith Clark, *Black Manhood*.

56. James Campbell questions these assertions of solidarity as unsubstantiated and claims that Baldwin stretched "his past life at its corners, to make it fit the dimensions of the present idea" (*Talking*, 248).

57. The *Harper's* piece was first titled "The Hard Kind of Courage" and became "A Fly in Buttermilk" in the essay collection *Nobody Knows My Name*; the other piece, "A Letter from the South: Nobody Knows My Name," gave its title to the collection. Leeming, *James Baldwin*, 136–37. After 1963, the more attention Baldwin seemed to pay to the South, the more ambivalent became the critiques of his works, as if his attention to the nether region of the country somehow compromised his northeast U.S.–French coolness and appeal. "The Negro Assays the Negro Mood," *New York Times*, March 12, 1961.

58. On authorial identity politics, see E. Patrick Johnson, *Appropriating Blackness*; and Stuart Hall, "Cultural Studies and Its Theoretical Legacies."

59. I am grateful to Nicholas F. Radel for pointing out this term to me and for his invaluable comments and advice on the queer references in this chapter.

60. See D'Emilio, *Lost Prophet*; Stokes, *The Color of Sex*; and Michaels, *Our America*.

61. I disagree with Daryl C. Dance's statement that Baldwin's southern experience involved a "loss of manhood" ("You Can't Go Home Again," 60).

62. As an (im)migrant of sorts, Baldwin knew well that an unproblematic return home was not possible—he was changed by his sojourn abroad and had to accept the mixed blessings of his new vantage point. Baldwin confirms his commitment to being the prophet of the word in "The Discovery of What It Means to Be an American," where he claims that writers both witness reality *and* transform it into art that shapes their readers' imagination and self-knowledge as social subjects: "[The] interior life is a real life, and the intangible dreams of people have a tangible effect on the world" (12). Like *Giovanni's Room*, Baldwin's southern writings confirm his interest in the interplays of exterior and interior and material and spatial consequences of desire.

63. Baldwin discusses a similar instance in reference to his trip to the South in 1960. In one of the interviews he mentions that his light was always on at the motel where he was staying because he was typing up his notes at night and felt unsafe and "terribly visible" as a northerner and intellectual. When he later arrived in Paris, he had a similar reaction to the one that he had in New York after his first southern trip: he yielded to post-traumatic panic at a friend's house and "was afraid to be alone" (*Conversations*, 70).

64. Note to the author, July 2006.

65. Weatherby provides an extensive summary of critical reactions to *No Name in the Street* (*Artist on Fire*, 308–12).

66. Critics who attend to this scene include Dance, Hakutani ("No Name," 285), and Hardy (*James Baldwin's God*, 70–71). There is a clear tradition of constructing Baldwin as oversexed, which I discuss in the introduction. In "Blues for Mister Baldwin," Joseph Featherstone obliquely criticizes Baldwin's preoccupation with sexuality in a homophobic context (155).

67. No one I have consulted was able to confirm the identity of the politician or the exact location of the event.

68. See Gayle Rubin's seminal piece "The Traffic in Women."

69. The books by Maurice Wallace, Michelle Wallace, Stokes, Michaels, and Gunning are relevant here. Lynn Orilla Scott mentions Baldwin's focus on heteronormative masculinity in her introduction: "He saw that machismo and queer baiting by 'heterosexual' men concealed both a fear of and a longing for male touch and intimacy, both of which were paradoxically projected onto the black male body by the white male" (xviii).

70. In that sense, he was also implicitly casting Cleaver's attack on him and Cleaver's aligning himself with Norman Mailer's "White Negro" as a form of literary race rape. This is a fascinating issue, also in light of the revelation that Mailer once lived with a black man during his early years in California. Baldwin talked about this in his interview with Quincy Troupe in 1987, shortly before he died, and the fact that this is virtually a deathbed confession makes the revelation convincing. Daniel Baldwin, Jimmy's father, had been married before his move to New York

and had several children from his first marriage. One of Jimmy's stepbrothers who lived in California told him about having shared an apartment with Mailer as a kind of "black husband." See also Reid-Pharr, *Conjugal Union*.

71. See also the discussions of this story in Margolis, "The Negro Church," 63–64. On the rules of black macho, see Michelle Wallace, *Black Macho*, 68.

72. See also E. Patrick Johnson on the "sadism" of heterosexuality in *Appropriating Blackness*, 50–51; and Stokes on Thomas Dixon's "restaging of sexual assault" in *The Color of Sex*, 146–47.

73. He claims in *Nobody Knows My Name*, "I decided to return here because I was afraid to" (xii–xiii). In his first confrontation with the landscape of the region, Baldwin thus observes and experiences, *through* his fear and sense of his paradoxical "denaturalization" as a northerner, what Homi Bhabha refers to as "the question of social visibility, the power of the eye to naturalize the rhetoric of national affiliation and its forms of collective expression" ("DissemiNation," 295).

74. This fragment could be read as an example of what Homi Bhabha terms the "construction of nationness as a form of social and textual affiliation" ("DissemiNation," 292). In this context, Baldwin's enactment of the "production of the nation as narration" in *No Name in the Street* can also be seen as taking place in a process of splitting, as Bhabha defines it, "between the continuist, accumulative temporality of the pedagogical, and the repetitious, recursive strategy of the performative" (297).

75. I belabor this point to signal that in this instance Baldwin in fact anticipates some of the "grand theory" to come, that is, what Julia Kristeva and Homi Bhabha say about nation and narration and temporality, especially Bhabha's point that "national time becomes concrete and visible in the chronotope of the local, particular, graphic" and that "narrative synchrony" has or implies a "graphically visible position in space" (*Nation and Narration*, 295). I contend that Baldwin shows how this model works already in *No Name in the Street*, and takes it even further by interrogating his own position and entry point into the region as a visitor, narrator, and character in the story built around specific spatial encounters with the South.

76. The spatial analysis aims to show how Baldwin's narrative design enables nonlinear or back-and-forth readings. Such a strategy demonstrates how southern and American homosexual panic simultaneously arises from and shapes social space, or how racialized and sexualized national identity is experienced, perceived, and imagined through spatial practices and their representations.

77. See also the discussion of this scene in Yoshinobu Hakutani, "No Name in the Street," 286. (On p. 278, Hakutani confuses chronology between *No Name in the Street* and *The Fire Next Time*.)

78. Barton, *Sites of Memory*, 1.

79. Upton, *Architecture in the United States*, ii.

80. See D'Emilio, *Lost Prophet*; and Polsgrove, *Divided Minds*.

81. See Newton's interview in *Playboy* and Johnson's discussion of this event in *Appropriating Blackness* (52–57).

82. Maurice Wallace's discussion of the "spectragraphic gaze" in *Constructing the Black Masculine* is helpful to my discussion here. My reading of this specific instance in Baldwin's text of the paradoxical, momentary advantage in terms of the ocular and architectural does not, obviously, suggest any permanent reversal of social hierarchies. *No Name in the Street* is a text that reveals the workings of the spatial politics of segregation and elucidates Baldwin's larger understanding of the complex fault lines between gender, sex, and race he experienced and then narrated in the collection. This in turn helps us to understand his narrator's paradoxical ability to feel something akin to pity or compassion for his white oppressors. As we shall see, once again, this ability has to do with Baldwin's perception of his own location in the restaurant scene as both inside and outside the nation as a black and queer artist.

83. Frederick Douglass's *Narrative* mentions a hiding place from which the young Douglass watches his Aunt Hester being whipped. Marlon Ross and I have discussed this instance as implying, perhaps, that Douglass fears being sexually violated in the way that she has been by her master.

84. See especially Parker, "Preposterous Events"; Radel, "Can the Sodomite Speak?"; and DiGangi, *Homoerotics*.

85. Michael Kimmel, Patricia Hill Collins, and Russ Castranovo take on the postslavery landscape of power and desire in the nineteenth and twentieth centuries that affected the rise of specific kinds of manhood, especially the ambivalent and effeminate "Genteel Patriarch in the South" (Kimmel, *Manhood in America*, 16–20).

86. Warren's *So Black and Blue* discusses Ellison's strategy in ways that resonate with what I show Baldwin is doing with racialized homophobia in *No Name in the Street*: "Rather than systematize his insights, Ellison allowed them to stand, sometimes contradictorily, alongside one another, a practice that made him . . . a master of the occasion of criticism, turning a single instance into an X ray of the social organism infected by race at that historical moment" (22).

87. As evidenced by the field-building works of Alan Bray and Jonathan Goldberg and others, queer studies originates in interpretations of literature and culture of the early modern period, and so its key terms and definitions owe as much to the surviving representations of that period as to the influence of Foucault's work on sexuality. On Baldwin's theoretical complexity, see also Fields, "Looking," 473.

88. See also the works on gender of Smith-Rosenberg, D'Emilio and Freedman, Mumford, and Dixon.

89. Radel mentions another important instance proving that Baldwin inverts the normative white racist power structure here by pointing to Morrison's use of a scene in *Beloved* where the white guards make the black male slaves perform oral sex on them. Radel explains that in this scene the act "does not denote 'homosexuality' or 'sodomy.' It just seems a normative display of patriarchal racist

power. Morrison's brilliance (and homophobia) is in showing the other side of this display of power, but she also reveals its normativity in white power structures" (unpublished notes).

90. See Jean-François Lyotard on landscape, face, and melancholia in *The Inhuman*, where he writes about the "scapeland" of writing; Baldwin mentions something similar in "The Preservation of Innocence" (*Collected Essays*, 594).

91. See Hardy, *James Baldwin's God*, especially chapter 5, on Baldwin's ambivalence about his experiences with, and the rhetoric of, black holiness culture in *The Fire Next Time*. I disagree with Hardy, however, that "as Baldwin reckons with this heritage, he often *pretends to be scandalized* by the anger and thirst for vengeance . . . that often marks black religion" (79; italics mine). Baldwin does not "pretend" but instead consciously deploys and employs his passionate reactions to that rhetoric; it is a matter of style and composition, an artistic device rather than an act of pretending to be scandalized. We can, however, speak of his self-conscious performance of such rhetoric, especially in *The Fire Next Time* and his later works (e.g., Proudhammer's speech at a civil rights rally in *Train*).

92. Hardy uses the same reference to "religion as bloodless theater" in *James Baldwin's God* (3).

93. An undercurrent of erotic and religious references can be read throughout Baldwin's oeuvre: in *Go Tell It on the Mountain*, whose teenage protagonist's homoerotic desire first blossoms in the church; in *The Amen Corner*, whose sexually repressed Sister Margaret finds out that "love never dies"; in *If Beale Street Could Talk*, in which Mrs. Hunt channels her sex drive into love for Jesus; and in *Just above My Head*, whose main character is a queer gospel singer.

94. See also Richard Dyer on "sad white young men" as ultimate queers, or how white the stereotype has been; he sees black or mulatto men as seeming to have a much easier time accepting their sexuality in various texts written by whites (*The Culture of Queers*, 124).

95. See also his much more ambivalent and defensive discussion of Cleaver on pp. 170–72.

96. This echoes gay pop culture images by Paul Cadmus and Tom of Finland.

97. See Sedgwick's discussion of Billy Budd in *Epistemology of the Closet*.

98. Baldwin's narrator harbors suspicions that Tony might be lying, not so much about the case as about his sexuality.

99. On the inherent "perversity" of Jews and Blacks, see Sander Gilman, *The Jew's Body* and *Disease and Representation*.

100. In a lively letter to Cezzar dated September 27, 1974 (letter 50), Baldwin recounts in detail the vicissitudes and resolution of Tony Maynard's case. Maynard is finally free, "after three mistrials" and seven years of incarceration in Germany and the United States. Baldwin has just published *If Beale Street Could Talk* in Germany, which has become a bestseller; he has also appeared in a German TV special, *James Baldwin*, whose action "is a circle" that involves his "battle to save [Tony's] life." Baldwin traces the progress of the case in Germany, which at some

point involved his German publisher, who had "under-written" the Maynard case or given Jimmy a "blank check" to help his friend and who, after Tony had been beaten up in the Hamburg prison (as described in *No Name in the Street*), sued the German state "on Tony's behalf." Baldwin believes that his notoriety then caused the USIS to "ban" him by means of canceling his five-city tour of Germany, the tour for which USIS had signed a contract with his German publisher. After he was "banned," the publisher, who "had a best-seller on his hands," made the impossible happen or "raised the fucking roof," and so Jimmy and his brother David "sailed into that storm." Despite that, Baldwin then pointed out to his hosts that the "American crimes" of racism did not "excuse" the German ones; he advised his German listeners that if they wanted to understand the "celebrated American Negro Problem," to which Baldwin was so "eminent and celebrated" a witness, they had "merely to speak" with their own migrants and immigrants, "the Turk, the Greek, and the Spaniard," who were so "busily (and gratefully)" sweeping their cities' streets.

101. Baldwin makes clear the link between Gene's taking his own life and miscegenation but neglects to bring in his own love for the light-skinned Gene, which he admits only later in "The Price of the Ticket."

102. For brevity's sake, I will not discuss class and the different levels of danger that the two men obviously face. Baldwin explains these issues clearly in the text around that scene.

103. Note the erotic triangles: LeRoy-Eric-Rufus, Eric-Cass-Richard, Leona-Rufus-Vivaldo, Vivaldo-Eric-Ida, Vivaldo-Cass-Richard, and Leona-Cass-Rufus.

104. These observations close the three decades of Baldwin's encounters with the American South and provide a powerful lens for rereading his works on the region today.

105. Polsgrove, *Divided Minds*. See her description of Robert Coles's awakening to the spatial manifestations of segregation in Mississippi. "Robert Coles was an educated man. He was acquainted with Reinhold Niebuhr and Anna Freud. He had studied at Harvard. Yet he had never given much thought, he would later say, to the fact of American life that had burst astonishingly upon him" (xvii).

106. See also D'Emilio, *The World Turned*, especially his discussion of Bayard Rustin.

107. Nina Simone has a version of it that seems a likely source of Baldwin's title given that he and the queer diva were good friends, as does the Reverend E. D. Campbell, whose rendering also enacts a call-and-response performance of a baptismal ritual.

108. See Lynn Orilla Scott's treatment of these themes in *James Baldwin's Later Fiction*, 144–69.

109. See Reid-Pharr's important reading of *Giovanni's Room* in a similar context in "Tearing the Goat's Flesh" as a novel exploring the "nonexistence of the . . . Black homosexual . . . in the Western notions of rationality and humanity" (387).

110. Interview with Pakay, May 9–10, 1970, Istanbul.

111. Marlon Riggs confirms this in an interview with Ron Simmons, where they also

discuss Malcolm's bisexuality and perceptions and representations in the context of heroic black masculinity. See "Sexuality, Television, and Death," 135–54.

Conclusion

1. Interview with author, November 14, 2005. Walter Dallas attended the Yale Drama School years after Engin Cezzar did. He staged a powerful performance of *The Amen Corner* at the Center Stage in Baltimore in 1981, which Baldwin saw and it so inspired him that he asked Dallas to become his collaborator. Dallas told me that the play was staged in London but was unable to give me more detailed information. *The Welcome Table* appeared at the University of the Arts in Philadelphia during the 1990–91 season, following a videotaped reading of the play with Baldwin and student actors in 1986, and a studio reading in 1989 for Ruby Dee, David Baldwin, and other friends (Leeming, *James Baldwin*, 378). On May 27, 1995, Dallas directed a reading at Lincoln Center that starred Novella Nelson as Edith, Oni Faida Lampley as LaVerne, Faran Tahir as Mohammed, Mari Nelson as Regina, Robert Knepper as Rob, and Mark Feuerstein as Mark; the Lincoln Center project did not materialize into a performance because the Baldwin Estate did not allow it.
2. The play's title also echoes a line from a popular gospel song, "I'm Gonna Sit at the Welcome Table."
3. Quoted in James Campbell, "Room in the East," 5.
4. I refer to the 1987 manuscript of the play, annotated by Baldwin, that Walter Dallas kindly shared with me in 2006. As with the rest of the Baldwin papers, direct quotations are not permitted by the estate.
5. Beam, "Not a Bad Legacy, Brother" (185). Beam confirms Baldwin's stature as a father figure for black queers: "Because he could envision us as lovers, our possibilities were endless. We could be warriors, artists, and astronauts; we could be severe, sensitive, and philosophical. . . . Not a bad legacy for someone whom the Republic wished deaf and dumb by age fourteen" (186).
6. Leeming also mentions other "sisters," Maya Angelou, Verta Mae Grosvenor, Louise Meriwether, Paule Marshall, and Eleanor Traylor, as possible inspirations (*James Baldwin*, 377).
7. Leeming states that Baldwin began writing the play in 1967, while living in the Pasha's Library in Rumeli Hisarı in Istanbul (*James Baldwin*, 275), and completed it in a "rough form" the year he died (320). It began as a work clearly focused on sex and gender, tentatively titled *The 121st Day of Sodom*, "a takeoff on Sade's 120 *Days of Sodom*" and was to be "'a drawing room nightmare of six adventurers' in the south of France" (275).
8. Leeming writes that Faure "had written a history of Saint-Paul de Vence, and had a particular aversion to blacks, whom she associated with those who, from her point of view, had exiled her from Algeria, the land of her birth. . . . Later Mlle

Faure would come to admire and respect her tenant, and he her" (*James Baldwin*, 312).

9. Interview with Walter Dallas, Freedom Theater, Philadelphia, June 20, 2006.

10. James Baldwin, letter to Walter Dallas, July 21 [or 27], 1987.

11. See the following by Gates: "An Interview with Josephine Baker and James Baldwin," *Southern Review*, 21.3 (summer 1985): 594–602; "An Interview with Josephine Baker and James Baldwin (1973)," in *James Baldwin: The Legacy*, ed. Quincy Troupe (New York: Simon & Schuster, 1989); "The Welcome Table," in *English Inside and Out: The Places of Literary Criticism*, ed. Susan Gubar and and Jonathan Kramholtz (New York: Routledge, 1993), 47–60; "The Welcome Table [James Baldwin]," in *Thirteen Ways of Looking at a Black Man* (New York: Vintage, 1997), 3–20; "The Welcome Table: James Baldwin in Exile," in *Exile and Creativity: Signposts, Travelers, Outsiders, Backward Glances*, ed. Susan Rubin Suleiman (Durham: Duke University Press, 1996), 305–20.

12. "James Baldwin: Bir Gün Mutlaka mı?" (Definitely One Day?), in *Konuşa Konuşa* (İstanbul: Gür Yayınları, 1983). Translated by Aslı Gür.

13. Beam describes Baldwin's charismatic and gender-bending presence in "Not a Bad Legacy, Brother": "The first and only time I heard James Baldwin read, I sat perched on the edge of my chair catching every syllable that dropped from his lips. In the too-crowded, too-hot room, I watched him pat beads of perspiration with a flourish only a true diva could muster. He was a diva, yet up close he seemed quite fragile, having paid the price of the ticket for being arrogant, articulate, and black" (186).

14. Interview with author, May 8, 2006.

15. Baldwin, *No Name in the Street*, 172; hereafter cited as N N S.

16. bell hooks, *Talking Back*. hooks's term helps to explain what Baldwin faced as a black queer writer, a "sissified" male as Marlon Ross defines it, that is, one who talked back and sometimes used women's voices to do so as he did in *Beale Street* and *The Welcome Table*. hooks writes, "True speaking is not solely an expression of creative power; it is an act of resistance, a political gesture that challenges politics of domination that would render us nameless and voiceless" (8). See also Ross, "Camping the Dirty Dozens."

17. This passage and its imagery resonate with Julia Kristeva's concept of feminine language. See *Desire in Language* and "Stabat Mater" in *The Kristeva Reader*.

18. In this Baldwin anticipates Mark Anthony Neal's *New Black Man*, which uses black feminist theory to propose a model of black manhood that is anti-homophobic and anti-misogynistic.

19. Baldwin can also be seen knitting together the realms of the semiotic and the symbolic or, in Kristeva's formulation, the passionate, bodily sphere of the mother and the phallic and cerebral sphere of the father. See *Desire in Language* and *Strangers to Ourselves*.

20. E. Patrick Johnson's exploration of "quare" studies riffs on Baldwin's titles, *No Name in the Street* and *Nobody Knows My Name*. He credits his southern grand-

mother with helping him to embrace the concept as denoting "something or someone who is odd, irregular, or slightly off kilter" and as referring to "something excessive—something that might philosophically translate into an excess of discursive and epistemological meanings grounded in African American cultural rituals and lived experience" ("'Quare' Studies," 2).

21. Leeming, "The White Problem," 21.
22. Walker, "In Search of Our Mother's Gardens," originally published in *Ms.*, May 1974.
23. Nellie McKay, "The Narrative Self," 96. See also Susan Lori Parks, who credits Baldwin with helping her to become a playwright, in Monte Williams, "From a Planet Closer to the Sun," *New York Times*, April 17, 1996, C1, C8.
24. "Authors and Their Books: James Baldwin Discusses *Tell Me How Long the Train's Been Gone*," with columnist Robert Cromie of the *Chicago Tribune*, audiotape (Motivational Programming Corporation, 1969).
25. E-mail correspondence with author, April 6, 2008.
26. Interview with author, June 6, 2006.

BIBLIOGRAPHY

Archival Sources

Baldwin, James. Archive at the Schomburg Center for Research in Black Culture, New York.
———. Letters to Engin Cezzar. Unpublished. James Baldwin Estate.

Interviews by the Author

Avni Bey (Salbaş). Personal interview. September 10, 2005.
Balamir, Oktay. Personal interviews. September 6–7, 2005.
Campbell, James. Personal interview. June 28, 2007.
Çapan, Cevat. Personal interview. May 26, 2001.
Cezzar, Engin. Personal interviews. May 24–30, 2001.
Dallas, Walter. Personal interview. November 14, 2005 (via telephone); June 20, 2006.
Fortuny, Kim. Personal interviews. September 9–10, 2005.
Freely, John. Personal interview. September 9, 2005.
Garwood, Minnie. Personal interview. September 10, 2005.
Happersberger, Lucien. Personal interview. June 25, 2007.
Keith, Kenton. Personal interview. April 10, 2006 (via telephone).
Leeming, David. Personal interviews. July 30, 2003; April 30, 2004; June 16, 2006.
Oral, Zeynep. Personal interviews. May 31, 2001; December 9, 2004 (with Aslı Gür).
Pakay, Sedat. Personal interviews. June 21, 2002; June 15–16, 2005; June 16–17, 2006.
Poyrazoğlu, Ali. Personal interviews. April 5, 2004 (with Aslı Gür); September 8, 2005.

Rein, Brenda. Personal interviews. May 8, 2006 (via telephone); June 8, 2006 (via telephone); October 11, 2006.

Sevgen, Cevza. Personal interview. September 9, 2005.

Sururi, Gülriz. Personal interview. May 30, 2001.

Published Sources in English

Achebe, Chinua. "The Day I Finally Met Baldwin." *Callaloo: A Journal of African-American and African Arts and Letters* 25.2 (2002): 502–4.

Achilles, Jochen. "African American Drama and Interracial Negotiations in 1964: James Baldwin's *Blues for Mister Charlie*, Adrienne Kennedy's *Funnyhouse of a Negro*, and Imamu Amiri Baraka's *The Slave*." *English Literatures in International Contexts*. Ed. Heinz Antor and Klaus Stierstorfer. Heidelberg, Germany, 2000. 201–219.

Adams, Stephen. "Giovanni's Room: The Homosexual as Hero." *James Baldwin*. Ed. Harold Bloom. New York: Chelsea House, 1986. 131–39.

Adelsen, Charles E. "A Love Affair: James Baldwin and Istanbul." *Ebony* 25.5 (March 1970): 40–46.

Ahmann, Mathew H., and Stephen J. Wright, eds. *The New Negro*. Notre Dame, Ind.: Fides, 1961.

Akçam, Taner. *A Shameful Act. The Armenian Genocide and the Question of Turkish Responsibility*. Tran. Paul Bessemer. New York: Macmillan, 2006.

Albert, Richard N. "The Jazz-Blues Motif in James Baldwin's 'Sonny's Blues.'" *College Literature* 11.2 (spring 1984): 178–85.

Aldrich, Robert F. *Colonialism and Homosexuality*. New York: Routledge, 2003.

Alexander, Meena. *The Shock of Arrival: Reflections on Postcolonial Experience*. New York: South End Press, 1996.

Allen, Brooke. "The Better James Baldwin." *New Criterion* 16.8 (1998): 28–36.

Anderson, Michael. "Trapped inside James Baldwin." *New York Times Book Review*, March 29, 1998, 13.

Andrews, Walter, and Mehmet Kalpaklı. *The Age of Beloveds: Love and the Beloved in Early-Modern Ottoman and European Culture and Society*. Durham, N.C.: Duke University Press, 2005.

Anzaldúa, Gloria. *Borderlands/La Frontera: The New Mestiza*. San Francisco: Aunt Lute Books, 1987.

Appiah, Kwame Anthony. *Cosmopolitanism: Ethics in a World of Strangers*. New York: W. W. Norton, 2006.

Armstrong, Hamilton Fish. *Where the East Begins*. New York: Harper and Brothers, 1929.

Ashman, Anastasia M., and Jennifer Eaton Gökmen, eds. *Tales from the Expat Harem: Foreign Women in Modern Turkey*. Emeryville, Calif.: Seal Press, 2006.

"At the Root of the Negro Problem . . ." *Time* 81.20 (May 1963): 26–27.

Auger, Philip George. *Native Sons in No Man's Land: Rewriting Afro-American Manhood in the Novels of Baldwin, Walker, Wideman, and Gaines*. New York: Garland, 2000.

Avedon, Richard, and James Baldwin. *Nothing Personal*. New York: Atheneum, 1964.

Awkward, Michael. "Negotiations of Power: White Critics, Black Texts, and the Self-Referential Impulse." *American Literary History* 2.4 (winter 1990): 581–606.

——. *Scenes of Instruction: A Memoir*. Durham, N.C.: Duke University Press, 1999.

Bachelard, Gaston. *Poetics of Space*. Trans. Maria Jolas. Boston: Beacon Press, 1969.

Baker, Houston A., Jr. "The Embattled Craftsman: An Essay on James Baldwin." *Journal of African–Afro-American Affairs* 1.1 (1977): 28–51.

Bakhtin, Mikhail. *The Dialogic Imagination. Four Essays*. Trans. Caryl Emerson and Michael Holquist. Ed. Michael Holquist. Austin: University of Texas Press, 1981.

——. "Response to a Question from the *Novy Mir* Editorial Staff." *Speech Genres and Other Late Essays*. Trans. Vern W. McGee. Ed. Caryl Emerson and Michael Holquist. Austin: University of Texas Press, 1986. 1–9.

Baldwin, James. *The Amen Corner*. New York: Dial, 1968.

——. *Another Country*. New York: Dial, 1962.

——. "As Much Truth as One Can Bear." *New York Times Book Review*, January 14, 1962, 25.

——. "Authors and Their Books: James Baldwin Discusses *Tell Me How Long the Train's Been Gone* with columnist Robert Cromie of *Chicago Tribune*." Audiotape. Motivational Programming Corporation, 1969.

——. *Blues for Mister Charlie*. New York: Dial, 1964.

——. *The Devil Finds Work*. New York: Dial, 1976.

——. "The Discovery of What It Means to Be an American." *Nobody Knows My Name: More Notes of a Native Son*. New York: Dial 1961. Reprinted in *James Baldwin: Collected Essays*. New York: Library of America, 1998. 137–42.

——. *Early Novels and Stories*. New York: Library of America, 1998.

——. *The Evidence of Things Not Seen*. New York: Holt, Rinehart and Winston, 1985.

——. *The Fire Next Time*. New York: Dial, 1963. Reprinted in *Price of the Ticket*, 333–80.

——. *Giovanni's Room*. New York: Dial, 1956.

——. *Go Tell It on the Mountain*. New York: Alfred A. Knopf, 1953.

——. " 'Go the Way Your Blood Beats': An Interview with Richard Goldstein." *James Baldwin: The Legacy*. Ed. Quincy Troupe. New York: Touchstone, 1989. 173–85.

——. *Going to Meet the Man*. New York: Dial, 1965.

——. *Harlem Quartet*. Paris: Stock, 1987.

——. *If Beale Street Could Talk*. New York: Dial, 1974.

——. "Introduction: Nobody Knows My Name." *James Baldwin: Collected Essays*. New York: Library of America, 1998. 135–36.

——. Interview with Sedat Pakay. Istanbul, May 9–10, 1970. CD recording. Sedat Pakay and Hudson Film Works.

——. Introduction to *Duties, Pleasures, and Conflicts: Essays in Struggle*. By Michael Thelwell. Amherst: University of Massachusetts Press, 1987.

——. *James Baldwin: Collected Essays*. New York: Library of America, 1998.

——. *Jimmy's Blues: Selected Poems*. London: Michael Joseph, 1983.

———. *Just above My Head.* New York: Dial, 1979.

———. *Little Man, Little Man: A Story of Childhood.* Illustrated by Yoran Cazac. New York: Dial, 1976.

———. "The Negro Assays the Negro Mood." *New York Times Sunday Magazine*, March 12, 1961.

———. "The New Lost Generation." *Price of the Ticket*, 305–313.

———. *No Name in the Street.* New York: Dial, 1972. Reprinted in *Price of the Ticket*, 449–552.

———. *Nobody Knows My Name: More Notes of a Native Son.* New York: Dial 1961. Reprinted in *James Baldwin: Collected Essays.* New York: Library of America, 1998. 131–285.

———. *Notes of a Native Son.* Boston: Beacon Press, 1955.

———. *One Day, When I Was Lost: A Scenario Based on "The Autobiography of Malcolm X."* New York: Dial, 1972.

———. *The Price of the Ticket: Collected Nonfiction, 1948–1985.* New York: St. Martin's, 1985.

———. *Tell Me How Long the Train's Been Gone.* New York: Dial, 1968.

———. "This Morning, This Evening, So Soon." *Going to Meet the Man.* New York: Vintage, 1993. 143–94. Originally published in 1960.

Baldwin, James. With Engin Cezzar. *Dost Mektupları.* Trans. Seçkin Selvi. Istanbul: Yapı Kredi Yayınları/Edebiyat Dizisi, 2007.

Baldwin, James, and Nikki Giovanni. *A Dialogue.* Philadelphia, Pa.: Lippincott, 1973.

Baldwin, James, and Sol Stein. *Native Sons: The Newly Discovered Correspondence and Photographs, as well as a Never-Before Published Story and Play.* New York: Ballantine, 2004.

Baldwin, James, et al. *Black Anti-Semitism and Jewish Racism.* New York: R. W. Baron, 1969.

———, et al. "Police Shooting of Oakland Negro." Letter to editor. *New York Times*, May 6, 1968.

Balfour, Katharine Lawrence. *The Evidence of Things Not Said: James Baldwin and the Promise of American Democracy.* Ithaca, N.Y.: Cornell University Press, 2001.

Ball, Arnetha F., and Sarah Warshauer Freedman. *Bakhtinian Perspectives on Language, Literacy, and Learning.* New York: Cambridge University Press, 2004.

Bartels, Emily C. *Spectacles of Strangeness: Imperialism, Alienation, and Marlowe.* Philadelphia: University of Pennsylvania Press, 1993.

Barton, Craig. *Sites of Memory: Perspectives on Architecture and Race.* New York: Princeton Architectural Press, 2001.

Beam, Joseph. "James Baldwin: Not a Bad Legacy, Brother." *Brother to Brother: New Writings by Black Gay Men.* Ed. Essex Hemphill. Boston: Alyson Publications, 1991. 184–86.

Bercovitch, Sacvan. "Emerson the Prophet: Romanticism, Puritanism, and Auto-American Biography." *Emerson: Prophecy, Metamorphosis, and Influence.* Ed. David Levin. New York: Columbia University Press, 1975. 1–27.

———. *The Office of the Scarlet Letter.* Baltimore: Johns Hopkins University Press, 1991.

———. *The Puritan Origins of the American Self.* New Haven, Conn.: Yale University Press, 1975.

Bereket, Tarik, and Barry D. Adam. "The Emergence of Gay Identities in Contemporary Turkey." *Sexualities* 9.2 (2006): 131–51.

Berman, Paul, ed. *Blacks and Jews: Alliances and Arguments.* New York: Delacorte Press, 1994.

Bernstein, Matthew, and Gaylyn Studlar, eds. *Visions of the East: Orientalism in Film.* New Brunswick, N.J.: Rutgers University Press, 1997.

Betsky, Aaron. *Queer Space: Architecture and Same-Sex Desire.* New York: William Morrow, 1997.

Bhabha, Homi K. "DissemiNation: Time, Narrative, and the Margins of the Modern Nation." *Nation and Narration.* Ed. H. Bhabha. New York: Routledge, 1993. 291–322.

———. *The Location of Culture.* New York: Routledge, 1994.

———, ed. *Nation and Narration.* New York: Routledge, 1990.

Bigsby, C. W. E. "The Committed Writer: James Baldwin as Dramatist." *Twentieth Century Literature: A Scholarly and Critical Journal* 13.1 (1967): 39–48.

———. "The Divided Mind of James Baldwin." *Modern Critical Views: James Baldwin.* Ed. Harold Bloom. New York: Chelsea House, 1986. 113–30.

Blair, Sara. "Photo-Text Capital: James Baldwin, Richard Avedon, and the Uses of Harlem." *Harlem Crossroads: Black Writers and the Photograph in the Twentieth Century.* Princeton, N.J.: Princeton University Press, 2007.

Bloom, Harold, ed. *James Baldwin.* New York: Chelsea House, 1986.

Bluefarb, Sam. "James Baldwin's 'Previous Condition': A Problem of Identification." *Negro American Literature Forum* 3.1 (1969): 26–29.

Bobia, Rosa. *The Critical Reception of James Baldwin in France.* New York: Grove/Atlantic, 1998.

Boelhower, William Q. "The Immigrant Novel as Genre." MELUS 1 (spring 1981): 3–13.

Boggs, Nicholas. "Of Mimicry and (*Little Man Little*) Man: Toward a Queersighted Theory of Black Childhood." *James Baldwin Now.* Ed. Dwight A. McBride. New York: New York University Press, 1999: 122–60.

Boone, Joseph A. *Queer Frontiers: Millennial Geographies, Genders, and Generations.* Madison: University of Wisconsin Press, 2000.

Boyd. Herb. *Baldwin's Harlem: A Biography of James Baldwin.* New York: Atria Books, 2008.

———, ed. *The Harlem Reader: A Celebration of New York's Most Famous Neighborhood.* New York: Three Rivers Press, 2003.

Boyd, Hilary Sumner, and John Freely. *Strolling through Istanbul: A Guide to the City.* New York: Columbia University Press, 2000.

Bray, Alan. *Homosexuality in Renaissance England.* New York: Columbia University Press, 1995.

Breen, Nelson E. "To Hear Another Language." *Callaloo: A Journal of African-American and African Arts and Letters* 12.3 (1989): 431–52.

Britt, David D. "America: Another Country." *Ba Shiru: A Journal of African Languages and Literature* 4 (1972): 47–51.

Brodkin, Karen. *How Jews Became White Folks and What That Says about Race in America.* New Brunswick, N.J.: Rutgers University Press, 1998.

Bruck, Peter. "Dungeon and Salvation: Biblical Rhetoric in James Baldwin's *Just above My Head.*" *History and Tradition in Afro-American Culture.* Ed. Gunter H. Lenz. Frankfurt: Campus, 1984. 130–46.

Bruinessen, Martin van. "Race, Culture, Nation and Identity Politics in Turkey." Paper presented at the Mica Ertegün Annual Turkish Studies Workshop on Continuity and Change: "Shifting State Ideologies from Late Ottoman to Early Republican Turkey, 1890–1930," Department of Near Eastern Studies, Princeton University, April 24–26, 1997. http://www.let.uu.nl.

Butler, Cheryl B. *The Art of the Black Essay: From Meditation to Transcendence.* New York: Routledge, 2003.

Butler, Judith P. *Bodies That Matter: On the Discursive Limits of "Sex."* New York: Routledge, 1993.

———. *The Psychic Life of Power: Theories in Subjection.* Stanford University Press, 1997.

———. *Undoing Gender.* New York: Routledge, 2004.

Byerman, Keith E. "Words and Music: Narrative Ambiguity in 'Sonny's Blues.'" *Studies in Short Fiction* 19.4 (fall 1982): 367–72.

Byrd, Rudolph P. *Traps: African American Men on Gender and Sexuality.* Bloomington: Indiana University Press, 2001.

Calvino, Italo. *Invisible Cities.* Trans. William Weaver. New York: Harcourt, 1974.

Campbell, James. *Exiled in Paris: Richard Wright, James Baldwin, Samuel Beckett, and Others on the Left Bank.* New York: Scribner, 1995.

———. "Room in the East: James Baldwin's Letters to Istanbul." *Times Literary Supplement,* June 15, 2007, 3–5.

———. *Talking at the Gates: A Life of James Baldwin.* New York: Penguin Books, 1992.

Campbell, Robert. *The Chasm: The Life and Death of a Great Experiment in Ghetto Education.* Boston: Houghton Mifflin, 1974.

Carson, Warren J. "Manhood, Musicality, and Male Bonding in *Just above My Head.*" *Re-viewing James Baldwin: Things Not Seen.* Ed. D. Quentin Miller and David Adams Leeming. Philadelphia, Pa.: Temple University Press, 2000. 215–32.

Cartey, Wilfred. "The Realities of Four Negro Writers." *Columbia University Forum* 9.3 (1966): 34–42.

———. "The Realities of Four Negro Writers." *Roots* 1.1 (1970): 145–59.

Carton, Evan. "The Politics of Selfhood: Bob Slocum, T. S. Garp, and Auto-American-Biography." *Novel: A Forum on Fiction* 20.1 (fall 1986): 41–61.

Castillo, Greg. "Soviet Orientalism: Socialist Realism and Built Tradition." *Traditional Dwellings and Settlements Review* 8.2 (1997): 32–47.

Castranovo, Russ. "Race and Other Clichés." *American Literary History* 14.3 (fall 2002): 551–65.

Chametzky, Jules, ed. *A Tribute to James Baldwin: Black Writers Redefine the Struggle.* Amherst, Mass.: Institute for the Advanced Study in the Humanities, 1989.

Champion, Ernest A. "James Baldwin and the Challenge of Ethnic Literature in the Eighties." MELUS 8.2 (1981): 61–64.

———. *Mr. Baldwin, I Presume: James Baldwin–Chinua Achebe, a Meeting of the Minds.* Lanham, Md.: University Press of America, 1995.

Champion, Laurie. "Assimilation versus Celebration in James McPherson's 'The Story of a Dead Man' and James Baldwin's 'Sonny's Blues.'" *Short Story* 8.2 (2000): 94–106.

Chancy, Myriam J. A. "Brother/Outsider: In Search of a Black Gay Legacy in James Baldwin's *Giovanni's Room.*" *The Gay 90's: Disciplinary and Interdisciplinary Formations in Queer Studies.* Genders, no. 26. Ed. Thomas Foster, Carol Siegel, and Ellen E. Berry. New York: New York University Press, 1997. 155–90.

Christian, Barbara. *Black Feminist Criticism: Perspectives on Black Women Writers.* Athene Series. New York: Teachers College Press, 1997.

Clark, Keith. *Black Manhood in James Baldwin, Ernest J. Gaines, and August Wilson.* Urbana: University of Illinois Press, 2002.

Clark, Kenneth B. *King, Malcolm, Baldwin: Three Interviews.* Middletown, Conn.: Wesleyan University Press, 1985.

Clark, Michael. "James Baldwin's 'Sonny's Blues': Childhood Light and Art." *College Language Association Journal* 29.2 (December 1985): 197–205.

Clarke, John Henrik, ed. *Harlem, U.S.A.: The Story of a City within a City Told by James Baldwin and Others.* Berlin: Seven Seas, 1964.

Cleaver, Eldridge. *Soul on Ice.* With an introduction by Maxwell Geismar. New York: McGraw-Hill, 1967.

Conger, Lesley. "Jimmy on East 15th Street." *African American Review* 29.4 (1995): 557–66.

Connell, R. W. *Masculinities.* Cambridge, UK: Polity Press, 1995.

Constantine-Simms, Delroy. *The Greatest Taboo: Homosexuality in Black Communities.* Los Angeles: Alyson Books, 2000.

Cooper, Grace C. "Baldwin's Language: Reflection of African Roots." MAWA *Review* 5.2 (1990): 40–45.

Coulibaly, Yedieti E. "Weeping Gods: A Study of Cultural Disintegration in James Baldwin's *Go Tell It on the Mountain* and Chinua Achebe's *Things Fall Apart.*" *Annales de l'Universite d'Abidjan* 9D (1976): 531–42.

Cruz-Malavé, Arnaldo, and Martin F. Manalansan IV. *Queer Globalizations: Citizenship and the Afterlife of Colonialism.* New York: New York University Press, 2002.

Csapó, Csaba. "Defiance against God: A Gay Reading of *Go Tell It on the Mountain* by James Baldwin." *AnaChronist* (2000): 315–26.

Curtis, C. Michael, ed. *God: Stories.* Boston: Houghton Mifflin, 1998.

Dance, Daryl C. "You Can't Go Home Again: James Baldwin and the South." *Critical*

Essays on James Baldwin. Ed. Fred L. Standley and Nancy V. Burt. Boston: G. K. Hall, 1988. 54–61.

Darsey, James. "Baldwin's Cosmopolitan Loneliness." *James Baldwin Now.* Ed. Dwight A. McBride. New York: New York University Press, 1999. 187–207.

DeGout, Yasmin Y. "Dividing the Mind: Contradictory Portraits of Homoerotic Love in *Giovanni's Room.*" *African American Review* 26.3 (1992): 425–35.

Delbanco, Nicholas. *Anywhere Out of the World. Essays on Travel, Writing, Death.* New York: Columbia University Press, 2005.

———. *Running in Place: Scenes from the South of France.* New York: Atlantic Monthly Press, 1989.

Deloria, Philip J. *Indians in Unexpected Places.* Lawrence: University Press of Kansas, 2004.

D'Emilio, John. *Lost Prophet: The Life and Times of Bayard Rustin.* New York: Free Press, 2003.

———. *The World Turned: Essays on Gay History, Politics, and Culture.* Durham, N.C.: Duke University Press, 2002.

D'Emilio, John, and Estelle B. Freedman. *Intimate Matters: A History of Sexuality in America.* New York: Harper and Row, 1988.

Demirtürk, E. Lâle. "Teaching African-American Literature in Turkey: The Politics of Pedagogy." *College Literature* 26.2 (spring 1999): 166–75.

Diedrich, Maria. "James A. Baldwin: Obituaries for a Black Ishmael." *James Baldwin: His Place in American Literary History and His Reception in Europe.* Ed. Maria Diedrich. Frankfurt: Peter Lang, 1991. 129–40.

Dievler, James A. "Sexual Exiles: James Baldwin and *Another Country.*" *James Baldwin Now.* Ed. Dwight A. McBride. New York: New York University Press, 1999. 161–83.

DiGangi, Mario. *The Homoerotics of Early Modern Drama.* New York: Cambridge University Press, 1997.

Dixon, Melvin. *Ride Out the Wilderness: Geography and Identity in Afro-American Literature.* Urbana: University of Illinois Press, 1987.

Drucker, Peter. "'In the Tropics There Is No Sin': Sexuality and the Gay-Lesbian Movements in the Third World." *New Left Review* 1.218 (July-August 1996): 75–101.

Dupee, F. W. "James Baldwin and 'The Man.'" *Modern Critical Views: James Baldwin.* Ed. Harold Bloom. New York: Chelsea House, 1986. 11–15.

Duyan, Veli, and Gülsüm Camur Duyan. "Gays and Lesbians' HIV/AIDS Knowledge and Their Attitudes toward the Persons Living with HIV/AIDS in Turkey." *HIV AIDS Review* 3.4 (2004): 15–20.

Dyer, Richard. *The Culture of Queers.* New York: Routledge, 2002.

———. *The Matter of Images: Essays on Representation.* New York: Routledge, 1993.

Eckman, Fern Marja. *The Furious Passage of James Baldwin.* New York: M. Evans, 1966.

Edwards, Brent Hayes. *The Practice of Diaspora: Literature, Translation, and the Rise of Black Internationalism.* Cambridge: Harvard University Press, 2003.

Eissenstat, Howard. "Metaphors of Race and Discourse of Nation: Racial Theory and State Nationalism in the First Decades of the Turkish Republic." *Race and Nation:*

Ethnic Systems in the Modern World. Ed. Paul Spickard. New York: Routledge, 2005. 239–56.

Ellis, Havelock. Introduction to *Four Plays.* By Christopher Marlowe. Ed. Havelock Ellis. New York: Heritage Press, 1966.

Epstein, Joseph, ed. *The Norton Book of Personal Essays.* New York: W. W. Norton, 1997.

Erduran, Refik. "Shock Sensation in Istanbul as Homo Play on Prisons Directed by Baldwin." *Variety,* January 14, 1970, 91.

Fabre, Michel. *From Harlem to Paris: Black American Writers in France, 1840–1980.* Chicago: University of Illinois Press, 1991.

Fanon, Frantz. *Black Skin, White Masks.* Trans. Charles Lam Markmann. London: MacGibbon and Kee, 1968.

Featherstone, Joseph. "Blues for Mr. Baldwin." *Critical Essays on James Baldwin.* Ed. Fred L. Standley and Nancy V. Burt. Boston: G. K. Hall, 1988. 152–55.

Ferguson, Roderick A. *Aberrations in Black: Toward a Queer of Color Critique.* Minneapolis: University of Minnesota Press, 2004.

Fiedler, Leslie A. "A Homo Sexual Dilemma." *Critical Essays on James Baldwin.* Ed. Fred L. Standley and Nancy V. Burt. Boston: G. K. Hall, 1988. 146–49.

Field, Douglas. "Looking for Jimmy Baldwin: Sex, Privacy, and Black Nationalist Fervor." *Callaloo* 27.2 (2004): 457–80.

———, ed. *Historical Guide to James Baldwin.* Oxford: Oxford University Press, 2009.

Fortuny, Kim. *American Writers in Istanbul: Melville to Baldwin.* Syracuse: Syracuse University Press, forthcoming.

Foucault, Michel. "Of Other Spaces." *Diacritics* 16 (spring 1986): 27.

Freely, John. *Inside the Seraglio: Private Lives of the Sultans in Istanbul.* New York: Penguin Books, 2000.

———. *Stamboul Sketches.* With photographs by Sedat Pakay. Istanbul: Redhouse Yayinevi, 1974.

Freely, Maureen. *The Life of the Party.* New York: Simon and Schuster, 1984.

Fremont-Smith, Eliot. "Another Track." Review of *Tell Me How Long the Train's Been Gone.* By James Baldwin. Books of the Times, *New York Times,* May 31, 1968.

Fuss, Diana. *Essentially Speaking: Feminism, Nature, and Difference.* New York: Routledge, 1989.

———. *The Sense of an Interior: Four Writers and the Rooms That Shaped Them.* New York: Routledge, 2004.

Gates, Henry Louis, Jr. "The 'Blackness of Blackness': A Critique of the Sign and the Signifying Monkey." *Critical Inquiry* 9.4 (June 1983): 685–723.

———. "Cabin Fever." *New York Times Book Review,* October 22, 2006, 31.

———. "An Interview with Josephine Baker and Baldwin." *James Baldwin: The Legacy.* Ed. Quincy Troupe. New York: Simon and Schuster, 1989. 161–72.

———. *The Signifying Monkey: A Theory of Afro-American Literary Criticism.* New York: Oxford University Press, 1988.

———. "The Welcome Table." *English Inside and Out: The Places of Literary Criticism.* Ed. Susan Gubar and Jonathan Kramholtz. New York: Routledge, 1993. 47–60.

———. "The Welcome Table [James Baldwin]." *Thirteen Ways of Looking at a Black Man*. New York: Vintage, 1997. 3–20.

———. "The Welcome Table: James Baldwin in Exile." *Exile and Creativity: Signposts, Travelers, Outsiders, Backward Glances*. Ed. Susan Suleiman. Durham, N.C.: Duke University Press, 1998. 305–320.

———, ed. *Bearing Witness: Selections from African-American Autobiography in the Twentieth Century*. New York: Pantheon Books, 1991.

Germaner, Semra, and Zeynep İnankur. *Orientalism and Turkey*. Istanbul: Turkish Cultural Service Foundation, 1989.

Gilman, Sander L. *Disease and Representation: Images of Illness from Madness to AIDS*. Ithaca, N.Y.: Cornell University Press, 1988.

———. *The Jew's Body*. New York: Routledge, 1991.

Gilroy, Paul. *Against Race: Imagining Political Culture beyond the Color Line*. Cambridge, Mass.: Belknap Press, 2000.

———. *The Black Atlantic: Modernity and Double Consciousness*. Cambridge, Mass.: Harvard University Press, 1993.

Girard, René. *Deceit, Desire, and the Novel: Self and Other in Literary Structure*. Baltimore: Johns Hopkins University Press, 1976.

Gititi, Gitahi. "Menaced by Resistance: The Black Teacher in the Mainly White School/ Classroom." *Race in the College Classroom: Pedagogy and Politics*. Ed. Bonnie TuSmith and Maureen T. Reddy. New Brunswick, N.J.: Rutgers University Press, 2002. 176–88.

Glave, Thomas. *Words to Our Now: Imagination and Dissent*. Minneapolis: University of Minnesota Press, 2005.

Goldberg, Jonathan, ed. *Queering the Renaissance*. Durham, N.C.: Duke University Press, 1994.

———. *Sodometries: Renaissance Texts, Modern Sexualities*. Stanford: Stanford University Press, 1992.

Goldman, Suzy Bernstein. "James Baldwin's 'Sonny's Blues': A Message in Music." *Negro American Literature Forum* 8.3 (1974): 231–33.

Gounard, Jean-Francois. *The Racial Problem in the Works of Richard Wright and James Baldwin*. Trans. Joseph J. Rodgers Jr. Westport, Conn.: Greenwood Press, 1992.

Graham-Brown, Sarah. *Images of Women: The Portrayal of Women in Photography of the Middle East, 1860–1950*. London: Quarter Books, 1988.

Griffin, Farah Jasmine. *"Who Set You Flowin'?" The African-American Migration Narrative*. New York: Oxford University Press, 1995.

Griffin, John Howard. *Black Like Me*. New York: Penguin, 1960.

Grosz, Elizabeth. "Bodies-Cities." *Sexuality and Space*. Ed. Beatriz Colomina. New York: Princeton Architectural Press, 1992. 241–53.

Gruesser, John Cullen. *The Unruly Voice: Rediscovering Pauline Elizabeth Hopkins*. Urbana: University of Illinois Press, 1996.

Guglielmo, Thomas A. *White on Arrival: Italians, Race, Color, and Power in Chicago, 1890–1945*. New York: Oxford University Press, 2003.

Gunning, Sandra. *Race, Rape, and Lynching: The Red Record of American Literature, 1890–1912.* New York: Oxford University Press, 1996.

Gunning, Sandra, Tera W. Hunter, and Michele Mitchell, eds. *Dialogues of Dispersal: Gender, Sexuality, and African Diasporas.* Malden, Mass.: Blackwell, 2004.

Guthrie, Tyrone. "A Director's View of *The Cherry Orchard.*" *The Cherry Orchard.* By Anton Chekhov. Minneapolis: University of Minnesota Press, 1965.

Hakutani, Yoshinobu. "If the Street Could Talk: James Baldwin's Search for Love and Understanding." *The City in African-American Literature.* Ed. Yoshinobu Hakutani and Robert Butler. Madison, N.J.: Fairleigh Dickinson University Press, 1995. 150–67.

———. "*No Name in the Street:* James Baldwin's Image of the American Sixties." *Critical Essays on James Baldwin.* Ed. Fred L. Standley and Nancy V. Burt. Boston: G. K. Hall, 1988. 277–89.

Halberstam, Judith. *In a Queer Time and Place: Transgender Bodies, Subcultural Lives.* New York: New York University Press, 2005.

Hale, Dorothy J. "Bakhtin in African American Literary Theory." ELH 61.2 (summer 1995): 445–71.

Hall, Kim F. *Things of Darkness: Economies of Race and Gender in Early Modern England.* Ithaca, N.Y.: Cornell University Press, 1995.

Hall, Stuart. *Critical Dialogues in Cultural Studies.* Ed. David Morley and Kuan-Hsing Chen. New York: Routledge, 1996.

———. "Cultural Studies and Its Theoretical Legacies." *Critical Dialogues in Cultural Studies.* Ed. David Morley and Kuan-Hsing Chen. New York: Routledge, 1996. 262–75.

Hamamoto, Takeo. "Wright, Ellison, Baldwin." *America Bungaku No Shintenkai: Dai 2-Ji Sekaitaisen Go No Shosetsu.* Ed. Toshihiko Ogata: Yamaguchi, Kyoto, 1983. 183–202.

Handlin, Oscar. *A Pictorial History of Immigration.* New York: Crown, 1972.

———. *The Uprooted: The Epic Story of the Great Migrations That Made the American People.* Boston: Little Brown, 1973.

Hansberry, Lorraine. *To Be Young, Gifted, and Black: Lorraine Hansberry in Her Own Words.* With an introduction by James Baldwin. Englewood Cliffs, N.J.: Prentice-Hall, 1969.

Hardy, Clarence E., III. *James Baldwin's God: Sex, Hope, and Crisis in Black Holiness Culture.* Knoxville: University of Tennessee Press, 2003.

Harris, George S. *Troubled Alliance: Turkish-American Problems in Historical Perspective, 1945–1971.* Washington: American Enterprise Institute for Public Policy Research, 1972.

Harris, Trudier. *Black Women in the Fiction of James Baldwin.* Knoxville: University of Tennessee Press, 1985.

———. "The Eye as Weapon in *If Beale Street Could Talk.*" MELUS 5.3 (1978): 54–66.

———, ed. *New Essays on "Go Tell It on the Mountain."* New York: Cambridge University Press, 1996.

Hatzimanolis, Efi. "Immigrant Writing Coming of Age? The Getting of Genre in Angelika Fremd's *Heartland*." *Journal of Narrative Technique* 21.1 (1991): 24–31.

Hemphill, Essex. "Living the Word/Looking for Home." *Queer Representations: Reading Lives, Reading Cultures*. Ed. Martin Duberman. New York: New York University Press, 1997. 305–10.

———. "Undressing Icons." *Brother to Brother: New Writings by Black Gay Men*. Boston: Alyson Publications, 1991. 181–83.

———, ed. *Brother to Brother: New Writings by Black Gay Men*. Boston, Mass.: Alyson Publications, 1991.

Henderson, Mae G. "In Another Country: Afro-American Expatriate Novelists in France, 1946–1974." *Dissertation Abstracts International* 45.3 (1984): 845A.

———. "James Baldwin: Expatriation, Homosexual Panic, and Man's Estate." *Callaloo: A Journal of African-American and African Arts and Letters* 23.1 (2000): 313–27.

———. "Speaking in Tongues: Dialogics, Dialectics, and the Black Woman Writer's Literary Tradition." *African American Literary Theory: A Reader*. Ed. Winston Napier. New York: New York University Press, 2000. 348–69.

Hentoff, Nat. "James Baldwin Gets Older and Sadder." *New York Times*, April 11, 1965.

Herbert, John. *Fortune and Men's Eyes*. New York: Grove Press, 1967.

Hernton, Calvin C. "James Baldwin: Dialogue and Vision." *American Writing Today*. Ed. Richard Kostelanetz. Washington: Communication Agency, 1982. 323–31.

Hicks, Granville. *Literary Horizons: A Quarter Century of American Fiction*. New York: New York University Press, 1970.

Hill-Lubin, Mildred A. "Achebe and Baldwin at the African Literature Association Conference in Gainesville." *Okike: An African Journal of New Writing* 17 (1980): 1–5.

———. "African Religion: That Invisible Institution in African and African-American Literature." *Interdisciplinary Dimensions of African Literature*. Ed. Kofi Anyidoho et al. Washington: Three Continents, 1985. 197–210.

Himes, Chester. *Cast the First Stone: A Novel*. Chatham, N.J.: Chatham Bookseller, 1973.

———. *A Rage in Harlem*. New York: Avon, 1965.

Hoffman, Eva. *Lost in Translation: Life in a New Language*. New York: Penguin, 1989.

Hoffman, Michael J., and Patrick D. Murphy. *Essentials of the Theory of Fiction*. 3rd ed. Durham, N.C.: Duke University Press, 2005.

hooks, bell. *Talking Back: Thinking Feminist, Thinking Black*. Boston, Mass.: South End Press, 1989.

Hutner, Gordon. Introduction to *Immigrant Voices: Twenty-four Narratives on Becoming American*. New York: Signet Classic, 1999. ix–xxi.

Huttunen, Tuomas. "M. G. Vassanji's *The Gunny Sack*: Narrating the Migrant Identity." *Tales of Two Cities: Essays on New Anglophone Literature*. Ed. John Skinner. Anglicana Turkuensia no. 22. Turku, Finland: University of Turku, 2000. 3–20.

Hyam, Ronald. *Empire and Sexuality: The British Experience*. New York: Manchester University Press, 1990.

Inge, Thomas M., Maurice Duke, and Jackson R. Bryer, eds. *Black American Writers: Bib-*

liographical Essays. Vol. 2: Richard Wright, Ralph Ellison, James Baldwin, and Amiri Baraka. New York: St. Martin's, 1978.

Izgarjan, Aleksandra. "On the 'Untranslatability' of African American Vernacular English." BAS: British and American Studies / Revista de Studii Britanice si Americane 4.1 (1999): 156–67.

Jackson, Jacquelyn Logan. "The Black Novelist and the Expatriate Experience: Richard Wright, James Baldwin, Chester Himes." Dissertation Abstracts International 45.1 (1984): 183A.

Jacobson, Matthew Frye. Barbarian Virtues: The United States Encounters Foreign People at Home and Abroad, 1876–1917. New York: Hill and Wang, 2000.

———. Whiteness of a Different Color: European Immigrants and the Alchemy of Race. Cambridge, Mass.: Harvard University Press, 1998.

James, C. L. R. Mariners, Renegades, and Castaways: The Story of Herman Melville and the World We Live In. New York: C. L. R. James, 1953.

James, Henry. The Art of the Novel: Critical Prefaces by Henry James. With an introduction by Richard P. Blackmur. New York: Charles Scribner's Sons, 1934.

Jenkins, Hester Donaldson. Behind Turkish Lattices. Piscataway, N.J.: Gorgias Press, 2004.

Johnson, E. Patrick. Appropriating Blackness: Performance and the Politics of Authenticity. Durham, N.C.: Duke University Press, 2003.

———. "Feeling the Spirit in the Dark: Expanding Notions of the Sacred in the African-American Gay Community." Callaloo: A Journal of African-American and African Arts and Letters 21.2 (1998): 399–416.

———. " 'Quare' Studies, or (Almost) Everything I Know About Queer Studies I Learned from My Grandmother." Text and Performance Quarterly 21.1 (January 2001): 1–25.

Johnson, E. Patrick, and Mae G. Henderson, eds. Black Queer Studies: A Critical Anthology. Durham, N.C.: Duke University Press, 2005.

Johnson, Willie. "If I Had My Way I'd Tear This Building Down." Columbia Records, 1928.

Johnson-Roullier, Cyraina E. Reading on the Edge: Exiles, Modernities, and Cultural Transformation in Proust, Joyce, and Baldwin. Albany: State University of New York Press, 2000.

Jothiprakash, R. Commitment as a Theme in African American Literature: A Study of James Baldwin and Ralph Ellison. Bristol, Ind.: Wyndham Hall Press, 1994.

Kaiser, Ernest, ed. A Freedomways Reader: Afro-America in the Seventies. 2nd ed. New York: International, 1977.

Kaplan, Amy. "Violent Beginnings and the Question of Empire Today." Presidential Address to the American Studies Association, Hartford, Connecticut, October 17, 2003. American Quarterly 56.1 (2004): 1–18.

Kaplan, Cora. " 'A Cavern Opened in My Mind': The Poetics of Homosexuality and the Politics of Masculinity in James Baldwin." Representing Black Men. Ed. Marcellus Blount and George P. Cunningham: New York: Routledge, 1996. 27–54.

Kasprzycki, Nancy. "The Migrant Novel and Its Characteristics." *Commonwealth Novel in English* 7–8 (1997): 169–78.

Kazan, Elia. *A Life*. New York: Knopf, 1988.

Keizer, Arlene R. *Black Subjects: Identity Formation in the Contemporary Narrative of Slavery*. Ithaca, N.Y.: Cornell University Press, 2004.

Kenan, Randall. *James Baldwin*. Lives of Notable Gay Men and Lesbians. New York: Chelsea House, 1994.

Kiernan, Kathy, and Michael Moore, eds. *First Fiction: An Anthology of the First Published Stories by Famous Writers*. Boston: Little Brown, 1994.

Kimmel, Michael S. *Manhood in America: A Cultural History*. New York: Oxford University Press, 2006.

King, Lovalerie, and Lynn Orilla Scott, eds. *James Baldwin and Toni Morrison: Comparative Critical and Theoretical Essays*. New York: Palgrave/Macmillan, 2006.

Kinnamon, Keneth. *James Baldwin: A Collection of Critical Essays*. Englewood Cliffs, N.J.: Prentice-Hall, 1974.

Klein, Christina. *Cold War Orientalism: Asia in the Middlebrow Imagination, 1945–1961*. Berkeley: University of California Press, 2003.

Klein, Marcus. *After Alienation: American Novels in Mid-Century*. Cleveland: World Publishing Company, 1964.

Kollhofer, Jakob, ed. *James Baldwin: His Place in American Literary History and His Reception in Europe*. Frankfurt: Peter Lang, 1991.

Kramer, Lloyd. "James Baldwin in Paris: Exile, Multiculturalism, and the Public Intellectual." *Historical Reflections / Réflexions Historiques* 27.1 (2001): 27–47.

Kranes, David. "Play Grounds." *Journal of Gambling Studies* 2.1 (1995): 91–102.

Kristeva, Julia. *Desire in Language: A Semiotic Approach to Literature and Art*. Ed. Leon S. Roudiez. Trans. Thomas Gora, Alice Jardine, and Leon S. Roudiez. Oxford: Blackwell, 1980.

———. *The Kristeva Reader*. Ed. Toril Moi. New York: Columbia University Press, 1986.

———. *Strangers to Ourselves*. Trans. Leon S. Roudiez. New York: Columbia University Press, 1994.

———. *Tales of Love*. Trans. Leon S. Roudiez. New York: Columbia University Press, 1987.

Kubitschek, Missy Dehn. "Subjugated Knowledge: Toward a Feminist Exploration of Rape in Afro-American Fiction." *Studies in Black American Literature: Black Feminist Criticism and Critical Theory*. Ed. Joe Weixlmann and Houston A. Baker Jr. Greenwood, Fla.: Penkevill, 1988. 43–56.

Kun, Josh. "Life According to the Beat: James Baldwin, Bessie Smith, and the Perilous Sounds of Love." *James Baldwin Now*. Ed. Dwight A. McBride. New York: New York University Press, 1999. 307–28.

Lamming, George. *The Pleasures of Exile*. Ann Arbor: University of Michigan Press, 1992.

Lazarus, Emma. *Songs of a Semite: The Dance to Death and Other Poems*. New York: "The American Hebrew," 1882.

Lee, Dorothy H. "The Bridge of Suffering." *Callaloo: A Journal of African-American and African Arts and Letters* 6.2 (1983): 92–99.

Leeming, David. *Amazing Grace: A Life of Beauford Delaney.* New York: Oxford University Press, 1998.

———. "An Interview with James Baldwin on Henry James." *Henry James Review* 8.1 (fall 1986): 47–56.

———. *James Baldwin: A Biography.* New York: Henry Holt, 1994.

Leeming, David, et al. "The White Problem." In "James Baldwin's Grand Tour." Special issue, PEN *America: A Journal for Writers and Readers* 1.2 (2001): 17–54.

Lefebvre, H. *The Production of Space.* Trans. Donald Nicholson-Smith. Oxford: Blackwell, 2000.

Leonard, John. Review of *Just above My Head.* By James Baldwin. Books of the Times, *New York Times,* September 21, 1979.

Lewis, Bernard. *Race and Slavery in the Middle East: An Historical Enquiry.* Oxford: Oxford University Press, 1990.

Lewis, Reina. *Gendering Orientalism: Race, Femininity, and Representation.* New York: Routledge, 1996.

———. *Rethinking Orientalism: Women, Travel, and the Ottoman Harem.* New Brunswick, N.J.: Rutgers University Press, 2004.

Lilly, Mark. *Gay Men's Literature in the Twentieth Century.* New York: New York University Press, 1993.

Lipsitz, George. *American Studies in a Moment of Danger.* Minneapolis: University of Minnesota Press, 2001.

Little, Douglass. *American Orientalism: The United States and the Middle East since 1945.* Chapel Hill: University of North Carolina Press, 2002.

Long, Lisa A., ed. *White Scholars / African American Texts.* New Brunswick, N.J.: Rutgers University Press, 2005.

Lorde, Audre. *Sister Outsider.* Freedom, Calif.: Crossing Press, 1984.

———. *Uses of the Erotic: The Erotic as Power.* New York: Out and Out Books, 1982. Originally published in 1978 in a private edition for distribution at the Conference on Feminist Perspectives on Pornography, San Francisco.

Lowe, Lisa. *Critical Terrains: French and British Orientalisms.* Ithaca, N.Y.: Cornell University Press, 1991.

———. *Immigrant Acts: On Asian American Cultural Politics.* Durham, N.C.: Duke University Press, 1996.

Ludington, Nick. "Baldwin, in Istanbul, Denies He's Given Up the Struggle." *New York Post,* December 12, 1969.

Luibhéid, Eithne. *Entry Denied: Controlling Sexuality at the Border.* Minneapolis: University of Minnesota Press, 2002.

Luibhéid, Eithne, and Lionel Cantú Jr., eds. *Queer Migrations: Sexuality, U.S. Citizenship, and Border Crossings.* Minneapolis: University of Minnesota Press, 2005.

Lyotard, Jean-François. *The Inhuman: Reflections on Time.* Stanford: Stanford University Press, 1988.

Macebuh, Stanley. *James Baldwin: A Critical Study*. New York: Third Press, 1973.

Mądra-Shallcross, Bożena. *Dom romantycznego artysty* [The Home of the Romantic Artist]. Kraków: Wydawnictwo Literackie, 1992.

Mailer, Norman. *Advertisements for Myself*. Cambridge, Mass.: Harvard University Press, 1992.

Major, Clarence. *The Dark and Feeling: Black American Writers and Their Work*. New York: Third Press, 1974.

Maksudyan, Nazan. "The Turkish Review of Anthropology and the Racist Face of Turkish Nationalism." *Cultural Dynamics* 17.3 (2005): 291–322.

Mandelker, Amy. *Bakhtin in Contexts: Across the Disciplines*. Chicago: Northwestern University Press, 1996.

Margolis, Edward. *Native Sons: A Critical Study of Twentieth-Century Black American Authors*. Philadelphia, Pa.: Lippincott, 1968.

———. "The Negro Church: James Baldwin and the Christian Vision." *James Baldwin*. Ed. Harold Bloom. New York: Chelsea House, 1986. 59–76.

Mariani, Philomena, ed. *Critical Fictions: The Politics of Imaginative Writing*. Seattle: Bay Press, 1991.

Mather, Cotton. *The Wonders of the Invisible World: Being an Account of the Tryals of Several Witches Lately Executed in New-England*. London: J. R. Smith, 1862.

M'Baye, Babacar. "Africanisms, Race Relations, and Diasporic Identities in 'Mules and Men,' 'Go Tell It on the Mountain,' and 'Mumbo Jumbo.'" *Dissertation Abstracts International, Section A: The Humanities and Social Sciences* 63.10 (2003): 3612.

McAlister, Melani. *Epic Encounters: Culture, Media, and the U.S. Interests in the Middle East, 1945–2000*. Berkeley: University of California Press, 2001.

McBride, Dwight A. "Can the Queen Speak? Racial Essentialism, Sexuality, and the Problem of Authority." *The Greatest Taboo: Homosexuality in Black Communities*. Ed. Delroy Constantine-Simms. Los Angeles: Alyson Publications, 2000. 24–43.

———. "Straight Black Studies: On African American Studies, James Baldwin, and Black Queer Studies." *Black Queer Studies: A Critical Anthology*. Ed. E. Patrick Johnson and Mae G. Henderson. Durham, N.C.: Duke University Press, 2005. 68–89.

———, ed. *James Baldwin Now*. New York: New York University Press, 1999.

McClane, Kenneth A. "Sonny's Blues." In *You've Got to Read This: Contemporary American Writers Introduce Stories That Held Them in Awe*. Ed. Ron Hansen and Jim Shepard. New York: Harper Perennial, 1994.

McKay, Nellie. "The Narrative Self: Race, Politics, and Culture in Black Women's Autobiography." *Women, Autobiography, Theory*. Ed. Sidonie Smith and Julia Watson. Madison: University of Wisconsin Press, 1998. 96–107.

Mendoza, Louis, and S. Shankar, eds. *Crossing into America: The New Literature of Immigration*. New York: New Press, 2003.

Meyer, Howard N., ed. *Integrating America's Heritage: A Congressional Hearing to Establish a National Commission on Negro History and Culture*. College Park, Md.: McGrath, 1970.

Michaels, Walter Benn. *Our America: Nativism, Modernism, and Pluralism.* Durham, N.C.: Duke University Press, 1995.

Miles, Tiya. *Ties That Bind: The Story of an Afro-Cherokee Family in Slavery and Freedom.* Berkeley: University of California Press, 2005.

Miller, Joshua L. "The Discovery of What It Means to Be a Witness: James Baldwin's Dialectics of Difference." *James Baldwin Now.* Ed. Dwight A. McBride. New York: New York University Press, 1999. 154–89.

Miller, Quentin D., ed. *Re-viewing James Baldwin: Things Not Seen.* Philadelphia, Pa.: Temple University Press, 2000.

Miłosz, Czesław. "My Faithful Mother Tongue." *The Separate Notebooks.* Trans. Robert Hass and Robert Pinsky et al. New York: Ecco Press, 1984. 193.

Moller, Karin. *The Theme of Identity in the Essays of James Baldwin: An Interpretation.* Goteborg: Acta Universitatis Gothoburgensis, 1975.

Moon, Sahng Young. "African Americans and Colonialism: James Baldwin's Essays in the Era of the Civil Rights Movement." *Journal of English Language and Literature* 47.4 (2001): 941–57.

Moore, Elizabeth Roosevelt. "Being Black: Existentialism in the Work of Richard Wright, Ralph Ellison, and James Baldwin." *Dissertation Abstracts International, Section A: The Humanities and Social Sciences* 62.12 (2002): 4217–18.

Moore, Gerald. "If You Ain't White You're Considered Black." *Transition* 3.12 (1964): 49–51.

Moore, Gerian Steven. "Modes of Black Discourse in the Narrative and Structure of James." Ph.D. diss., University of Michigan, 1989.

Morrison, Toni. *Playing in the Dark: Whiteness and the Literary Imagination.* Cambridge, Mass.: Harvard University Press, 1992.

Mosher, Marlene. "Baldwin's 'Sonny's Blue's.'" *Explicator* 40.4 (summer 1982): 59.

———. "James Baldwin's Blues." *College Language Association Journal* 26.1 (1982): 112–24.

Mullen, Bill V. *Afro-Orientalism.* Minneapolis: University of Minnesota Press, 2004.

Mumford, Kevin J. *Interzones: Black/White Sex Districts in Chicago and New York in the Early Twentieth Century.* New York: Columbia University Press, 1997.

Muñoz, José Esteban. *Disidentifications: Queers of Color and the Performance of Politics.* Minneapolis: University of Minnesota Press, 1999.

Murray, Donald C. "James Baldwin's 'Sonny's Blues': Complicated and Simple." *Studies in Short Fiction* 14 (1977): 353–57.

Naber, Nadine. "Arab American Femininities: Beyond Arab Virgin / American(ized) Whore." *Feminist Studies* 32.1 (spring 2006): 87–111.

Navasky, Victor. *Naming Names.* New York: Viking, 1980.

Naylor, Gloria, ed. *Children of the Night: The Best Short Stories by Black Writers, 1967 to the Present.* Boston: Little, Brown, 1995.

Neal, Mark Anthony. *New Black Man.* New York: Routledge, 2005.

Nelson, Emmanuel. "Critical Deviance: Homophobia and the Reception of James Baldwin's Fiction." *Journal of American Culture* 14.3 (fall 1991): 91–96.

Nero, Charles. "Fixing Ceremonies: An Introduction." *Ceremonies: Prose and Poetry*, by Essex Hemphill. San Francisco: Cleis Press, 2000. xi–xxiii.

———. "Re/Membering Langston: Homophobic Textuality and Arnold Rampersad's *Life of Langston Hughes*." *Queer Representations: Reading Lives, Reading Cultures*. Ed. Martin Duberman. New York: New York University Press, 1997. 188–96.

Newton, Huey. "Huey Newton: A Candid Conversation with the Embattled Leader of the Black Panther Party." Interview, *Playboy*, May 1973, 73–90.

Nicol, Davidson. *Modern African Writing: La Derniere Annèe de Malcolm X*. Paris: Presence Africaine, 1967.

Nkosi, Lewis. "The Mountain." *Transition: An International Review*, no. 79 (1999): 102–125.

Norse, Harold. *Memoirs of a Bastard Angel. A Fifty-Year Literary and Erotic Odyssey*. New York: Thunder's Mouth Press, 1989.

Nwankwo, Ifeoma Kiddoe. *Black Cosmopolitanism: Racial Consciousness and Transnational Ideology in the Americas*. Philadelphia: University of Pennsylvania Press, 2005.

Oates, Joyce Carol. "Tragic Rites in Dostoevsky's *The Possessed*." *Contraries: Essays by Joyce Carol Oates*. New York: Oxford, 1981.

Obeidat, Marwan M. *American Literature and Orientalism*. Berlin: Klaus Schwartz, 1998.

O'Daniel, Therman B., ed. *James Baldwin: A Critical Evaluation*. Washington: Howard University Press, 1977.

Ogbaa, Kalu. "Protest and the Individual Talents of Three Black Novelists." *College Language Association Journal* 35.2 (1991): 159–84.

Ohi, Kevin. "'I'm Not the Boy You Want': Sexuality, 'Race,' and Thwarted Revelation in Baldwin's *Another Country*." *African American Review* 33.2 (1999): 261–81.

Olson, Barbara K. "'Come-to-Jesus Stuff' in James Baldwin's *Go Tell It on the Mountain* and *The Amen Corner*." *African American Review* 31.2 (1997): 295–301.

Ongiri, Amy Abugo. "We Are Family: Black Nationalism, Black Masculinity, and the Black Gay Cultural Imagination." *College Literature* 24.1 (1997): 280–94.

———. "We Are Family: Miscegenation, Black Nationalism, Black Masculinity, and Black Gay Cultural Imagination." *Race-ing Representation: Voice, History, and Sexuality*. Ed. Kostas Myrsiades and Linda Myrsiades. Lanham, Md.: Rowman and Littlefield, 1998.

Øverland, Orm. *Immigrant Minds, American Identities: Making the United States Home*. Chicago: University of Illinois Press, 2000.

Pakay, Sedat. Artist's statement in "The Mountain," by Lewis Nkosi. *Transition* 8.3 (1979): 124.

———. "Knowing Jimmy." University of Michigan, Ann Arbor. January 8, 2004.

Paliwal, G. D. "African Consciousness in Modern American Fiction: A Note on Novels by Wright, Ellison and Baldwin." *Rajasthan University Studies in English* 10 (1977): 62–70.

Pamuk, Orhan. *Istanbul: Memories and the City*. Trans. Maureen Freely. New York: Knopf, 2005.

Panichas, George Andrew, ed. *The Politics of Twentieth-Century Novelists*. New York: Hawthorn Books, 1971.

Parker, Patricia. "Preposterous Events." *Shakespeare Quarterly* 43 (1992): 186–213.

Pavlic, Edward M. *Crossroads Modernism: Descent and Emergence in African-American Literary Culture*. Minneapolis: University of Minnesota Press, 2002.

Peterson, Dale E. "Response and Call: The African American Dialogue with Bakhtin." *American Literature* 65.4 (December 1993): 761–75.

———. *Up from Bondage: The Literatures of Russian and African American Soul*. Durham, N.C.: Duke University Press, 2000.

Petry, Ann. *The Street*. Boston: Houghton Mifflin, 1946.

Petzen, Jennifer. "Home or Homelike?" *Space and Culture* 7.20 (2004): 20–32.

Pinn, Anthony B., ed. *By These Hands: A Documentary History of African American Humanism*. New York: New York University Press, 2001.

Polsgrove, Carol. *Divided Minds: Intellectuals and the Civil Rights Movement*. New York: W. W. Norton, 2001.

Pomerantz, Charlotte, ed. *A Quarter-Century of Un-Americana, 1938–1963: A Tragico-Comical Memorabilia of HUAC, House Un-American Activities Committee*. New York: Marzani and Munsell, 1963.

Porter, Horace A. *Stealing the Fire: The Art and Protest of James Baldwin*. Middletown, Conn.: Wesleyan University Press, 1989.

Povey, John. "Achebe and Baldwin in C.B. Land—10-4 Good Buddy!!! A Dialogue at the African Literature Association Meeting, Gainesville, Florida, March 1980." *Pacific Coast Africanist Association Occasional Paper* 3 (1981): 7–9.

Pratt, Louis H. *James Baldwin*. Boston: Twayne, 1978.

Pratt, Mary Louise. *Imperial Eyes: Travel Writing and Transculturation*. New York: Routledge, 1992.

Puzo, Mario. "His Cardboard Lovers." *Critical Essays on James Baldwin*. Ed. Fred L. Standley and Nancy V. Burt. Boston: G. K. Hall, 1988. 155–58.

Radel, Nicholas F. "Can the Sodomite Speak? Sodomy, Satire, Desire, and the Castlehaven Case." *Love, Sex, Intimacy, and Friendship between Men, 1550–1800*. Ed. Katherine O'Donnell and Michael O'Rourke. New York: Palgrave Macmillan, 2003. 148–67.

Raphael-Hernandez, Heike, ed. *Blackening Europe: The African American Presence*. New York: Routledge, 2004.

Reed-Danahay, Deborah E., ed. *Auto/Ethnography: Rewriting the Self and the Social*. Oxford: Berg, 1997.

Reid-Pharr, Robert F. *Conjugal Union: The Body, the House, and the Black American*. New York: Oxford University Press, 1999.

———. "Cosmopolitan Afrocentric Mulatto Intellectual." *American Literary History* 31.1 (spring 2001): 169–79.

———. "Dinge." *Women and Performance: A Journal of Feminist Theory* 8.2 (1996): 75–85.

———. *Once You Go Black: Choice, Desire, and the Black American Intellectual*. New York: New York University Press, 2007.

———. "Tearing the Goat's Flesh: Homosexuality, Abjection, and the Production of a Late Twentieth-Century Black Masculinity." *Studies in the Novel* 28.3 (1996): 372–94.

Reilly, John M. "'Sonny's Blues': James Baldwin's Image of Black Community." *Negro American Literature Forum* 4.2 (1970): 56–60.

Richter, David H. *The Critical Tradition: Classic Texts and Contemporary Trends.* 3rd ed. Boston: Bedford/St. Martin's, 2007.

Riggs, Marlon. "Sexuality, Television, and Death: A Black Gay Dialogue on Malcolm X." *Malcolm X: In Our Own Image.* Ed Joe Wood. New York: St. Martin's Press, 1992. 135–54.

Rive, Richard. "Writing and the New Society." *Contrast* 12.3 (1979): 60–67.

Robert, Mary, and Deniz Kandiyoti. "Photo Essay: Transsexuals and the Urban Landscape in Istanbul." *Middle East Report* 206: *Power and Sexuality in the Middle East* (spring 1998): 20–25.

Robertson, Patricia R. "Baldwin's 'Sonny's Blues': The Scapegoat Metaphor." *University of Mississippi Studies in English* 9 (1991): 189–98.

Robinson, Angelo DeWayne. "'I'm Not the Boy for You': Images of African American Male Homosexuality." *Dissertation Abstracts International, Section A: The Humanities and Social Sciences* 62.10 (2002): 3394–95.

Robinson, Marc. *Altogether Elsewhere: Writers in Exile.* Boston, Mass.: Faber and Faber, 1994.

Roediger, David R., ed. *Black on White: Black Writers on What It Means to Be White.* New York: Schocken Books, 1998.

———. *Colored White: Transcending the Racial Past.* Berkeley: University of California Press, 2002.

———. "First Word in Whiteness: Early Twentieth-Century European Experiences." *Critical White Studies: Looking behind the Mirror.* Ed. Richard Delgado and Jean Stefancic. Philadelphia, Pa.: Temple University Press, 1997. 354–56.

———. *The Wages of Whiteness: Race and the Making of the American Working Class.* New York: Verso, 1991.

Roediger, David R., and James Barrett. "Inbetween Peoples: Race, Nationality, and the 'New-Immigrant' Working Class." *Colored White: Transcending the Racial Past.* Berkeley: University of California Press, 2002. 138–68.

Rogoff, Irit. "'Other's Others': Spectatorship and Difference." *Vision in Context: Historical and Contemporary Perspectives on Sight.* Ed. Teresa Brennan and Martin Jay. New York: Routledge, 1996. 187–202.

———. *Terra Infirma: Geography's Visual Culture.* New York: Routledge, 2000.

Rose, Toby, and Katherine B. Payant, eds. *The Immigrant Experience in North American Literature: Carving Out a Niche.* Westport, Conn.: Greenwood Press, 1999.

Ross, Marlon. "Beyond the Closet as Raceless Paradigm." *Black Queer Studies: A Critical Anthology.* Ed. E. Patrick Johnson and Mae G. Henderson. Durham, N.C.: Duke University Press, 2005. 161–89.

———. "Camping the Dirty Dozens: The Queer Resources of Black Nationalist Invective." *Callaloo: A Journal of African-American and African Arts and Letters* 23.1 (winter 2000): 290–312.

———. *Manning the Race: Reforming Black Men in the Jim Crow Era.* New York: New York University Press, 2004.

———. "Race, Rape, Castration: Feminist Theories of Sexual Violence and Masculine Strategies of Black Protest." *Masculinity Studies and Feminist Theory: New Directions.* Ed. Judith Kegan Gardiner. New York: Columbia University Press, 2002. 305–343.

———. "White Fantasies of Desire: Baldwin and the Racial Identities of Sexuality." *James Baldwin Now.* Ed. Dwight A. McBride: New York: New York University Press, 1999. 13–55.

Roth, Philip. "Blues for Mr. Charlie." *Modern Critical Views: James Baldwin.* Ed. Harold Bloom. New York: Chelsea House, 1986. 37–44.

Roth, Wolff-Michael. "Auto/biography as Method: Dialectical Sociology of Everyday Life." Review essay of *Our Lives as Database—Doing a Sociology of Ourselves: Czech Social Transitions in Autobiographical Research Dialogue,* ed. Zdenfek Konopásek. *Forum Qualitative Sozialforschung / Forum: Qualitative Social Research* 3.4 (July 2002). Online journal. http://www.qualitative-research.net/.

Rubin, Gayle. "The Traffic in Women: Notes on the 'Political Economy' of Sex." *Toward an Anthropology of Women.* Ed. Rayna R. Reiter. New York: Monthly Review Press, 1975. 157–210.

Ruff, Shawn Stewart, ed. *Go the Way Your Blood Beats: An Anthology of Lesbian and Gay Fiction by African American Writers.* New York: H. Holt, 1996.

Rusk, Lauren. *The Life Writing of Otherness: Woolf, Baldwin, Kingston, and Winterson.* New York: Routledge, 2002.

Russell, Dick. *Black Genius and the American Experience.* New York: Carroll and Graf, 1998.

Ryan, Katy. "Falling in Public: Larsen's *Passing,* McCarthy's *The Group,* and Baldwin's *Another Country.*" *Studies in the Novel* 36.1 (spring 2004): 95–114.

Said, Edward. *The Edward Said Reader.* Ed. Moustafa Bayoumi and Andrew Rubin. New York: Vintage, 2000.

———. "Intellectual Exile: Expatriates and Marginals." *The Edward Said Reader.* Ed. Moustafa Bayoumi and Andrew Rubin. New York: Vintage, 2000. 368–81.

———. *Orientalism.* New York: Vintage Books, 1979.

Samuels, Gertrude. "A New Lobby—Ex-Cons." *New York Times,* October 19, 1969.

Sanders, Leslie. "Text and Contexts in Afro-American Criticism." *Canadian Review of American Studies / Revue Canadienne d'Etudes Americaines* 14.3 (1983): 344–52.

Sarotte, Georges Michel. *Like a Brother, Like a Lover: Male Homosexuality in the American Novel.* Trans. Richard Miller. Garden City, N.Y.: Anchor Press/Doubleday, 1978.

Schick, Irvin. *The Erotic Margin: Sexuality and Spatiality in Alterist Discourse.* London: Verso, 1999.

———. "The Fair Circassian: Some Racial and Sexual Slippages of Orientalism." Unpublished paper.

Schick, Irvin, and Ertuğrul Ahmet Tonak, eds. *Turkey in Transition: New Perspectives.*

Trans. Rezan Benatar, Irvin C. Schick, and Ronnie Margulies. New York: Oxford University Press, 1987.

Scott, Darrieck. "More Than You'll Ever Be: Antonio Fargas, Eldridge Cleaver, and Toni Morrison's Beloved." *Dangerous Liaisons: Blacks, Gays, and the Struggle for Equality.* Ed. Eric Brandt. New York: New Press, 1999. 217–42.

Scott, Lynn Orilla. *James Baldwin's Later Fiction: Witness to the Journey.* East Lansing: Michigan State University Press, 2002.

Sedgwick, Eve Kosofsky. *Between Men: English Literature and Male Homosocial Desire.* New York: Columbia University Press, 1985.

———. *Epistemology of the Closet.* Berkeley: University of California Press, 1990.

———. *Tendencies.* Durham, N.C.: Duke University Press, 1993.

Şhafak, Elif. *The Saint of Incipient Insanities.* New York: Farrar, Straus and Giroux, 2004.

Shawcross, John T. "Joy and Sadness: James Baldwin, Novelist." *Callaloo: A Journal of African-American and African Arts and Letters* 6.2 (1983): 100–11.

Sherard, Tracey. "Sonny's Bebop: Baldwin's 'Blues Text' as Intracultural Critique." *African American Review* 32.4 (1998): 691–705.

Shin, Andrew, and Barbara Judson. "Beneath the Black Aesthetic: James Baldwin's Primer of Black American Masculinity." *African American Review* 32.2 (1998): 247–61.

Shohat, Ella, and Robert Stam. *I'm Thinking Eurocentrism: Multiculturalism and Media.* New York: Routledge, 1994.

Siegal, Ronald. *Islam's Black Slaves: The Other Black Diaspora.* New York: Farrar, Straus and Giroux, 2001.

Silvera, Frank. "Toward a Theater of Understanding." *Negro Digest* 18.6 (1969): 33–35.

Simmons, Ron. "Some Thoughts on the Challenges Facing Black Gay Intellectuals." *Brother to Brother: New Writings by Black Gay Men.* Ed. Essex Hemphill. Boston: Alyson Publications, 1991. 211–28.

Singh, Amritjit. "Self-Definition as a Moral Concern in the Twentieth-Century Afro-American Novel." *Indian Journal of American Studies* 8.2 (1978): 23–38.

Sivan, Miriam. "Out of and Back to Africa: James Baldwin's *Go Tell It on the Mountain.*" *Christianity and Literature* 51.1 (2001): 29–41.

Smith, Patricia Juliana, ed. *The Queer Sixties.* New York: Routledge, 1999.

Smith, Sidonie, and Julia Watson. Introduction to *Women, Autobiography, Theory.* Ed. Sidonie Smith and Julia Watson. Madison: University of Wisconsin Press, 1998.

Smith-Rosenberg, Carroll. *Disorderly Conduct: Visions of Gender in Victorian America.* New York: A. A. Knopf, 1985.

Sollors, Werner. *Beyond Ethnicity: Consent and Descent in American Culture.* New York: Oxford University Press, 1986.

———, ed. *The Invention of Ethnicity.* New York: Oxford University Press, 1989.

———. *Neither Black nor White yet Both: Thematic Explorations of Interracial Literature.* New York: Oxford University Press, 1997.

Sollors, Werner, and Maria Diedrich. *The Black Columbiad: Defining Moments in African American Literature and Culture.* Cambridge, Mass.: Harvard University Press, 1994.

Somerville, Siobhan B. *Queering the Color Line: Race and the Invention of Homosexuality in American Culture*. Durham, N.C.: Duke University Press, 2000.

Spillers, Hortense. "The Politics of Intimacy." *Sturdy Black Bridges: Visions of Black Women in Literature*. Ed. Roseann P. Bell, Bettye J. Parker, and Beverly Guy-Sheftall. Garden City, N.Y.: Anchor Press/Doubleday, 1979. 87–106.

Spurlin, William J. "Queer Identity and Racial Alienation: The Politics of Race and Sexuality in James Baldwin and in the 'New' South Africa." *Journal of Literary Studies* 15.1–2 (1999): 218–37.

Standley, Fred L., and Nancy V. Burt, eds. *Critical Essays on James Baldwin*. Boston, Mass.: G. K. Hall, 1988.

Standley, Fred L., and Louis H. Pratt, eds. *Conversations with James Baldwin*. Jackson: University Press of Mississippi, 1989.

Standley, Fred L., and Nancy V. Standley. *James Baldwin: A Reference Guide*. Boston, Mass.: G. K. Hall, 1980.

Steet, Linda. *Veils and Daggers: A Century of National Geographic's Representation of the Arab World*. Philadelphia: Temple University Press, 2000.

Stevens, Laura M. "Transatlanticism Now." *American Literary History* 16.1 (2004): 93–102.

Stilgoe, John R. Introduction to *Poetics of Space*. By Gaston Bachelard. Trans. Maria Jolas. Boston, Mass.: Beacon Press, 1969.

Stockton, Kathryn Bond. *Beautiful Bottom, Beautiful Shame: Where Black Meets Queer*. Durham, N.C.: Duke University Press, 2006.

Stokes, Mason. *The Color of Sex: Whiteness, Heterosexuality, and the Fictions of White Supremacy*. Durham, N.C.: Duke University Press, 2001.

Stuckey, Sterling. "Foreshadowings and Fulfillment: The Ring Shout, the Blues and Jazz in the Works of Douglass, Melville, and Baldwin." *Letterature d'America: Rivista Trimestrale* 21.86 (2001): 45–61.

Suleiman, Susan Rubin, ed. *Exile and Creativity: Signposts, Travelers, Outsiders, Backward Glances*. Durham, N.C.: Duke University Press, 1998.

Sullivan, Dan. "Theater: A Distressing *Fortune and Men's Eyes*." *New York Times*, February 24, 1967.

Sylvander, Carolyn Wedin. *James Baldwin*. New York: Ungar, 1980.

Talaga, Tanya. "Obituary: John Herbert Turned Trauma into Acclaimed Theater Career." *Toronto Star*, June 25, 2001.

Tatum, Alfred W. "Against Marginalization and Criminal Reading Curriculum Standards for African American Adolescents in Low-Level Tracks: A Retrospective of Baldwin's Essay." *Journal of Adolescent and Adult Literacy* 43.6 (2000): 570–72.

Taubman, Howard. "Theater: 'Blues for Mister Charlie.'" *New York Times*, April 24, 1964.

Taylor, Charles Lavalle. "Figurations of the Family in Fiction by Toni Morrison, John Updike, James Baldwin, and Philip Roth." Ph.D. diss., University of Michigan, 1996.

Taylor, Gordon O. "Voices from the Veil: Black American Autobiography." *Georgia Review* 35.2 (1981): 341–61.

Thelwell, Michael. *Duties, Pleasures, and Conflicts: Essays in Struggle.* Amherst: University of Massachusetts Press, 1987.

Thomas, Kendall. "'Ain't Nothin' like the Real Thing': Black Masculinity, Gay Sexuality, and the Jargon of Authenticity." *Representing Black Men.* Ed. Marcellus Blount and George P. Cunningham. New York: Routledge, 1996. 55–69.

Thompson, Thelma B. "Romantic Idealists and Conforming Materialists: Expressions of the American National Character." *MAWA Review* 3.1 (1988): 6–9.

Tifft, Wilton S. *Ellis Island.* Chicago: Contemporary Books, 1990.

Tóibín, Colm. "The Last Witness." *London Review of Books* 23.18 (2001): 15–20.

Tomlinson, Robert. "'Payin' One's Dues': Expatriation as Personal Experience and Paradigm in the Works of James Baldwin." *African American Review* 33.1 (1999): 135–48.

Trachtenberg, Alan. *Shades of Hiawatha: Staging Indians, Making Americans, 1880–1930.* New York: Hill and Wang, 2004.

Troupe, Quincy, ed. *James Baldwin: The Legacy.* New York: Simon and Schuster, 1989.

———. "The Last Interview (1987)." *James Baldwin: The Legacy.* Ed. Quincy Troupe. New York: Simon and Schuster, 1989. 186–212.

Tuan, Yi-Fu. *Space and Place: The Perspective of Experience.* Minneapolis: University of Minnesota Press, 2001.

Turner, Alice K., ed. *Playboy Stories: The Best of Forty Years of Short Fiction.* New York: Dutton, 1994.

Upton, Dell. *Architecture in the United States.* New York: Oxford University Press, 1998.

Vickery, John B., and J'nan M. Sellery. *The Scapegoat: Ritual and Literature.* Boston, Mass.: Houghton Mifflin, 1971.

Vitkus, Daniel J. "Turning Turk in *Othello*: The Conversion and Damnation of the Moor." *Shakespeare Quarterly* 48.2 (summer 1997): 145–76.

Von Eschen, Penny M. *Satchmo Blows Up the World: Jazz Ambassadors Play the Cold War.* Cambridge, Mass.: Harvard University Press, 2004.

Waldrep, Shelton. "'Being Bridges': Cleaver/Baldwin/Lorde and African-American Sexism and Sexuality." *Critical Essays: Gay and Lesbian Writers of Color.* Ed. Emmanuel S. Nelson. New York: Haworth Press, 1993. 167–80.

Walker, Alice. *In Search of Our Mothers' Gardens: Womanist Prose.* San Diego, Calif.: Harcourt Brace Jovanovich, 1983.

Walker, Willie Earl, III. "Prophetic Articulations: James Baldwin and the Racial Formation of the United States." *Dissertation Abstracts International, Section A: The Humanities and Social Sciences* 60.4 (1999): 1173.

Wall, Cheryl A. *Worrying the Line: Black Women Writers, Lineage, and Literary Tradition.* Chapel Hill: University of North Carolina Press, 2005.

Wallace, Maurice. *Constructing the Black Masculine: Identity and Ideality in Black Men's Literature and Culture.* Durham, N.C.: Duke University Press, 2002.

———. "On Being a Witness: Passion, Pedagogy, and the Legacy of James Baldwin." *Black Queer Studies: A Critical Anthology.* Ed. E. Patrick Johnson and Mae G. Henderson. Durham, N.C.: Duke University Press, 2005. 276–88.

Wallace, Michelle. *Black Macho and the Myth of the Superwoman.* New York: Verso, 1978.

Walters, Wendy W. *At Home in Diaspora: Black International Writing.* Minneapolis: University of Minnesota Press, 2005.

Warren, Kenneth W. "Appeals for (Mis)recognition: Theorizing the Diaspora." *Cultures of United States Imperialism.* Ed. Amy Kaplan and Donald E. Pease. Durham, N.C.: Duke University Press, 1993. 392–406.

———. *Black and White Strangers: Race and American Literary Realism.* Chicago: University of Chicago Press, 1993.

———. "From under the Superscript: A Response to Michael Awkward." *American Literary History* 4.1 (spring 1992), 97–103.

———. *So Black and Blue: Ralph Ellison and the Occasion of Criticism.* Chicago: University of Chicago Press, 2003.

Washington, Bryan R. *The Politics of Exile: Ideology in Henry James, F. Scott Fitzgerald, and James Baldwin.* Boston, Mass.: Northeastern University Press, 1995.

Waters, Mary C. *Black Identities: West Indian Immigrant Dreams and American Realities.* Cambridge: Harvard University Press, 1999.

Waters, Wendy W. *At Home in the Diaspora: Black International Writing.* Minneapolis: University of Minnesota Press, 2005.

Watkins, Mel. "An Appreciation." *James Baldwin: The Legacy.* Ed. Quincy Troupe. New York: Simon and Schuster, 1989. 107–23.

———. "The Fire Next Time This Time." Review of *No Name in the Street.* By James Baldwin. *New York Times,* May 28, 1972.

Watts, Daniel H., ed. *Nationalism, Colonialism, and the United States: One Minute to Twelve.* New York: Liberation Committee for Africa, 1961.

Weatherby, William J. *James Baldwin: Artist on Fire; A Portrait.* New York: D. I. Fine, 1989.

———. *Squaring Off: Mailer versus Baldwin.* New York: Mason/Charter, 1977.

Wein, George. *Myself Among Others: A Life in Music.* Cambridge, Mass.: Da Capo Press, 2003.

Weisenburger, Steven. "The Shudder and the Silence: James Baldwin on White Terror." *ANQ: A Quarterly Journal of Short Articles, Notes, and Reviews* 15.3 (2002): 3–12.

Weixlmann, Joe. "Staged Segregation: Baldwin's *Blues for Mister Charlie* and O'Neill's *All God's Chillun Got Wings.*" *Black American Literature Forum* 11.1 (1977): 35–36.

West, Cornel. *Democracy Matters: Winning the Fight against Imperialism.* New York: Penguin, 2004.

———. *Prophetic Thought in Postmodern Times: Beyond Eurocentrism and Multiculturalism.* Vol. 1. Monroe: Common Courage Press, 1993.

Whittemore, Katharine, and Gerald Marzorati. *Voices in Black and White: Writings on Race in America from Harper's Magazine.* New York: Franklin Square Press, 1992.

Wiegman, Robyn. *American Anatomies: Theorizing Race and Gender.* Durham, N.C.: Duke University Press, 1995.

Williams, John Alfred, ed. *The Angry Black: Stories and Articles by James Baldwin and Others.* New York: Lancer Books, 1962.

Winant, Howard. *The New Politics of Race: Globalism, Difference, Justice.* Minneapolis: University of Minnesota Press, 2004.

Woods, Gregory. *A History of Gay Literature: The Male Tradition.* New Haven, Conn.: Yale University Press, 1998.

Woods, Lebbeus. *War and Architecture. Rat i Arhitektura.* Pamphlet Architecture 15. Princeton Architectural Press, 1993.

Wright, Michelle. "'Alas, Poor Richard!' Transatlantic Baldwin, the Politics of Forgetting, and the Project of Modernity." *James Baldwin Now.* Ed. Dwight A. McBride. New York: New York University Press, 1999. 208–32.

Yeğenoğlu, Meyda. *Colonial Fantasies: Towards a Feminist Reading of Orientalism.* New York: Cambridge University Press, 1998.

Yezierska, Anzia. *How I Found America: Collected Stories.* New York: Persea Books, 1991.

———. *Red Ribbon on a White Horse.* New York: Scribners, 1950.

Yoshihara, Mari. *Embracing the East: White Women and American Orientalism.* New York: Oxford University Press, 2003.

Yüzgün, Arslan. "Homosexuality and Police Terror in Turkey." *Journal of Homosexuality* 24.3–4 (1994): 159–69.

Zaborowska, Magdalena J. "Americanization of a 'Queer Fellow': Performing Jewishness and Sexuality in Abraham Cahan's *The Rise of David Levinsky.*" *American Studies in Scandinavia* 29.1 (1997): 18–27.

———. *How We Found America: Reading Gender through East European Immigrant Narratives.* Chapel Hill: University of North Carolina Press, 1995.

———. "'In the Same Boat': James Baldwin and the Other Atlantic." *Historical Guide to James Baldwin.* Ed. Douglas Field. Oxford: Oxford University Press, 2009.

———. "Mapping Transcultural Masculinities: James Baldwin's Innocents Abroad, or *Giovanni's Room* Revisited." *Other Americans, Other Americas: The Politics and Poetics of Multiculturalism.* Ed. Magdalena J. Zaborowska. Aarhus, Denmark: Aarhus University Press, 1998. 119–31.

Zaborowska, Magdalena J., Sibelan Forrester, and Elena Gapova, eds. *Over the Wall / After the Fall: Post-Communist Cultures through an East–West Gaze.* Bloomington: Indiana University Press, 2004.

Baldwin's Works in Turkish

Baldwin, James. *Bir Başka Ülke* [Another Country]. Trans. Çiğdem Öztekin. İstanbul: Yapı Kredi Yayınları, 2005.

———. *Bundan Sonrası Ateş* [The Fire Next Time]. Trans. Kıvanç Güney. İstanbul: Yapı Kredi Yayınları, 2006.

———. "Bütün İnsanlar Kardeştir" [All Men Are Brothers]. *Tiyatro Dergisi* 13 (1969).

———. With Engin Cezzar. *Dost Mektupları* [Letters from a Friend]. Trans. Seçkin Selvi. İstanbul: Yapı Kredi Yayınları, 2007.

———. *Giovanni'nin Odası* [Giovanni's Room]. Trans. Tektaş Ağaoğlu. İstanbul: Ağaoğlu Yayınevi, 1964.

———. *Giovanni'nin Odası* [Giovanni's Room]. Trans. Çiğdem Öztekin. İstanbul: Yapı Kredi Yayınları, 2006.

———. *Kara Yabancı* [Another Country]. Trans. Tanju Kurtarel. İstanbul: Ağaoğlu Yayınevi, 1970.

———. *Ne Zaman Gitti Tren* [Tell Me How Long the Train's Been Gone]. Trans. Oktay Balamir. İstanbul: Sander Yayınları, 1973.

———. *Ne Zaman Gitti Tren* [Tell Me How Long the Train's Been Gone]. Trans. Dilek Cenkçiler. İstanbul: Yapı Kredi Yayınları, 2007.

———. *Sokağın Dili Olsa* [If Beale Street Could Talk]. Trans. Seçkin Cılızoğlu. İstanbul: Sander Yayınları, 1974.

———. *Sokağın Dili Olsa* [If Beale Street Could Talk]. Trans. Seçkin Selvi. İstanbul: Yapı Kredi Yayınları, 2007.

Other Sources in Turkish

Ağaoğlu, Tektaş. "James Baldwin'le Konuşma" [Interview with James Baldwin]. *Yeni Dergi* (Ankara: De Yayınevi) 1, no. 2 (November 1964): 15–22.

Akçura, Gökhan. *Kırkıncı Sanat Yılında Engin Cezzar Kitabı* [The Book of Engin Cezzar in His Fortieth Year in the Arts]. İstanbul: Yapı Kredi Yayınları, 1996.

Birsel (Oral), Zeynep. "James Baldwin Hisar'da Son Romanını Bitirdi" [James Baldwin Finished His Latest Novel at Hisar]. *Yeni Gazete*, October 27, 1966.

Cezzar, Engin. With İzzeddin Çalışlar. *Engin Cezzar'ı Takdimimdir* [Introducing Engin Cezzar]. İstanbul: Doğan Kitapçılık, 2005.

"Gülriz Sururi'nin İstediği Bu Muydu?" [Was This What Gulriz Sururi Wanted?]. *Akşam*, December 21, 1969.

Gülriz Sururi and Engin Cezzar Troupe. *Tiyatro Dergisi* (İstanbul) 13, December 1969.

Güvemli, Zahir. "'Cezzarlar' cüretli' Bir Oyunu Sahneye Koydular: Düşenin Dostu" [Cezzars Are Staging a 'Daring' Play: Düşenin Dostu]. *Yeni Gazete*, December 18, 1969.

Halman, Talat S. "Amerikalı Zenci Yazar James Baldwin Anlatıyor" [The Black American Writer James Baldwin Tells about It]. *Cep Dergisi* (İstanbul: Varlık Yayınları), no. 3 (January 1967): 71–77.

Herbert, John. 1970. *Düşenin Dostu* [Friend of the Fallen]. Trans. Ali Poyrazoğlu and Oktay Balamir. İstanbul: Sander Yayınları.

Kohen, Sami. "I Am Warning Them!" [İkaz Ediyorum]. Interview with James Baldwin. *Milliyet*, July 25 1966, 5.

Oral, Zeynep. *Bir Ses* [A Voice]. İstanbul: Doğan Kitapçılık, 1982.

———. "James Baldwin: Bir Gün Mutlaka mı?" [Definitely One Day?]. *Konuşa Konuşa* [By Talking It Over]. İstanbul: Gür Yayınları, 1983. 273–83.

———. "Siyah Öfke Dindi . . ." [The Black Fury Calmed Down . . .]. Sözden Söze [From One Conversation to Another]. 2nd ed. İstanbul: Cem Yayınevi, 1990. 79–85.

Örs, Cüneyt. "Düşenin Dostu Olur mu, Olmaz mı Siz Onu Zenci Yazara Sorun?" [Ask the Black Author Whether the Fallen Has Any Friends or Not?]. Yeni İstanbul, December 22, 1969, 5.

Poyrazoğlu, Ali. "Düşenin Dostu Adlı Oyunumuzu Sahneye Koyacak Olan Ünlü Roman ve Tiyatro Yazarı James Baldwin ile Bir Konuşma" [An Interview with James Baldwin, the Famous Author and Director of Our Play Called Düşenin Dostu]. Tiyatro Dergisi (İstanbul: Gülriz Sururi ve Engin Cezzar Topluluğu), no. 12 (October 1969).

Schick, Irvin. Çerkes Güzeli-Bir Şarkiyatçı İmgenin Serüveni. İstanbul: Oğlak, 2004.

Solelli, Sezai. "Bu Yıl İstanbul Tiyatroları" [This Year at the Istanbul Theaters]. Ses, no. 36 (September 5, 1970).

———. "Düşenin Dostu" [The Friend of the Fallen]. Ses, no. 53 (December 27, 1969).

———. "Cezzarlar'ın Yeni Oyunu" [Cezzars' New Play]. Ses, no. 47 (November 15, 1969).

———. "Tiyatroda Küfür" [Profanity in the Theater]. Ses, no. 50 (December 6, 1969, 20).

Sururi, Gülriz. Bir An Gelir [There Comes a Time]. İstanbul: Doğan Kitap, 2003.

———. Kıldan İnce Kılıçtan Keskince [Thinner than Hair, Sharper than Sword]. İstanbul: Milliyet Yayınları, 1978.

Tamer, Ülkü. "Amerika'da Siyah Düşmanlığı: Harlem Altıları" [Hostility toward Blacks in America: The Harlem Six]. Cep Dergisi (İstanbul: Varlık Yayınları), no. 4 (February 1967): 33–36.

Films

I Heard It through the Grapevine. Dir. Dick Fontaine and Pat Hartley. 1982.

James Baldwin. A Clark Television production for BBC Worldwide Television. Princeton, N.J.: Films for the Humanities and Sciences, 1997.

James Baldwin: Author. Black Americans of Achievement Video Collection. Bala Cynwyd: Schlessinger Video Productions, 1994.

James Baldwin: From Another Place. Dir. Sedat Pakay. Hudson Film Works, 1973.

Looking for Langston: A Meditation on Langston Hughes (1902–1907) and the Harlem Renaissance. Dir. Isaac Julien. VHS. New York: Waterbearer Films, 1992.

The Price of the Ticket. Dir. Karen Thorsen. California Newsreel, 1989.

INDEX

Baldwin, James (*continued*)
253, 258, 260, 261; as transnational
writer, xix–xxi, 2–7, 24, 27, 32, 47, 56,
69, 93–117, 121–31, 201–3, 217–23,
250–51; in Turkey, 9, 13, 23, 68, 80,
84, 88, 96, 106, 168, 188–90, 218,
250, 255, 256–57, 287 n. 69; Turkey
as authorial setting of, xxii–iii, xvii, 1–
6, 7–16, 18, 21–22, 24–25, 40–41, 43,
53, 56–57, 79, 89, 91–92, 93, 103, 107,
109, 116–19, 138–39, 191, 202, 203–8,
209, 218, 222, 225, 246, 258, 262, 294
n. 51, 318 n. 32; Turkish translations
of works by, 7, 36, 51, 70, 117, 137,
138, 144, 280–81 n. 13, 297 n. 80;
urban imaginary in, 107–8, 123, 138,
143, 195, 293 n. 45; women in works
of, 122, 142, 147–49, 153–54, 168,
174–75, 214, 215, 282 n. 26; women's
relationships with, 17, 38, 46, 62, 65,
72–73, 107, 161–62; women writers
and, xiv, xvi, 107, 143–44, 261, 268
n. 23, 282–83 n. 26, 314 n. 3, 317–
18 n. 29, 318 n. 38, 324–25 n. 89, 327
n. 6, 329 nn. 22–23; Wright and, xix,
4, 95, 114, 199, 231, 270 n. 14, 295
n. 64, 317 n. 29
Baldwin, Paula Maria (sister), 71, 82
Baldwin-Cezzar letters, 104, 108, 218,
262, 272 n. 28, 293 n. 42, 295 n. 57;
Baldwin's dwellings described in,
41–43, 58, 280 n. 12; Baldwin's works
mentioned in, 17, 91, 109, 112, 142,
143, 144, 181, 249, 282–83 n. 26,
285 n. 53, 288 nn. 1–2, 304 n. 7, 305
n. 18, 306 n. 19, 312 n. 75, 325 n. 100;
collection of, 51–54, 257–58, 271
n. 22, 274 n. 48, 277 n. 79, 283 n. 33,
305 n. 13; relationship with Cezzar in,
48–49, 51, 53–54, 74, 75–76, 78, 85,
88, 146, 155, 209, 214, 250, 257–58,
280 n. 13, 284 n. 36, 286 n. 63, 291
n. 21, 319 n. 43; Turkey mentioned in,

20, 51, 53, 58, 88, 316 n. 23; Turkish
edition of, 12, 51, 52–54
Balfour, Lawrie, 277 n. 77, 279 n. 90,
279 n. 92, 292 n. 39
Balmumcu, 10, 208
Baraka, Amiri (LeRoi Jones), 25, 192,
199, 313 n. 89, 315 nn. 11–12
Bartels, Emily C., 297 n. 77
Barton, Craig E., 229
Beam, Joseph, 250–51, 327 n. 5, 328
n. 13
Bebek, 38, 40, 56–57, 58, 59, 98, 104,
207, 286 n. 59
Belafonte, Harry, 301 n. 1
Bercovitch, Sacvan, xix, 213, 318 n. 39
Berger, Aliye, 17, 74
Bergman, Ingmar, 141–42
Bernstein, Matthew, 138, 299 n. 94
Bey, Avni (Avni Salbaş), 8, 13–14, 28,
275 n. 50, 284 n. 37
Beyoğlu (Turkey), 117
Bhabha, Homi, 323 nn. 73–75
Bir Başka Ülke (trans. of *Another Country*),
117, 271 n. 25, 297 n. 80
Birsel, Zeynep, 163
"Black Boy Looks at the White Boy, The"
(Baldwin), 299 n. 91
Blackface, 21, 59, 68, 251
Black Muslims, 19, 86
Black Panthers, 36, 93, 203, 214, 218,
254, 313 n. 88
Black Power, 21, 178, 245, 321 n. 55; and
black masculinity, 199, 202
Black queer studies, 6, 22, 233, 269 n. 4,
276 n. 67, 324 n. 87
Blues for Mister Charlie (Baldwin), 27, 66,
96, 141–42, 143, 146, 148, 153–54,
243, 252, 278 n. 89, 302 n. 1, 303–4
n. 6, 304 n. 7, 307 n. 35, 307 n. 38,
316 n. 26
Bodrum (Turkey), xvii, 9, 23, 84, 88, 96,
150, 250, 255–57; map of xxx
Boğaziçi Üniversitesi (Bosphorus Uni-

Costa-Gavras (Constantin Gavras), 50, 84, 256–57, 274 n. 43, 274 n. 45
Crawford, Cheryl, 142
"Creative Process, The" (Baldwin), 268 n. 23
Cromie, Robert, 214, 262, 319 n. 41, 329 n. 24
Cullen, Countee, 270 n. 10
Cultural Experiment, A (Moravia), 11, 304 n. 7
Cyprus, 12, 274 n. 45, 287 n. 70

Dallas, Walter, xxvi, 249, 252, 253, 254, 303 n. 4, 327 n. 1, 327 n. 4
Dance, Daryl C., 322 n. 61
"Dark Days" (Baldwin), 206
"Dark Runner" (Baldwin), 277 n. 80
Davis, Angela, 218, 316 n. 23
Davis, Gary, 319 n. 51
Davis, Miles, 51, 117
Davis, Sammy, Jr., 302 n. 1
Delaney, Beauford, 9, 27, 75, 110, 145, 213; as Baldwin's mentor, 3–4, 5, 108, 123; images of, 9, 76; in Turkey, 57–58, 293 n. 43
Delbanco, Nicholas, 255, 270 n. 15, 313 n. 90
Deloria, Philip, 19, 271 n. 23, 276–77 n. 72
D'Emilio, John, 324 n. 88
Devil Finds Work, The (Baldwin), 206, 210, 238, 272 n. 27, 318 n. 32
Devrim, Şirin, 17, 286 n. 61
De Witt Clinton High School, 2–3
dialogic imagination, xv, xxi, 108
Dialogic Imagination, The (Bakhtin), xiii–xiv
Dickens, Charles, 212, 224
Diedrich, Maria, 6
Dievler, James A., 269 n. 7, 289 n. 3, 289 n. 10, 297 n. 81, 298 n. 87
Dilmen, Güngör, 12, 83
"Discovery of What It Means to Be an

American, The" (Baldwin), 270 n. 13, 289 n. 5, 322 n. 62
Dixon, Melvin, xiv, 278–79 n. 90
Dodson, Owen, 303 n. 3
Dost Mektupları (Letters from a Friend), 52, 250, 256, 257, 274 n. 48, 280–81 n. 13, 305 n. 13, 305–6 n. 18
Dostoyevsky, Fyodor, 111, 190, 212–13, 292 n. 38
Douglas, Alfred, 313 n. 1
Douglass, Frederick, 261, 281 n. 18, 324 n. 83
Du Bois, W. E. B., xix, 17, 28, 83, 96, 213, 266 n. 14, 275 n. 58, 318 n. 39
Dunbar, Paul Lawrence, 316 n. 18
Dupee, F. E., 21
Düşenin Dostu (trans. of Fortune and Men's Eyes), xxiii, 7, 36, 139, 156, 162, 193, 196, 211; actors in, 168, 169, 170–73; audience response to, 165–66, 167, 180, 187, 212; Baldwin's interpretation of, 148, 153–54, 163, 168, 175–78, 180–81, 187–89, 194, 202, 227, 238, 317–18 n. 29; Baldwin's other works and, 218, 219, 227, 238, 246, 249, 250, 252–53; ban on, 183–84, 312 nn. 78–79; Cherry's collaboration on, 178–79, 190–91, 272 n. 35, 311 n. 72; drag performances in, 151, 173, 184, 189; gay life in Turkey and, 149, 150, 157–58, 160; national tour of, 181–82; production and staging of, 145–49, 157–58, 159, 183, 190, 250, 252; rehearsals of, 160–61, 168–70, 173–75, 178–80; stage design and music in, 155, 178–80, 218, 246, 311–12 n. 72; Sururi's comments on, 157–59, 173–74, 187; translation of, 139, 145, 146, 149–51, 306 n. 24; Turkish cultural climate in, 155, 157–59, 163–64, 166–67, 177; Turkish media response to, 163–64, 180, 185–87, 187–89, 189–92, 197–99,

306 n. 23, 312 n. 74, 312 nn. 83–84;
Turkish theater and, 154–55, 157, 160,
163–64, 185–89, 203; United States
media response to, 16, 20, 180, 183,
184, 186, 189–92, 197–98, 203, 258,
276 n. 72, 312 n. 75, 312 n. 81
Dyer, Richard, 300 n. 104, 325 n. 94

East, 84, 224, 264, 284 n. 40, 291 n. 21,
297 n. 77; in *Another Country*, xxii,
95–98, 116, 121–23, 126–37, 298
n. 85; Baldwin's authorship and,
7–8, 15–20, 32, 33, 71, 89, 91, 98,
102, 205, 253, 262; erotic imaginary
and, xxii, 11, 20–22, 116–17, 125–34,
135–37, 248, 271 n. 20, 272 n. 36,
275 n. 51, 290 n. 13, 290 n. 19, 291
n. 20, 297 n. 78, 299 nn. 94–95, 300
n. 99; eroticized Turkey and, 6, 11,
12, 19, 20–22, 79, 92–102, 103, 122,
125, 129, 190, 198, 248, 271 n. 20, 275
n. 51, 276 n. 68, 290 n. 13, 292 n. 37;
exile and, 15–20, 281–82 n. 21, 300
n. 99, 300 n. 101; fantasies of gender
and sexuality and, 6, 19–20, 98, 117,
121–22, 128, 271 n. 20, 290 n. 13, 290
n. 19, 299 n. 95, 300 n. 98, 300 n. 100;
homoeroticism and, 21, 80, 95, 122,
132, 165, 198, 242, 283 n. 31, 286–87
n. 63, 299 n. 95; as liminal location,
92, 99, 126, 135, 138, 197, 202, 203,
266 n. 11, 271 n. 19, 289 n. 7, 290
n. 13; perceptions in American culture of, 19, 98, 18, 83, 98, 290 n. 18;
race and, 71, 102, 116, 124, 127, 130,
132–33, 138; religion and, 124, 126,
129, 130, 238, 271 n. 19, 291 n. 23;
urban imaginary and, 107–9, 123, 133,
138, 298 n. 88
Eastern Europe, 18, 124, 137, 275–76
n. 63
Ebony (magazine), 16, 20, 184, 189, 191–
92, 197–98, 203, 209, 258

Eckman, Fern Marja, 12, 20, 109, 114,
115–16, 129, 199, 267 n. 18, 296 n. 68,
316 n. 26
Edwards, Brent Hays, 5, 6, 267 n. 20
Eliot, T. S., 105, 111, 296 n. 76
Ellis, Havelock, 298 n. 89
Ellison, Ralph, xvi, 285 n. 51, 324 n. 86
Eminönü (Istanbul), 36, 98
"Encounter on the Seine" (Baldwin),
289 n. 5
"Equal in Paris" (Baldwin), 110, 277
n. 80, 289 n. 5, 316 n. 23
Erbaşar, Bülent, 170–73
Erduran, Refik, 180, 183, 186
Erdek (Turkey), xxx, 13
erotics, 32, 267 n. 21; authorship and,
xxi, 2, 12, 21–22, 24, 81, 124, 138, 155,
194, 198, 230–31; Baldwin and, xxi,
2, 6, 22–23, 24, 27, 48, 49, 65, 73,
81, 95, 118, 120, 124–25, 128, 137–38,
162, 168, 192, 194, 198, 209, 230, 245,
256, 287 n. 64, 293 n. 44; Baldwin's
works and, 22–23, 27, 49, 73, 91,
116–21, 128, 125–34, 135–37, 209,
234, 242, 250–52, 301 nn. 108–9, 325
n. 93; the East and, xxii, 11, 20–22,
117, 125–34, 135–37, 271 n. 20, 272
n. 36, 275 n. 51, 290 n. 13, 290 n. 19,
291 n. 20, 297 n. 78, 299 n. 95, 300
n. 99; eroticized Turkey and, 6, 11, 12,
19, 20–22, 79, 92–102, 122, 125, 129,
190, 271 n. 20, 275 n. 51, 276 n. 68,
290 n. 13, 292 n. 37; exile and, xxi,
67–68, 127, 250, 300 n. 101; location
and, xx, 20, 81, 93, 118, 124, 192, 266
n. 11, 275 n. 51, 276–77 n. 72, 290
n. 13; race, sex, and, 2, 6, 19, 27, 65,
67–68, 73, 95, 116, 118, 119, 121, 122,
125, 209–10, 230–31, 242, 245, 256.
See also homoeroticism
Espadon, L' (Gürmen), 12, 84, 275 n. 45;
Baldwin's and Cezzar's script of,
256–57, 274 n. 45

Essence (magazine), 79, 145

Essex, Hemphill, xiv, 73, 231, 278 n. 86, 315 n. 10, 316 n. 18

Ethnopornography, 128

Evers, Medgar, 8, 11

"Everybody's Protest Novel" (Baldwin), 114, 281 n. 19, 317–18 n. 29

Evidence of Things Not Seen, The (Baldwin), 27, 154, 243, 261

Evil Empire, 18, 275–76 n. 63

exile, xiii, 279 n. 93, 296 n. 73, 327 n. 8; authorship and, 6, 15, 18, 23, 25, 28, 35–36, 40, 44, 89, 109, 154, 201, 202, 262, 269 n. 8, 270 n. 14, 278 n. 83, 288–89 n. 3, 289 n. 10; Baldwin and, 2–8, 11, 15–28, 35, 42, 44–45, 65, 88–89, 91, 109, 122, 146, 154, 191, 195, 201–9, 250, 162, 209, 250, 252, 269 n. 8, 270 n. 14, 278 n. 83, 288–89 n. 3, 289 n. 10, 294 n. 51, 297 n. 80, 298 n. 87; as dwelling, 23, 42, 44–45, 65, 88, 146, 262, 281–82 n. 21; the erotic and, xxi, 127, 250, 300 n. 101; intellectual, xix, xxi, 2, 5, 6, 16, 28, 195, 202, 281–82 n. 21, 313 n. 92; queerness and, 3, 6, 122, 191, 202; race and, 2, 6, 26, 40, 122, 269 n. 8, 278 n. 83, 294 n. 51; sex and, 20, 26, 122, 127, 191, 209, 250, 269 n. 7, 294 n. 51, 298 n. 87; Turkey as space of, 6, 8, 15–20, 21, 23, 28, 35–36, 45, 53, 88, 91, 115, 145, 146, 154, 191, 202–3, 211, 270 n. 14

Fabre, Michel, 293 n. 48, 296 n. 75

fairy tale, 127–31, 268 n. 23

Fanon, Frantz, 18, 217

Faulkner, William, 111

Faure, Jeanne, 252, 327–28 n. 8

FBI Story, The, 36

Featherstone, Joseph, 294 n. 56, 322 n. 66

feminism, 6, 7, 17, 161; Baldwin's works and, 260, 261–62, 328 n. 18; the erotic and, 267 n. 21; Orientalism and, 102, 299 n. 94; social space and, 219, 299 n. 94; theory, autobiography, and, xv, xx, 266–67 n. 17

Ferguson, Roderick, 270–71 n. 18

Fiedler, Leslie A., 294–95 n. 56

Field, Douglas, 273 n. 41, 314 n. 8

Fire Next Time, The (Baldwin), xiv, xviii, xx, 95, 112, 205, 259, 293 n. 45, 307 n. 34, 319 n. 45, 323 n. 77, 325 n. 91; Baldwin's oeuvre and, xxi, 5, 24, 27, 96, 113, 217, 238, 250, 279 n. 92, 289 n. 8; sexual liberation and, 21–22, 200–201, 209, 267 n. 21; translations of, 7, 8, 15, 24, 32, 56, 69–71, 92, 102, 105, 163, 262, 203, 271 n. 25, 272 n. 26, 306 n. 29

Fireside Pentecostal Assembly Church, 2

Fitzgerald, F. Scott, 25

Flack, Roberta, 319 n. 52

Flaubert, Gustave, 297 n. 78, 319 n. 40

"Fly in Buttermilk, The" (Baldwin), 220, 321 n. 57

Fonger, Lee, 291 n. 24

Fontaine, Richard, 265 n. 6

Fortune and Men's Eyes, 7, 10, 16, 23, 47, 56, 61, 75, 96; action and characters of, 151–53, 167–68, 170–73; authorship of, xxiii, 22, 36, 139, 142, 147, 149, 152–53, 306 n. 26, 308 n. 39; Baldwin's interpretation of, 141, 148, 153–54, 163, 168, 175–78, 180–81, 187–89, 194, 202, 227, 238, 317–18 n. 29; Baldwin's other works and, 218, 219, 227, 238, 246, 249, 250, 252–53; as directed by Baldwin, 148, 153–54, 155, 163, 168, 175–78, 178–79, 180–81, 187–89, 190–91, 194, 202, 218, 227, 238, 246, 272 n. 35, 284 n. 39, 311 n. 72, 304 n. 7, 317–18 n. 29; prisons and incarceration in,

"Going to Meet the Man" (Baldwin), 8, 131, 178, 206, 227, 231, 317–18 n. 29

Going to Meet the Man (Baldwin), 108, 220, 243, 279 n. 91, 294–95 n. 56

Goldberg, Jonathan, 324 n. 87

Golden Horn (Istanbul), 60

Goldstein, Richard, 22, 210

Go Tell It on the Mountain (Baldwin), xvi, xviii–xix, xx, 4, 19, 93, 178, 221, 268 n. 2, 270 n. 12, 279 n. 92, 295 n. 67, 325 n. 93

Go Tell It on the Mountain (film), 273–74 n. 42

"Go the Way Your Blood Beats," 318 n. 34

Graham-Brown, Sarah, 290 n. 18

Greenwich Village: as authorial location, 2, 48, 108, 117–18, 121, 132–33, 293 n. 43; Baldwin's coming of age and, 269 n. 7, 276 n. 70, 288–89 n. 3; metropolitan culture in, 51, 86; queer identity in, 3, 103

Greenwood, Keith, 291 n. 24

Griffin, Farah, 317 n. 28

Griffin, John Howard, 230

Gorki, Maxim, 270 n. 11

Grosz, Elizabeth, 281 n. 16

Gülriz Sururi–Engin Cezzar Theater, xxiii, 8, 10, 36, 302 (chap. 3 note)

Gunning, Sandra, 271 n. 22, 300 n. 102, 317 n. 28, 322 n. 69

Gürmen, Osman Necmi, 12, 274 n. 45

Guthrie, William Tyrone, 174, 252, 311 n. 68

Güvemli, Zahir, 187–90

"Gypsy" (Roma), 38, 150

Hair (musical), 10, 77, 286 n. 58

Hakutani, Yashinobu, 322 n. 66, 323 n. 77

Halberstam, Judith, 291–92 n. 26

Haley, Alex, 10, 11, 46, 58, 144, 217

Hall, John, 114, 202, 223–24

Hall, Kim F., 292–93 n. 40, 296–97 n. 77

Hall, Stuart, 267 n. 18, 321 n. 58

Hallelujah Chorus, 303 n. 4

Hamam (hammam), 122, 165

Hamlet, 55, 59

Handy, W. C., 113

Hansberry, Lorraine, 143–44, 282–83 n. 26

Happersberger, Lucien, 9, 272 n. 31, 288–89 n. 3, 293 n. 44

Hardy, Clarence E., III, 322 n. 66, 325 nn. 91–92

harem, 80, 98, 126, 128, 292 n. 37, 300 n. 100

Harlem, xiii, 2–5, 12, 27, 46, 50, 92, 111–36, 143, 199, 205, 211, 237, 260, 269 n. 7, 274 n. 47, 298 n. 84, 301 n. 110, 307 n. 34

Harris, George S., 271 n. 21, 285 n. 54

Harris, Trudier, 267 n. 19, 278–79 n. 90, 298 n. 85, 299 n. 97

Hartley, Pat, 265 n. 6

Hassell, Bernard, 10, 252, 286 n. 58

Hemingway, Ernest, 25, 105, 111, 281 n. 19, 296 n. 75

Henderson, Mae G., 6, 265 n. 1, 269 n. 4, 319 n. 49

Herbert, John, xxiii, 22, 36, 139, 142, 147, 149, 152–53, 306 n. 26, 308 n. 39

"Here Be Dragons" (Baldwin), xxiv, 21, 251, 267 n. 21, 269 n. 4

Heston, Charlton, 144, 280 n. 4

Hikmet, Nazım, 181, 313 n. 86

Himes, Chester, 274 n. 47

Hoffman, Eva, xvii

Hollywood, 11, 19, 53, 61, 75, 144–45, 214, 217, 243, 273 n. 39, 306 n. 20

homemaking, 41, 43–44, 278 n. 81

Home of the Brave (film), 210

homoeroticism, 112, 185, 245, 276–77 n. 72, 315 n. 10; Baldwin's works and,

119, 216, 228, 230–31, 240, 242, 301
n. 109, 325 n. 93; Orient and, 122,
242, 283 n. 31; social space and, 233–
36; in Turkey, 21, 79, 96–97, 158, 191,
198, 286–87 n. 63

homophobia, 146, 147, 216, 273, 325
n. 89; Baldwin and, xvii, 21, 189, 278
n. 86, 280 n. 3, 298 n. 84, 315 nn. 10–
11; race and, 226–27, 231, 240, 241–
42, 245, 315 nn. 14–15, 316 n. 18; in
Turkey, 13, 159, 189; in United States,
xxiii, 33, 38, 114, 119, 198, 200, 201,
209, 216, 280 n. 3

homosexuality, xvii, 118, 188, 221, 234,
244, 245; orientalism and, 98, 122,
271 n. 20, 277 n. 72, 283 n. 31; in
prisons, 7, 142, 146, 188; segregation
and, 201–2, 216, 219, 236, 323 n. 76

homosexual panic, xxiii, 153, 197, 239,
241, 319 n. 49; race and, 199, 219,
228, 232, 234, 236, 244, 324 n. 86;
segregation and, 201–2, 216, 219,
232, 234, 323 n. 76

homosociality, 96, 119, 121, 125, 146,
148, 151–53, 216, 222, 225–31, 240,
243, 321 n. 51

hooks, bell, 260, 267 n. 18, 315 n. 14,
328 n. 16

Horne, Lena, 302 n. 1

houri (huri), 126, 128, 299 n. 95

Hughes, Langston, 270 n. 10, 315 n. 15

Hurston, Zora Neale, 261, 317–18 n. 29,
318 n. 38

Hutter, Don, 213

Hyam, Ronald, 138

Idiot, The (Dostoyevsky), 212

If Beale Street Could Talk (Baldwin), xxiii,
xxiv, 17, 21, 70, 154, 202, 267 n. 19,
295–96 n. 67, 325 n. 93, 325–26
n. 100; transgender elements in, 213,
328 n. 16

I Heard It through the Grapevine (film), 265
n. 6, 313 n. 89

immigration, xv, xix–xx, xxii–xxiii, 44–
45, 78, 83, 233, 266 n. 10, 266 n. 17,
278 n. 81, 281 n. 20, 304–5 n. 11;
Baldwin as immigrant writer, xvii,
220, 223; in Baldwin's works, 105,
115, 118, 123–26, 129, 137–38, 268
n. 24, 296 n. 60; in Turkey, 28, 310
n. 60; in Western Europe, 273 n. 38,
326 n. 100

İnankur, Zeynep, 274 n. 49, 291 n. 20,
298 n. 85, 299 n. 95

Islam, 5, 55, 238, 282 n. 22, 287 n. 72;
in Turkey, 14, 83–84, 85–86, 96, 102,
154–55, 308 n. 40; Western approaches to, 117, 130, 272–73 n. 37,
297 n. 79

Israel, 8, 15, 82, 276 n. 64, 297 n. 79

Istanbul, xxii–xxiv, 31, 300 n. 100; autoethnography and, xx, 45–46, 54–61,
64, 73–74; as authorial location,
xxii–iii, xvii, 1–6, 7, 8–10, 11–13,
14–15, 18, 21–22, 24–25, 40–41, 43,
53, 56–57, 79, 89, 91–92, 93, 103,
107, 109, 116–19, 138–39, 191, 202,
203–8, 209, 218, 222, 225, 246, 258,
262, 294 n. 51, 318 n. 32; as Baldwin's transitory home, 28, 41–45, 52,
86–89, 92, 101–3, 109–10, 138, 205;
high society in, 9, 142, 151, 211–12;
images of, xxxi, xvi, xxxii, 30, 37, 40,
63, 97, 100, 101, 140, 194, 204, 207,
212, 248; in James Baldwin (Pakay), 18,
33–41, 88–89, 96, 98, 203–4, 207;
Orientalization of, 12, 14, 20, 93, 123,
124, 126, 190–91; social issues in,
155, 157–59, 163–64, 166–67, 177; as
space of exile, 15–20, 21, 23, 28, 53,
115, 145, 146, 211; urban imaginary of,
28, 107–8, 276 n. 68

İsvan, Ahmed, 310–11 n. 61

n. 105; the South in, xxiii, 200, 201, 202, 216, 217, 221–22, 228, 229, 230–31, 234, 236, 241–42, 243–44; spatial focus of, 21, 219, 244, 323 nn. 76–77, 314–15 n. 10, 324 n. 82; transgender metaphors in, 213, 253, 260–62; Turkey as authorial location of, xxii–xxiii, 6, 21, 24, 43, 53, 202, 203–8, 209, 218, 222, 225, 246, 258, 318 n. 32; United States reception of, 24, 215, 216, 322 n. 65, 323 n. 74, 324 n. 86

No Papers for Mohammed (Baldwin), 11, 252, 273 n. 38

"Northern Protestant, The" (Baldwin), 141–42, 302 n. 2

"Notes for a Hypothetical Novel" (Baldwin), 112, 268 n. 23

Notes of a Native Son (Baldwin), xiv, 5, 23, 70, 214, 220, 277 n. 80, 279 n. 92

"Notes of a Native Son" (Baldwin), 217

"Notes on the House of Bondage" (Baldwin), 23, 79, 195, 206

Nothing Personal (Baldwin), 3, 318 n. 37

Norse, Harold, 3–4, 267 n. 7, 269 nn. 8–9

Oates, Joyce Carol, 294 n. 55

Obeidat, Marwan M., 99, 117, 271 n. 19, 291 n. 21, 296–97 n. 77

One Day When I Was Lost (Baldwin), 8, 11, 145, 280 n. 4

121st Day of Sodom, The, 59, 327 n. 7

"Open Letter to Mr. Carter, An" (Baldwin), 206

Oral, Zeynep, xxiii, 8, 16, 17, 145, 146, 156, 166, 193, 302, 306 n. 22, 309 nn. 56–57; Baldwin's friendship with, 162, 169–70, 177, 209, 211, 255–57, 309 n. 54, 311 n. 66; Baldwin's working relationship with, 160–63, 168, 174; on Baldwin's works, 69, 168; on *Düşenin Dostu*, 163–64, 168–69, 170, 173–75, 179–80; images of, 147, 162,

170, 194; on race and sexuality, 69, 71, 163–66, 206, 311 n. 64; on social issues in Turkey, 178, 206, 310–11 n. 61

Orient, 271 nn. 20–21; American orientalism, 277 n. 73, 290 n. 18; eroticizing of, 6, 12, 14, 20, 22, 79, 92–102, 123–26, 129, 190–91, 290 n. 18, 292 n. 37; gendering of, 290 n. 18; homoeroticized, 122; literary references to, 19, 99, 116–17, 125, 130, 296–97 n. 77, 297 n. 78; as location for xenological erotica, 128; location of, 266 n. 11, 290 n. 13; orientalist approaches to, xxii, 79, 98, 103, 107, 116, 123–25, 128, 138, 290 n. 13; "queer orientalism," 295 n. 66; as "tableau of queerness," 117, 295 n. 66. *See also* East

Othello (Shakespeare), 59–60, 130

Øverland, Orm, 44, 278 n. 81, 281 n. 20

Öztekin, Çiğdem, 117, 271 n. 25, 297 n. 80

Painter, Mary, 51, 116, 252, 296 n. 72

Pakay, Sedat, 1, 25, 58, 203, 280 n. 4, 289–90 n. 12, 301 n. 110, 306 n. 20; author's interview of, 31, 68, 144–45, 262–64, 280 n. 7, 284 n. 37, 291 n. 24; on Baldwin's appearance, 31, 68; Baldwin's friendship with, 68, 74

Pamuk, Orhan, 28, 276 n. 68

Paris, 4–5, 9–10, 17, 41–42, 51, 70, 77, 82, 92, 109–10, 113, 220, 257, 275 n. 58, 288–89 n. 3, 289 n. 5, 293 n. 44, 293 n. 48, 322 n. 63

Parker, Alan, 159

Parks, Suzan-Lori, xiv, 329 n. 23

Pasha's Library, 58–60, 81, 161, 287–88 n. 73, 327 n. 7

Pearl, Arnold, 273 n. 39, 305 n. 17, 306 n. 21

Peterson, Dale E., xiv, 267 n. 20

189, 286 n. 56; images of, 76, 156;
interview of, 61, 64, 66, 284 n. 47;
memoirs of, 45, 74, 187, 282 n. 22,
284 n. 45; on race in Turkey, 71, 73
surveillance, 83, 275 n. 53, 275 n. 59,
314 n. 5; "back entry" vantage point
and, 228–36; Baldwin's fear of, 17,
18, 52, 83, 220, 287 n. 68; of Baldwin's "marked" body in the South,
229, 234–35; as mechanism of social
control, 219
Switzerland, xxvi, 68–69, 272 n. 31, 273
n. 38

Tacer, Cengiz, 33, 262
Tahir, Kemal, 187, 312–13 n. 86
"Take Me to the Water" (Baldwin), 214,
217, 222, 237, 239, 241, 245, 260–61
Taksim Square (Istanbul), 36, 38, 42,
54, 55–57, 98, 101, 104, 204, 207, 211,
255, 318 n. 35
Taubman, Howard, 142, 303–4 n. 6
Tea and Sympathy (Anderson), 185, 312
n. 82
Tell Me How Long the Train's Been Gone
(Baldwin), 302 n. 1, 305 n. 12; autobiography in, 214, 262, 319 n. 41,
329 n. 24; race and sexuality in, 22,
73, 209; Turkey and, 8, 11, 21, 22–24,
49, 52, 59, 70, 73, 92, 142–44, 305
n. 15; United States reception of, 21,
142–44, 92, 209, 279 n. 70, 305 n. 14,
325 n. 91
Temiz, Okay, 179, 311–12 n. 72
tespih, 33–34, 36, 89, 93, 280 n. 6
theater, 49, 54, 59, 61, 67, 139; Baldwin
and, 27, 66, 96, 141–42, 143–44, 145,
146, 148, 153–54, 186, 243, 249–50,
252–55, 278 n. 89, 302 n. 1, 302 n. 3,
303 n. 6, 304 n. 7, 307 n. 35, 307
n. 38, 316 n. 26, 325 n. 93, 327 n. 1;
Gülriz Sururi-Engin Cezzar Theater,
xxiii, 8, 10, 36, 302

Thelwell, Michael, 43, 259–60, 278
n. 88, 281 n. 15
"This Morning, This Evening, So Soon"
(Baldwin), 78, 268 n. 24, 301 n. 114
Thomas, Kendall, 19, 201, 276 n. 69, 315
n. 16
Thorsen, Karen, 31, 32, 45, 54, 69, 92,
106, 109, 279 n. 1, 280 n. 3, 286 n. 60,
289 nn. 5–6, 289 n. 12, 292 n. 38, 293
n. 47, 293 n. 50, 305 n. 15, 313 n. 89,
315 n. 12, 319 n. 43
Time (magazine), 20, 26, 199, 255
Tiyatro Dergisi (newsletter), 146, 163,
302, 311 n. 67; Baldwin's comments
in, 148, 174–76, 188, 306 n. 25
"To Be Baptized" (Baldwin), 217–18,
237–41, 245, 260
Tonak, Ahmet, 316 n. 24
totalitarianism, 203
transgender person, xxiv, xxvii, 67, 184,
198, 213, 247, 251, 253, 258, 260, 261,
308 n. 45
translations, 68, 72, 106, 265 n. 5,
281–82 n. 21, 284 n. 42; of Baldwin-
Cezzar letters, 250, 280–81 n. 13,
305–6 n. 18; of Baldwin's works, 7,
22, 36, 51, 70, 117, 137–39, 144, 271
n. 25, 272 n. 26, 297 n. 80, 305 n. 15;
of Fortune and Men's Eyes, xxiii, 150,
180, 186
Troupe, Quincy, 199, 200, 315 n. 12, 315
n. 15, 316 n. 18, 322 n. 70, 328 n. 11
Turkey: Armenians in, 17, 46, 107, 185,
212, 297 n. 79, 310 n. 60; Baldwin's
works translated in, 7, 36, 51, 70, 117,
137, 138, 144, 280–81 n. 13, 297 n. 80;
baths in, 21, 80, 122, 165, 198, 286–87
n. 63, 299 n. 95; blackness and race
in, 8, 14, 20, 71, 86–87, 165, 166–67,
205, 285–86 n. 54, 310 n. 60; class
strife and poverty in, 102, 159, 178;
homophobia in, 13, 159, 189; homosexuality in, 14, 19, 68, 80, 96–97,

Turkey (continued)
106, 157, 158–60, 164, 166, 168, 185, 188–90, 218, 308 n. 46, 324 n. 89; Kurds in, 71, 86–87, 166–67, 205, 310 n. 60; military coups in, 16, 205, 310–11 n. 61; NATO membership of, 18, 99, 177, 271 n. 21, 311 n. 70; orientalizing of, 6, 22, 79, 92–102, 125, 129, 190, 292 n. 37; as secular Muslim culture, xxii, xxiii, 6, 7, 11, 19, 21, 36, 83, 86, 96–97, 102, 145–46, 155, 166, 185, 202, 272 n. 36; sociability in, xx–xxi, xxiv, 14, 23, 87, 96; theater in, 154–55, 157, 160, 163–64, 185–89, 203; transgender people in, 158, 184, 189, 308 n. 45, 308–9 n. 47; United States military presence in, 11, 18, 99, 295–96 n. 54; United States opposed in, 18, 26, 99, 177, 285–86 n. 54

Tuwim, Julian, 285 n. 51

Tyson, Cicely, 303 n. 4

Uncle Tom's Cabin (Stowe), 114

Upton, Dell, 230, 323 n. 79

urban imaginary: in Another Country, 107, 123, 135, 293 n. 43, 301 n. 114; in Baldwin's works, 107–8, 123, 138, 143, 195, 293 n. 45; Istanbul of, 28, 107–8, 276 n. 68. See also social space

USIS (United States Information Service), 17, 326 n. 100

U.S. Navy, 18, 99

Üsküdar (Istanbul), 11, 272 n. 36

Vidal, Gore, 21

Vietnam War, 17, 18, 19, 109, 177, 272 n. 34

Village Voice, 210

Vitkus, Daniel J., 130

Von Eschen, Penny, xvii, 6, 267 n. 20, 271 n. 22, 291 n. 21

Walker, Alice, xiv, 261, 329 n. 22

Wall, Cheryl A., 215, 317 n. 29, 318 n. 38

Wallace, Maurice, 19, 199, 270 n. 18, 275 n. 59, 276 n. 69, 292 n. 35, 314 n. 5, 322 n. 69, 324 n. 82

Wallace, Michelle, 198, 227, 322 n. 69, 323 n. 71

Warner Brothers, 273 n. 39, 306 n. 21

Warren, Kenneth W., xxvii, 233, 268–69 n. 3, 295 n. 56, 324 n. 86

Washington, Bryan R., 278 n. 83, 296 n. 73

Waters, Mary C., 301 n. 106

Watkins, Mel, 215, 319 n. 45

Weatherby, William J., 5, 12, 16

Wein, George, 303 n. 4

Welcome Table, The (Baldwin), xxiv, xxvi, 303 n. 4, 314 n. 9, 328 n. 11; autobiography in, 261–62, 264; Black Panthers' influence on, 254, 258, 259; Dallas's collaboration on, 249–50, 252–55; genre and subject of, 251–52, 255; inspirations for, 11, 255, 327 n. 2; letters on, 253–55, 257–58; performances of, 253, 327 n. 1; race and sexuality in, 21, 245, 250–51, 252; transgender perspectives in, 213, 247, 252–53, 254, 258, 259–61, 328 n. 16; Turkish roots of, 23, 59, 87, 173, 249, 253, 255–58

Wiegman, Robyn, 227, 228

Williams, Tennessee, 137, 143

Winant, Howard, 99–100

West, Cornel, 18, 26, 117, 267 n. 18, 320 n. 54

"White Man's Guilt" (Baldwin), 206

"White Racism or World Community" (Baldwin), 206

Wilde, Oscar, 313 n. 1

Worth, Eugene, 4, 115–16, 288 n. 3, 295–96 n. 67

Wright, Michelle, 6, 267 n. 20, 295 n. 64

Woods, Lebbeus, 109, 293 n. 49

Woods, Gregory, 295 n. 66, 298 n. 86

World War II, 3, 216, 239, 271 n. 21; the "East" formed after, 18, 83, 98, 290 n. 18; race and sexuality after, 269 n. 7, 299 n. 93

Wright, Richard, xix, 270 n. 14; Baldwin's meeting with, 4; black masculinity and, 114, 199, 231, 317 n. 29; as Occidental tourist, 95; "protest tradition" and, 295 n. 64, 317 n. 29

xenological erotica, 128. *See also* erotics; homoeroticism

xenotopia, 300 n. 99

Yale Drama School, 8, 303 n. 5, 327 n. 1

Yeats, W. B., 113

Yeğenoğlu, Meyda, 290 n. 19, 299 n. 94

Yeni Cami (Valide Sultan Mosque), 36

Yeni Dergi (journal), 130, 206

Yeni Gazete (newspaper), 146, 147, 161, 187, 189

Yerag, A., 185, 312 n. 83

Young People's Socialist League (YPSL), 4

Zonguldak (Turkey), xxx, 181

Magdalena J. Zaborowska is an associate professor in the Program in American Culture and the Center for Afro-american and African Studies at the University of Michigan, Ann Arbor. She is the author of *How We Found America: Reading Gender through East European Immigrant Narratives* (1995). She is the editor of the following: *Other Americans, Other Americas: The Politics and Poetics of Multiculturalism* (1998); with Sibelan Forrester and Elena Gapova, *Over the Wall / After the Fall: Post-Communist Cultures through an East–West Gaze* (2004); and, with Tracy Fessenden and Nicholas Radel, *The Puritan Origins of American Sex: Religion, Sexuality, and National Identity in American Literature* (2001).

Library of Congress Cataloging-in-Publication Data

Zaborowska, Magdalena J.

James Baldwin's Turkish decade : erotics of exile /

Magdalena J. Zaborowska

p. cm.

Includes bibliographical references and index.

ISBN 978-0-8223-4144-4 (cloth : acid-free paper)

ISBN 978-0-8223-4167-3 (pbk. : acid-free paper)

1. Baldwin, James, 1924–1987—Homes and haunts—

Turkey. 2. African American authors—Biography. 3. African

Americans—Turkey—Biography. 4. Americans—Turkey—

Biography. 5. Turkey—Biography. I. Title.

PS3552.A45Z98 2008

818'.5409—dc22 [B] 2008028960